MW01626329

Sargent and the Sea

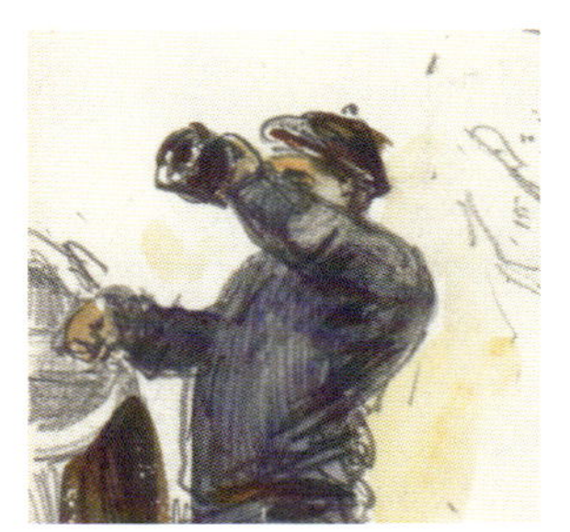
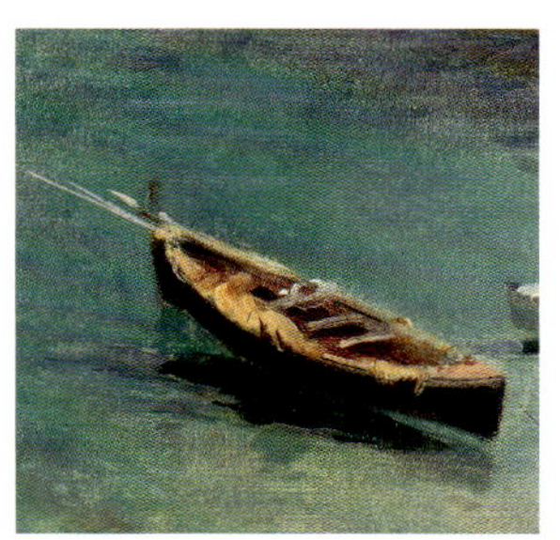
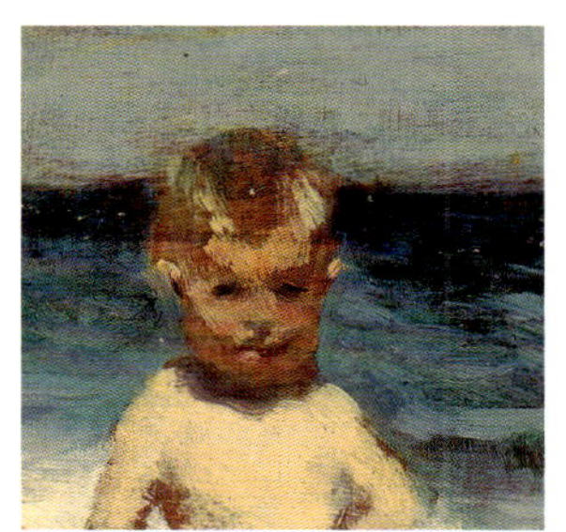
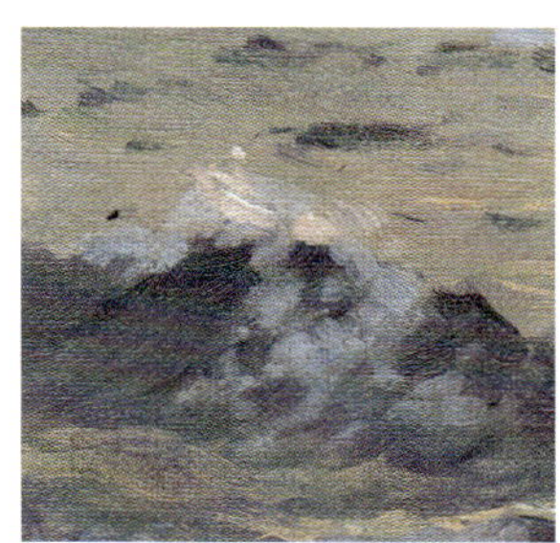

Sargent

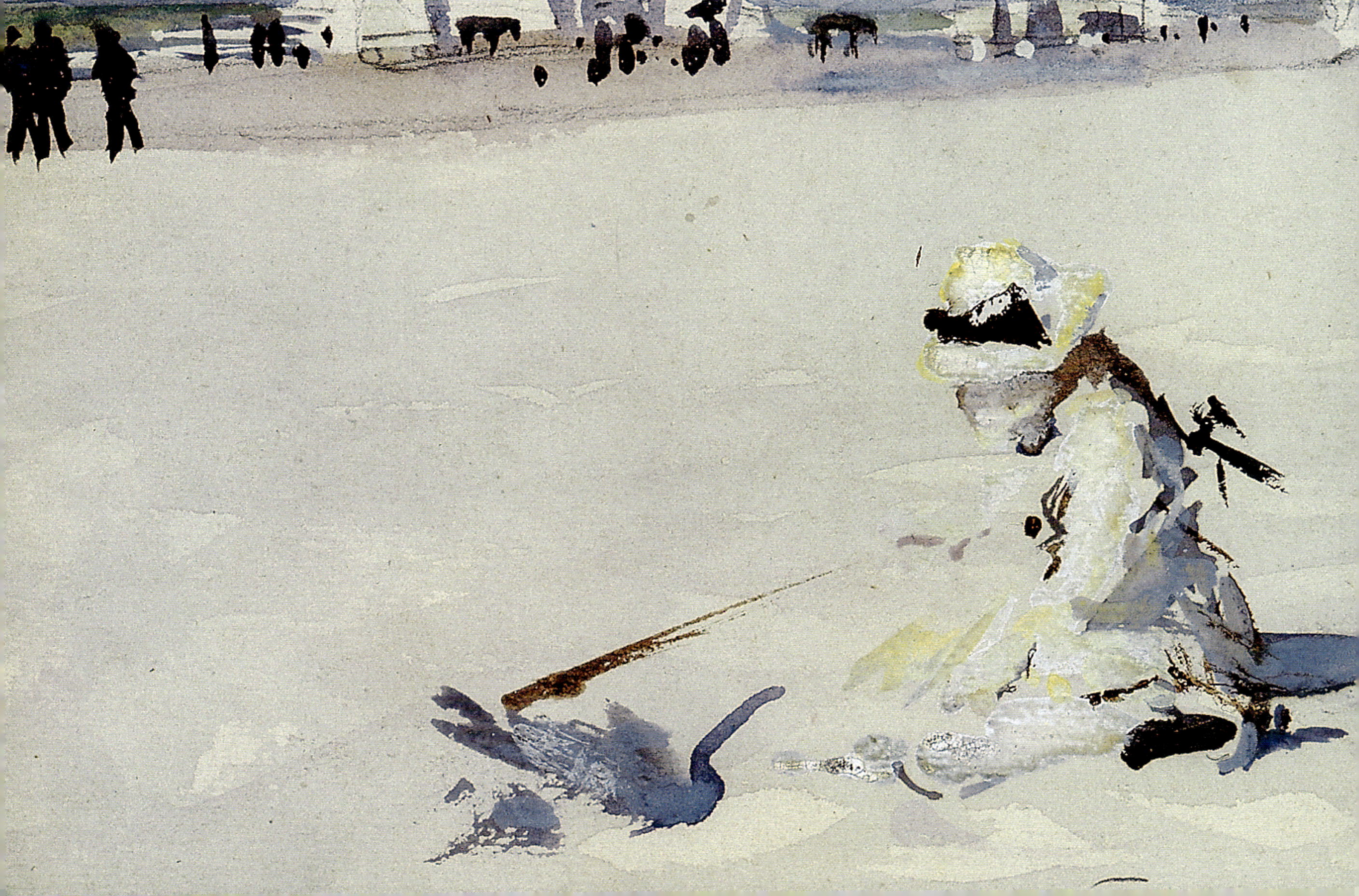

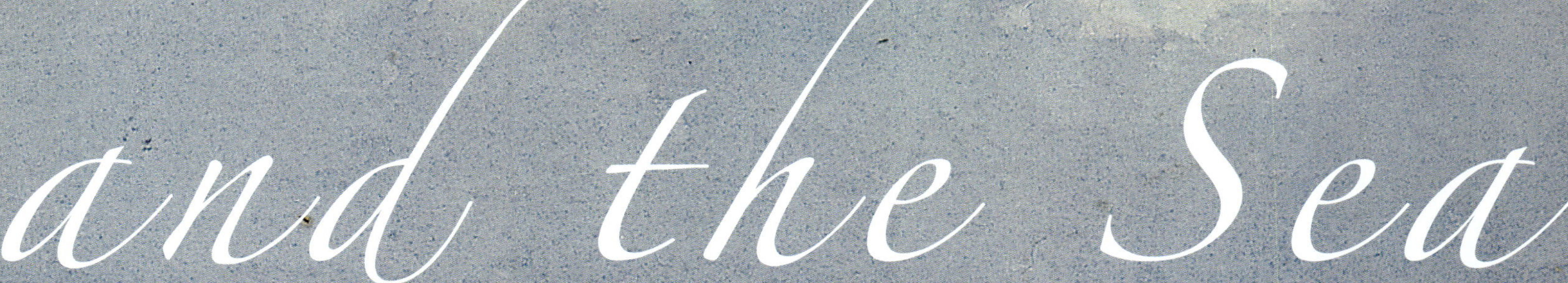

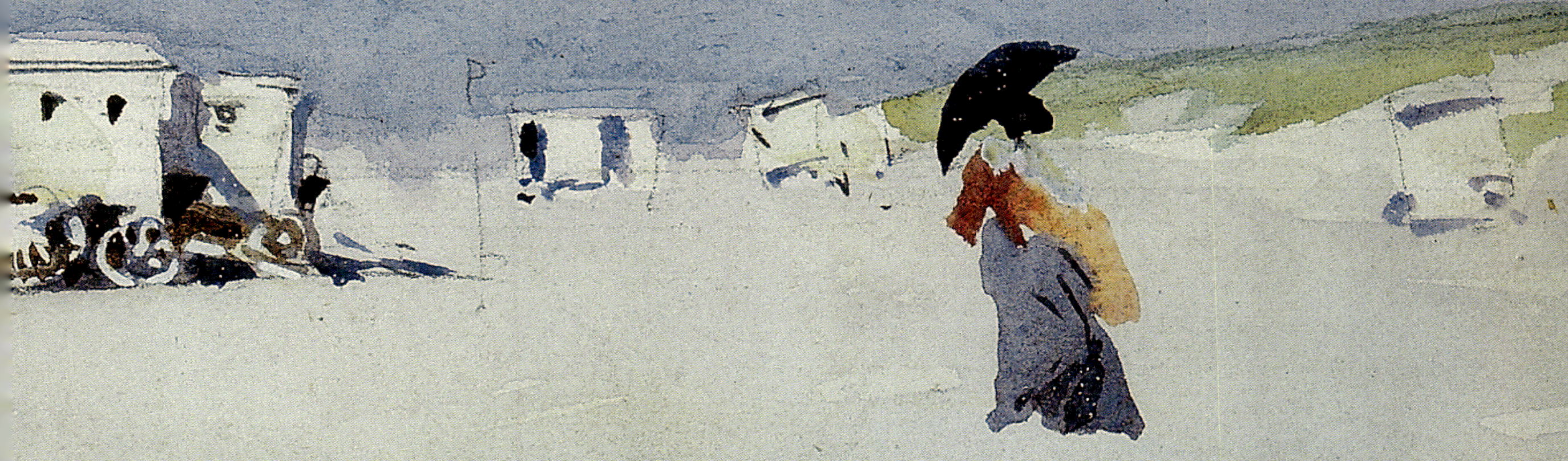

edited by SARAH CASH

with essays by Sarah Cash, Stephanie L. Herdrich, Erica E. Hirshler, Richard Ormond, and Marc Simpson

Yale University Press, New Haven and London
in association with
Corcoran Gallery of Art, Washington, D.C.

Published on the occasion of the exhibition *Sargent and the Sea*, organized by Sarah Cash at the Corcoran Gallery of Art, Washington, D.C., with the collaboration of Richard Ormond.

Corcoran Gallery of Art, September 12, 2009 to January 3, 2010
Museum of Fine Arts, Houston, February 14 to May 23, 2010
Royal Academy of Arts, London, July 10 to September 26, 2010

Sargent and the Sea is organized by the Corcoran Gallery of Art, Washington, D.C., and made possible by the generous support of the Terra Foundation for American Art, Christie's, The Mr. & Mrs. Raymond J. Horowitz Foundation for the Arts, Inc., and Altria Group, Inc. Additional support for the exhibition is provided by the *American Masterpieces* initiative of the National Endowment for the Arts and The Joseph F. McCrindle Foundation.

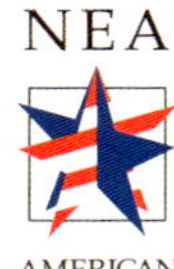

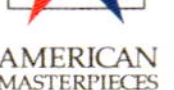

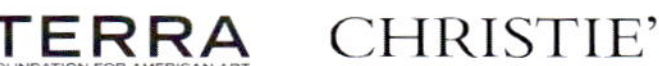

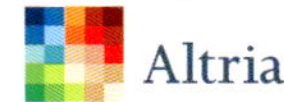

Designed by Sally Salvesen
Printed in Singapore by CS Graphics

Library of Congress Cataloging in Publication Data
Cash, Sarah.
Sargent and the sea / Sarah Cash and Richard Ormond.
p. cm.
Includes bibliographical references and index.
ISBN 978-0-300-14360-7 (cloth: alk. paper)
0-88675-082-2 (paperback: alk. paper)
1. Sargent, John Singer, 1856–1925—Exhibitions. 2. Sea in art—Exhibitions. I. Sargent, John Singer, 1856–1925. II. Ormond, Richard. III. Title.
N6537.S32A4 2009
759.13–dc22
2009015240

Half title page: Details of figs. 94, 173, 161, and 26

Title spread: Detail of *On the Sands* (fig. 158)

Fig. 1 (page vi): Fratelli Vianelli, Portrait photograph of John Singer Sargent, Venice, *c.* 1874. Private Collection. (Exhibition)

Fig. 2 (page viii): Detail from *Two Boys on a Beach with Boats* (fig. 165)

Fig. 3 (page xiv): Detail from Sketch for *En Route pour la pêche* and *Fishing for Oysters at Cancale* (fig. 145)

Contents

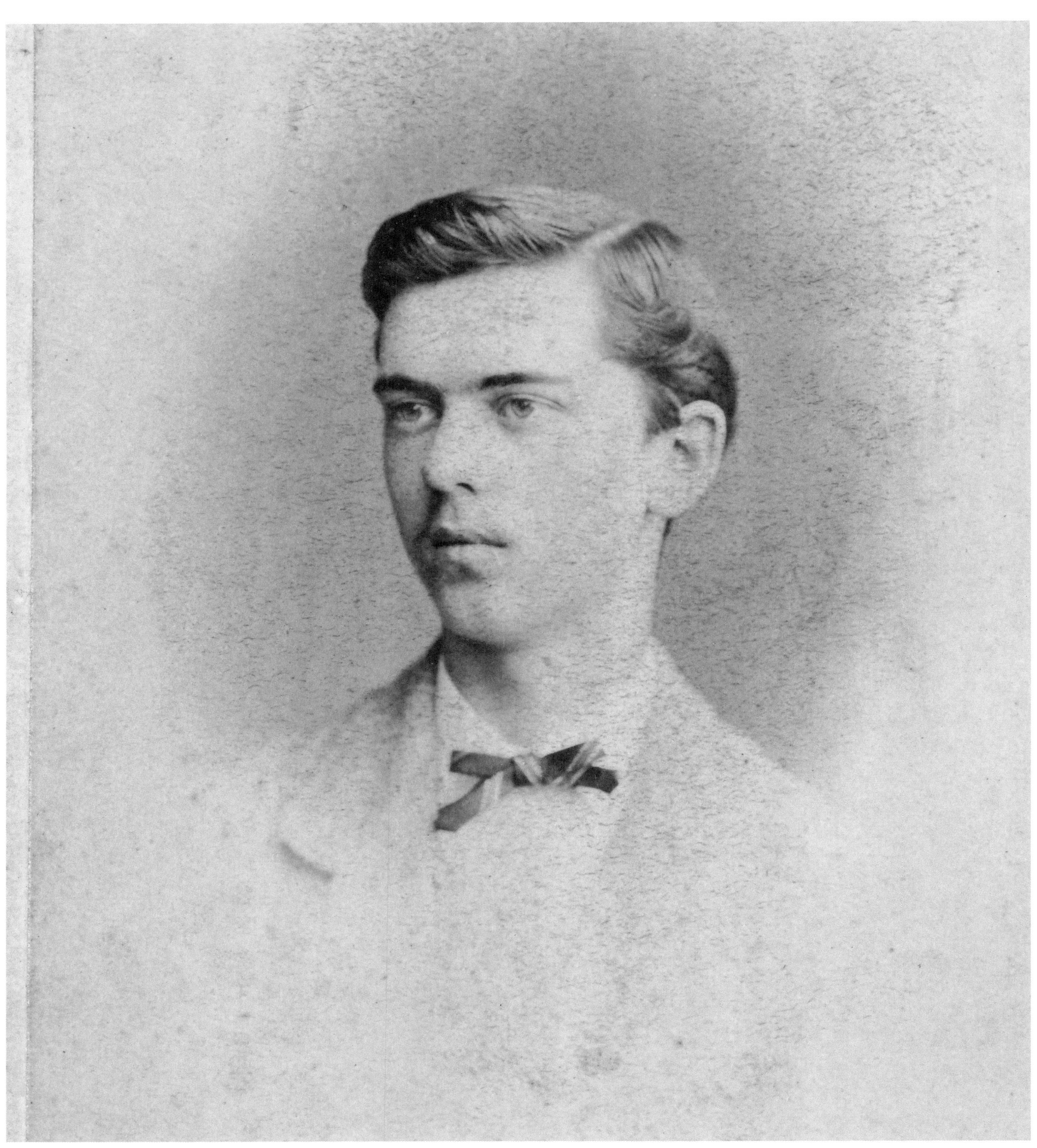

Director's Foreword

In the greatest late nineteenth-century landscape and genre painting, the issue is not usually about how well the scene and its contents are depicted. The greatest works are to do with atmosphere. In Monet's landscape art, for example, we can sense the air itself; we can feel the heat or cold; we can hear the whisperings of leaves and grass; we can smell and feel the burblings and grumblings of human biology and psychology; and so we can position ourselves emotionally in that very specific time and place. It was an extraordinary moment in the history of depictive art.

John Singer Sargent (1856–1925) was an artist of that moment, one of the most technically gifted painters in a period characterized by superlative technique. Alongside James McNeill Whistler, he was the greatest American painter of the age, and one who earned his place among his contemporaries, in a European environment bristling with already legendary figures.

Sargent was most revered, of course, as a portraitist, and that aspect of his career has been celebrated by a number of exhibitions over the last decades. Like a number of his great French contemporaries, however, he was not exclusively interested in the depiction of humanity. Especially in his early career, he concerned himself also with open space, and everything that this implied for painterly technique. This manifested itself most consistently in his interest in marine life. For the first time then, this exhibition brings together Sargent's seascapes. Some of these works are central to the artist's œuvre; the superb *En Route pour la pêche* (1878), for example, reveals to us that even at this early stage, the artist was already one of the most gifted and spontaneous artists in the story of American art. What the Corcoran painting also reveals to us, is that while Sargent worked in the age of Impressionism, and shared the Impressionists' artistic heritage, in his use of color, he was distinct from them. Rather, he carries the idea of Realism into a new terrain, and anticipated the generation of American artists of the early twentieth century, known as The Eight or the Ashcan school, who for the first time perhaps established the idea of a wholly American vision.

This exhibition has been some years in the making. I am extremely grateful to the curators who made it possible, Sarah Cash, the Bechhoefer Curator of American Art, and Richard Ormond. And as always, the wonderful staff of the Corcoran Gallery have excelled in creating this exhibition.

Paul Greenhalgh, *Director and President*
Corcoran Gallery of Art / Corcoran College of Art + Design

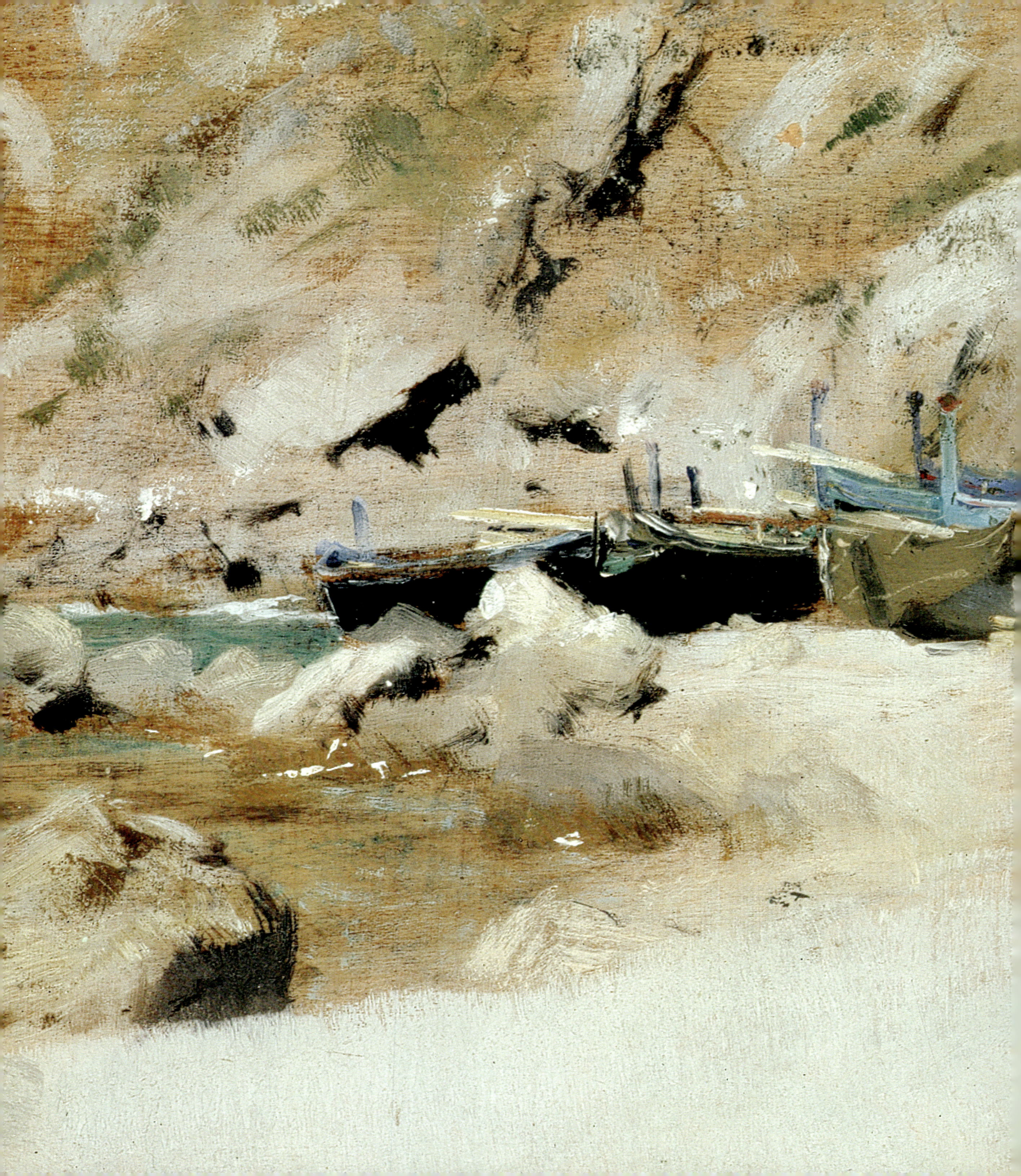

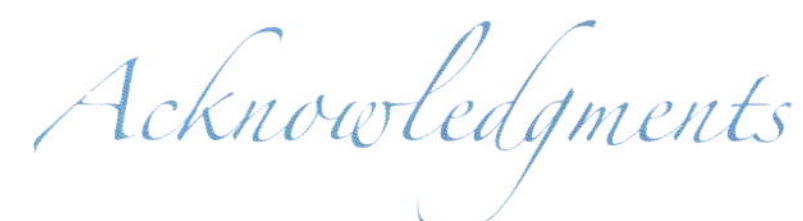

Sargent and the Sea was conceived in 1998 as an exhibition focused solely on the Corcoran Gallery of Art's early John Singer Sargent masterpiece *En Route pour la pêche* (*Setting Out to Fish*) and its preparatory and related works. Over subsequent years the project gestated during other endeavors and institutional changes, while benefiting immeasurably from conversations with my ultimate collaborator Richard Ormond; these exchanges occurred as he delved deeply into the artist's early marine work in preparation for the fourth volume of the John Singer Sargent catalogue raisonné. Paul Greenhalgh, President and Director of the Corcoran, and Philip Brookman, Chief Curator and Director of Research, have strongly supported the concept of the show, and I am very grateful for their enthusiasm and assistance.

The present exhibition and catalogue owe their ultimate form not only to Richard Ormond's distinguished scholarship but also to his unflagging enthusiasm for his ancestor's rich œuvre. In addition to contributing an enlightening essay to this volume, he lent his expertise to the Corcoran on every aspect of the project—notably providing an initial checklist and facilitating contact with many lenders—and patiently answered countless questions. I cannot overstate the value of his kind and wise counsel during my first foray into Sargent scholarship. These last debts are also owed to my three other partners in this endeavor: Stephanie L. Herdrich, Research Associate, American Paintings and Sculpture, The Metropolitan Museum of Art; Erica E. Hirshler, Croll Senior Curator of Paintings, Art of the Americas, Museum of Fine Arts, Boston; and Marc Simpson, Associate Director, Williams College Graduate Program in the History of Art and Curator of American Art, Sterling and Francine Clark Art Institute. They not only provided outstanding contributions to this book but also graciously assisted with many complex details of key loans from their respective institutions.

Shown at three venues and, appropriately, on both sides of the ocean that provided inspiration for so many of Sargent's marines, this exhibition would not have been realized without the collaboration of many institutional colleagues and private individuals—far more than can be named here. In Washington, the Corcoran Gallery of Art staff has provided invaluable support in every aspect of organizing this exhibition and its publication, beginning in its earliest stages when former Chief Curator Jacquelyn Days Serwer championed the idea of it. In addition to Paul Greenhalgh,

Mariana Nork and members of the Development team, particularly Janice Marks, Kate Denton, Joe Callahan, John Scherfel, and Rachel Frank, oversaw key fundraising. Elizabeth Parr skillfully coordinated the administration of the exhibition. The always upbeat Dana Gildenhorn deserves special recognition for her attention to complex details of checklists and loans, as well as rights and reproductions for this book. In the latter she was ably assisted by Ila Furman. Over the course of the project several energetic interns provided invaluable assistance: Matthew Bacon, Diana Kaw, Margaret Morrison, Ellen Rawson, Ingrid Seggerman, Elizabeth Shook, and Amy Torbert. Former and present Corcoran Library Directors Douglas Litts and Mario Ascencio, as well as Pat Reid, handled library requests with dispatch. Dare Hartwell, Carol Ann Small, and Ken Ashton expertly prepared a number of objects for the exhibition. Nancy Swallow adroitly organized all aspects of loans, insurance, packing, and transportation. Michael Baltzer, Cory Hixson, and Charles Sthreshley implemented Linda McNamara's superb exhibition plans, while John deWolf and Maria Habib designed the graphics. Sarah Durkee and her creative team, especially Michelle Clair and Linda Powell, oversaw all educational undertakings, including an Exploration Gallery and a major scholarly symposium. Kristin Guiter and Jessica Semler guided the marketing and public relations for the exhibition.

We are delighted to have the Museum of Fine Arts, Houston, as the exhibition's second venue, and thank above all Emily Ballew Neff, Curator of American Painting and Sculpture, for coordinating the presentation with her usual collegiality. We are also grateful to Director Peter C. Marzio and Chief Adminstrator of Exhibitions Karen B. Vetter, as well as to Gwendolyn H. Goffe, Willard Holmes, Amy Purvis, and the museum's dedicated staff of educators, registrars, art handlers, and designers. Several Museum trustees generously made the Houston showing possible: Nancy and Rich Kinder; Cornelia and Meredith Long; Mr. Fayez Sarofim; and Ms. Ann G. Trammell.

Sargent is revered in London, where he settled permanently by 1886, and so we are fortunate that *Sargent and the Sea* will be seen there at the Royal Academy of Arts. We acknowledge the cooperation of Charles Saumarez Smith, Secretary and Chief Executive, as well as that of Cayetana Castillo, Adrian Locke, Beth B. Schneider, and MaryAnne Stevens.

We extend our deepest gratitude to our funders and lenders, listed elsewhere in this volume, without whom this undertaking would not have been possible. The latter, who understood that the inclusion of every possible early Sargent marine was crucial to the success of this tightly focused exhibition, welcomed Richard Ormond and me into their homes, storerooms, and conservation studios. Many other people helped make these loans possible as well. Foremost recognition goes to Warren Adelson, who not only offered valuable advice and assisted in securing several loans, but also facilitated a key grant. The staff at Adelson Galleries, including Lisa Bush Hankin and especially Elizabeth Oustinoff, contributed assistance in many ways and provided inspiring quarters for project meetings. Richard Ormond's research partner in the Sargent catalogue raisonné, Elaine Kilmurray, cheerfully lent her own wealth of knowledge at critical moments.

Three museums in particular allowed significant loans while building projects challenged the accessibility of their collections. At the Metropolitan Museum of Art we thank Marjorie Shelley, Sherman Fairchild Conservator in Charge, Paper Conservation, who oversaw treatment of the Sargent scrapbook, and especially H. Barbara Weinberg, Alice Pratt Brown Curator, American

Paintings and Sculpture. At the Museum of Fine Arts, Boston, we are especially grateful to Malcolm Rogers, Ann and Graham Gund Director, and to Elliot Bostwick Davis, John Moors Cabot Chair, Art of the Americas; and at the Harvard Art Museum to Miriam Stewart, Assistant Curator of Drawings, and Kathryn Press, Assistant Registrar.

The following individuals kindly facilitated contact with lenders, aided in the examination of works of art, answered research queries, and secured catalogue and other research photographs: Judith Barter, Art Institute of Chicago; Teresa A. Carbone, Brooklyn Museum; Eric Widing, Christie's; Mark Cole, Cleveland Museum of Art; Jenny Sponberg, Curtis Galleries, Inc.; Leah Decker; David Dufour; Timothy Anglin Burgard, Jane Glover, and Sue Grinols, Fine Arts Museums of San Francisco; Elizabeth Fonseca; Barbara Dayer Gallati; Kim Housego; Jill Cogen and Natalie Russell, The Huntington; Nicola and Richard Irwin; John Rowe, Joseph F. McCrindle Foundation; Cornelius Lansing; Catherine Levy; Martha Long and Meredith Long, Meredith Long & Company; Elizabeth Athens, Elaine Bradson, Rebecca Capua, and Deanna Cross, Metropolitan Museum of Art; Maria Miller; Erin McCutcheon, Elizabeth Mitchell, Kim Pashko, and Jennifer Riley, Museum of Fine Arts, Boston; Allison Luchs, National Gallery of Art; Helena E. Wright, National Museum of American History, Smithsonian Institution; Nathan Pendlebury, National Museums Liverpool; Margaret C. Conrads and Scott Heffley, Nelson-Atkins Museum of Art; David Burnhauser, Linda Ferber, Susan Kriete, and Roberta J. M. Olson, New-York Historical Society; Christopher Newall; Leonée Ormond; Meg Perlman; Nancy Ash, Sarah Cantor, and Shelley Langdale, Philadelphia Museum of Art; Julie Reynolds; Lesley Shaw; Gun-Britt Hietanen and Henry Wiklund, Society of Swedish Literature in Finland; Deborah Sole; Gavin Spanierman; Merry Armata and Teresa O'Toole, Sterling and Francine Clark Art Institute; Birgitta and Ulfs Dahlberg, Stor Sarvlaks Manor; Stephen Deuchar, Carole Towers, and Chris Woods, Tate, London; Elizabeth Kennedy and Cathy Ricciardelli, Terra Foundation for American Art; Stuart and Katterina Wrede; and Carol Jones and David McCaslin, Yale University Library.

In addition to the conservators acknowledged herein, several others have generously shared their knowledge of Sargent's working methods and otherwise assisted in the technical aspects of the project: Harriet Irgang; Sian Jones; Patricia Favero and Elizabeth Steele, The Phillips Collection; and Bonnie Rimer. Dorothy Mahon at the Metropolitan Museum of Art accompanied me to view several paintings in New York private collections, providing thoughtful advice and later treating a key painting along with M. Alan Miller. At the Museum of Fine Arts, Boston, Rhona MacBeth and above all Lydia Vagts and Jean Woodward enthusiastically investigated Sargent's working methods in creating the Cancale pictures.

The whereabouts of a small number of Sargent's early marines has escaped scholars even after exhaustive searches. After one particularly vigorous yet fruitless quest, the elusive painting surfaced with uncanny timing; for her deft handling of initial communications surrounding that event, I am indebted to Erica Hirshler. For their assistance in these pursuits we thank in particular Sabina ffrench Blake, Emma Chambers, Lissa Cooley, Reba Dein, Kay Foster, and John Robertson.

The production and elegant design of this catalogue are due to the efforts of Sally Salvesen, Yale University Press, London, who enthusiastically nurtured the volume from the time Richard Ormond and I shared the idea with her in the spring of 2007. Her colleague Catherine Bowe meticulously organized images and checked myriad details.

The authors benefited enormously from sharing information and their manuscripts with each other. We also thank those instrumental to our research and writing, many of whom are mentioned elsewhere here or in the essay notes. In addition, Stephanie L. Herdrich thanks for their support her Metropolitan Museum of Art colleagues Katie Steiner and H. Barbara Weinberg. Erica E. Hirshler extends gratitude to her fellow Museum of Fine Arts, Boston curator George T.M. Shackelford and to intern Elizabeth Mandel; to Melissa Buron and Lynn Orr, Fine Arts Museums of San Franscisco; and to Harry Clark. Richard Ormond acknowledges Dr. Pieter van der Merwe, National Maritime Museum, Greenwich. Marc Simpson would like to thank Gretchen Sinnett, Katie Steiner, Amy Torbert, and Fronia Wissman. I am grateful to Adam Greenhalgh, Dorothy Moss, Emily D. Shapiro, and Thayer Tolles. For enlightening Stephanie Herdrich and me on the history, topography, and piscary practices of Cancale, special recognition goes to Mary Margaret Chappell, like Sargent an American in Brittany. Through her (and, importantly, though her translations), our research benefited immeasurably from contact with several *Cancalais*: intrepid photographer Hervé Lambrecht; artist and *bisquine* expert Marek; and oystermen François-Joseph Pichot and his father Joseph Pichot-Louvet (to whom Richard Ormond led me). For granting me a workspace and stack access at the Smithsonian American Art Museum/National Portrait Gallery Library, I thank Cecilia Chin.

I take the liberty of ending on a personal note. This book is dedicated to the memory of my parents, George and Barbara Cash; my father, in particular, was an ardent admirer of Sargent's early career. Memories of their keen aesthetic sensibilities as well as their enthusiasm and aptitude for art in its many forms—and above all their support of my career and family—continue to nourish and inspire me. My most loyal sustainers have been my husband, Glenn R. MacCullough, and our beloved son Colin; together we share Sargent's passion for travel to new and exotic places. They endured my preoccupation with this project not only when I undertook many trips and labored on evenings and weekends, but also during our own family voyages across land and sea.

Sarah Cash
Washington, D.C.
May 2009

Corcoran Gallery of Art and College of Art and Design
Board of Trustees

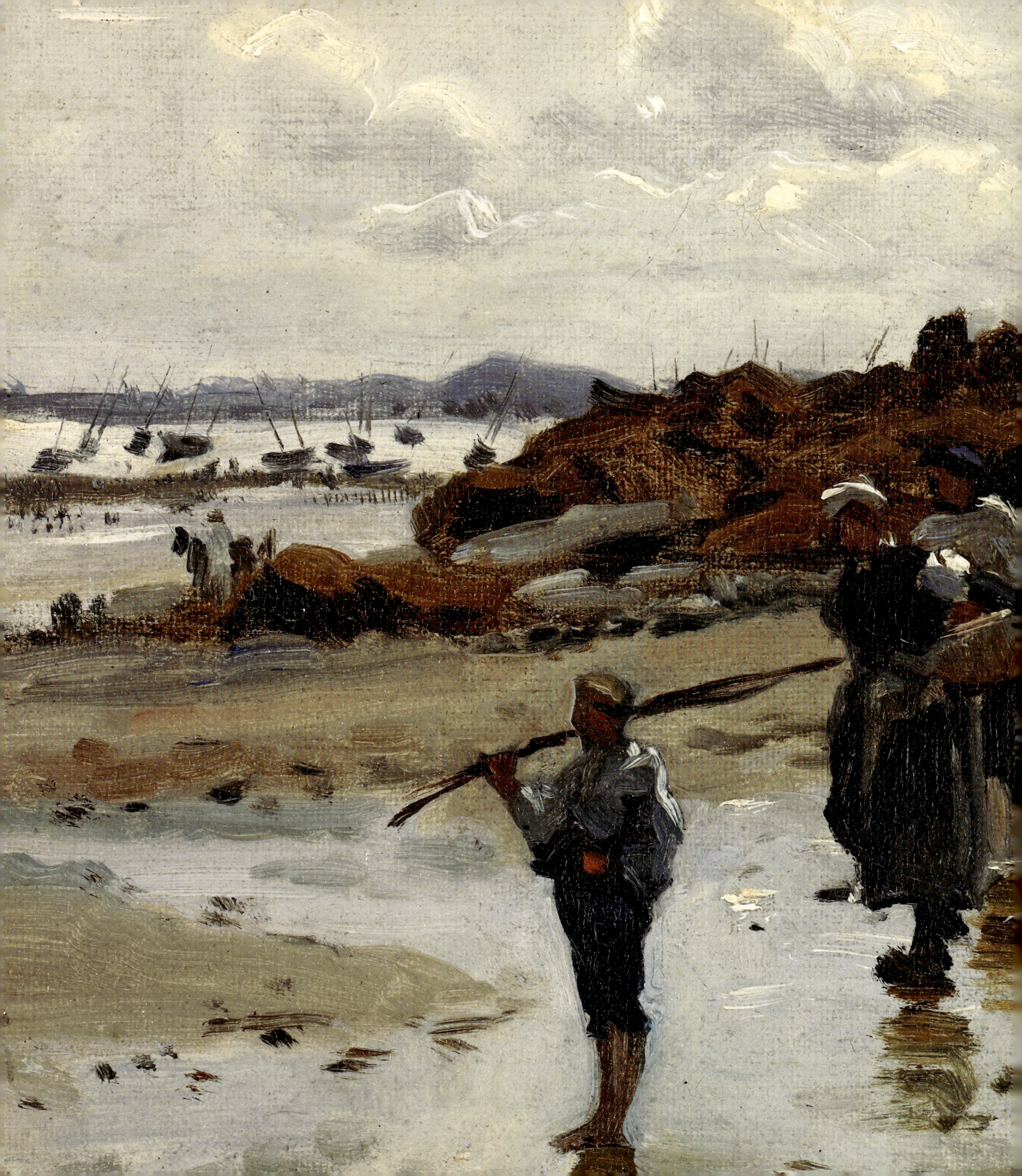

Lenders to the Exhibition

Colby College, Special Collections, Waterville, Maine

Corcoran Gallery of Art, Washington, D.C.

Curtis Galleries, Minneapolis

Fine Arts Museums of San Francisco

Collection of Isabel Fonseca, London

Frank M. Gren "Annapolis Collection"

Harvard Art Museum, Fogg Art Museum

The Metropolitan Museum of Art

Mr. and Mrs. William J. Miller, Jr.

Museum of Fine Arts, Boston

The Nelson-Atkins Museum of Art, Kansas City, Missouri

The New-York Historical Society

Philadelphia Museum of Art

Private Collections

The Fayez Sarofim Collection

William Kelly Simpson, New York

Archives of American Art, Smithsonian Institution

The Society of Swedish Literature in Finland

Sterling and Francine Clark Art Institute, Williamstown, Massachusetts

Tate, London

Terra Foundation for American Art, Chicago

Virginia Commonwealth University, James Branch Cabell Library,
Special Collections & Archives

Note to the Reader

All works are by John Singer Sargent unless otherwise specified. Except where new titles, dates, and dimensions have been assigned based on the scholarship presented herein, this information derives from Richard Ormond and Elaine Kilmurray, *John Singer Sargent: Figures and Landscapes, 1874–1882*, vol. 4 of *The Complete Paintings* (New Haven and London: Yale University Press, 2006) and, for works on paper in the collection of The Metropolitan Museum of Art, from Stephanie L. Herdrich and H. Barbara Weinberg, *American Drawings and Watercolors in The Metropolitan Museum of Art: John Singer Sargent* (New York: The Metropolitan Museum of Art, 2000). More data, including inscriptions on the verso of double-sided objects and details of paper color and type, may be found in those two publications. Regarding the John Singer Sargent Scrapbook in the collection of The Metropolitan Museum of Art, the designation "In the John Singer Sargent Scrapbook" indicates that the sketch in question is affixed in that volume, whereas the designation "From the John Singer Sargent Scrapbook" indicates that the sketch is no longer affixed there.

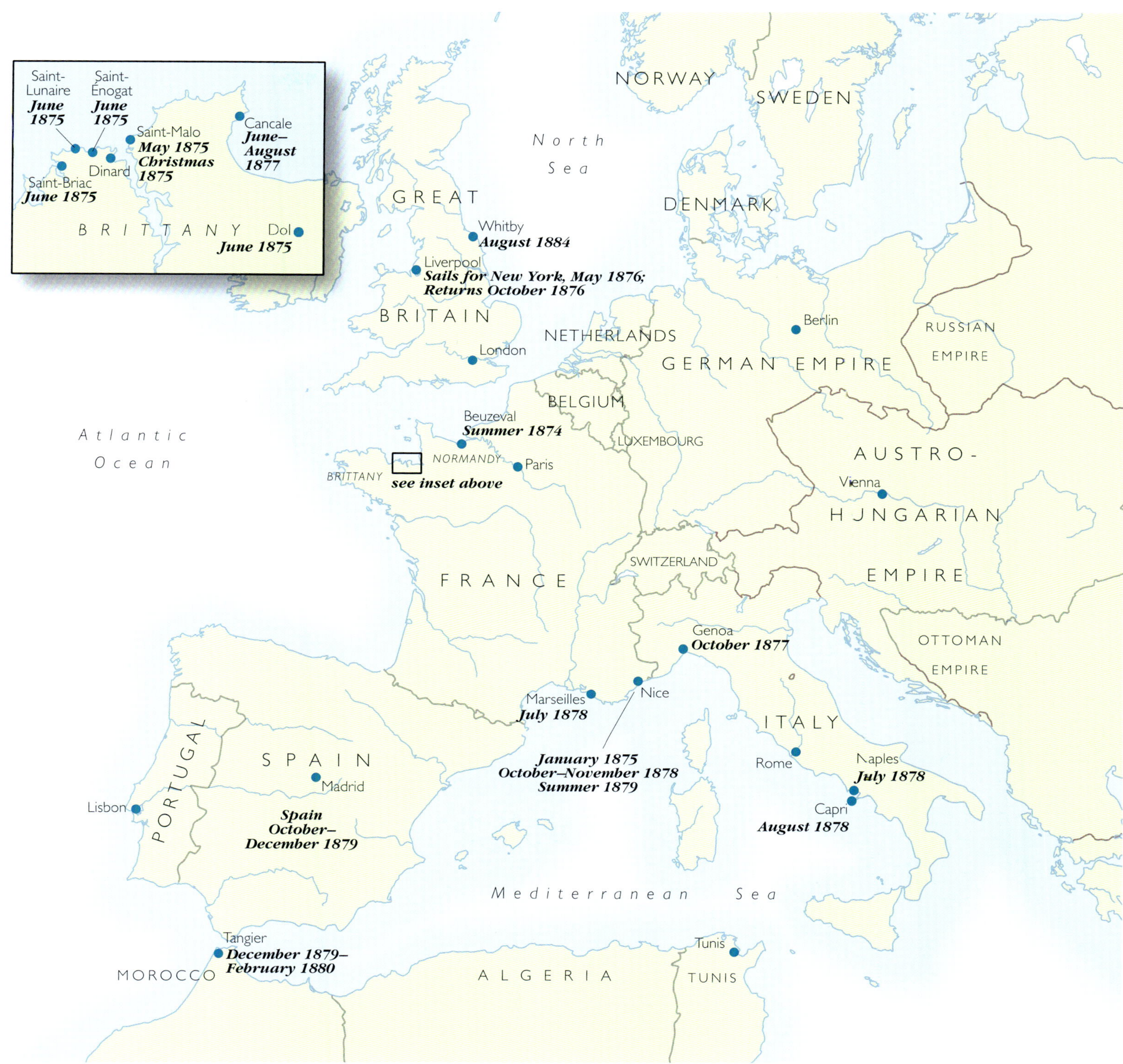

Fig. 4 Map documenting the locales and periods of John Singer Sargent's travel when he created his marines of 1874-1880 and 1884; during this time the artist was based in Paris.

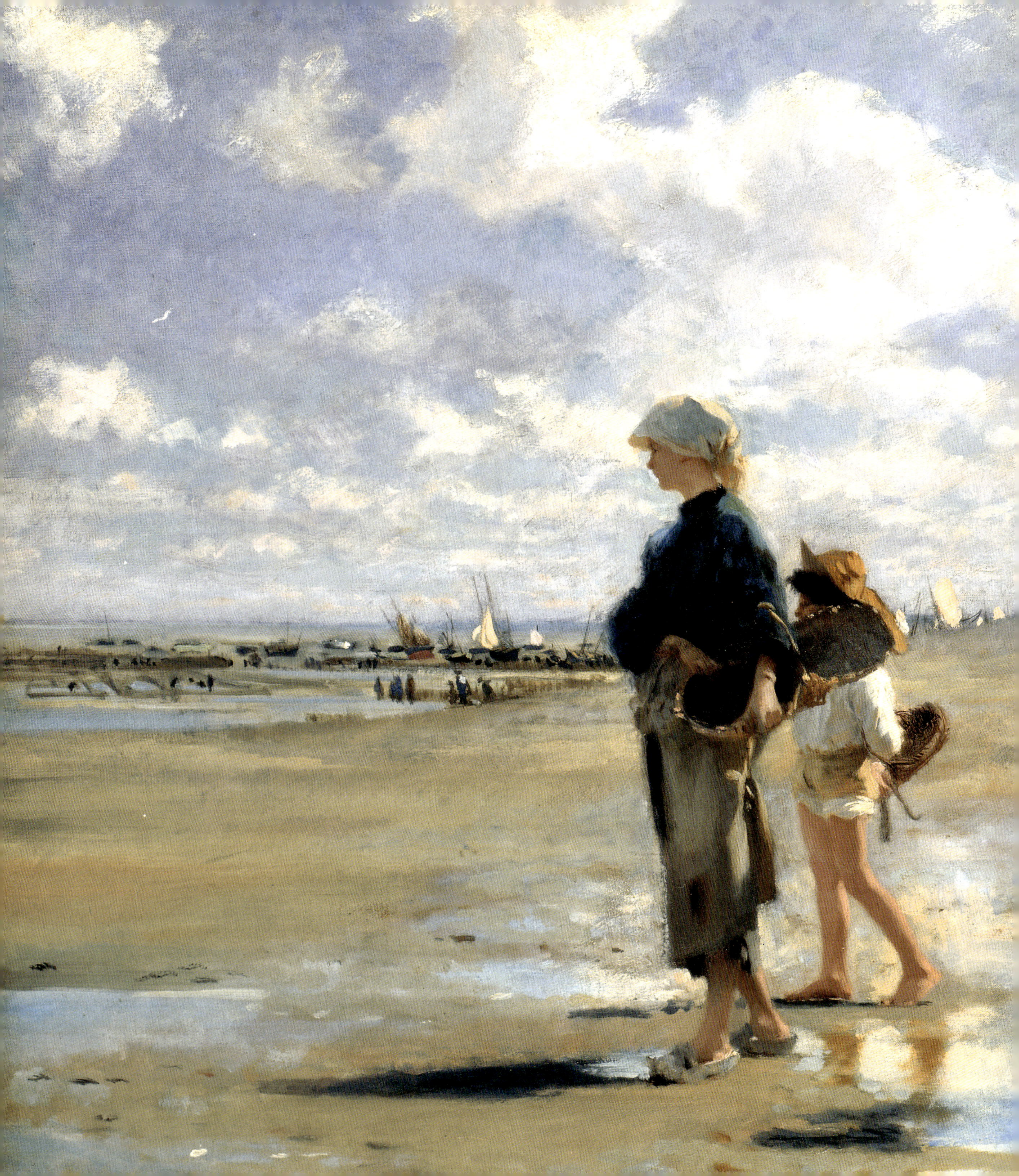

Sargent and the Sea: Introduction

RICHARD ORMOND

John Singer Sargent's early sea-pieces and beach scenes have not hitherto been gathered together, nor has the artist been remotely considered a marine painter. The extent of his engagement with marine subjects has only recently been recognized.[1] The aim of this exhibition is to put the sea back center-stage, and to demonstrate what a large part it played in the evolution of the artist's style and his artistic preferences. Those of us involved in the project like to think of ourselves as pioneers, shining a searchlight on a forgotten episode of Sargent's art. The recent discovery of three previously unknown seascapes (see figs. 24, 25, 26) has confirmed our thesis that in the years 1874–1879 he was primarily a marine painter. This essay attempts to explain how this happened and what was significant about the pictures exhibited here as a group for the first time.

In order to set the scene it is important to rehearse the outlines of Sargent's career. He was born in Florence in January 1856 to American expatriate parents, Dr Fitzwilliam Sargent and Mary Newbold Sargent, who had given up America for a roving, unsettled existence, traversing Europe as the seasons dictated. He was the eldest of three children, a year older than his sister Emily, and fourteen years senior to Violet, the baby of the family.[2] Sargent grew up with a keen appreciation of European art and culture. He was widely traveled and well read, he spoke four languages, and he showed a precocious talent as a watercolorist and draughtsman. Sargent was also a gifted pianist who was good enough to have become a professional musician. In later life he helped many younger composers and musicians, and he played a prominent role in the musical life of London.

Responding to their son's vocation, in the absence of their own, Sargent's parents agreed to let him train professionally as an artist. In the spring of 1874, at the age of eighteen, he entered the atelier of the fashionable French portrait painter Carolus-Duran in Paris. Sargent is depicted at work in the atelier by his close friend J. Carroll Beckwith, who studied with him (fig. 6) and with whom he shared a separate studio. Beckwith did a number of drawings of fellow students at this time, including a fine profile study of the young Sargent that captures his good looks (fig. 7). Sargent took to his master's lessons in the art of painting as a duck to water, laying the foundations for that wizardry with the brush that would always single him out. In 1877 he exhibited his first work at the Paris Salon, the state-sponsored annual display of contemporary

Facing page: Fig. 5 Detail of fig. 8, *En Route pour la pêche (Setting Out to Fish)*, 1878. Corcoran Gallery of Art, Washington, D.C., Museum Purchase, Gallery Fund, 17.2. (Exhibition)

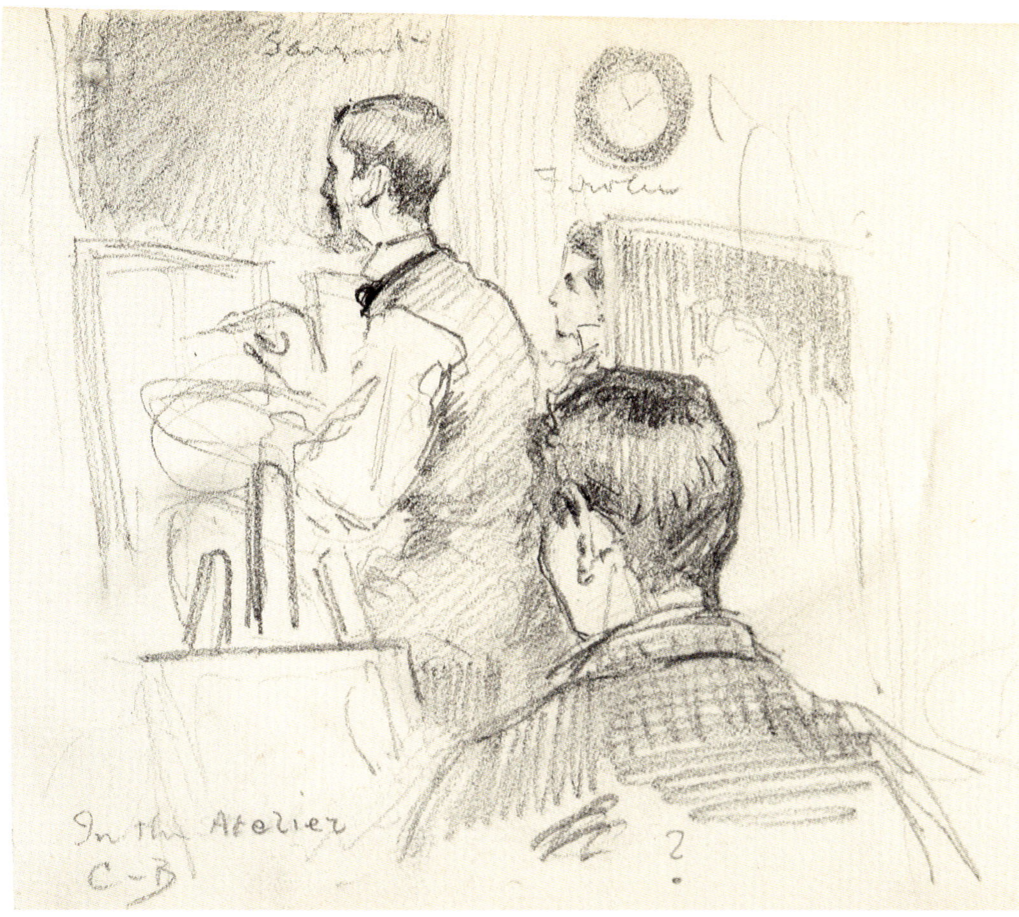

Fig. 6 James Carroll Beckwith (1852–1917), *In the Atelier of Carolus-Duran: Portrait of John Singer Sargent Painting at the Easel in the Company of Frank Fowler and an Unidentified Artist*, *c.* 1874–76. Graphite on paper, $3\frac{15}{16} \times 4\frac{1}{4}$ in (9.7×10.8 cm). Collection of The New-York Historical Society. Gift of the National Academy of Design, 1935.85.2.245. (Exhibition)

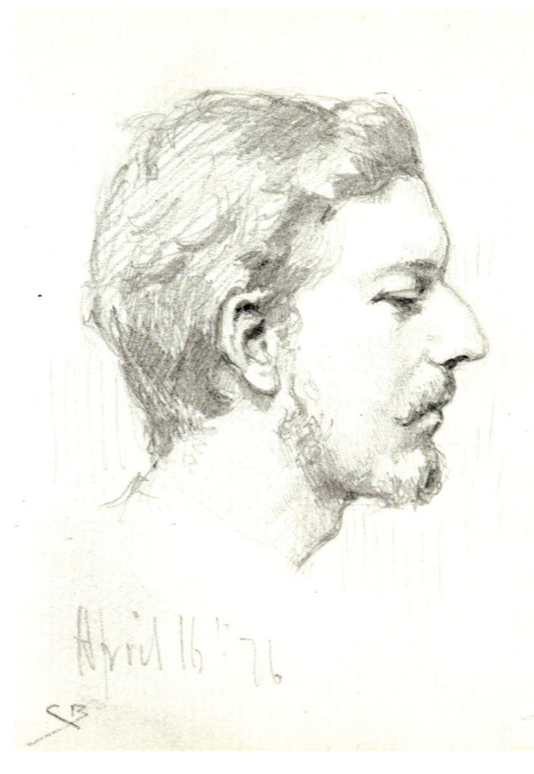

Fig. 7 James Carroll Beckwith (1852–1917), *Profile Portrait of John Singer Sargent*, 1876. Graphite on paper, $3\frac{3}{4} \times 2\frac{1}{2}$ in (9.5×6.4 cm). Collection of The New-York Historical Society. Gift of the National Academy of Design, 1935.85.2.176. (Exhibition)

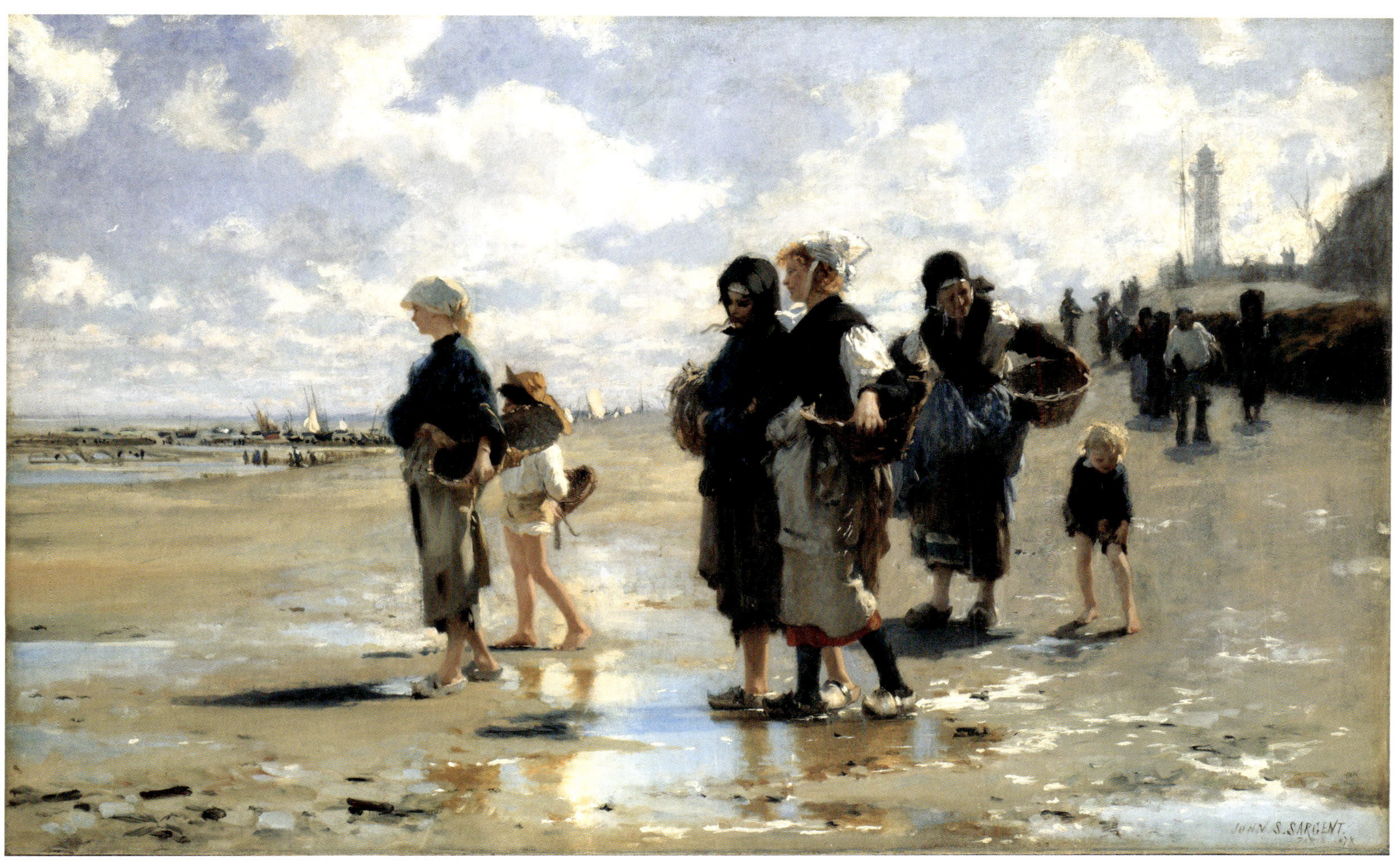

Fig. 8 *En Route pour la pêche (Setting Out to Fish)*, 1878. Oil on canvas, 31⅛ × 48⅜ in (78.8 × 122.8 cm). Inscribed, lower right: *JOHN S. SARGENT. / PARIS 1878.* Corcoran Gallery of Art, Washington, D.C., Museum Purchase, Gallery Fund, 17.2. (Exhibition)

art, with a portrait of his childhood friend *Fanny Watts* (Philadelphia Museum of Art). This was followed a year later by *En Route pour la pêche (Setting Out to Fish)*, the centerpiece of the current exhibition (fig. 8).

Over the following years Sargent was represented at the Salon with portraits and subject pictures that earned him an enviable reputation as one of the rising stars of his generation. He combined bold, unconventional compositions with a progressive style of painting that emphasized texture, tone, and the mark of the individual brushstroke.

Among his masterpieces of these early years were *The Daughters of Edward Darley Boit* (1882, Museum of Fine Arts, Boston), four young girls dispersed within an atmospheric interior; his great Spanish dance picture *El Jaleo* (1882, Isabella Stewart Gardner Museum, Boston); and the notorious portrait of *Madame X (Madame Pierre Gautreau)* (1883–84, Metropolitan Museum of Art, New York), which caused a scandal at the Salon of 1884. Partly because of this, Sargent's career went into a temporary dip and he was persuaded by his friends, especially the novelist Henry James, to move to London. However, English taste was more conservative than the French and he found it difficult to establish himself. In the interim he turned to landscape, painting a series of vivid Impressionist sketches at

Broadway in the Cotswolds, inspired by his friend Claude Monet whom he visited at Giverny. These sketches culminated in his plein air masterpiece, *Carnation, Lily, Lily, Rose* (1885–86, Tate, London), a vision of two young girls lighting Japanese lanterns at dusk in a forest of flowers, which made a hit at the London Royal Academy exhibition of 1887.

The artist's breakthrough as a portrait painter came in the same year, in America not England. Commissioned to paint the wife of a wealthy New York banker, the result was *Mrs Henry Marquand* (1887, Princeton University Art Museum, New Jersey), after which he was fêted in his native country and liberally patronized. A second visit to America in 1890 yielded more than forty portraits and confirmed his position as the leading American portraitist of his generation. In the same year he received a commission to decorate the Boston Public Library with a cycle of murals illustrating the *Triumph of Religion*, in the Special Collections Hall on the second floor.[3] Sargent regarded this cycle as his greatest contribution to the art of his time and he labored on it for thirty years. It was followed by two later schemes of mural decoration, in the Museum of Fine Arts, Boston (a series of classical themes in the entrance staircase and upper rotunda),[4] and in the Widener Library at Harvard University (two murals on the staircase commemorating the war dead). In England it was the portrait of *Lady Agnew* (1892–93, National Gallery of Scotland, Edinburgh), exhibited at the Royal Academy in 1893, that was his passport to success. With its brilliant effects of light and color, it simply outshone everything else on the walls of the Academy. The high style and bravura painting of Sargent's portraits appealed to a new generation of cosmopolitan and liberated clients. By 1900 he had been taken up by the British aristocracy and he was portraying the great and the good on both sides of the Atlantic. Increasingly, however, he became frustrated by the treadmill of portraiture, his inability to finish his murals, and his desire for the freedom to paint subjects of his own choosing. In 1907 he shut up shop to the dismay of his society patrons, offering charcoal portraits ('mug shots' he called them) in lieu of oil paintings. His later years were devoted to the murals and, on extended summer sketching expeditions, to landscapes and figure scenes in oil and watercolor, painted in a brilliant Impressionist vein.

The First World War brought to an end the "gilded age" of which Sargent had been the grand recorder, "the Van Dyck of our times" as the sculptor Auguste Rodin dubbed him. Sargent spent part of the war years in America, working on his mural schemes, but he returned to Europe in 1918 and spent time on the western front, where he conceived his great war painting *Gassed* (1918, Imperial War Museum, London). He also painted the *General Officers of World War I* (1922, National Portrait Gallery, London), one of three groups of statesmen, generals, and admirals commissioned by Sir Abe Bailey. A large, reserved man, Sargent never married but was often surrounded in Chelsea, London, by his close-knit family and a circle of devoted friends. He died at his house, 31 Tite Street, on the night of 14–15 April 1925, on the eve of his departure for America to install the last phase of his mural scheme in the Museum of Fine Arts, Boston.

The Sargent of this exhibition is not the grand old man of the 1920s but a young art student at the start of his career with everything to play for. He had to learn his trade as well as forge his own artistic identity. There are surviving studies of models in oil and pencil that testify to his grounding in the disciplines of academic art. When released from the restraints of the atelier, his preference was for plein air sketches which reflect an awareness of the latest trends in French art. His summer vacations were spent on the north French coast so it is scarcely surprising that he turned to marine subjects (the sea lay outside his bedroom window), but his attraction to them went deeper than that. He came of seafaring stock and a tradition of shipowning that went back generations.[5]

The founder of the Sargent family fortunes was Epes Sargent (1690–1762), a prosperous merchant and shipowner and a pillar of the community, first in Gloucester, Massachusetts, later in Salem. His son Winthrop Sargent (1727–1793), the artist's great great grandfather, acted as government agent in Gloucester during the American Revolutionary War, and he was one of the delegates to the state convention ratifying the Federal Constitution. His son Fitzwilliam Sargent (1768–1822) continued the shipowning business, establishing the India Company for trade with the East, and amassing a large fortune in the process. Failing health forced him to hand over the reins of the business to his son Winthrop Sargent (1792–1874), the artist's grandfather. The latter successfully managed the company until, in 1829, a disastrous series of losses at sea led to the failure of the business and the consequent loss of property.

The artist's father, another Fitzwilliam Sargent (1820–1889), was just ten at the time of the crash, which cast a long shadow over the family. An impoverished and chastened Winthrop withdrew to Philadelphia where he engaged in the commission business (probably some form of agency or insurance business), later managing a farm left to his youngest son Gorham Parsons Sargent, and serving with the Presbyterian Board of Publication as secretary in charge of foreign missions. Fitzwilliam meanwhile had studied medicine at the University of Pennsylvania, establishing a position as a rising surgeon at Wills Hospital in Philadelphia. In 1850 he married Mary Newbold Singer, daughter of a well-to-do merchant in the city; her mother's family, the Newbolds, were also in trade.

As he grew up, Fitzwilliam must have been keenly aware that, but for the crash, he would, as the eldest son, have inherited the family's shipping business. Perhaps it was the consciousness of his family's seafaring past that made him so touchingly interested in the United States navy, or perhaps his own thwarted ambitions in that direction. As Vernon Lee (the pseudonym of the writer Violet Paget, a close childhood friend of the painter) put it:

> That delicate, taciturn, austere—and oh so, so little of a jolly Tar!—father, was evidently fascinated by the profession from which fate had excluded him. He frequented American warships and admirals (considerably unlike himself in person), and I cannot but fancy that his nautical patriotism had been heightened by, and in turn heightened, the rancours he nurtured concerning the *Alabama* business, then recent history, and the British attitude towards what he spoke of as "The Rebels."[6]

According to Vernon Lee the young John was taken to entertainments on board US flagships at Villefranche, the port serving Nice, "and his toy boats were the badge of his naval future."[7]

Among the admirals whom Dr Fitzwilliam Sargent cultivated was Admiral Augustus Case (1812–1893), a veteran of the American Civil War, then living in Europe, and the two families became friendly. It was Admiral Case who would, memorably, purchase Sargent's early Salon painting *En Route pour la pêche* (fig. 8), thus giving his career a "push" at just the right moment. Significantly, Case's son Gus

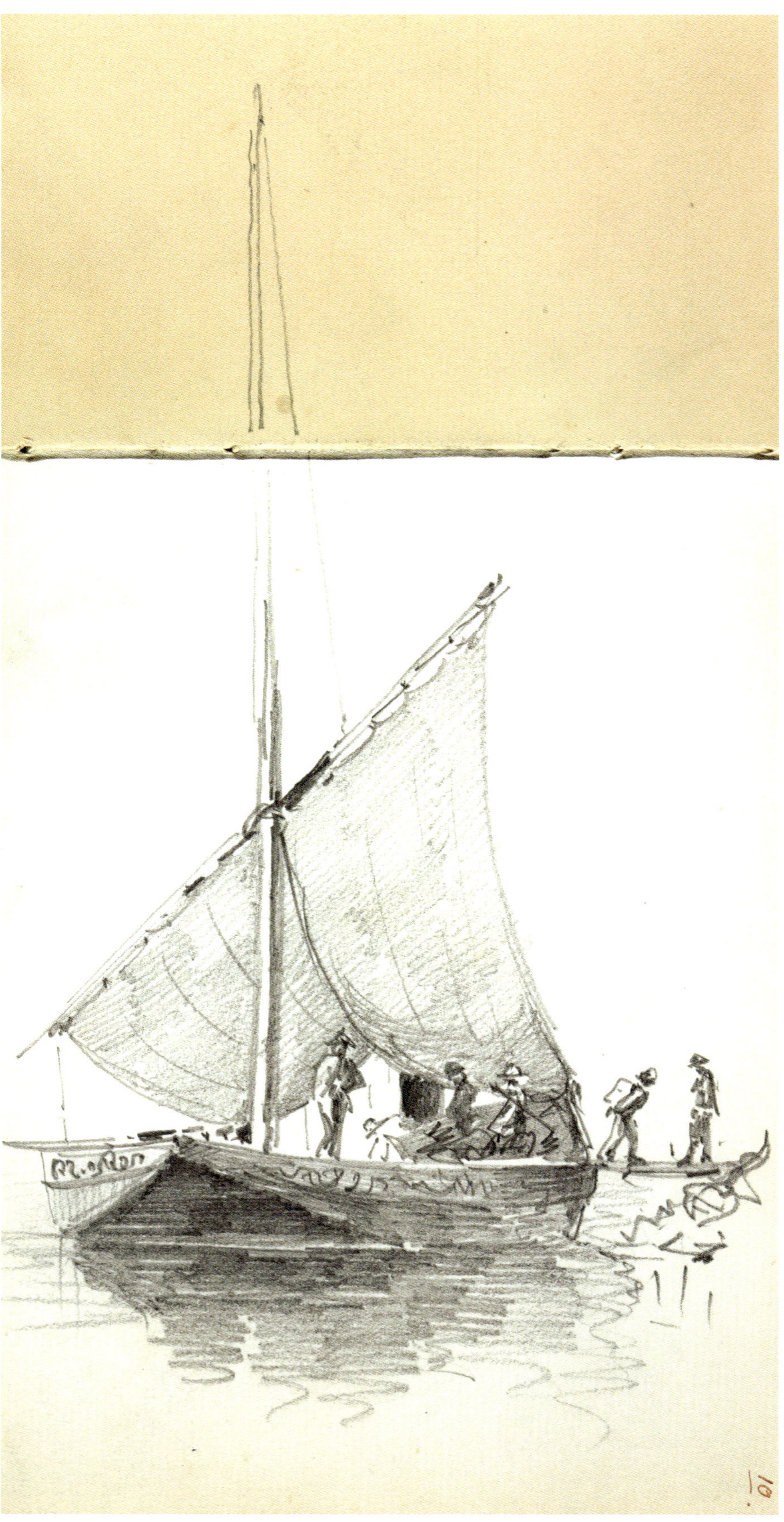

signed up for the United States navy as did his son-in-law Charles Deering. The two young men were good friends of the artist, who may have felt a tinge of envy when they sailed off to the east with the American fleet.[8] If Fitzwilliam had harbored dreams of a naval career for his son John, he came to recognize that his son's vocation lay in quite a different direction. It is a tribute to his liberal attitudes that he actively supported his son's choice of profession and put no barriers in his way.

Like his father, the young Sargent must have grown up with stories of his family's maritime past. He was proud of his ancestry and he later contributed pictures and funds to the Sargent-Gilman historic home in Gloucester, Massachusetts, which remains a public museum to this day. The artist was never far from the sea and was attracted to ships and boats from a young age. Among his earliest drawings, done when he was nine and sent to an uncle in Philadelphia, are sketches of sailing ships that were probably copied from illustrated magazines. In April 1865, at the same age, Sargent confided his impressions of Bordeaux to his friend Ben del Castillo:

> Bordeaux is a fine old city. The quai on which our hotel was is very wide, and the river has a great lot of large ships in it and a great many steamers. We left so early the next morning that I had not

Fig. 9 *Sailboat*, 1872. Graphite on paper, 6⅛ × 4⁷⁄₁₆ in (15.6 × 11.3 cm). Inscribed, lower right: *10*. Harvard Art Museum, Fogg Art Museum. Gift of Mrs Francis Ormond, 1937.7.9.10. (Exhibition)

> time to draw any of them; but they would have been too difficult for me, I think.[9]

To the same correspondent he wrote a month later that he had made a picture of the battery at San Sebastian in northern Spain, and "a good many ships."[10] He later described his visit to England in some detail, recalling a trip to see Isambard Kingdom Brunel's huge iron ship *Great Eastern*, then employed in cable laying:

> On our way to Paris we stopped at Sheerness to see the Great Eastern. We took a little row boat and a couple of sailors rowed us to her, about three miles. We went on board, and saw a great many pieces of the cable, and the first officer gave Mama a piece of it. Yesterday we went to the hotel de Cluny . . . We saw a very curious ship that looked as if it had been made of gold. It was full of men holding ropes in their hands, while others were ready to beat on drums. I believe it was presented to one of the Kings of France by an Emperor of China.[11]

These letters demonstrate Sargent's powers of observation and his eye for detail. No drawings of the *Great Eastern* are extant, but his early sketchbooks contain studies of boats drawn mostly on the Italian lakes, like the *Sailboat* of 1872 in the Fogg Art Museum (fig. 9).[12]

Sargent also sharpened his eye for maritime scenes by mining images from the popular press. Vernon Lee recalled the artist copying an illustration from a magazine during the winter of 1867–68:

> I can see in my mind's eye (for I saw it with the bodily one within the last half century, and even hope to find it in some mislaid portfolio) a "picture" which he made for my album. I can see the clean juxtaposed blue and green of sky and waves, the splendid tossing lines of sea and ships, see even the bold pencil title in a clearer version of his grown-up writing, the title in a corner, "U.S. Ship (name, alas, forgotten!) Chasing the Slaver *Panther*."[13]

In Florence during the winter of 1869–70, Sargent ran across Captain Edward Augustus Silsbee of the American mercantile marine. Silsbee is remembered today as the man who courted Jane Clairmont, Byron's former mistress, in the hope of obtaining her Shelley manuscripts—a story that inspired Henry James to write *The Aspern Papers*. The young Sargent listened spellbound to the captain's stories, including one about himself. When in command of a steamer he fell into an oil tank, and it took so long to get him out that his curly hair "refused ever to curl again."[14]

Sargent's first serious experiments in marine art occurred during the summer vacation he took with his family shortly after joining Carolus-Duran's atelier in 1874. It was common practice for art students, and artists in general, to decamp to the countryside or the seaside over the summer to paint genre scenes as an antidote to the disciplines of the atelier. The north French coastline was immensely popular and whole communities of artists descended on the resorts of the region to record its topography and inhabitants. The artists were part of the middle-class exodus to the seaside which became such a feature of nineteenth-century social life. Like their clients, artists were attracted by the prospect of visiting exciting and unfamiliar places, the pleasures that going to the seaside involved (sun, beach, fresh air, fishing, sea bathing), and the opportunity to experience the traditional way of life and picturesque costumes of the local inhabitants. The vogue for sea pictures and

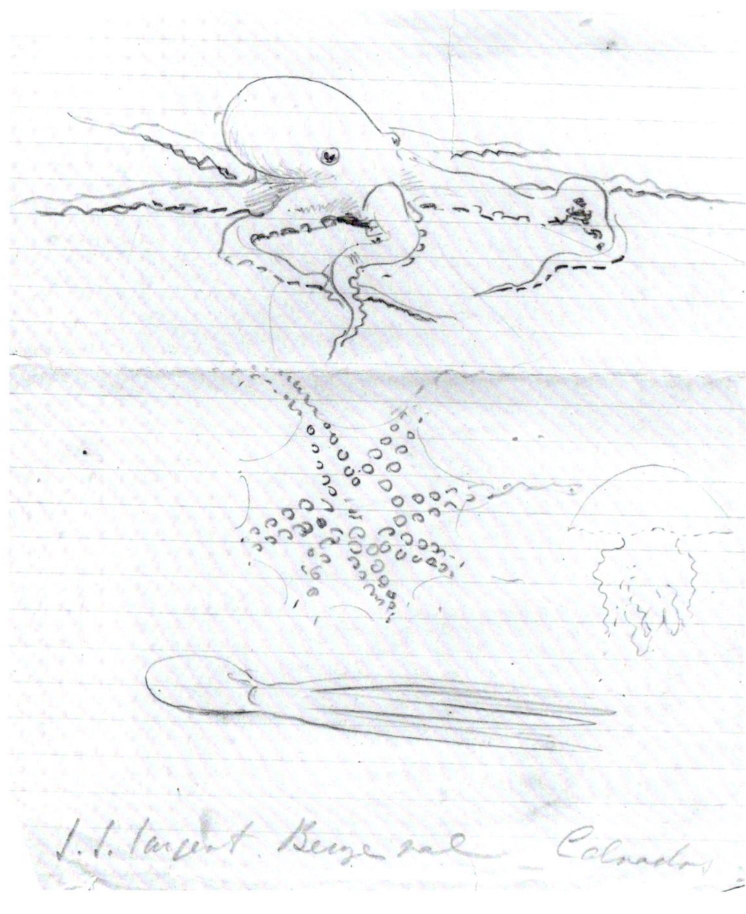

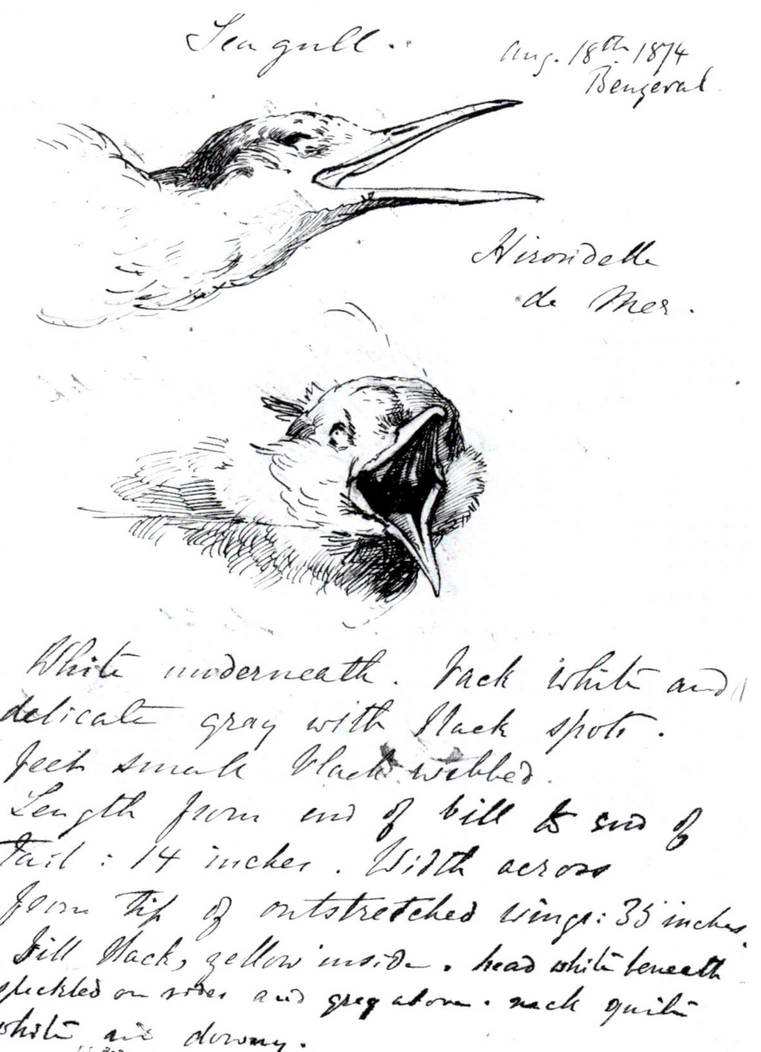

Fig. 10 *Octopus and Starfish*, Beuzeval (Calvados), Normandy, 1874. Graphite on paper, 6 3/8 × 8 in (16.2 × 20.3 cm) (irregular). Inscribed, bottom: *J.S. Sargent/Beuzeval/Calvados.* Private Collection. (Exhibition)

Fig. 11 *Seagull*, Beuzeval (Calvados), Normandy, 1874. Pen and ink on paper, 7 15/16 × 5 5/8 in (20.2 × 14.3 cm). Inscribed, top center and right: *Seagull/Aug. 18th 1874/Beuzeval.* The Metropolitan Museum of Art. Gift of Mrs Francis Ormond, 1950. (50.130.86 recto)

beach scenes was directly stimulated by the vacation industry because it reflected a self-image of what people on holiday had experienced and brought back with them. The same thing happened in the countryside, where pastoral imagery satisfied a deep longing for the simple life and unspoilt nature.

Sargent was not a free agent like most of his fellow students but lumbered with his family, who had settled temporarily in Paris. What took them to Beuzeval, now part of the township of Houlgate on the Calvados coast of Normandy, in late June 1874, is unknown. They may have followed the advice of family friends, the Watts's, who like them spent the summer in the Hotel Imbert, a building that still survives. The only record of their holiday is a letter written from the hotel by Dr Sargent to his close friend and fellow expatriate George Bemis on 8 September 1874. Lacking a birth certificate for his son, Dr Sargent needed a note from Bemis confirming Sargent's parentage and birth so that he could sit the Concours, a competitive exam for entry to the École des Beaux-Arts in Paris, the official French art school:

> We have had a very pleasant satisfactory summer here—much more agreeable good weather than the Engadine [Swiss Alps] would have been; good every thing, I may say, and we do not envy the Swiss their mountains or valleys or their air—
>
> It is possible that my wife may linger with the two younger children at Rouen after John and I shall have gone to Paris to attend to this concours matter.[15]

Of Sargent's artistic endeavors that summer little survives (one assumes he was not idle): a watercolor of two boys, Oscar and Bobino (see fig. 66), executed in the rather stilted style of his earlier, juvenile watercolors; a drawing of an octopus (fig. 10), anticipating his oil of the following summer (fig. 12); another of a seagull with extensive color notes (fig. 11). At Rouen he transcribed a harmony exercise demonstrating how to move from one musical key to another (private collection). That is the sum total of his surviving output, and it does not demonstrate any great advance in his artistic powers. At Nice, where he spent Christmas with his

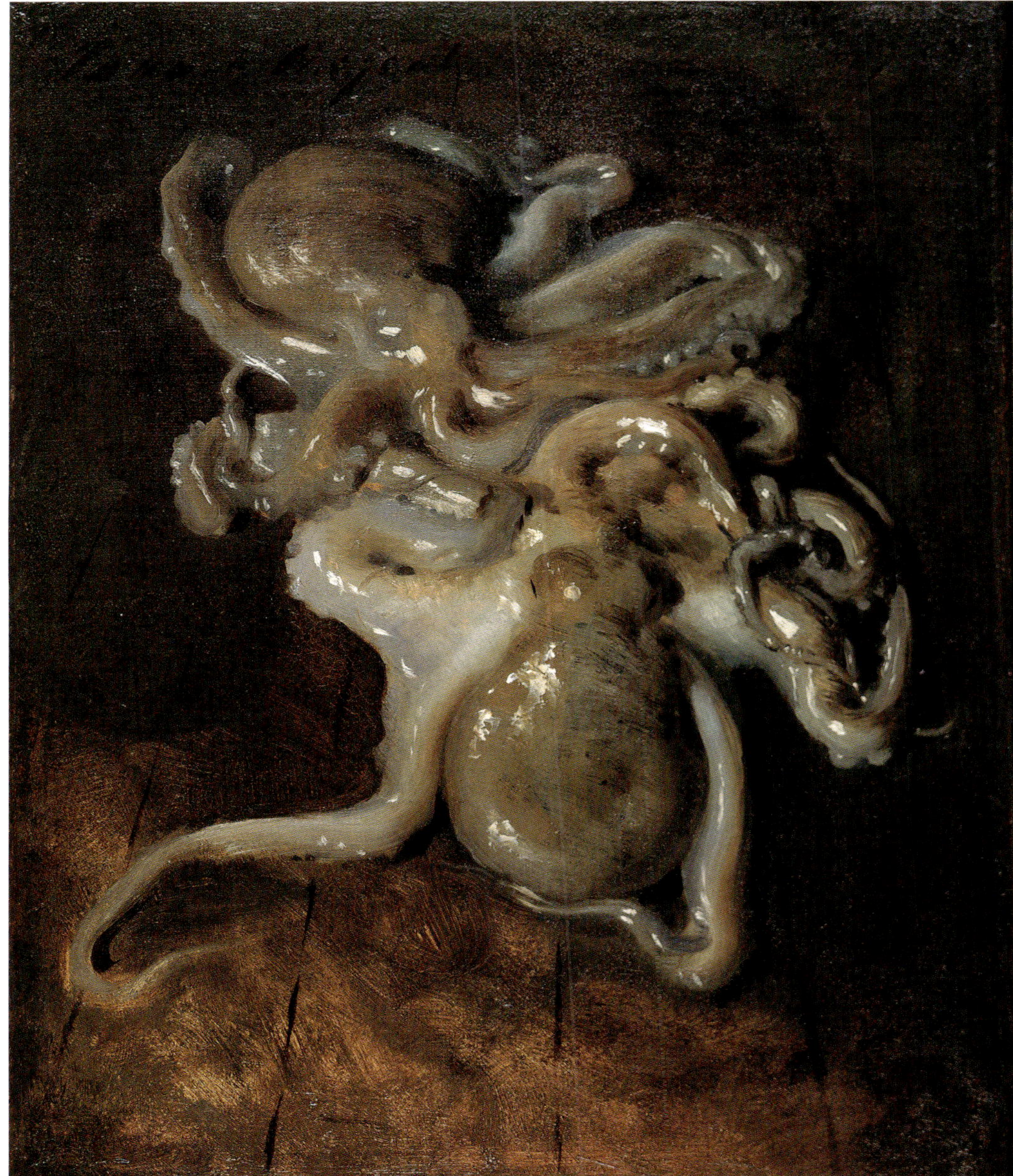

Fig. 12 *Two Octopi*, *c.* 1875. Oil on canvas, 16 × 12⅝ in (40.6 × 32.1 cm). Inscribed, upper left: *John S. Sargent*; upper right: *1875*. Private Collection.

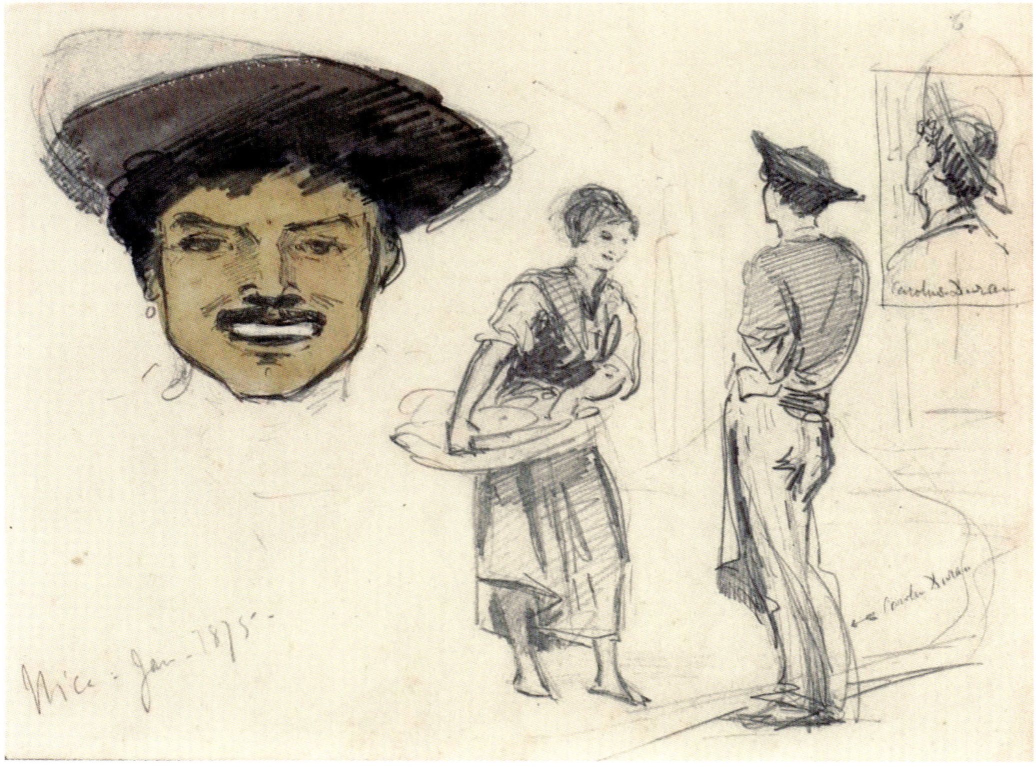

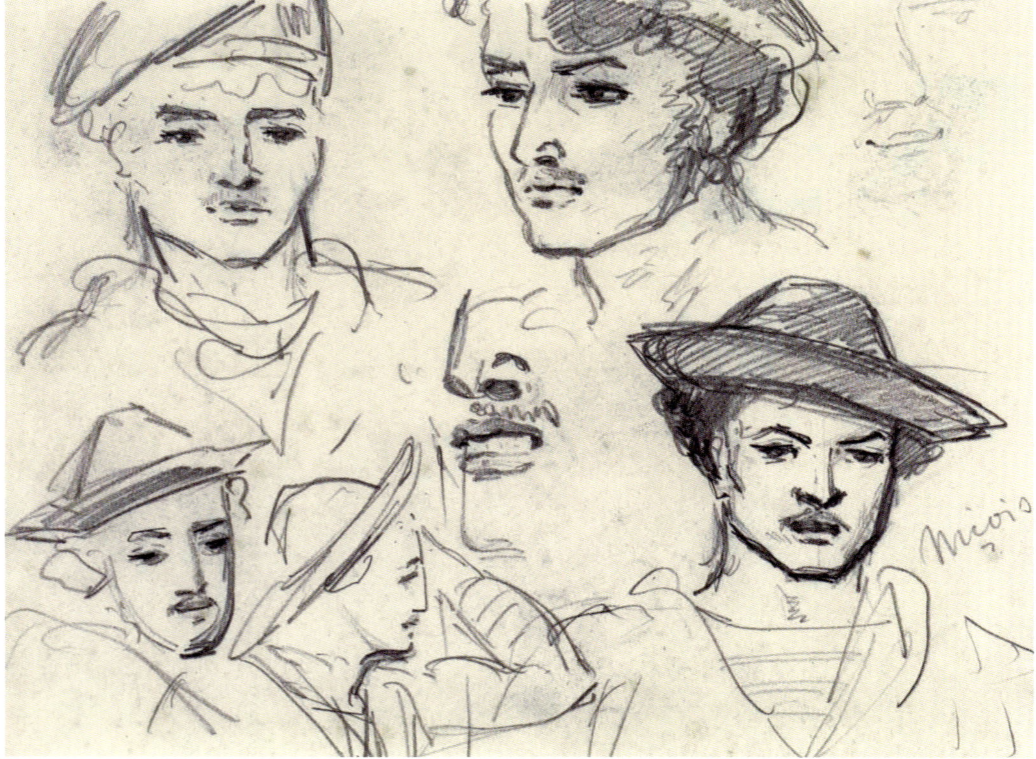

family, he continued to explore maritime imagery, executing a vivid double-sided drawing of sailors down at the port (figs. 13, 14).

The transformation in Sargent's artistic powers occurred over the winter of 1874–75. Suddenly, or so it seems, Sargent emerges as a fully-formed painter and draughtsman of considerable skill and sophistication. The portrait sketches of his family and friends are textbook illustrations of tonal painting *au premier point* (the brush falling in single decisive strokes). The little picture of a café scene with two wine glasses, *La Table sous la tonnelle* (fig. 15), inscribed "1874" but likely to date from the following year, is an astonishing performance for a nineteen-year-old. The treatment of sunlight flickering through trees, and the spirited brushwork, demonstrate the young painter's absorption of the latest styles in French painting, including that of Impressionism. His reputation as the star of the atelier was established through studies of this caliber. His work was now the benchmark against which other students measured their progress.

Figs. 13, 14 *Figure Studies*, Nice, 1875. Graphite with watercolor and black chalk on paper, $7\frac{3}{4} \times 10\frac{1}{16}$ in (19.8 × 25.6 cm). Inscribed, recto [sailors, woman with basket], lower left: *Nice. Jan. 1875*, upper right and lower right: *Carolus Duran*; verso [sailors], lower right: *Niçois*. William Kelly Simpson, New York. (Exhibition)

Sargent's art education at Carolus-Duran's atelier was supplemented by drawing classes at the École des Beaux-Arts, to which he had no difficulty in gaining admission (22 October 1874). He also attended evening classes in the atelier of the French realist painter Léon Bonnat. Apart from a superb presentation drawing of an antique classical plinth, with which he won the *concours d'ornament* in May 1877,[16] none of Sargent's surviving life studies can be certainly associated with the École. However, those drawings of models that we do know demonstrate an instinctive mastery of line and an ability to model form through the interplay of light and dark tones. Precision of drawing went hand in hand with bravura painting and laid the foundation for his highly developed technical skills.

The fruits of this rapidly acquired proficiency were to be demonstrated during a second vacation on the north French coast. This time the Sargent family traveled further west, spending the summer at the fishing village of Saint-Énogat, a few miles from Saint-Malo, the major port in that region of Brittany. The presence of several family friends—the Austins, Norrises, Sorchans, and Wattses—suggests that the choice of resort may have been a collective decision. A letter from Sargent to Ben del Castillo, written from the Maison Lefort at Saint-Énogat on 20 June 1875, describes the house and location:

> We enjoy our little country house very much with its pleasant garden and thoroughly rural entourage. I have reason to be contented and thankful for my quarters are charming. My bedroom is the most beautiful interior I have ever seen in anything short of a palace or a castle. It is furnished throughout in the mediaeval style. Its beamed ceiling and floor are of oak, its walls completely hung with stamped leathers and arras;

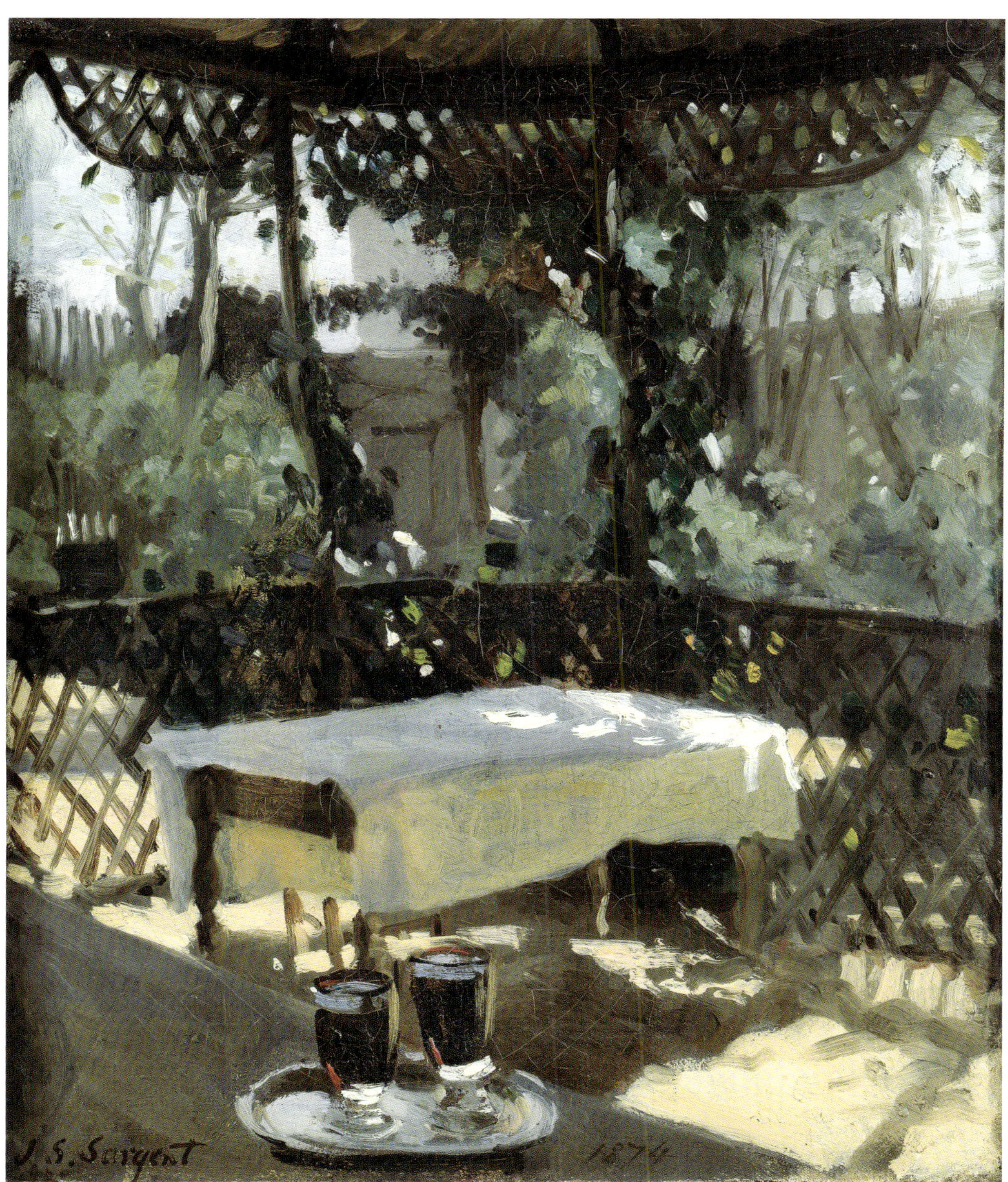

Fig. 15 *La Table sous la tonnelle*, *c.* 1875. Oil on canvas, 18 × 14½ in (45.7 × 36.8 cm). Inscribed, lower left: *J. S. Sargent*; lower center: *1874*. Private Collection.

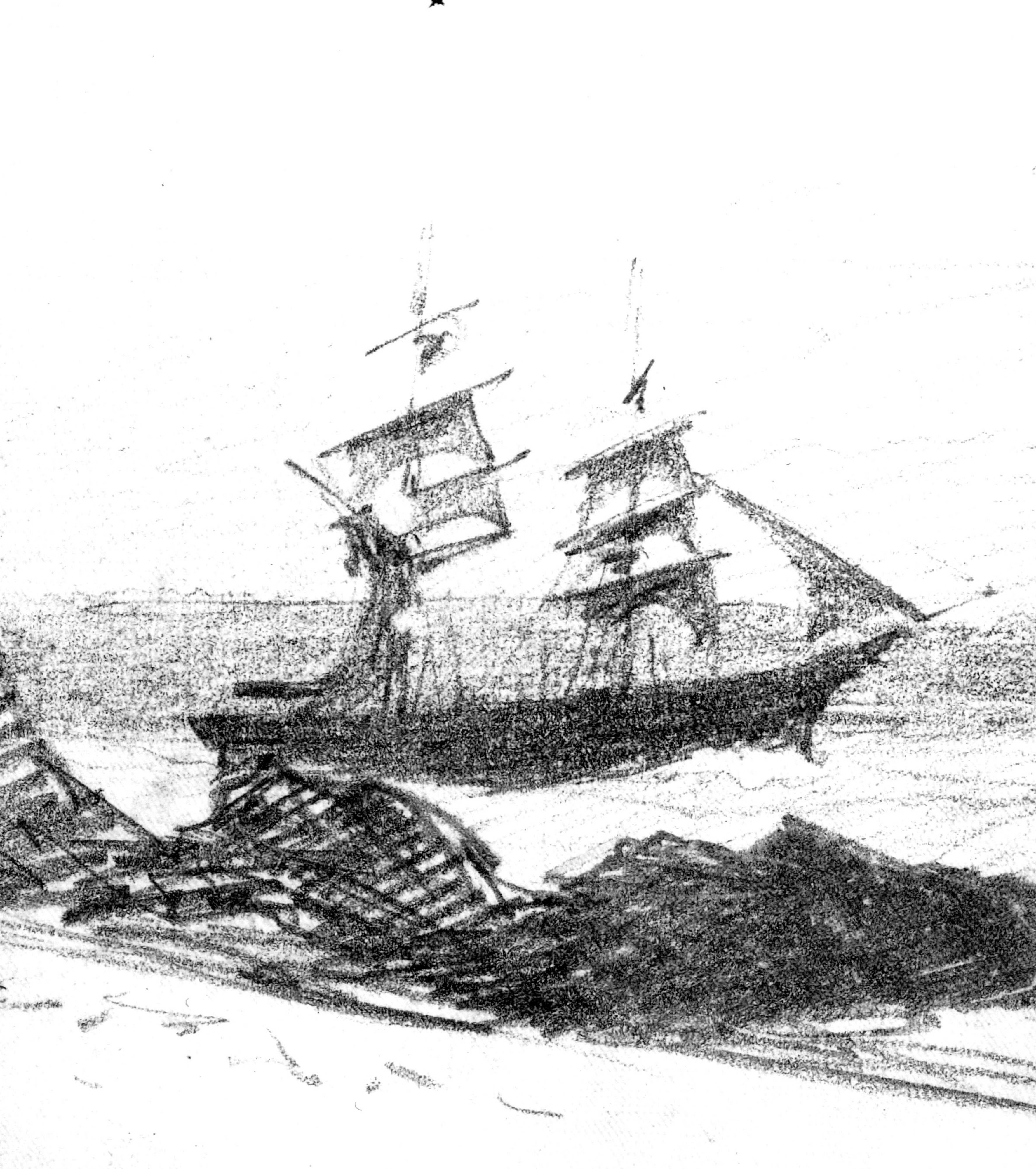

> the furniture is all antique and richly carved, especially the grand bedstead with canopy and bed posts, the immense wardrobe, and ebony cabinet . . . from them [the windows] you look right over and into the fig tree with its great shining green leaves and ripening fruit, then over the pear trees and cherry trees and flowers of the garden, to the wide cornfields, and over them to the sea.
>
> There is much to paint, but it has poured ever since we have been here, so I have accomplished little as yet.[17]

This letter is scarcely revealing of Sargent's artistic motivations. That he came to Saint-Énogat with a preconceived plan of action is probably unlikely given his youth and relative inexperience. There were plenty of distractions in the form of his pretty young Austin cousins and the lively Fanny Watts, not to speak of his family obligations. Dr Sargent writes to George Bemis of foraging for butter and eggs in the local farms, walks on the windmill-covered hills, expeditions to Saint-Malo and Saint-Servain, and cruises to the islands.[18]

The paintings and drawings that Sargent executed in Brittany in 1875 are works of real quality. The artist's focus is on scenes from the seashore and rustic subjects in the countryside. Thirteen of the sheets associated with this visit appear to have come from the same sketchbook. They show a serrated fore-edge, where the page was torn out of the sketchbook, and they are approximately of the same dimensions, 4 × 6½ in (10.16 × 16.51 cm). One of the drawings is dated "May 1875" (see fig. 16), although Dr Sargent informed Bemis that he and the family would not leave Paris till the end of June; Sargent himself may have gone to Brittany earlier. All but one of the drawings were mounted in a scrapbook now in the Metropolitan Museum of Art, New York, the significance of which is discussed by Stephanie Herdrich in her essay (see pp. 59–87).

The drawings represent a succession of thought-through compositions. They might have been turned into paintings, so clearly are the main features of each scene defined and blocked in. The drawing is swift and assured, grasping intuitively the fugitive effects of the weather and the movement of the sea. What was lurking in Sargent's mind as he created these bold images? That he was conscious of the long tradition of marine art is certain, for he was an inveterate museum-goer and knowledgeable about art history. His drawings echo the marine pictures of those Dutch seventeenth-century masters like Julius Porcellis and Simon de Vlieger, where rocky outcrops counterpoint wide expanses of sea (see fig. 80). He was not alone in this, for the Impressionists, too, looked back to the Dutch masters for inspiration when painting seascapes.[19] There is an immediacy to Sargent's imagery, lacking in his Dutch predecessors, a transcription of specific conditions at sea rather than generalized effects.

Sargent drew on the experience of these sketches in two oil paintings that the present author dates to 1875. *An Old Boat Stranded* (fig. 17) depicts the hulk of an old fishing boat stranded in the shallows of a cove, similar in composition to the drawing of *Two Small Boats Moored to Beach* (fig. 18). A yacht under full sail noses its way around the point like the ship in *Saint-Malo* (fig. 16). The artist exploits the romantic associations of the hulk, symbolic of the passage of time and dead men's lives, with the gleaming modernity of the yacht, the epitome of wealth and leisure. *An Old Boat Stranded* sadly is missing, so we cannot judge the impact of its color, but the way it is blocked in, with square brushstrokes, is very much in the spirit of the drawings. In character it bears the stamp of modern realism.

Facing page: Fig. 16 Detail of fig. 68, *Saint-Malo*, 1875. In the John Singer Sargent Scrapbook (50.130.154). The Metropolitan Museum of Art. Gift of Mrs Francis Ormond, 1950. (50.130.154w) (Exhibition)

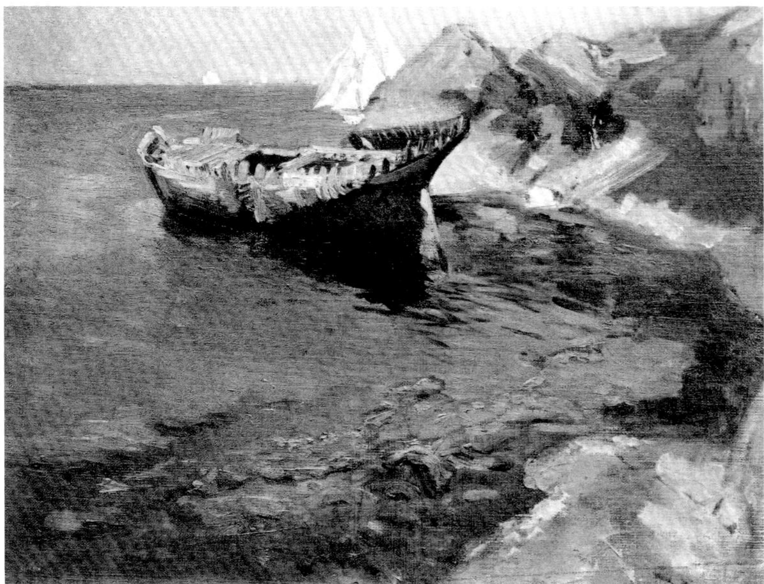

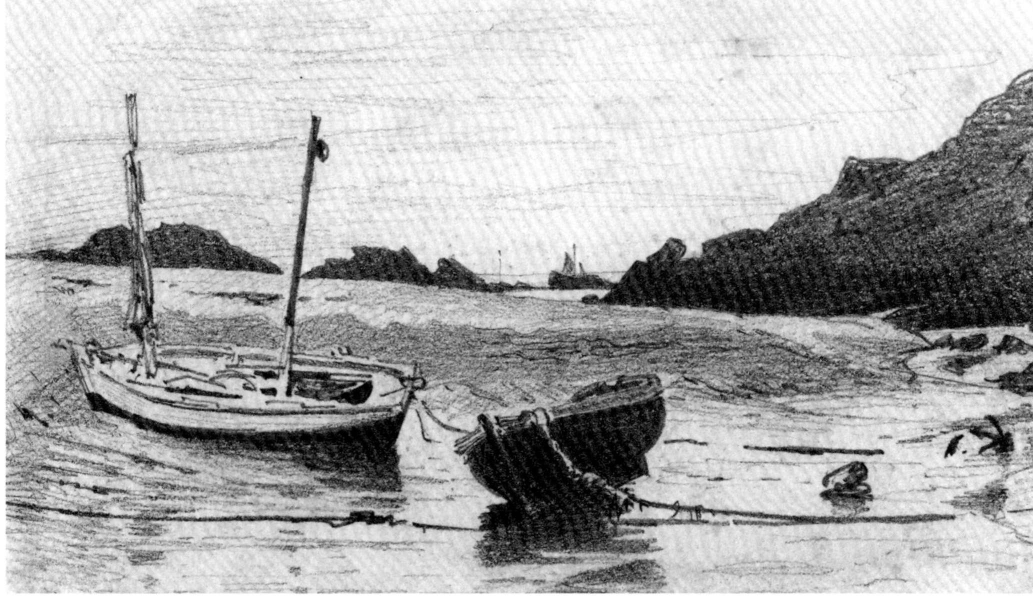

Fig. 17 *An Old Boat Stranded*, *c.* 1875. Oil on canvas, 13 × 16¾ in (33 × 42.5 cm). Untraced.

Fig. 18 *Two Small Boats Moored to Beach*, *c.* 1875. Graphite on paper, 3¹⁵⁄₁₆ × 6½ in (10 × 16.5 cm). In the John Singer Sargent Scrapbook (50.130.154). The Metropolitan Museum of Art, New York. Gift of Mrs Francis Ormond, 1950. (50.130.154hh) (Exhibition)

The second picture, *Seascape with Rocks* (fig. 19) is more muted and aesthetic in mood. Two bands of seaweed-covered rocks, set at an angle to one another, articulate the foreground. The gently rippling water in front gives way to a luminous sense of distance and space under an opalescent sky, an effect not unlike that in *Coastal Scene* (fig. 20). A sliver of land in the distance marks out the boundary of the wide passage of open water. The subtle adjustments of tone within a restricted color range (off whites and bluish grays) demonstrate a new sensitivity in the artist's treatment of light and the evocation of mood. We are lulled into a dreamy state of lassitude contemplating this hazy vision of the sea. One wonders whether the artist was as yet aware of the seascapes by James McNeill Whistler, an issue explored by Erica Hirshler (pp. 53–55).

The only certainly documented oil painting from 1875 is *Two Octopi* (fig. 12). This is an assured performance in the realist mode, depicting the gleaming bodies and tentacles of two freshly caught molluscs. The reference here is to the still-life pictures of dead fish by such established realist Salon painters as Théodule-Augustin Ribot and Antoine Vollon. Sargent's molluscs are less freighted with social meaning than those of his older contemporaries and more concerned with painterly issues of light, texture, and design. The two animals lie facing each other on the floorboards of the boat, their tentacles forming an intricate web of writhing forms. It is impossible not to feel sympathy for these fearsome-looking creatures so cruelly exposed in death. The artist conveys the moist flesh of the octopi in a tour-de-force of pictorial representation that recalls the still-lifes of fish by Edouard Manet. Sargent was just nineteen.

Sargent came of age as a marine painter in the series of pictures and drawings

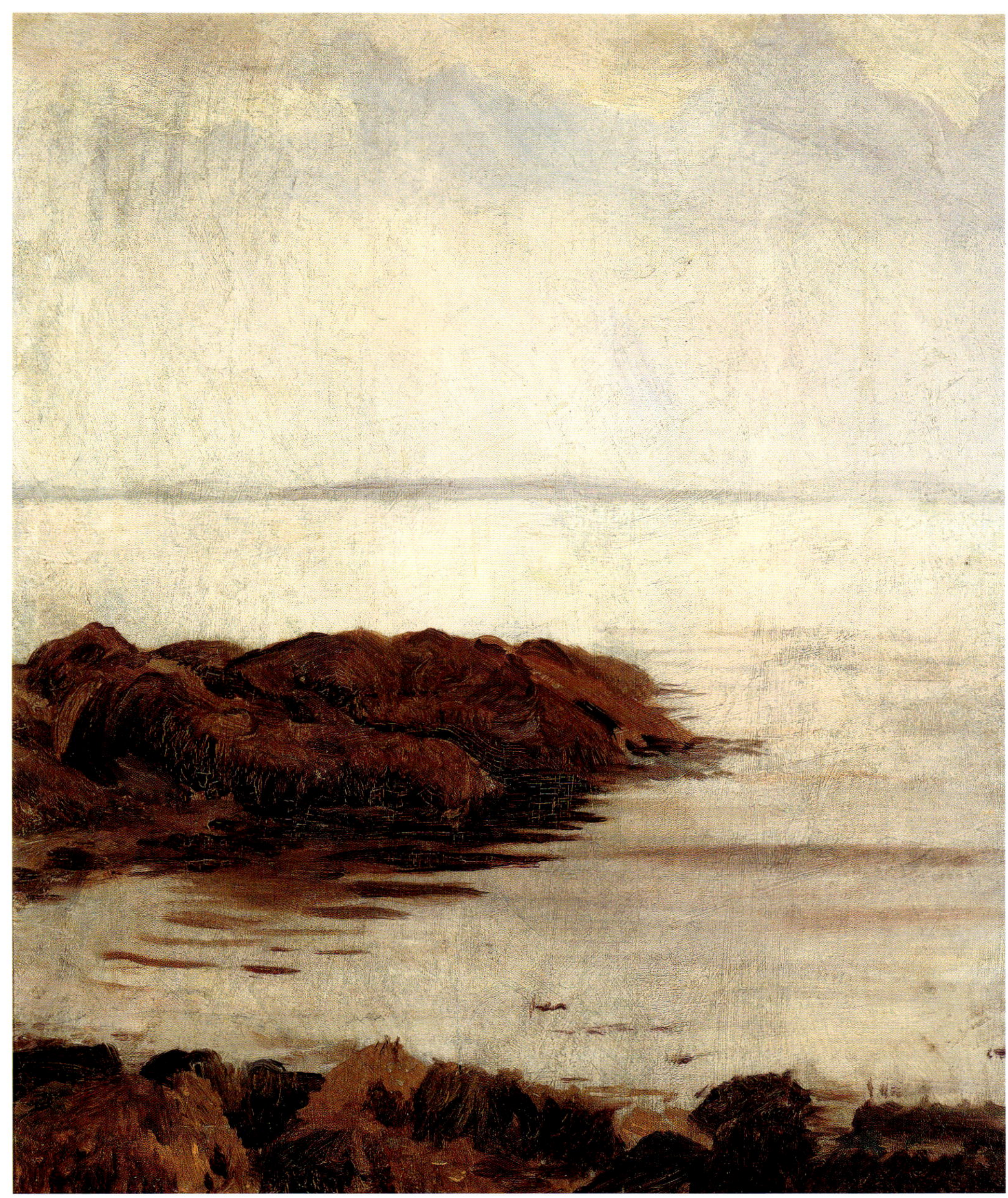

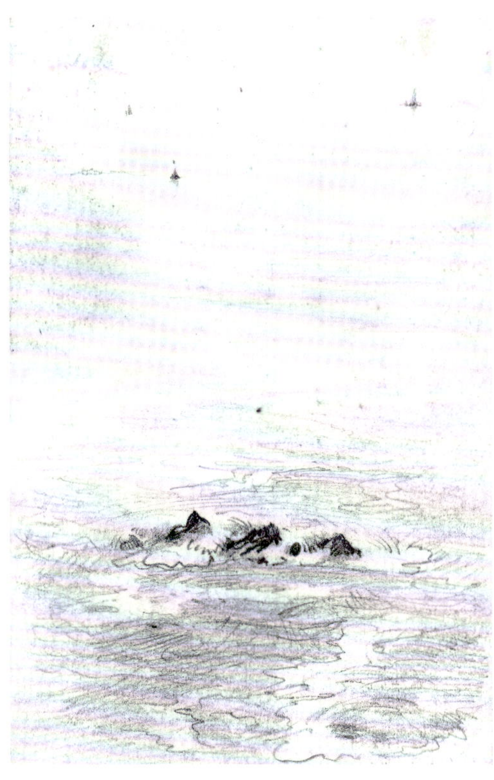

inspired by his transatlantic voyages of 1876, which are the subject of Erica Hirshler's essay (pp. 39–57). Exposure to the elements of the ocean released his imagination and his ambition. He was no longer looking out to sea from the comfort zone of the shore but caught up in the drama and wildness of the ocean itself, especially on the return voyage when he experienced the full force of an Atlantic gale. He traveled back to Europe from

Fig. 19 *Seascape with Rocks*, *c.* 1875–77. Oil on canvas, 17 × 14 in (43.2 × 35.6 cm). Corcoran Gallery of Art, Washington, D.C., Joseph F. McCrindle Collection, 2009.004. (Exhibition)

Fig. 20 *Coastal Scene*, *c.* 1875. Graphite on paper, 6⅝ × 4 in (16.8 × 10.2 cm). In the John Singer Sargent Scrapbook (50.130.154). The Metropolitan Museum of Art, New York. Gift of Mrs Francis Ormond, 1950. (50.130.154s) (Exhibition)

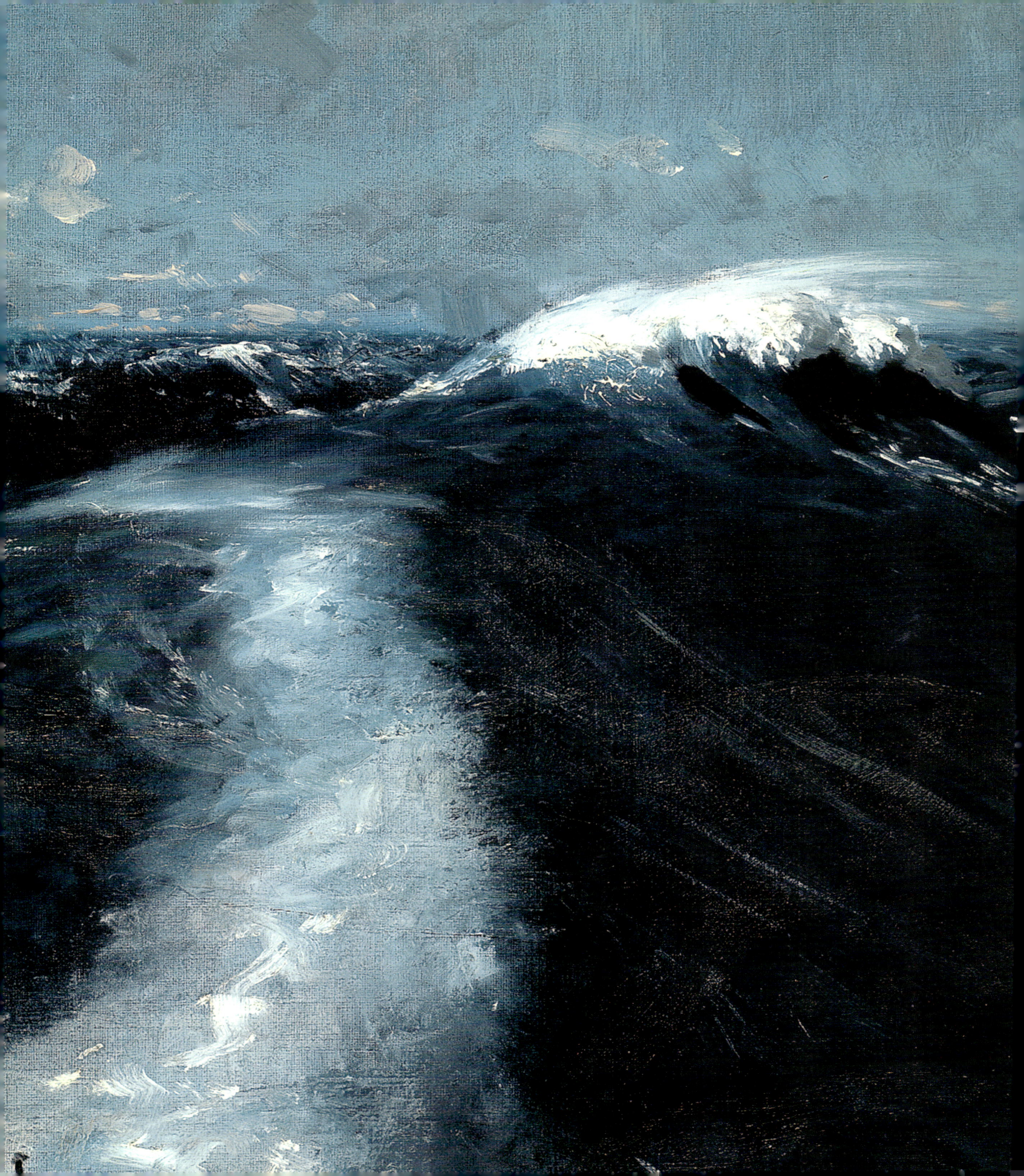

America in October 1876 aboard the *SS Algeria*, a Cunard liner. His painting *Atlantic Storm* (fig. 21) presents an awe-inspiring spectacle of the sea witnessed from the plunging deck of the ship. The wake streams out behind in a glistening web of white froth, and the huge, spume-crested waves seem likely at any moment to overwhelm the fragile craft.

This is sea painting on a grand scale. One is reminded again of the Dutch masters, Ludolph Bakhuizen and William Van de Velde the Younger in particular, whose storm pictures, represented in most of the great European collections of art, illustrate the destructive powers of nature and the fragility of human life. Nearer in time are the Romantics, pre-eminent among them J. M.W. Turner, which engage the emotions of the viewer in a more direct and sensational way. Turner's famous painting *Shipwreck* (fig. 22) was copied by Sargent at this early period in a drawing executed on the back of stationery from The Children's Hospital in Philadelphia (fig. 23). He would have seen Turner's work on his visits to London, but his drawing is likely to have been done from a print or reproduction. If it was executed in Philadelphia it would have to date from 1876. Stylistically it relates to other early marine drawings and reflects Sargent's lifelong admiration for the British painter. He inserted a print of Turner's *Calais Pier* in his early scrapbook (fig. 115). The American artist William Thorne recalled standing in front of a Turner marine painting in the Tate Gallery when Sargent remarked: "Thorne, when I'm in the mood he Turner seems to me the greatest of all the landscape masters."[20] Nearer to home in Paris, Théodore Géricault's celebrated *Raft of the Medusa* (1819) was to be seen in the Louvre, and in the Musée du Luxembourg hung wreck scenes by Théodore Gudin and Eugène Isabey.

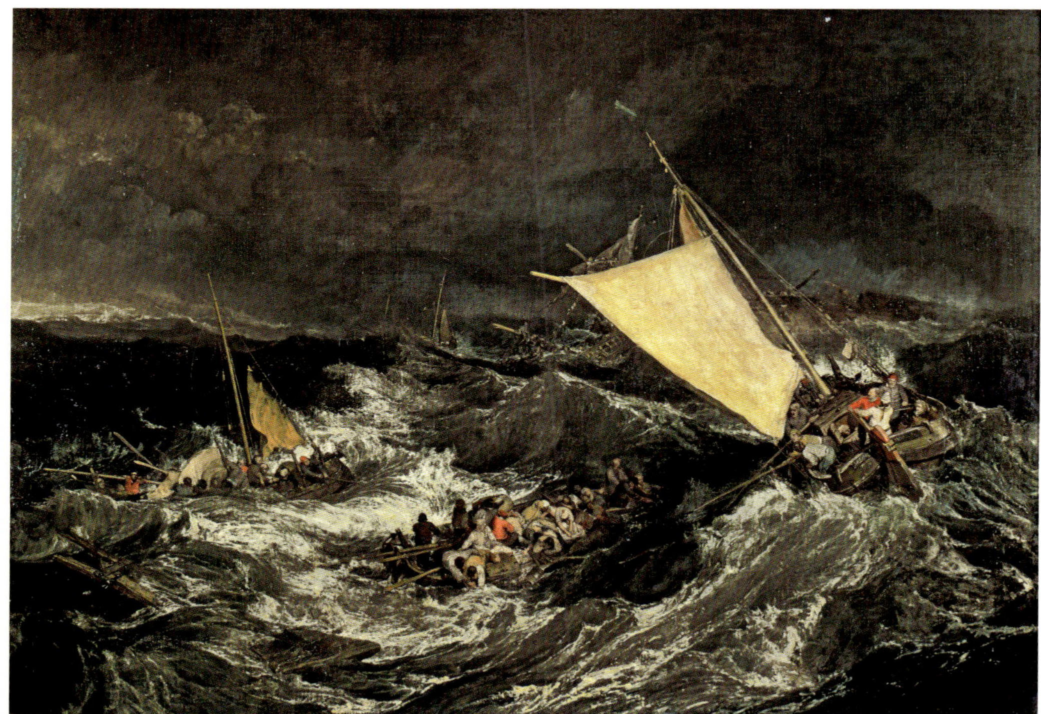

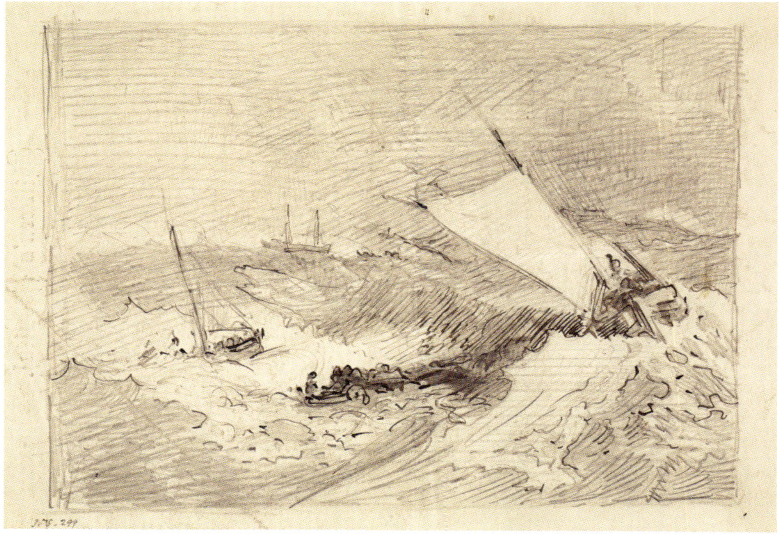

Facing page: Fig. 21 Detail of fig. 51, *Atlantic Storm*, 1876. Curtis Galleries, Minneapolis. (Exhibition)

Fig. 22 J.M.W. Turner, *Shipwreck*, 1805. Oil on canvas, 67⅛ × 95⅛ in (170.5 × 241.5 cm). Tate, London. Accepted by the nation as part of the Turner Bequest, 1856, N00476.

Fig. 23 *Sketch of boats in a stormy sea*, c. 1876. Graphite with pen and ink on paper (Stationery from The Children's Hospital, Philadelphia), 5 1/16 × 7 5/8 in. (12.8 × 19.4 cm). Museum of Fine Arts, Boston, Sargent Collection, Gift of Miss Emily Sargent and Mrs. Violet Ormond in memory of their brother John Singer Sargent, 28.923. (Exhibition)

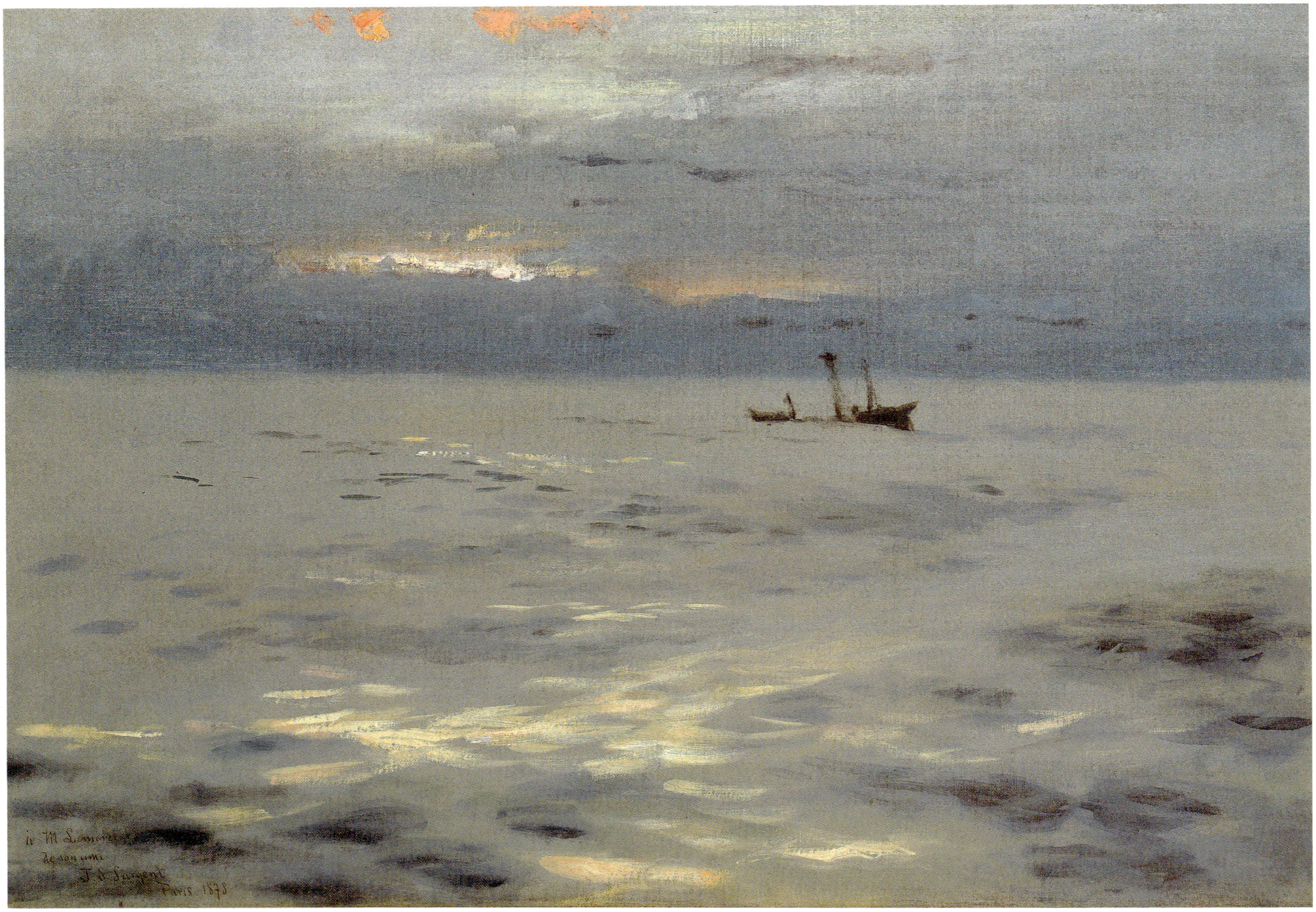

Fig. 24 *Atlantic Sunset*, *c.* 1876. Oil on canvas, 25½ × 36¼ in (64.8 × 92 cm). Inscribed, bottom left: *à M. Lemercier / de son ami / J.S. Sargent / Paris 1878*. Private Collection. (Exhibition)

Fig. 25 *The Derelict*, *c.* 1876. Oil on canvas, 13¼ × 20 in (33.7 × 50.8 cm). Inscribed, lower right: *à M. Hirsch son ami reconnaissant / J.S. Sargent*. Private Collection. (Exhibition)

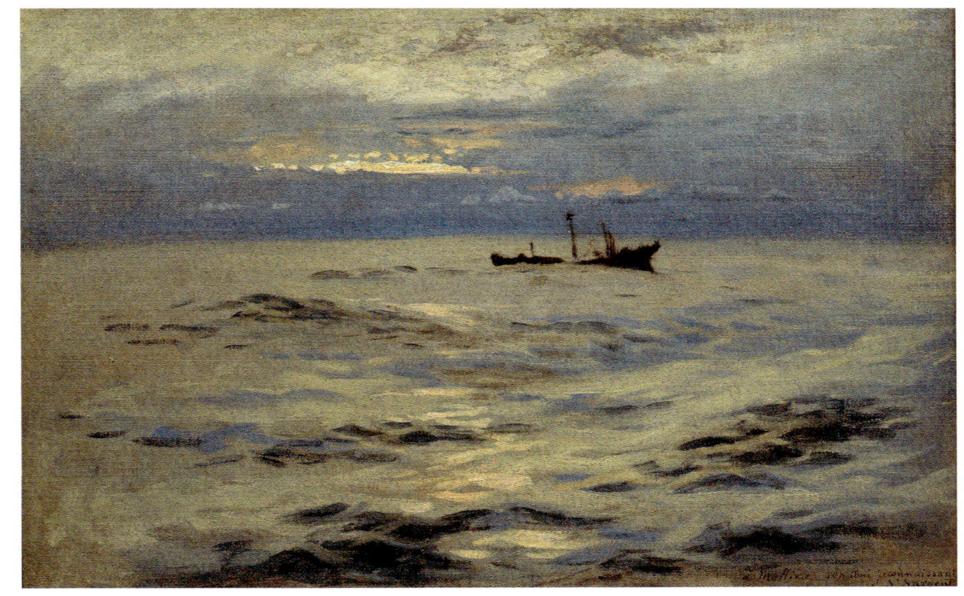

Sargent demonstrates his modernist credentials in the way he composes *Atlantic Storm*, squeezing the ship into the bottom of the picture space, arbitrarily cropping it and pitching the viewer headlong down the deck. It is the kind of approach Edgar Degas might have attempted, a telescopic foreshortening of space with simplified detail. The seascape in the background of the picture is more conventionally treated, in the realist *métier* of Gustave Courbet and Johan Barthold Jongkind, though neither of these artists painted at sea. They were always shoreline observers looking seaward. A second Sargent picture apparently recording this same Atlantic storm is *Mid-Ocean, Mid-Winter* (fig. 54).

Atlantic Storm and *Mid-Ocean, Mid-Winter* are well-documented pictures. The recent appearance of three hitherto unknown seascapes radically altered perceptions of Sargent's role as a marine painter. *Atlantic Sunset* (fig. 24) is a major addition to the artist's œuvre, a painting that conveys the immensity of the ocean at that crepuscular moment of the day so dear to the hearts of the aesthetes; it is the marine equivalent to Sargent's urban picture *In the Luxembourg Gardens* (1879, Philadelphia Museum of Art). Gleams from the setting sun light up the gray-blue tones of the water, and the distant bank of cloud is shot through with streaks of pink and orange. What looks like an abandoned sailing ship lies low in the water, casting a melancholy gloom over the scene. The picture is dated "1878" but this probably relates to the date of its presentation to the artist's landlord, Dr Abel Lemercier, not its date of execution.[21] Sargent spent the summer of 1878 in Capri, but *Atlantic Sunset* does not look like a Mediterranean scene and it is a fair assumption that the picture is a record of something he had seen on one of his transatlantic voyages. The existence of a smaller version, *The Derelict* (fig. 25), which turned up a few months before *Atlantic Sunset*, may be the plein air sketch on which the artist based the larger work. *Seascape* (fig. 26), the third of the rediscovered marine paintings, is a work in the same vein. The sun, low in the horizon and partially obscured, casts reflections across the sea and the white-crested waves in the foreground that chart the vessel's passage.

Sargent's imagination was stimulated by scenes inboard as well as those seaward. A series of drawings, in the tight, staccato style he had developed in Brittany the

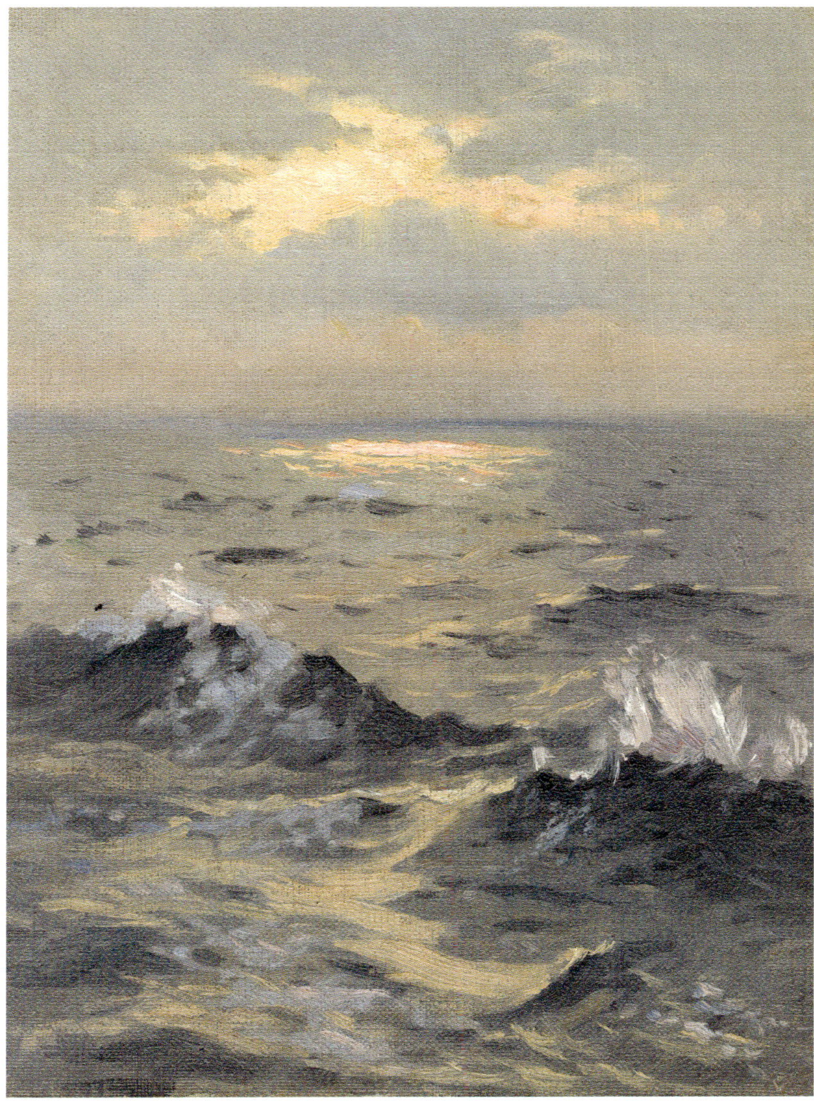

Fig. 26 *Seascape*, *c.* 1876. Oil on canvas, 11 × 8⁵⁄₁₆ in (28.6 × 21.1 cm). Frank M. Gren "Annapolis Collection." (Exhibition)

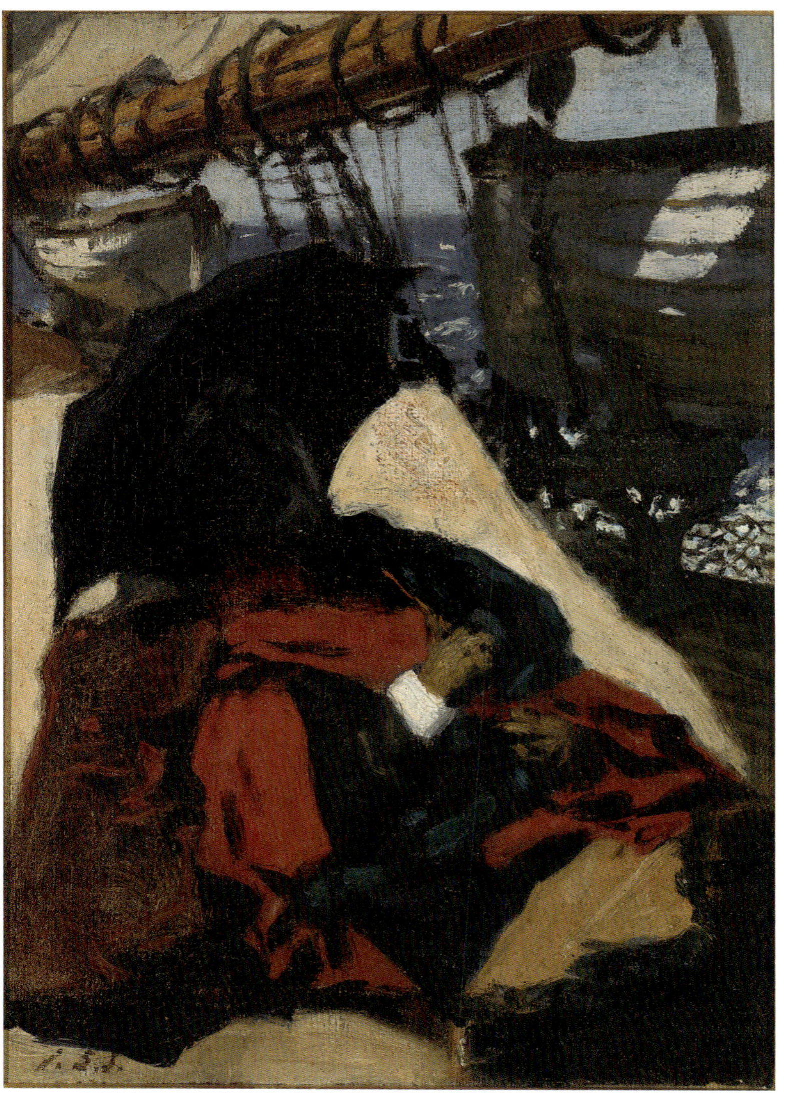

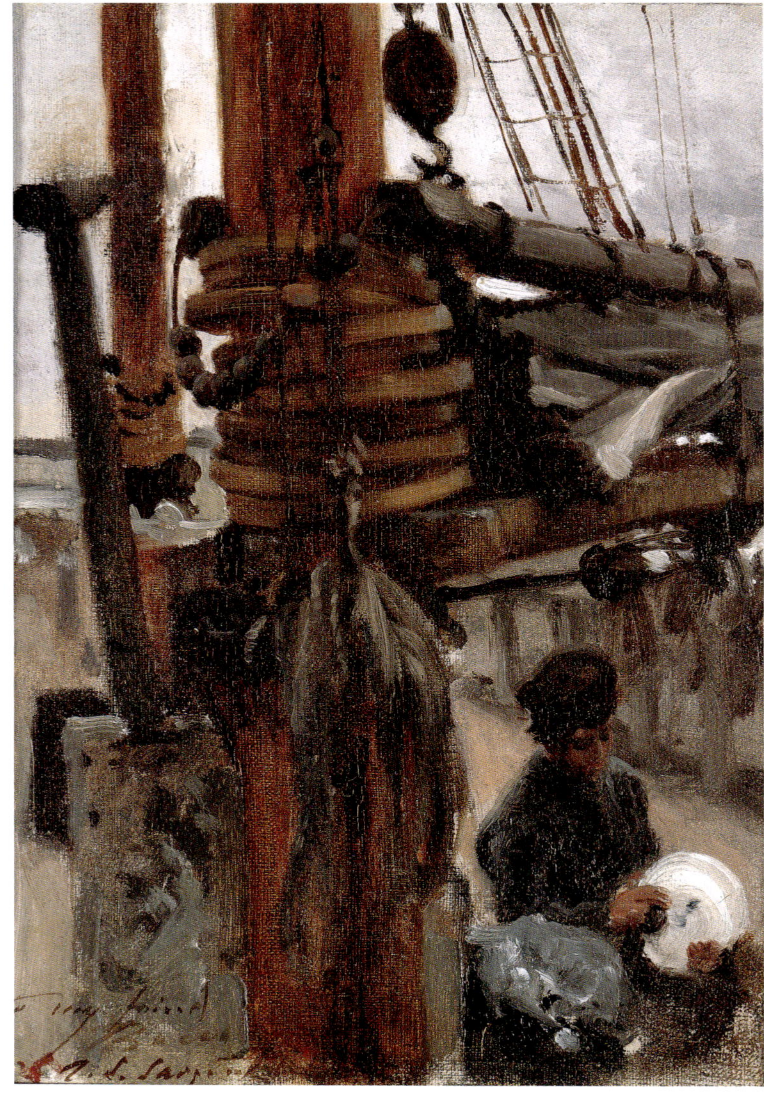

Fig. 27 *The Artist's Mother Aboard Ship*, 1876. Oil on canvas, 11 × 7¾ in (28 × 19.8 cm). Inscribed, lower left: *J.S.S.* The Fayez Sarofim Collection. (Exhibition, Washington and Houston only)

Fig. 28 *The Cook's Boy*, 1876. Oil on canvas mounted on board, 10⅞ × 7⅝ in (27.6 × 19.3 cm). Inscribed, lower left: *to my friend / Bacon / John S. Sargent.* Private Collection. (Exhibition, Washington and Houston only)

previous year, reveals the artist's close observation of detail in his depiction of ship's equipment and the working of the ship (see p. 77). The two oil sketches of scenes on deck, *The Artist's Mother Aboard Ship* and *The Cook's Boy* (figs. 27, 28) are works of a different stamp. The former shows Mrs Sargent resting in a deckchair, the boom of a sail above her and foam-capped waves behind. Her face is invisible under the shadow of her parasol, and her blanket and layers of costume create flat, semi-abstract blocks of color. The way that the artist crops and compresses the image to create the effect of a snapshot, an intimate view of someone unconscious of being observed, reminds the author of the work of Degas. A good parallel is Degas' picture called *At the Races* (fig. 29). A later example of the older artist's influence on Sargent can be seen in the latter's sketch of the *Rehearsal of the Pas de Loup Orchestra at the Cirque d'Hiver* of *c.* 1879,[22] which takes its cue from Degas' paintings of *The Ballet from "Robert le Diable"* (versions in The Metropolitan Museum of Art, New York, 1872, and Victoria & Albert Museum, London, 1876), and *Orchestra of the Paris Opera* (*c.* 1870, Musée d'Orsay, Paris). One of Degas' friends represented in the latter picture is the composer Emmanuel Chabrier, friend and patron of Manet and later of Sargent.[23] In conversation Degas was disparaging of Sargent's art, but he bothered to record his name and address in one of his notebooks, which suggests the possibility of contact between them.[24] Sargent did a drawing after the pastel of *L'Étoile* which Degas showed at the third Impressionist exhibition of 1877, and they exhibited together at the Cercle des arts libéraux, Paris, in 1881.[25]

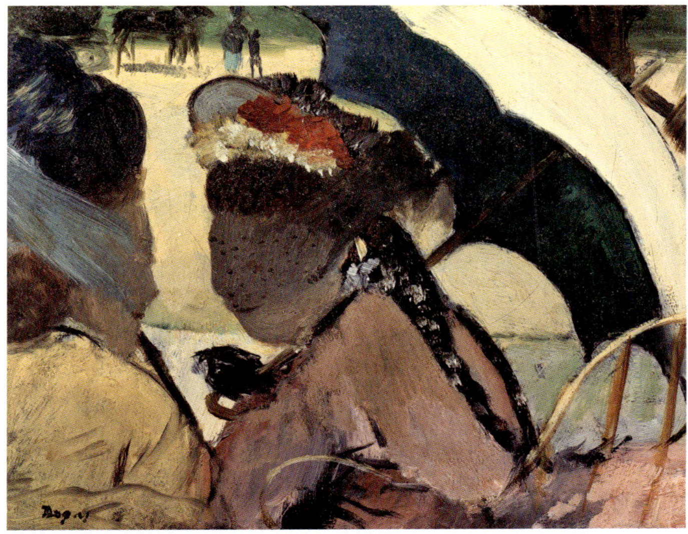

Fig. 29 Edgar Degas, *At the Races (Aux Courses)*, *c.* 1876–77. Oil on canvas, 7½ × 9⁹⁄₁₆ in (19 × 24 cm). Private Collection.

Sargent's journey to America in 1876 marked a rite of passage in his personal life: his first visit to his native land. The year 1877 witnessed a professional rite of passage: his first work to be exhibited, a portrait of *Fanny Watts* (1877, Philadelphia Museum of Art), was accepted at the Paris Salon of that year. Getting a picture into the Salon was the aim of every self-respecting student at Carolus-Duran's atelier. This was the acid test of a young artist's talent, and an essential step on the way to professional recognition. Sargent's portrait of Fanny Watts, a close friend and fellow-expatriate, was attractive and accomplished but it gave little hint of the electrifying portraits that were to follow, among them *Carolus-Duran* (1879, Sterling and Francine Clark Art Institute, Williamstown, Massachusetts), *Dr Pozzi* (1881, UCLA at the Armand Hammer Museum of Art and Cultural Center, Los Angeles), *The Daughters of Edward Darley Boit* (1882, Museum of Fine Arts, Boston), and *Madame X* (*Madame Pierre Gautreau*) (1883–84, The Metropolitan Museum of Art, New York).[26] The young Sargent was still a student at the atelier and the École des Beaux-Arts, and he was some way off from asserting his professional independence. His status as a star pupil was confirmed when in this same year, 1877, he was asked to assist his master on a ceiling decoration for the Palais du Luxembourg, celebrating *The Triumph of Marie de Medici* (1877, now in the Louvre).

Having opened an account at the Salon in 1877, the inevitable question followed: what next? Sargent had spent two summers sketching on the north French coast. A third summer had been spent visiting America, drawing scenes on board ships and painting seascapes as he voyaged across the Atlantic. His experience as a marine artist made the choice of a French seaside subject for his next Salon contribution an

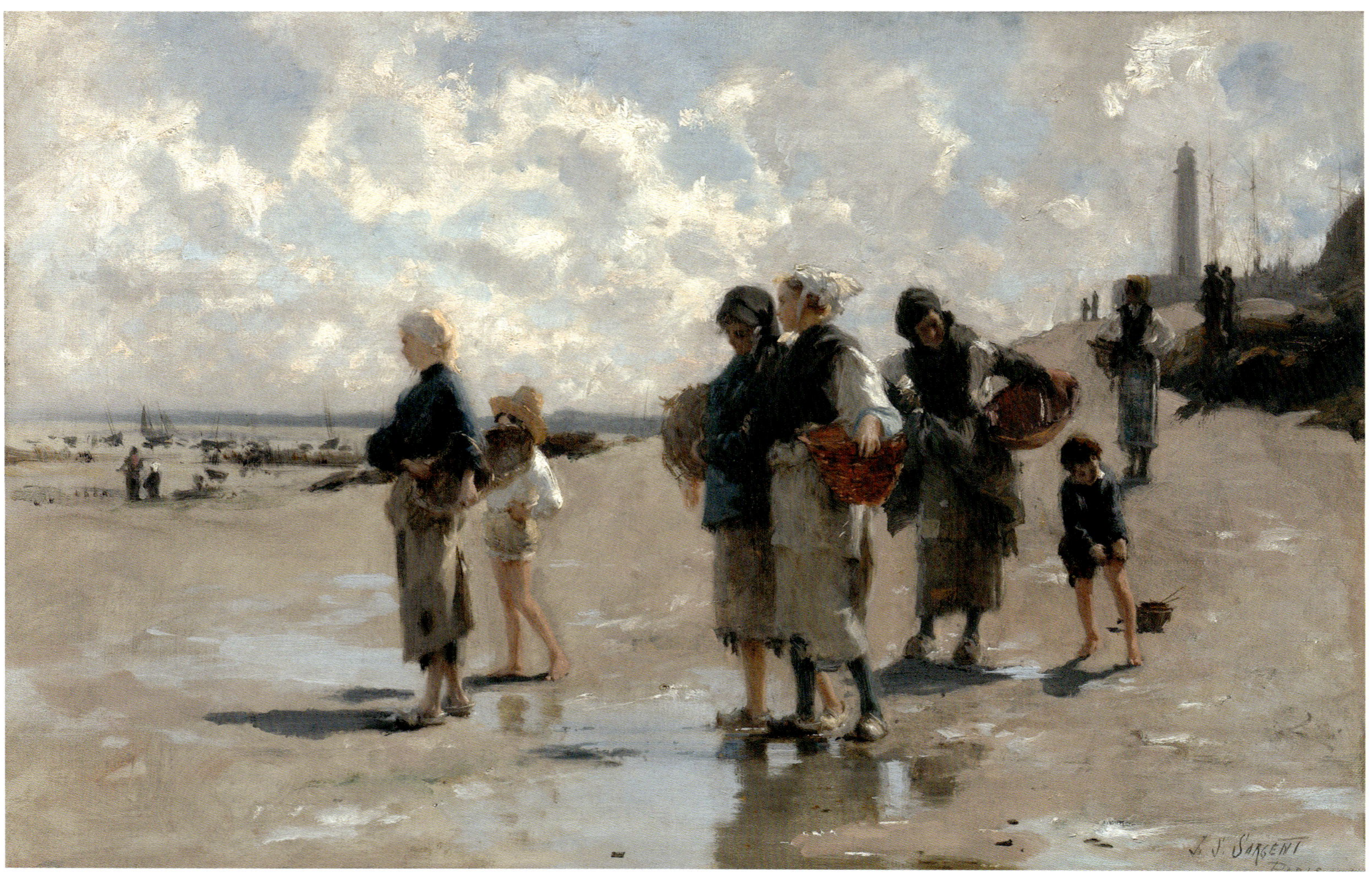

Fig. 30 *Fishing for Oysters at Cancale*, 1877–78. Oil on canvas, 16⅛ × 24 in (41 × 61 cm). Inscribed, lower right: *J. S. Sargent / Paris.* Museum of Fine Arts, Boston. Gift of Miss Mary Appleton, 35.708. (Exhibition)

obvious one. He left Paris for the Breton township of Cancale in June 1877 with a fellow art student, Eugène Lachaise, but without his parents. He seems to have come with a specific purpose in mind—to find a Salon subject. What determined the choice of Cancale is unknown. There were better-known resorts where artists congregated, such as Pont-Aven and Concarneau, but the famous oyster beds and fishing fleet at Cancale had drawn artists there before Sargent.

Sargent's choice of subject for his proposed Salon painting shows him opting for a well-established genre. Ambitious scenes of rural labor were associated with the Barbizon school and their successors. Such scenes were invariably weighted with social meaning, either highlighting the drudgery and poverty inseparable from agricultural labor, or extolling the simple joys and rituals of rural life as an unspoken antidote to the corruption of the city. Jules Breton was one of the most successful exponents of the genre, spanning both sides of the social divide in his scenes of harvesting and rural festivals. He had first made his name at the Paris Exposition Universelle of 1855, and his processional subjects, employing a wide cast of attractive

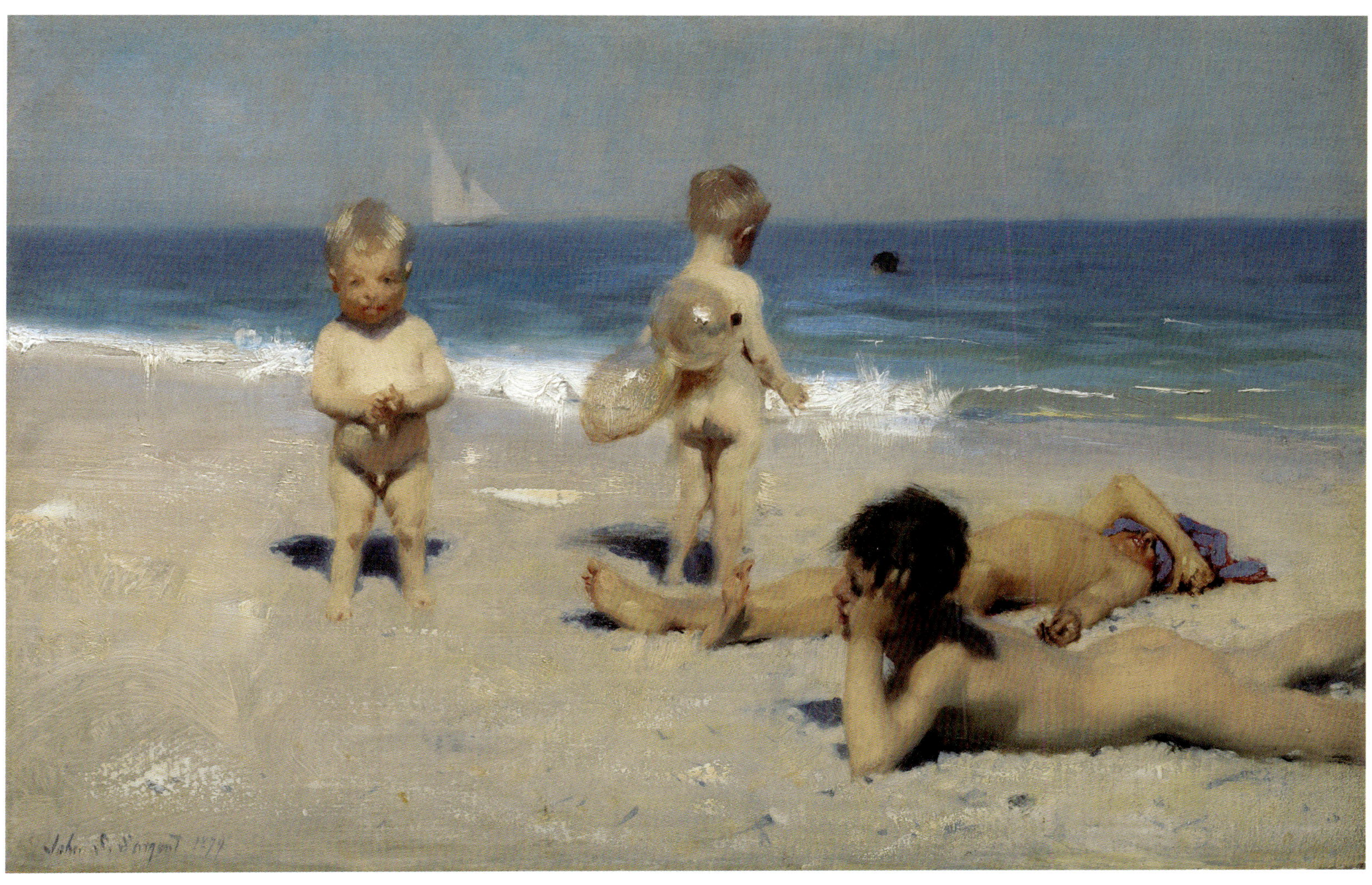

Fig. 31 *Neapolitan Children Bathing*, 1879. Oil on canvas, 10 9/16 × 16 3/16 in (16.8 × 41.1 cm). Inscribed, lower left: *John S. Sargent 1879*. Sterling and Francine Clark Art Institute, Williamstown, Massachusetts, 1955.852. (Exhibition)

female models, remained popular throughout the later nineteenth century. Breton was a generation older than Sargent, but he continued to exert a broad influence on younger painters.

Like the figures in scenes by Breton, such as *Le Rappel des glaneuses* (1859, Musée des Beaux-Arts, Arras), those in *En Route pour la pêche* (see fig. 8) are deliberately posed to give them a monumental presence. Nothing is casual in the way they stand, the intervals between them, nor the way in which their heads and upper bodies break the line of the horizon. Sargent is presenting us with a seductive vision of the fishing industry. There is no sign here of drudgery and toil, but then Sargent does not have a social message or critique in quite the same way that Breton does. He subverts the conventions of the genre by not wearing his heart on his sleeve and by painting his picture as an Impressionist might have done, as a study in color and light. White highlights fringe the foreground pools left by the retreating tide that mirror the blue sky. The wide expanse of the beach opens up behind the figures, creating a liberating sense of space and freedom. A distant cluster of fishing boats fringes the bay of Mont-Saint-Michel.

Clouds scudding across the sky complete this exhilarating scene of beach life on a fresh summer day. *En Route pour la pêche* is a formal art work masquerading as a plein air sketch, especially true of the smaller of the two versions (fig. 30). The artist takes a traditional subject and transposes it in another key to give it a modern edge. The academic mode is joined to Sargent's experience of avant-garde painting, Jules Breton crossed with Eugène Boudin and Claude Monet. The bridge between old and new would be a defining characteristic of Sargent's early art.

The painting of the Cancale fisherfolk in two separate versions represented a major commitment of Sargent's time and energy. Both versions are inscribed "Paris" and the artist must have been preoccupied with them during the fall and winter of 1877–78. The relationship between the two versions is described in depth in the essay by Sarah Cash (pp. 89–117). The artist sent the larger version to the Paris Salon in the spring of 1878, soon after submitting the smaller one to the recently founded Society of American Artists in New York. It was the latter picture that captured the headlines and made a lasting impression on critics and public alike.[27] From then onwards America would form an integral part of Sargent's exhibition strategy, establishing him over time as a pre-eminent American painter. In 1879 he played the same trick as he had in 1878, sending versions of the same subject, *A Capriote*, to exhibitions at the Salon and the Society of American Artists, while *Neapolitan Children Bathing* (fig. 31) went to the annual show of the National Academy of Design in New York.[28]

Sargent's summer painting expeditions would take him to a succession of exotic locations: Capri in 1878; Madrid, Granada, and Tangier in 1879; and Venice in 1880 and 1882. These cities were all on the international art circuit, much visited and much painted by artists of the time. Capri had been a popular destination since the early 1800s. Romantic pictures of the people and scenery of the island featured in exhibitions in Paris and London, Munich and Berlin, throughout the century. The presence of several artist friends in Capri during the summer of 1878 suggests that Sargent had consulted with them before selecting the island. At the end of the summer he came away with three exhibition pictures and a quantity of figure sketches and landscapes; it had been another productive interlude. The artist's island muse was Rosina Ferrara, a well-known Capri model. She posed for the three versions of *A Capriote*, a picture of her standing in the crook of an olive tree; for a finished head in profile; and for several versions of a picture showing her dancing the tarantella on the rooftop of a house, notable for their tonalities of white on white.[29]

The picture that concerns us here is *Neapolitan Children Bathing*, a picture literally dazzling to the eye, so intense is the effect of sunlight on the white sand and the bodies of the four boys (see Marc Simpson's essay, pp. 119–43). In contrast to *En Route pour la pêche*, the painting is small in scale, informal in composition, and hot in color. The informality is deceptive, for preliminary oil studies indicate that the composition was just as carefully planned as the Cancale beach scenes (see pp. 89–117). The two standing little boys break up the horizontals of the beach, sea, and horizon line, the younger of the two gazing out at us, the other turned seaward. The older boys lie sensuously on the sand, the curves of their bodies emphasized by the shadows they cast. The legs of the foremost boy are chopped off by the edge of the canvas to suggest the casualness of the artist's viewpoint.

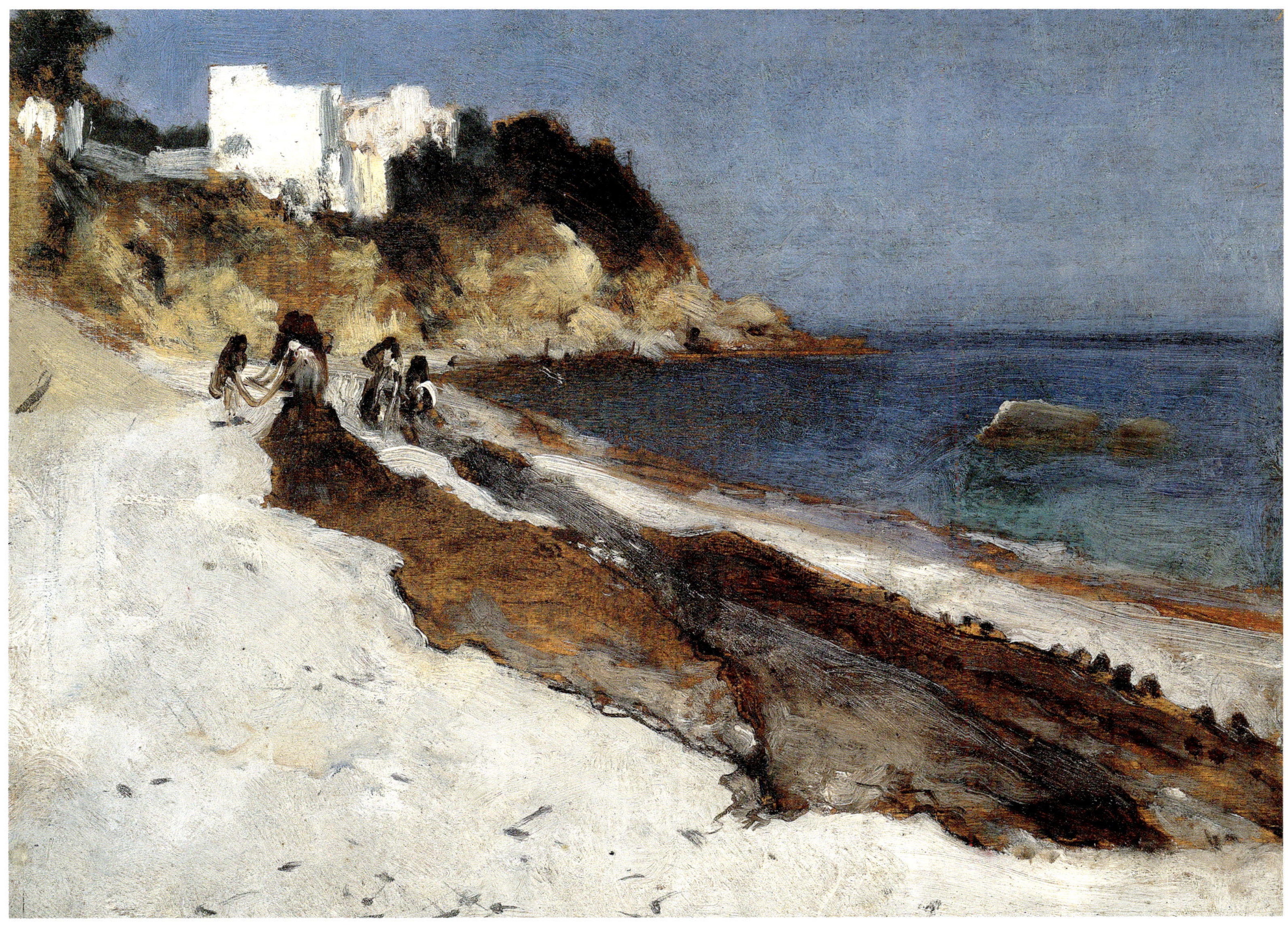

Fig. 32 *Moroccan Beach Scene*, *c.* 1880. Oil on panel, 10 × 13½ in (25.4 × 34.3 cm). Private Collection. (Exhibition)

Sargent painted one further beach scene during a visit to North Africa in 1880. This is *Moroccan Beach Scene* (fig. 32), a vibrant sketch painted in the same highly keyed color range as *Neapolitan Children Bathing*. A gaggle of local women are seen laying out fishing nets to dry. The white sand and dense blue sky evoke the brilliance and saturating heat of a sunlit day on the Mediterranean coast.

The final group of marine subjects from the early period of Sargent's art are the least well known and documented. Small in scale and mostly executed in watercolor, they record shipping scenes and fishing boats in various unidentified ports and harbors. There are few figures and relatively few signs of active work on the quayside. *Boats in Harbor I* (destroyed) was dated "1879" and this has been taken as the approximate date of the whole series, though some paintings may be earlier or later. The subject of this last picture exists in two versions, in oil and watercolor (figs.

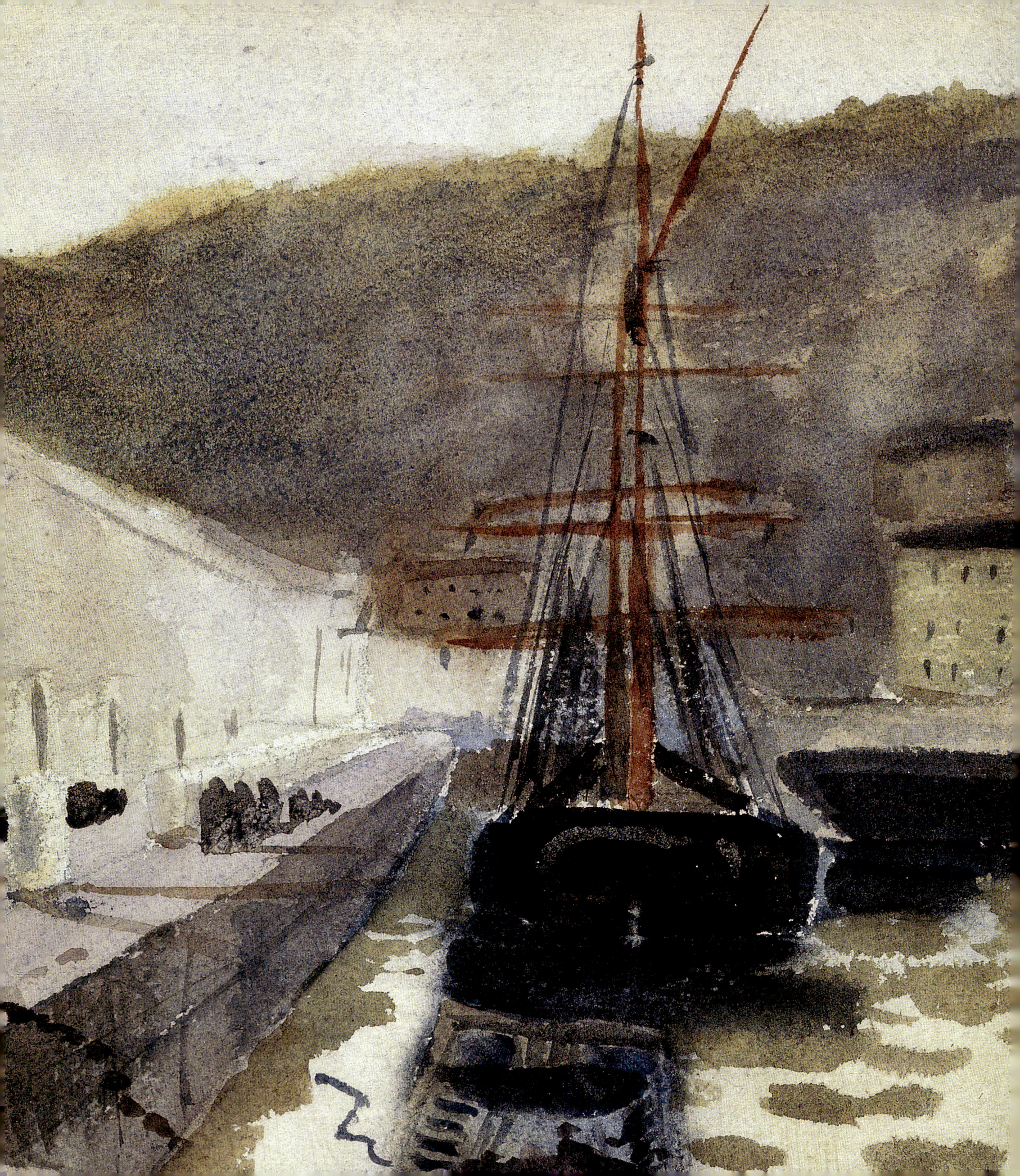

34, 36). There are close parallels between *Two Nude Figures Standing on a Wharf*, *Wharf Scene*, and *Ships and Boats* (figs. 35, 37, 38), in terms of style and composition. *Boats I* and *Boats II* represent views of the same small harbor (figs. 39, 40).

What prompted these port and harbor scenes it is difficult to know. It is possible that Sargent was stalking another Salon subject, except that none of the scenes he painted looks suitable for translation to a grand scale. The closest parallel to his scenes of shipping is to be found in the watercolors of canal scenes that he painted in Venice during the period 1880–82. None of the ports have been positively identified, although *Ships and Boats* (fig. 38) is inscribed "Nice" on the reverse. *Port Scene I* (fig. 41) may represent Genoa. Sargent is recorded as there with his family in October 1877. The sophisticated watercolor called *Port Scene II* (fig. 42) may possibly have been painted at Nice. It demonstrates the way that the bright Mediterranean sun beats down on the forms and drains them of color. In July 1878 he traveled to Naples by way of Marseille. He was with his family in Nice during part of October–November

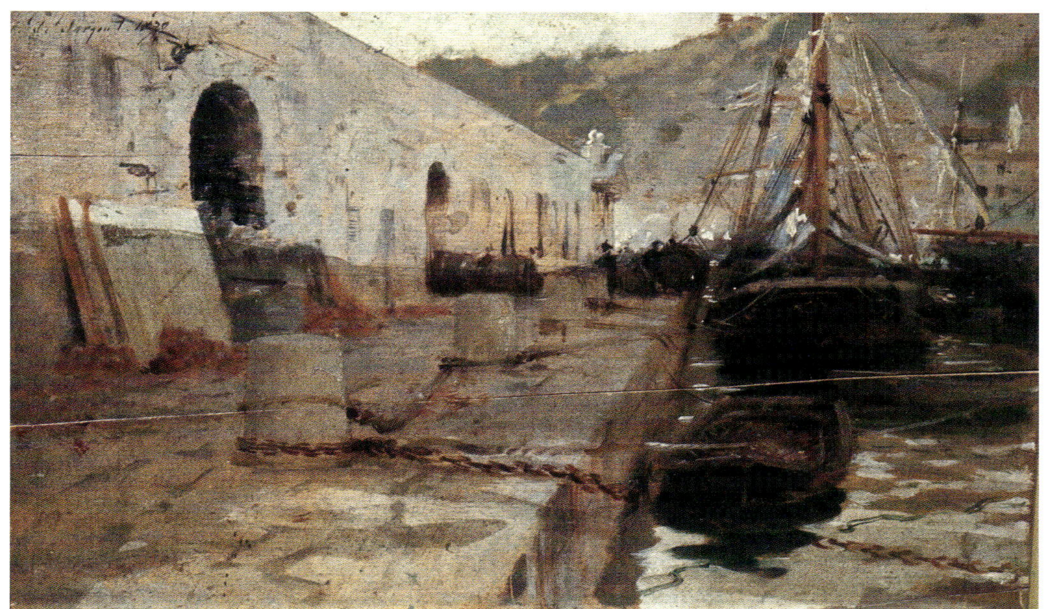

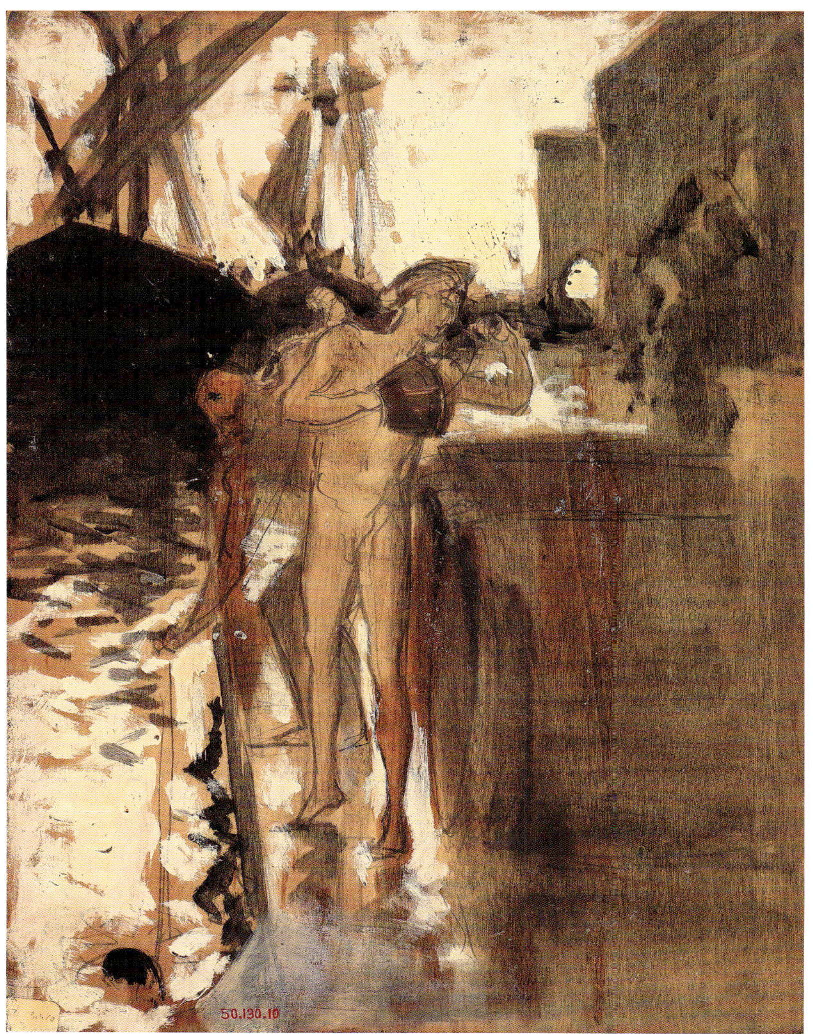

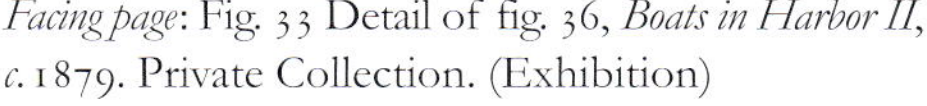

Facing page: Fig. 33 Detail of fig. 36, *Boats in Harbor II*, *c.* 1879. Private Collection. (Exhibition)

Fig. 34 *Boats in Harbor I*, 1879. Oil on panel, 10 × 13 in (25.3 × 33 cm). Inscribed top left: *to my friend Cox / J.S. Sargent 1879*. Destroyed (formerly collection of Dr Cornelius Lansing).

Fig. 35 *Two Nude Figures Standing on a Wharf*, *c.* 1879. Oil on panel, 13¾ × 10½ in (34.9 × 26.7 cm). The Metropolitan Museum of Art. Gift of Mrs Francis Ormond, 1950. (50.130.10b verso) (Exhibition)

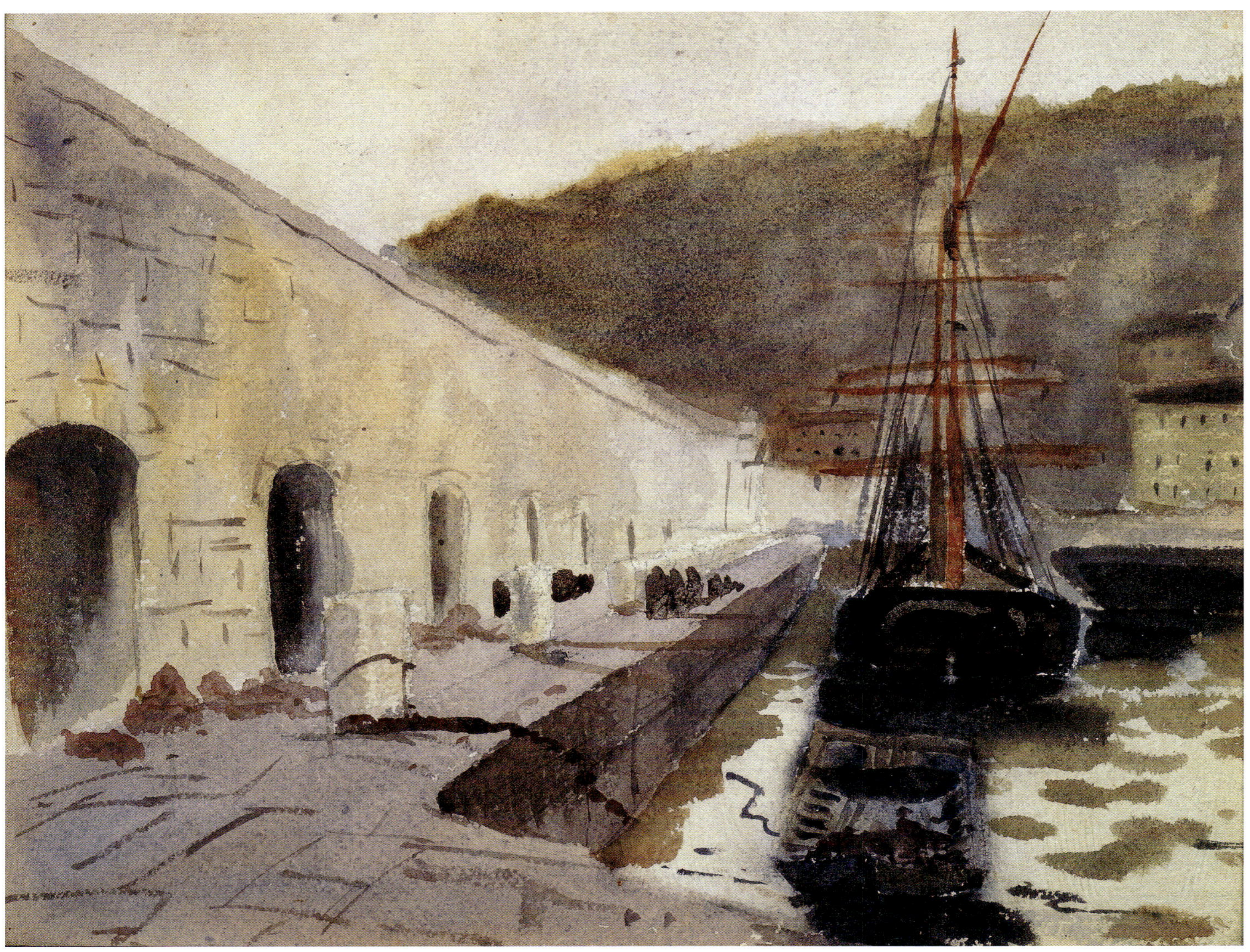

Fig. 36 *Boats in Harbor II*, *c.* 1879. Watercolor and graphite on paper, 8½ × 11 in (21.6 × 28 cm). Private Collection. (Exhibition)

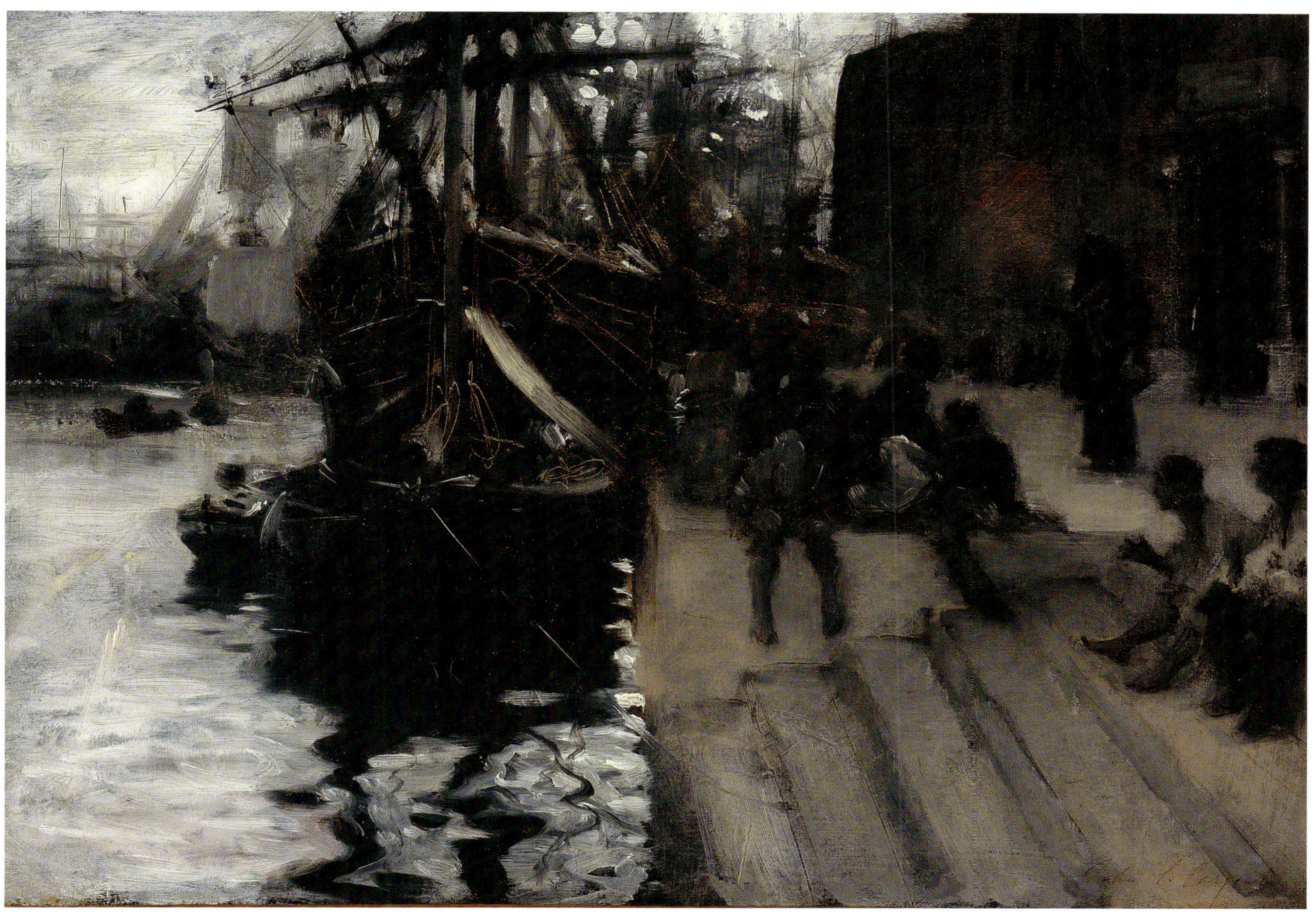

Fig. 37 *Wharf Scene*, *c.* 1879. Oil on canvas (grisaille), 12⅞ × 18 1/16 in (32.7 × 46 cm). Inscribed, lower right: *John S. Sargent*. Mr and Mrs William J. Miller, Jr. (Exhibition)

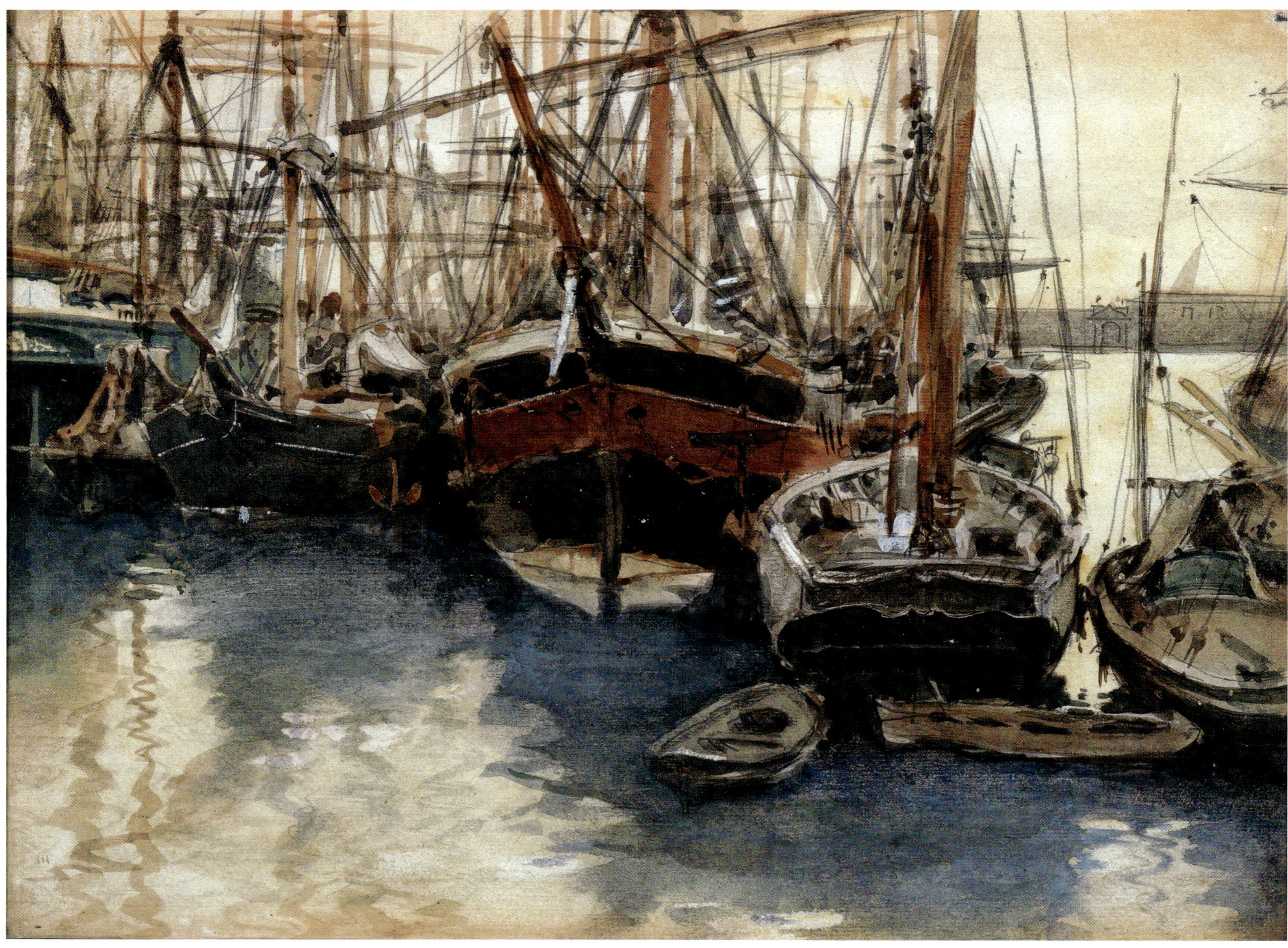

Fig. 38 *Ships and Boats*, *c.* 1879. Watercolor and graphite on paper, 9 × 11 in (22.8 × 28 cm). Private Collection. (Exhibition)

1878. He was there again during the summer of 1879, and in Spain and North Africa for part of the winter of 1879–80. He had every opportunity, therefore, for sketching shipping in a variety of Mediterranean ports during the period 1877–79.

Apart from *Port Scene I*, which shows a view of distant ships and buildings across a wide stretch of water, Sargent's port scenes follow a common format. The dockside from which he painted occupies a significant slice of the picture space, and there are buildings and fortifications to the side. *Low Tide at Cancale Harbor* (see fig. 147) is a forerunner of this type of composition. The area of water in the port scenes is usually smaller than the dock structure. Ships and boats are seen close-to, either bow or stern view. The complicated pattern of masts and riggings forms an integral part of the design. The only serious activity recorded in any of these scenes is the loading of a coastal vessel in *Boats in*

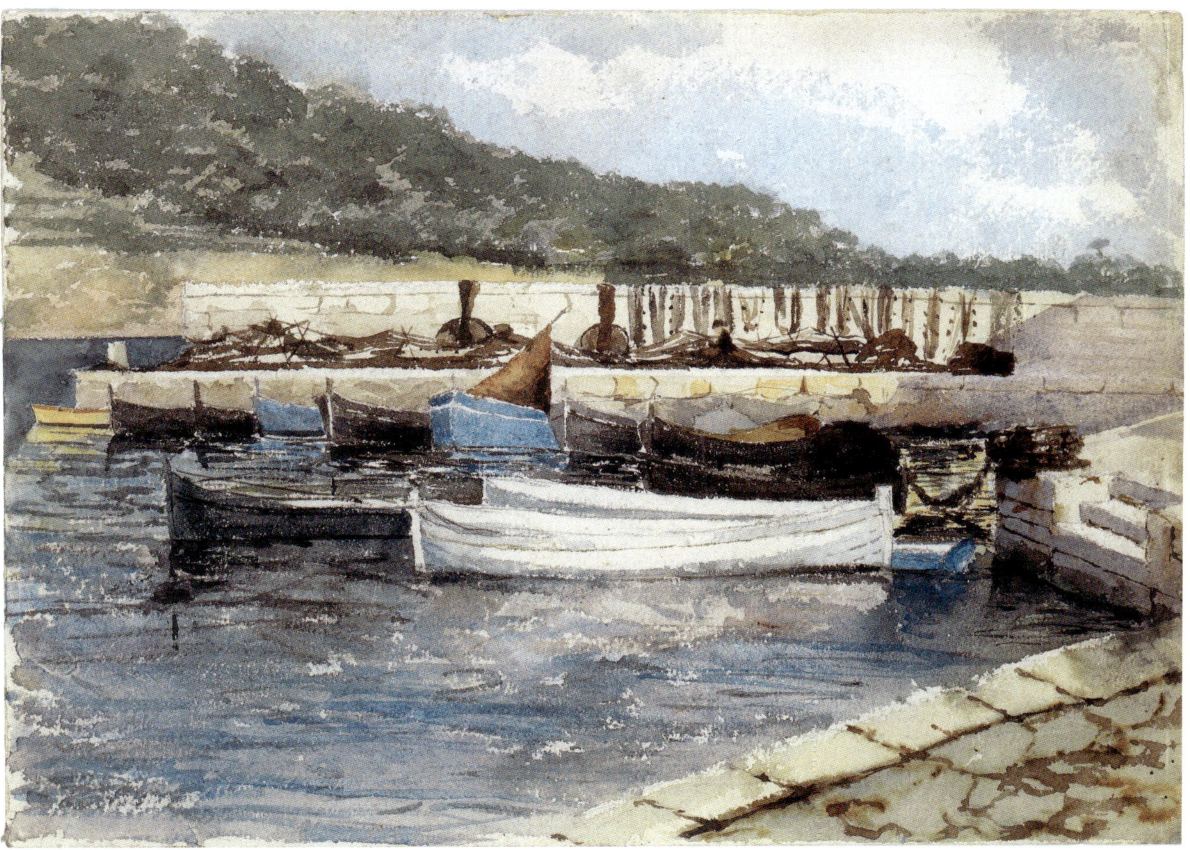

Fig. 39 *Boats I*, *c.* 1879. Watercolor and graphite on paper, 10 5/16 × 14 3/16 in (26.3 × 36.1 cm). The Metropolitan Museum of Art. Gift of Mrs Francis Ormond, 1950. (50.130.80q) (Exhibition, Washington and London only)

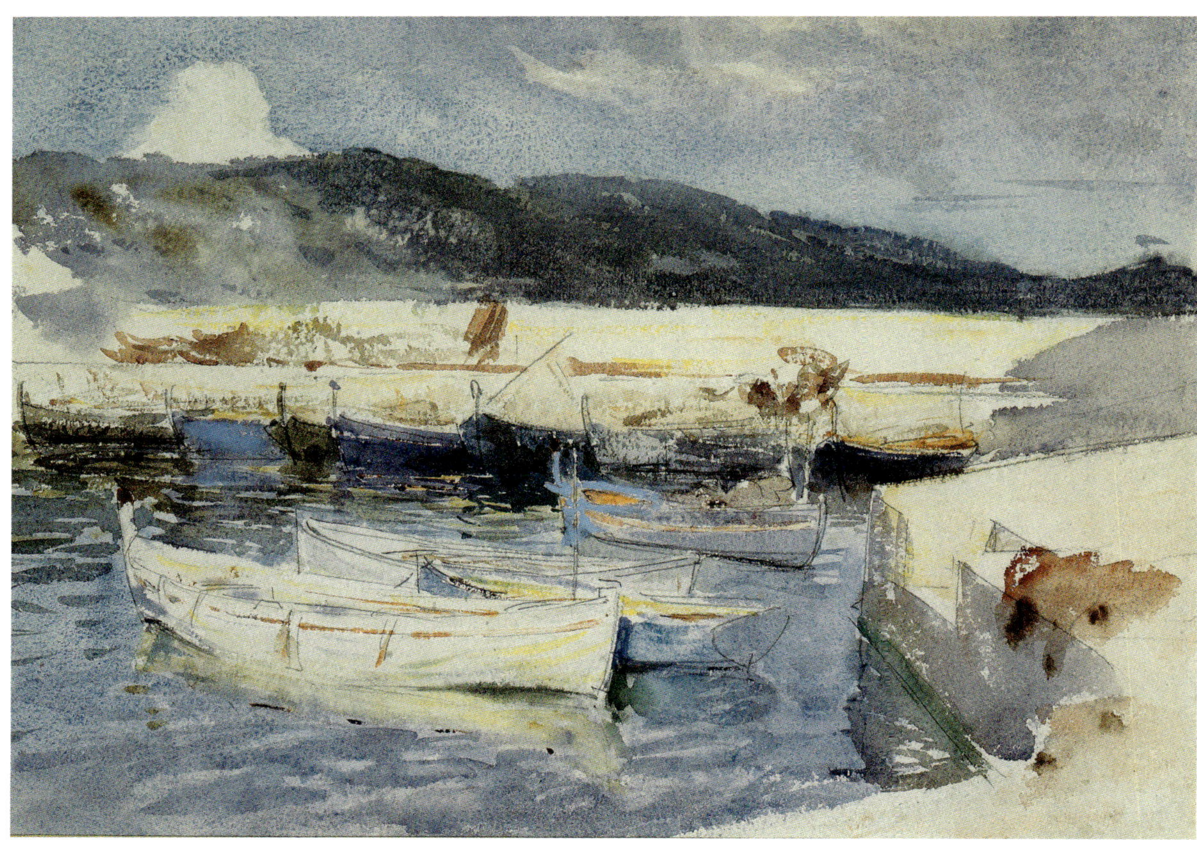

Fig. 40 *Boats II*, *c.* 1879. Watercolor and graphite on paper, 10 × 14 in (25.5 × 35.6 cm). Private Collection. (Exhibition)

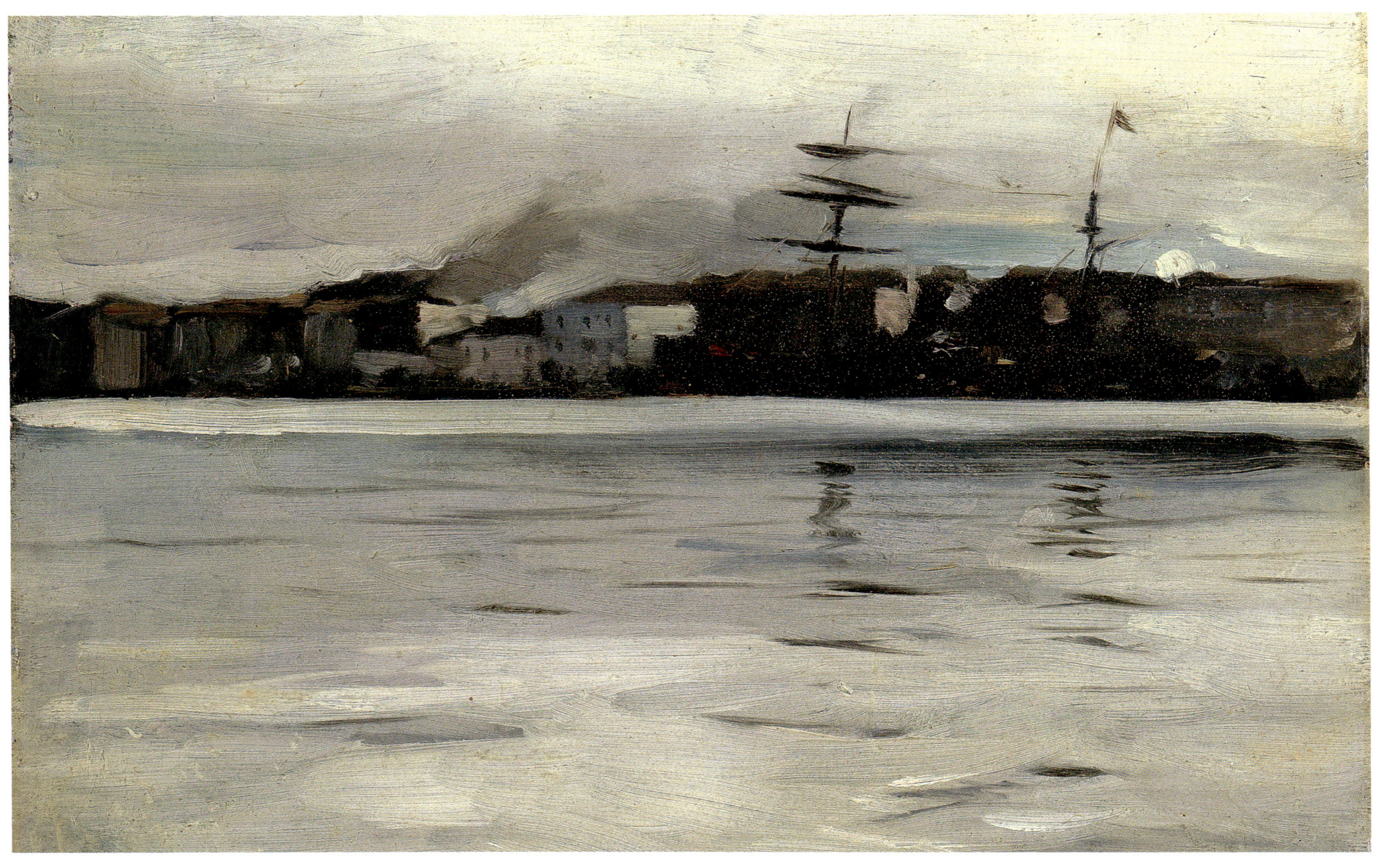

Fig. 41 *Port Scene I*, *c.* 1877. Oil on panel, 10 × 13½ in (25.3 × 34.5 cm). Private Collection. (Exhibition)

Harbor I (see fig. 34). The men in *Two Nude Figures Standing on a Wharf* (see fig. 35) are drawing up buckets of water and filling water barrels for an unspecified purpose. Their nudity and their idealized poses smack of academic composition. The figures in *Wharf Scene* (see fig. 37) are bystanders and idlers. Vessels of every description are massed together in *Ships and Boats* (see fig. 38), open water in front and a blizzard of spars above. This is a classic marine subject handled with a deft touch. Occasional accents of vivid blue punctuate the somber tones of brown and gray.

Painted on dull days, the port scenes are generally subdued in coloring; *Wharf Scene* (see fig. 37) is virtually a grisaille. Overall, the treatment of light is subtle and painterly, and the pictures give off a strong atmosphere. Like the back streets of Venice, which the artist painted a year or two later, the environment is gritty and working-class. This is the dirty business of

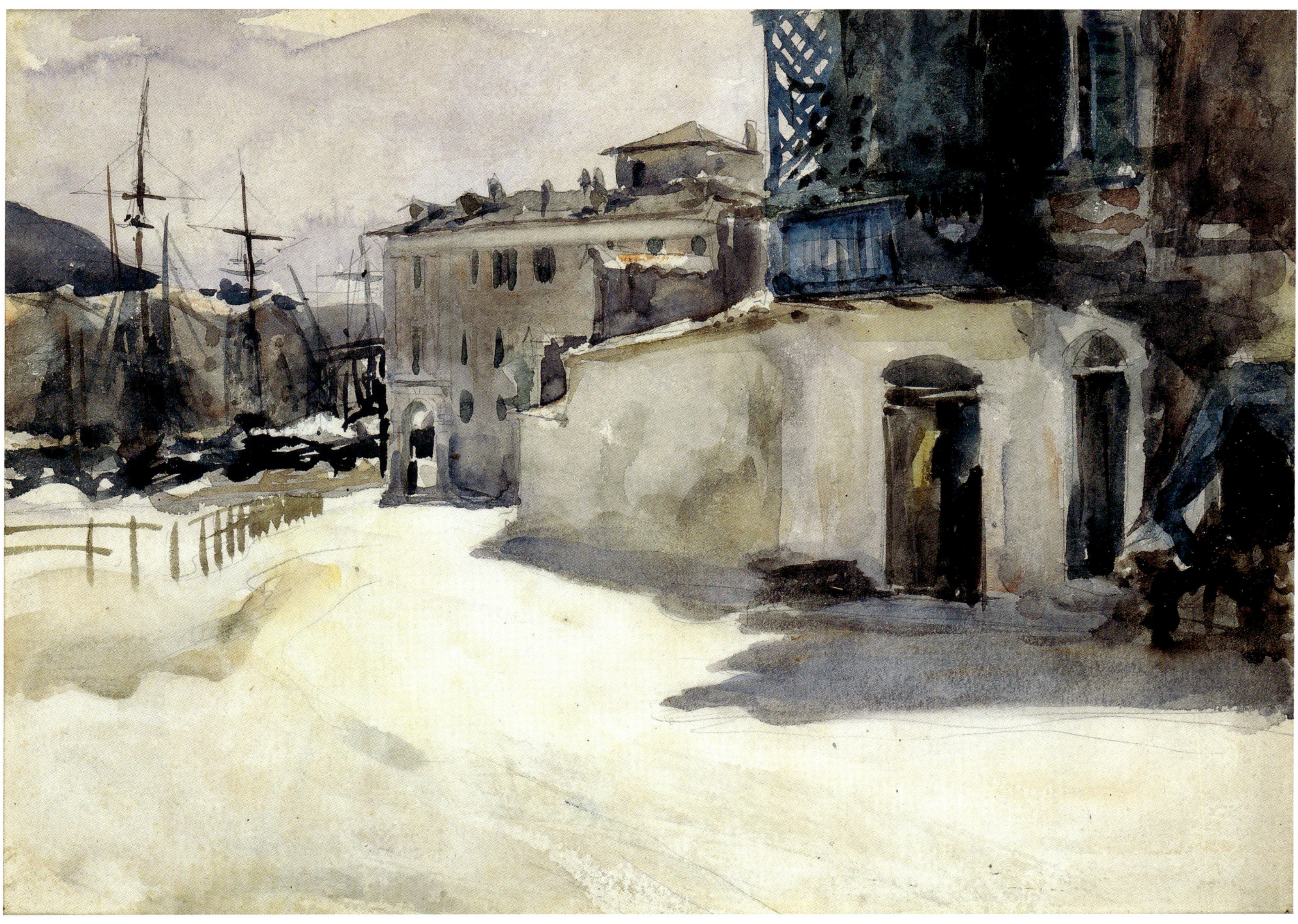

trade and shipping, of docks and warehouses and working boats. The pictures are works of social realism in their unsparing record of industrial conditions. The watercolors of fishing boats in harbor (see figs. 39, 40) are brighter and more colorful than the port scenes, but no less concerned with the details of commercial activity. The boats are carefully studied, nets and fishing tackle line the back of the harbor wall, and strongly articulated quays frame the scene. In *Filet et Barque* (fig. 43) we actually see a drag net (*drague*) in operation.

The interruptions in Sargent's art come abruptly and marine painting was no exception. The year 1879 effectively marks the end of this particular phase of his art. The journey to Spain and Tangier in 1879–80 fired the artist up with new ideas for figurative subjects, and the seaside was left behind. The Salon paintings inspired by this trip, *Fumée d'ambre gris* (1880, Sterling and Francine Clark Art Institute, Williamstown,

Fig. 42 *Port Scene II*, *c.* 1879. Watercolor and graphite on paper, 10 × 14 in (25.5 × 35.7 cm). Private Collection. (Exhibition)

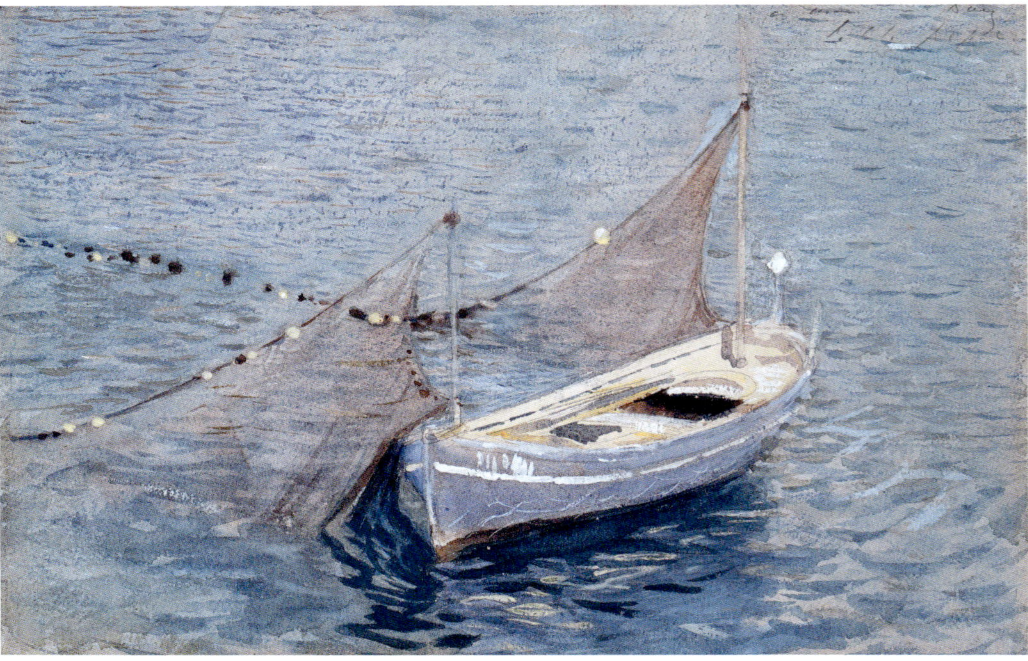

Fig. 43 *Filet et Barque*, *c.* 1879. Watercolor and graphite on paper, 10 × 13¾ in (25.3 × 35 cm). Inscribed, top right: *a mon ami Duez / J.S.S. popol* [?]. Private Collection. (Exhibition)

Massachusetts), a North African woman inhaling incense, and *El Jaleo* (1882, Isabella Stewart Gardner Museum, Boston), a raucous scene of flamenco dancing, show the artist exploring new subject areas. The positive reception accorded to his portrait of *Carolus-Duran* at the Salon of 1879 engendered more commissions that mark the beginning of his professional career as a portraitist. The early 1880s was to be a period of intense activity and it produced several masterpieces of portraiture and figure painting. The sea was not wholly forgotten, though it plays a subsidiary role in his work. In Venice he painted a sequence of canal scenes and one wide view across the lagoon that reflect his experience as a marine painter. On a visit to the English port of Whitby he was moved to record the fishing fleet out at sea on a gray day (fig. 44), a Whistlerian scene that is a throwback to the marine subjects of the 1870s, but this was to remain an isolated experiment. It was not until the period after 1900, when Sargent once again returned to landscape painting, that one finds a significant group of marine subjects: massed shipping in the port of Palma on the island of Majorca; sailing ships lying out in the Venetian lagoon; fishing boats off the Italian and Portuguese coasts; elegant yachts in Florida.

Sargent's early marine period lasted approximately from 1874 to 1879. It included the two early holidays in Normandy and Brittany (1874 and 1875), the transatlantic crossings of 1876, the Cancale episode of 1877, the Capri visit of 1878, and the Mediterranean harbor scenes here placed around 1879. These trips produced a substantial body of work, including a sequence of seascapes and a group of beach scenes, three of which were sent on exhibition. The circumstances of family holidays on the north French coast may have precipitated Sargent's interest in

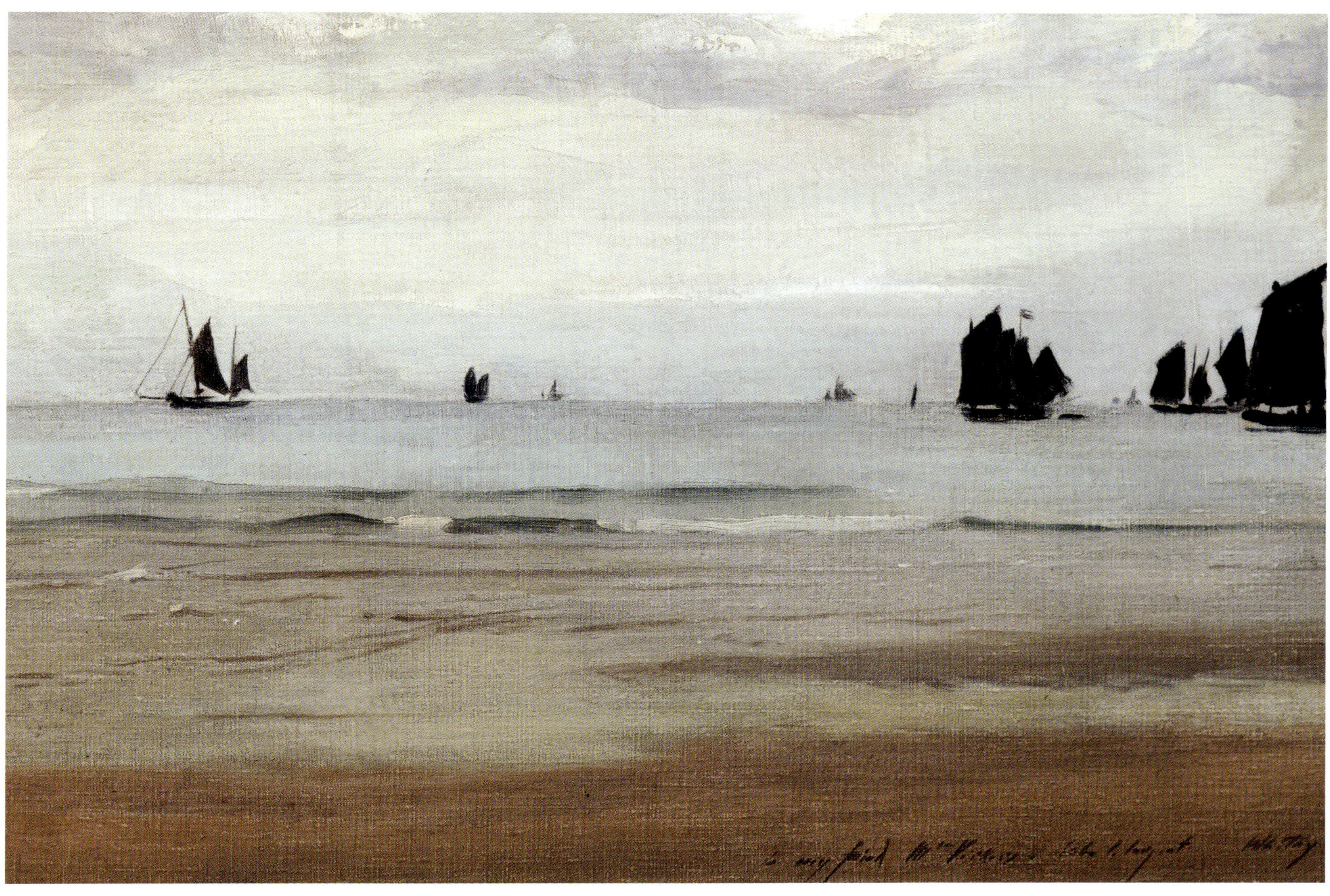

marine subjects, but he seems to have had a genuine yearning for the sea and a knowledge of ships that is well demonstrated in the pictures and drawings gathered together for this exhibition. He was an innovator pushing back the boundaries of marine art through his unconventional viewpoint, the realism with which he rendered light and tone, and his bold, free brushwork. Within his marine œuvre, there is an astonishing range and variety of work. He was never willing to follow a well-established path or to repeat a successful formula. He was always reaching out for new subjects, exploring new ideas, and developing new skills. That is what makes his painting so innovative and exciting.

Fig. 44 *Whitby Fishing Boats*, 1884. Oil on canvas, 18½ × 27 in (47 × 68.6 cm). Inscribed, lower right: *to my friend Mrs Vickers, John S. Sargent Whitby.* Private Collection. (Exhibition, Washington and London only)

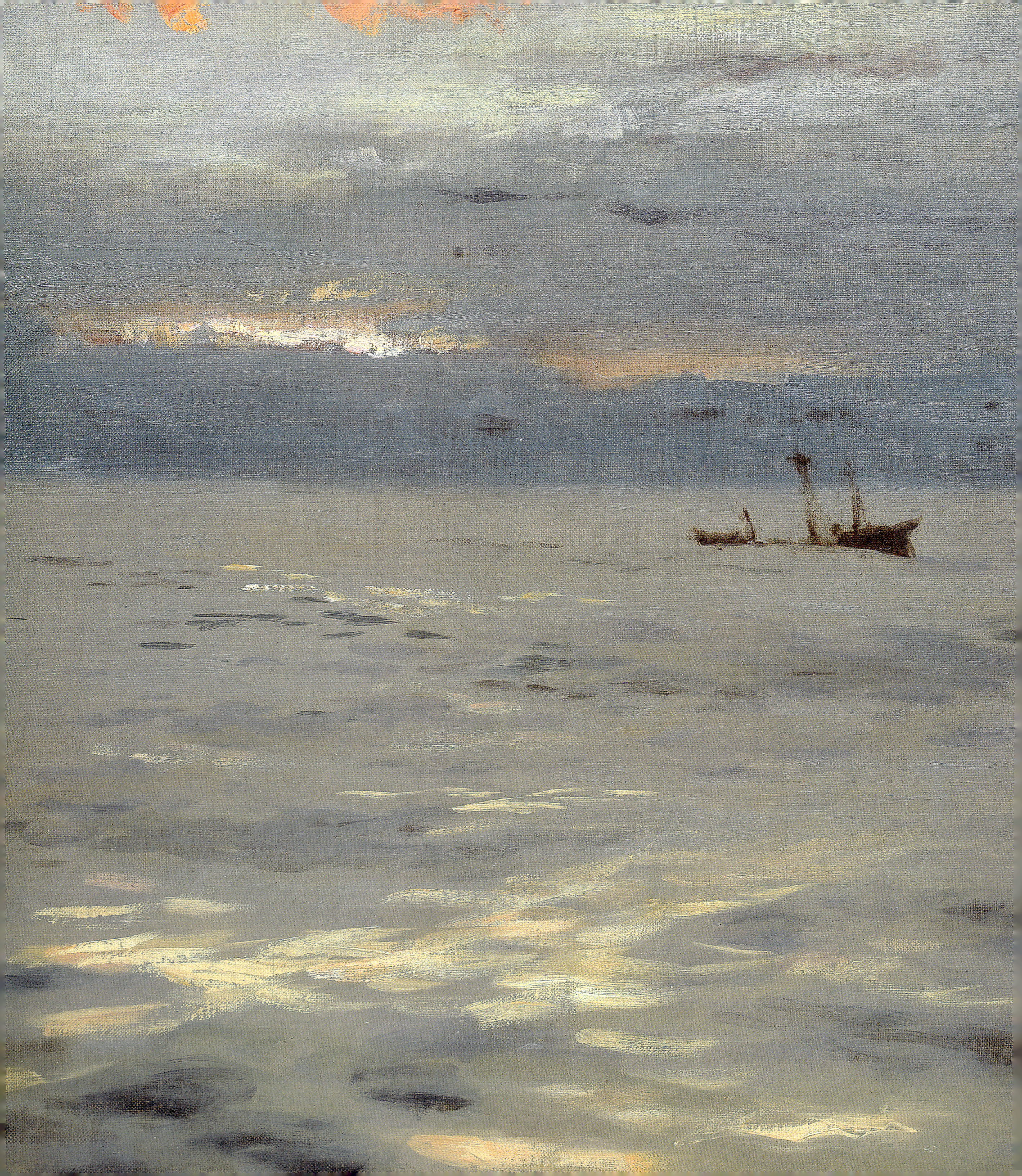

Uncharted Waters

ERICA E. HIRSHLER

"We need sometimes to escape into open solitudes, into aimlessness, into the moral holiday of running some pure hazard, in order to sharpen the edge of life," wrote the philosopher George Santayana in about 1912. In a provocative essay about travel, he claimed that locomotion was the key to intelligence. Santayana—himself a cosmopolitan and well-traveled man, born in Spain, raised and educated in Massachusetts, and resident in Europe—proposed that the unique ability of animals to move from place to place lent passion and desire to life. Human ambition and imagination were sparked by the knowledge of distant places and the possibility of getting to them. "What charm is equal to that of ports and ships and the thought of ceaseless comings and goings?" he asked.[1]

Ceaseless comings and goings served to sharpen the edges of both the life and the art of John Sargent, surely one of the most nomadic of all the great painters of the late nineteenth century. His restless pattern of travel, maintained throughout his career, had been determined for him at the very start by both his seafaring ancestors and his peripatetic parents (see Richard Ormond's Introduction, pp. 3–37). Born in Florence, trained in Paris, comfortable in a host of countries although perhaps never entirely at home in any of them, Sargent was described by his childhood friend Vernon Lee as an "accentless mongrel." In 1887 Henry James—echoing a host of other critics—asked whether Sargent could even be considered an American. The answer was, James wrote, "that we shall be well advised to claim him."[2] James was writing to introduce Sargent to an American audience before the painter's second trip to the United States; the author's words were buttressed by the successes Sargent had already achieved in Europe. By 1887 some of his greatest paintings—*En Route pour la pêche* (see fig. 8), *El Jaleo*, *The Daughters of Edward Darley Boit*, *Madame X (Madame Pierre Gautreau)*—were already behind him. But in the late 1870s, in terms of his nationality, his artistic progression, and his activities, the young John Sargent was both figuratively and literally at sea.

At this early point in his career, Sargent was faced with choices about the trajectory of his art. He needed to decide between the past and the future, whether to follow academic tradition or to join with more modern innovators. He had studied with success at both the time-honored École des Beaux-Arts and in the more adventurous studio of Carolus-Duran; he had drawn meticulous studies after classical sculpture and also visited the second Impressionist exhibition in April 1876, where some (unconfirmed) sources report that he first met Claude Monet. Sargent had not

Facing page: Fig. 45 Detail of fig. 50, *Atlantic Sunset*, *c.* 1876. Private Collection. (Exhibition)

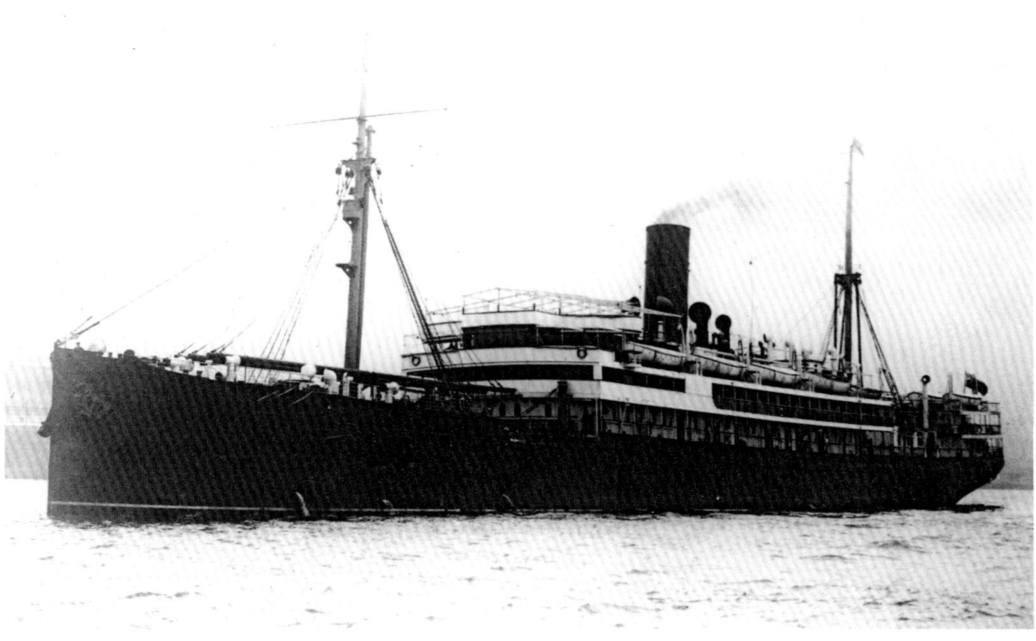

Fig. 46 The *SS Algeria*. Photograph. Merseyside Maritime Museum, Liverpool.

completed any major paintings in oil; his course was not yet set. If his artistic allegiances were still unclear, his national ties were also as yet undetermined. It was in part with the idea of proclaiming her son as an American that his mother took him to the United States for the first time in late May 1876, when he was almost twenty years old.

Mary Sargent hoped to give her son (at long last) some sort of personal anchor in Philadelphia, introducing him to the American cousins he had never met and showing him the American cities he had never seen. She booked passage for herself, her son, and her elder daughter, Emily, on the *SS Abyssinia*, an elegant Cunard steamship that made the Atlantic crossing from Liverpool to New York in a mere ten days; they stayed in the United States for just over four months. In early October 1876, they returned to Europe on the *SS Abyssinia*'s sister ship, the *SS Algeria* (fig. 46). Their second voyage lasted seventeen days, lengthened perhaps by the tremendous storm the vessel encountered along the way (see fig. 51). But rather than any of Sargent's experiences on American soil, none of which he seems to have painted, it is his observations aboard these ships—manifested in both the things he recorded and in those he ignored—that offer the most interesting insights into the course of his artistic vision.

Sargent's 1876 voyage was also different in another respect—he was returning to a native land he had never experienced. Crossing the ocean was not in itself unusual at this time; by 1868 the American journal *Putnam's Magazine* had already announced that "the era in which we live will be called the nomadic period. With the advent of ocean steam navigation and the railway system, began a travelling mania which has gradually increased until half the world's inhabitants, or at least half of its civilized portion, are on the move."[5] Most accounts of American travelers document their transatlantic passages eastward, toward Europe, and they describe their excitement about encountering the Old World and their enthusiasm for experiencing first hand the well-known sites they had previously explored only through illustrations and literary descriptions. On their return journeys, Americans expressed their homesickness, their desire to return to familiar people, places, and to the modern conveniences their compatriots took for granted. But unlike his fellow Americans crossing the ocean westward, Sargent was traveling to the United States for the first time.

Despite the descriptions and instructions that Sargent would have received from his mother, it was the Old World that would have been familiar to him rather than the New. His preconceptions may even have been more in keeping with the Europeans who were also making their maiden voyage to the United States. But as an American himself, familiar with other Americans and fluent in American English, Sargent might not have felt entirely aligned with them either. Could he have agreed with the (fictive) judgmental French passenger who found his fellow travelers "theatrically American . . . much given to a constant display of cheap patriotism"? The author continued, describing his perplexity with the American character—its heterogeneity, its freedoms, and particularly a twenty-year-old American girl he observed on the ship who had "bright eyes, a tireless tongue, and a frank independence of manner . . . in twenty-four hours she knew every unattached man on board the ship." While attesting to the girl's virtue, the author commented, "it is not surprising that neither Frenchmen or Englishmen understand [the Americans]," and he wondered whether perhaps the gregarious American temperament might be explained by the continent's "terrible" range of climate.[4] On board ship, Sargent was an observer suspended between two worlds—the comfortable experience of Europe, where he had been born and raised, and the unknown promise of America, which had always provided an identity and an attachment for his family. Both continents were equally foreign and familiar; the ocean voyage between them provided the painter with an opportunity for transition and contemplation.

Many writers have discussed the psychology of the transatlantic voyage and its function as a liminal space.[5] Passengers existed out of bounds; they had left the borders of one country but had not yet arrived in another. They met people whom they did not know and often whom they were unlikely to see again, chance encounters outside the boundaries of their usual society. "Once free from the wharf strings," wrote Clarence Buel in *Century Magazine*, "the steamer was nearly as independent of the ordinary world as a miniature planet."[6] Comfortably housed in all the luxury the Cunard Line could provide, first-class (or "saloon") passengers began their international adventure on board, for their fellow travelers were most likely to hail from disparate countries. Enclosed in this neutral environment, removed from hearth and home, travelers could use the voyage as an opportunity to reinvent themselves.

No details of the Sargent family's crossing survive. In all probability their trip resembled those taken by many other passengers of the period. Most of the ones who recorded their experiences aboard ship described their human interactions—their fellow passengers and their peculiarities, the rolling motion of the ship and frequent advent of seasickness, games above deck (ring toss) and below (whist and other games of chance), the size and decoration of the cabins and saloons, the quality of the food, and various romantic flirtations. As Charles Dickens put it in his own account of traveling to America, "a dozen murders on shore would lack the interest of these slight incidents at sea."[7] These episodes provided constant fodder for contemporary

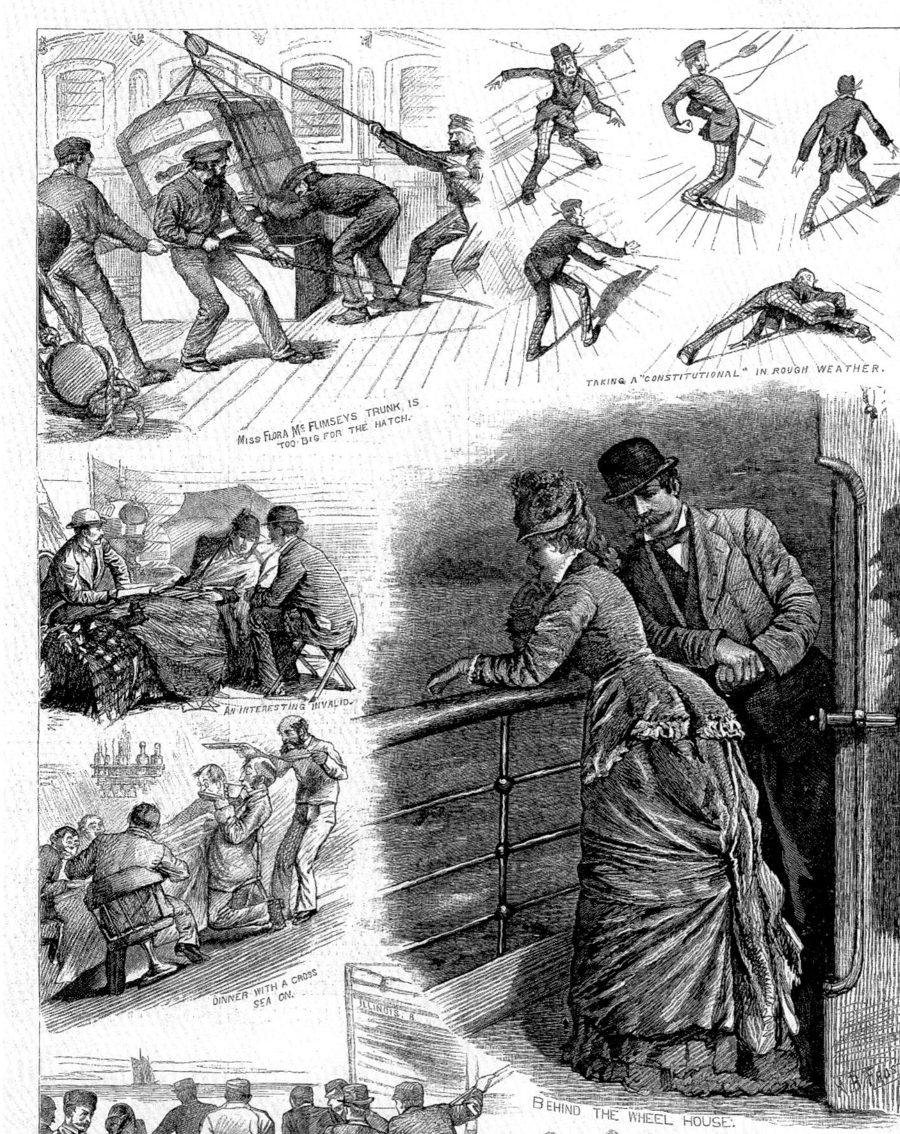

Fig. 47 Arthur B. Frost, *Incidents of an Ocean Trip*, from *Harper's Weekly*, August 10, 1878.

illustrators, among them Winslow Homer, who drew *Homeward Bound* for *Harper's Weekly* on his own return from Europe in 1868, and Arthur B. Frost, whose humorous *Incidents of an Ocean Trip* appeared in the same magazine ten years later (fig. 47). The American painter Henry Bacon, to whom Sargent gave four of his marine paintings, made such motifs one of the chief subjects of his art. In his lengthy description of one of his own December crossings, Bacon glossed over rough seas and any thoughts of the infinite he may have entertained, preferring instead to describe the personalities on board, their daily activities, and the captain's dinner.[8] These events provided Bacon with themes of modern life for a popular series of paintings in oil, among them *On the Open Sea—The Transatlantic Steamship "Péreire"* (fig. 48). One of Bacon's earliest transatlantic subjects, exhibited at the Salon in 1877, the canvas depicts an assortment of passengers on deck. The mood is one of suspended animation, of idle amusements undertaken to pass the time before something of interest took place—a flirtation, a storm, the sighting of land. In transit, Bacon's passengers live outside the routines of their everyday lives.

Bacon based his painting upon a pencil study he made in mid-January 1877, later reproduced in *The Art Amateur* as *In Mid-Ocean* (fig. 49). Presumably the sketch was made on his own crossing that month. The changes the artist made between his drawing and painting are worthy of note, for Bacon improved upon his actual experience, transforming the mood from one of endurance to one of amusement. The weather has changed for the better in the oil painting; the passengers no longer cover their ears, huddle beneath shawls, or grasp umbrellas. The sea is conspicuously calm and blue, and the smoke of the engines dissipates quickly into the breeze instead of hanging over the deck in a dense black cloud. Bacon's images brought James

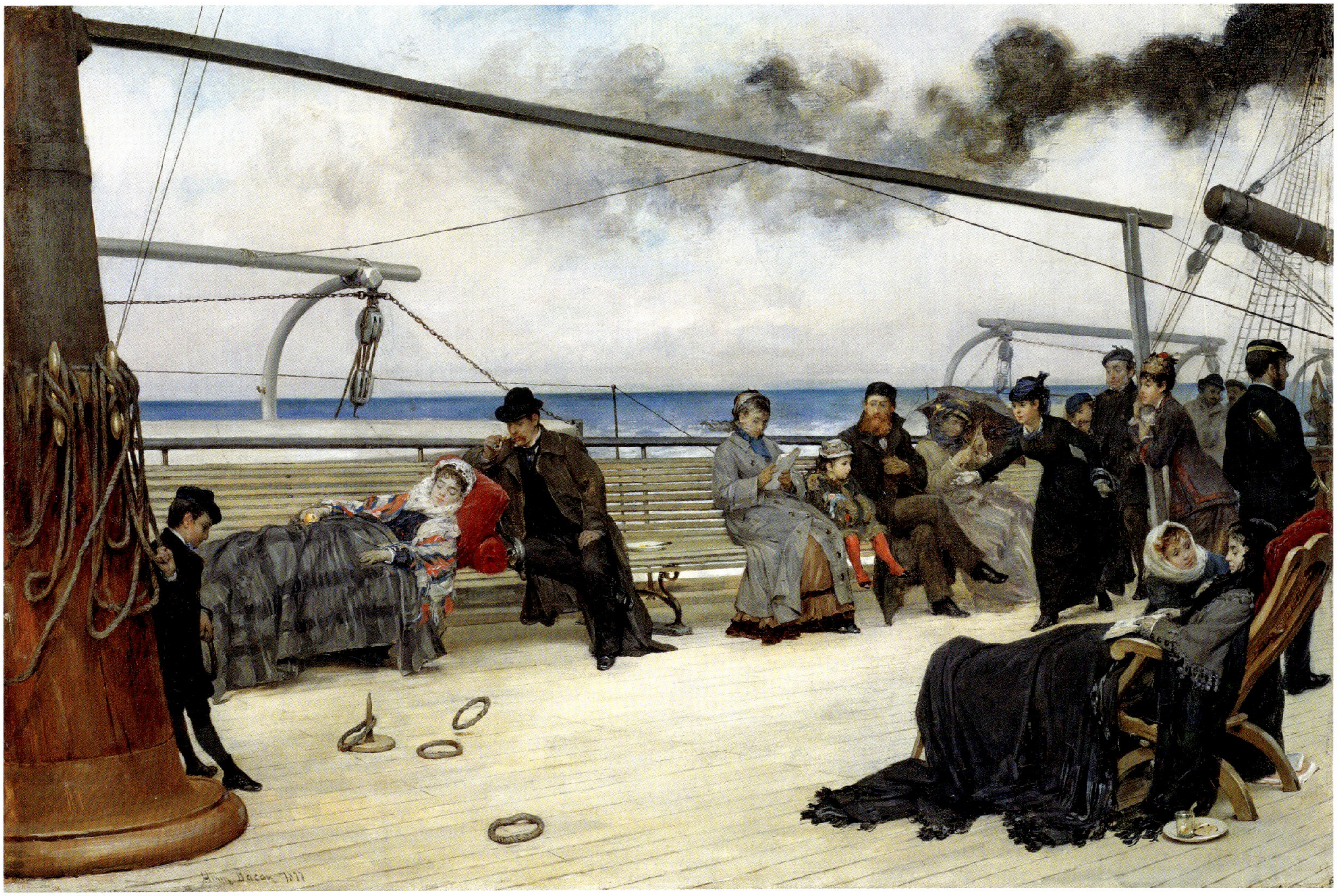

Fig. 48 Henry Bacon, *On the Open Sea – The Transatlantic Steamship "Péreire,"* 1877. Oil on canvas, 19¾ × 29⅛ in (50.16 × 73.98 cm). Museum of Fine Arts, Boston. Gift of Mrs Edward Livingston Davis, 13.1692.

Fig. 49 Henry Bacon, *In Mid-Ocean*, from *The Art Amateur* 7 (November 1882), p. 116.

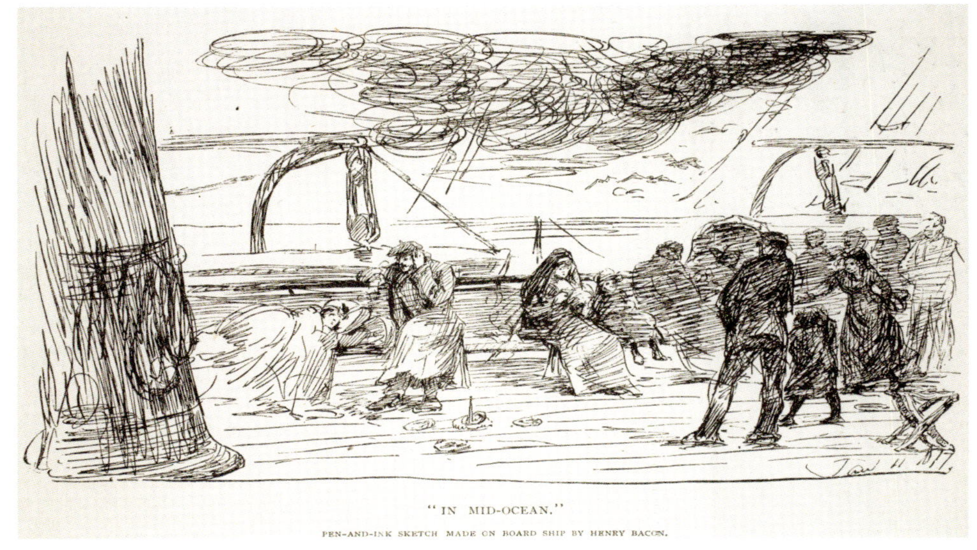

Tissot's flirtatious scenes of boating (both paintings and prints) out from the River Thames and onto the open seas, and his transatlantic paintings appealed to both actual and would-be travelers headed in either direction. His sentimental narratives of life aboard ship became very popular; by November 1882 the British journalist Richard Whiteing, who illustrated *In Mid-Ocean* amongst other works, could proclaim that Bacon's subjects would be familiar to his readers "through the engravings of them to be found on the walls of many an American home."[9]

Bacon and Sargent may have traveled together to America on the *SS Abyssinia* (Bacon also went from Paris to Philadelphia in 1876), and Sargent gave Bacon three small, informal shipboard sketches and one of his seascapes, perhaps as a souvenir of shared experiences (see figs. 27, 28, 54, and 153).[10] But their images of life at sea are very different. Sargent's art ignored the social and the specific in favor of the solitary and the universal. Occasionally he recorded people aboard ship, but (save for the unusual oil study of his mother in a deckchair, see fig. 27) he concentrated his attention on the crew at work and made mostly small sketches in pencil (see pp. 58–81). Unlike Bacon, Sargent did not paint his fellow first-class passengers either during his trip or later, in the studio. What he painted in oil was the sea—shifting without boundaries, no land in sight.

In a sense these images reflect Sargent's own position, not just physically, in the reality of his own passage, but also psychologically. Certainly he was aware of his own innate talent as a painter; that same year his fellow student and friend James Carroll Beckwith had reported of him, "his work makes me shake myself."[11] While Sargent would return to the École and to Carolus-Duran's studio to continue his training after his 1876 voyage, he must have understood that his own path as an aspiring artist was clear, that soon he could set his own course as a painter. It is not at all evident at this stage that Sargent would set his sights on portraiture; of the paintings he made between 1874 and 1878, only a handful are portraits, mostly sketches of friends and family. As Richard Ormond suggests in the introduction, perhaps Sargent would follow his family's seafaring path, using painting as his craft.

Sargent made two large seascapes in 1876, *Atlantic Sunset* and *Atlantic Storm*, along with three small and delicately beautiful oils, *The Derelict*; *Mid-Ocean, Mid-Winter*; and *Seascape* (figs. 50, 51, 53, 54, 56).[12] The two larger paintings might be placed on different shores of the aesthetic sea that Sargent was starting to navigate. *Atlantic Sunset* (fig. 50) is calm and reflective, with soft opalescent hues blending into each other. *Atlantic Storm* (see fig. 51) is active and violent, narrative, with dramatic lines and solid colors. Both allude to the dangers of a transatlantic crossing—the rough seas in one and the derelict craft in the other—but artistically they are opposites, one illustrative and one contemplative, divergent markers on the course of Sargent's artistic journey.

Atlantic Storm records the vertiginous pitch of a steamship's deck as it makes its way through high seas. Sargent experienced such a rough passage on his return from America to Europe, and he drew the sloping deck of the *SS Algeria* and the surrounding mountainous waves in a small sketchbook (see figs. 103 and 104). He would not have been able to spend much time working outside during such a gale, for as the writer Mark Twain noted of his own stormy crossing, "one could not promenade without risking his neck; at one moment the bowsprit was taking a deadly aim at the sun in mid-heaven, and at the next it was trying to harpoon a shark in the bottom of the ocean. What a weird sensation it is to feel the stern of a ship sinking swiftly from under you and see the bow climbing high away among the clouds!" Charles Dickens also described his experience of

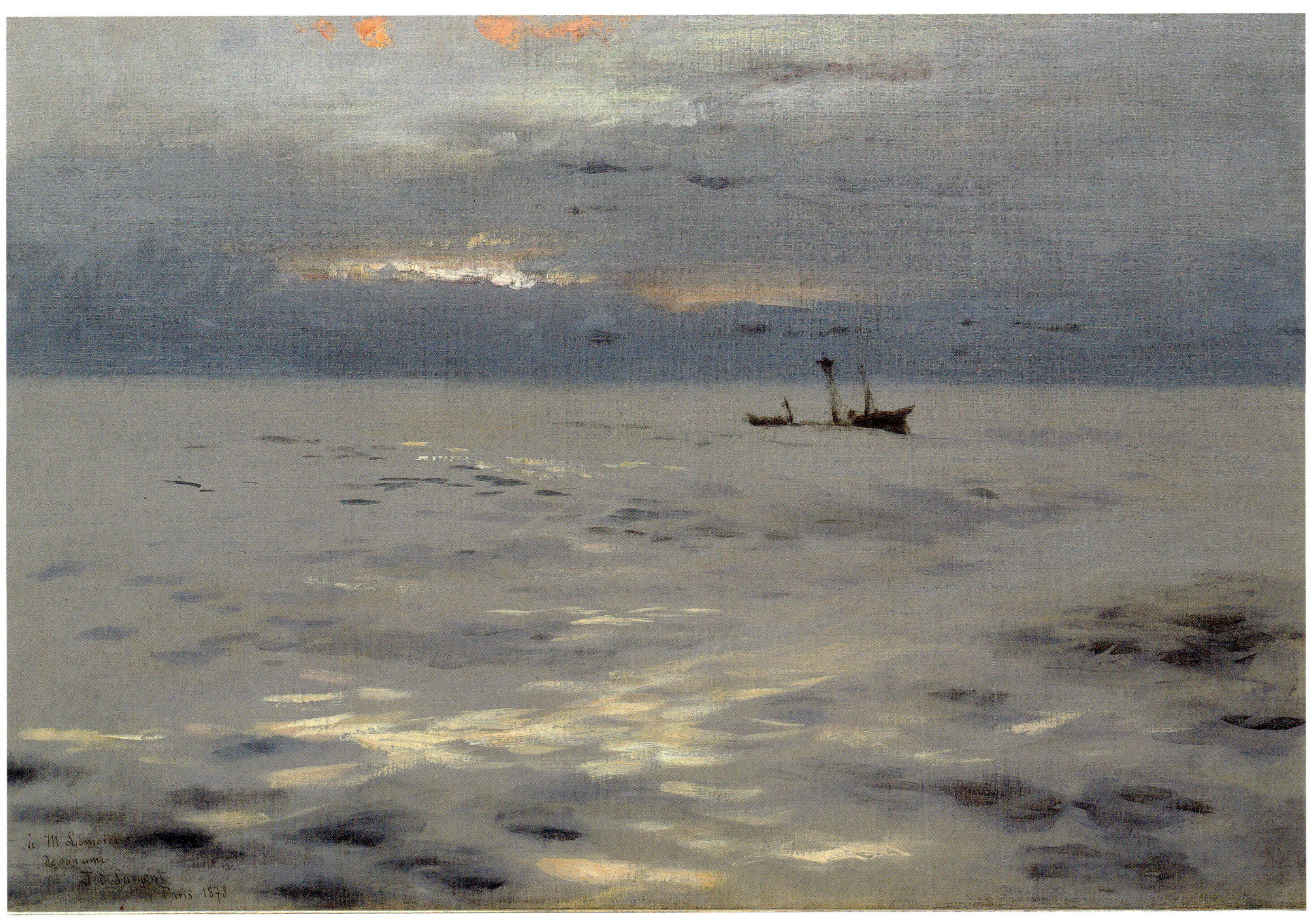

Fig. 50 *Atlantic Sunset*, *c.* 1876. Oil on canvas, 25½ × 36¼ in (64.8 × 92 cm). Inscribed, bottom left: *à M. Lemercier / de son ami / J.S. Sargent / Paris 1878.* Private Collection. (Exhibition)

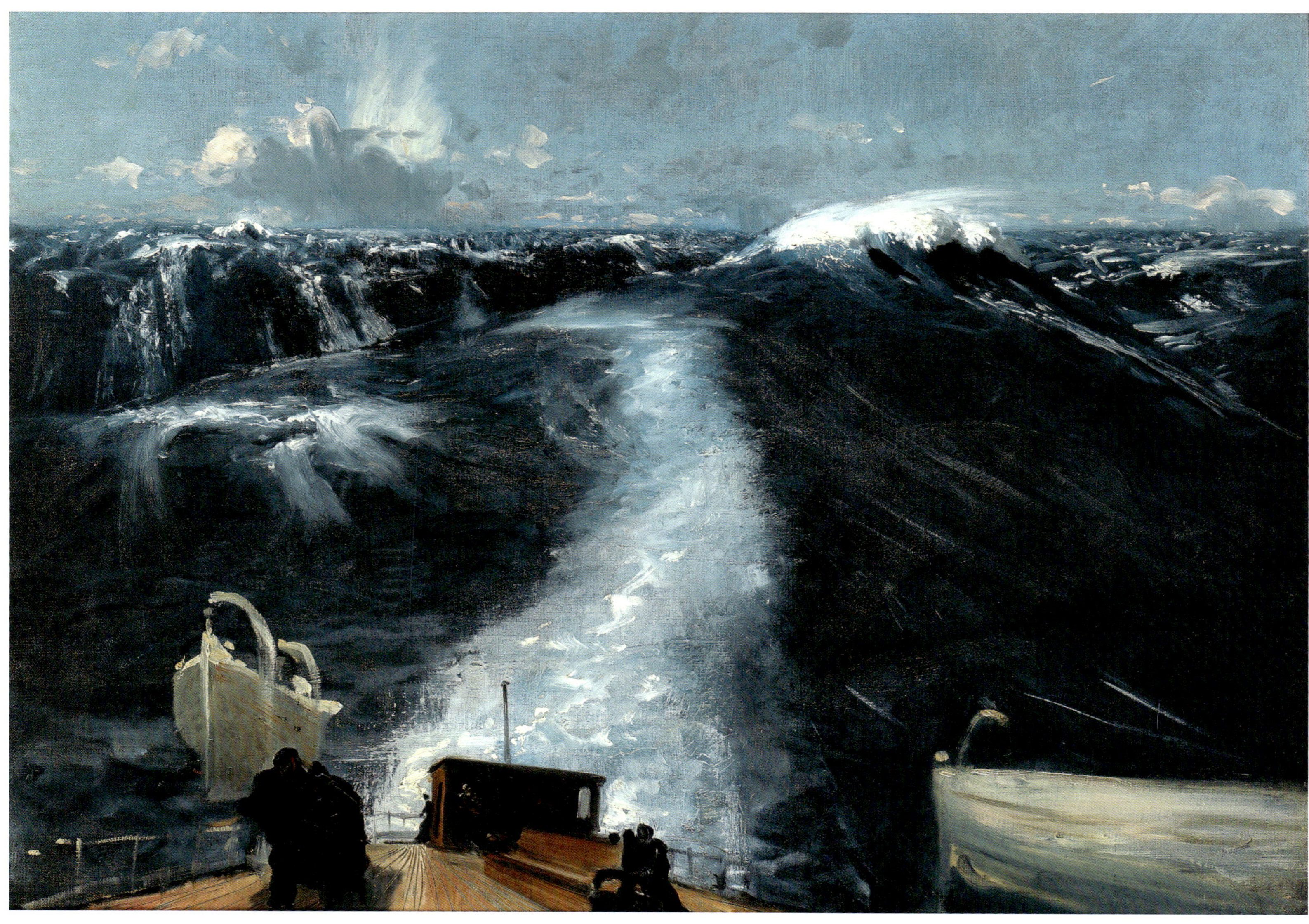

Fig. 51 *Atlantic Storm*, 1876. Oil on canvas, 23 × 32 in (58.5 × 81.5 cm). Curtis Galleries, Minneapolis. (Exhibition)

sailing through a storm with "everything . . . sliding and bumping about." He wrote that "the agitation of a steam-vessel is, on a bad winter's night in the wild Atlantic . . . impossible for the most vivid imagination to conceive . . . she is flung down on her side in the waves, with her mast dipping into them, and that, springing up again, she rolls over on the other side, until a heavy sea strikes her with the noise of a hundred great guns, and hurls her back—that she stops, and staggers, and shivers, as though stunned, and then, with a violent throbbing at her heart, darts onward like a monster goaded into madness."[13] These are not optimal conditions for painting, and Sargent's composition was almost certainly made in the studio.[14]

Sargent caught the *SS Algeria* on her upward rise, the ship's stern abruptly descending at the very bottom of the picture, almost swamped by the huge waves that rise behind it. The steep plunge of the deck, which rushes into the distance so precipitously, is almost comical in its unlikely tilt; a pair of dark figures struggle to walk up it, only slightly more stable than the hapless teetering figure in Arthur Frost's *Taking a Constitutional in Rough Weather* (fig. 52). While Sargent omitted various details of the furnishings of the *SS Algeria*, he included two of its lifeboats which, although misplaced from their actual locations, swing from their davits and provide small reassurance against the immensity of the sea. Sargent employed a high horizon line, giving over two thirds of his composition to the weight of the ocean, its slate-blue water and its immense waves, dark mountainous swells with snowy white crests. A strong wind blows the foam from the tops of the waves and animates the changeable sky. The main feature at the center of the composition is the wake of the ship, a short-lived trace of the course of man.

The ship's progress, visible only in the frothy path it leaves in the water, was

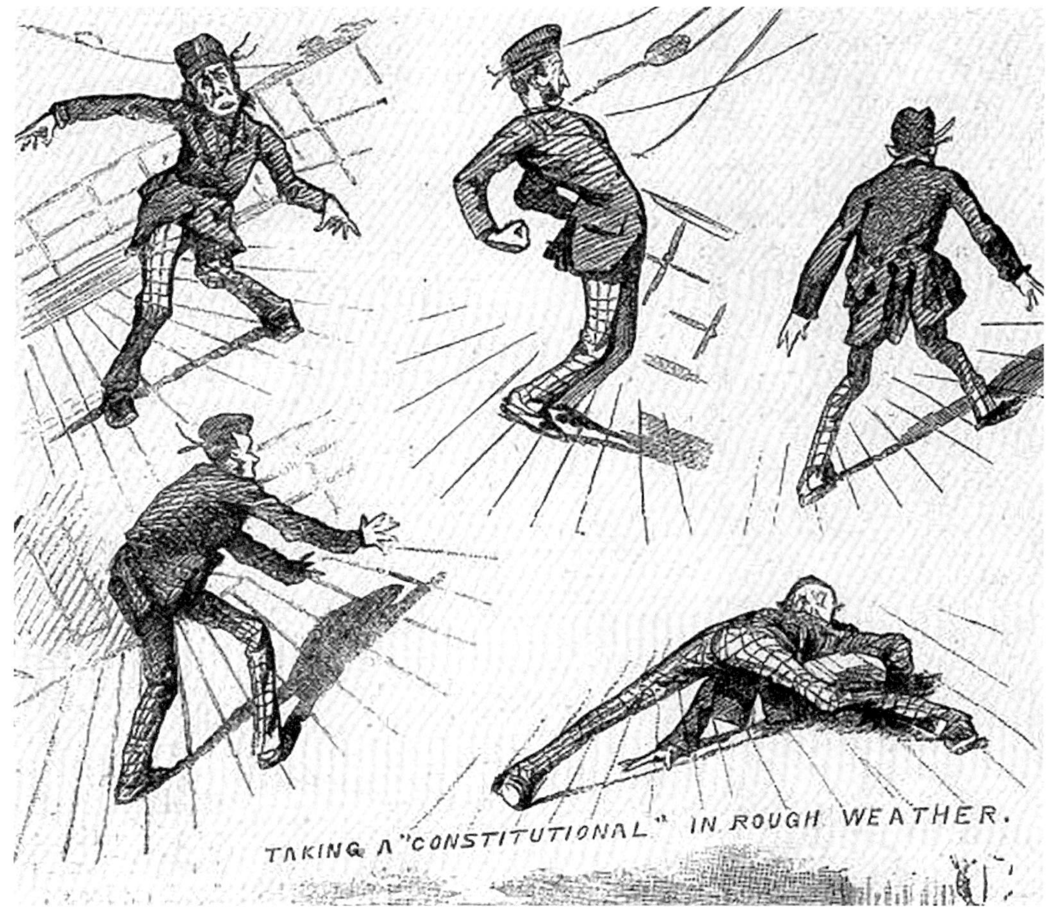

Fig. 52 Arthur B. Frost, *Taking a Constitutional in Rough Weather*, detail of fig. 47, Arthur B. Frost, *Incidents of an Ocean Trip*, from *Harper's Weekly*, August 10, 1878.

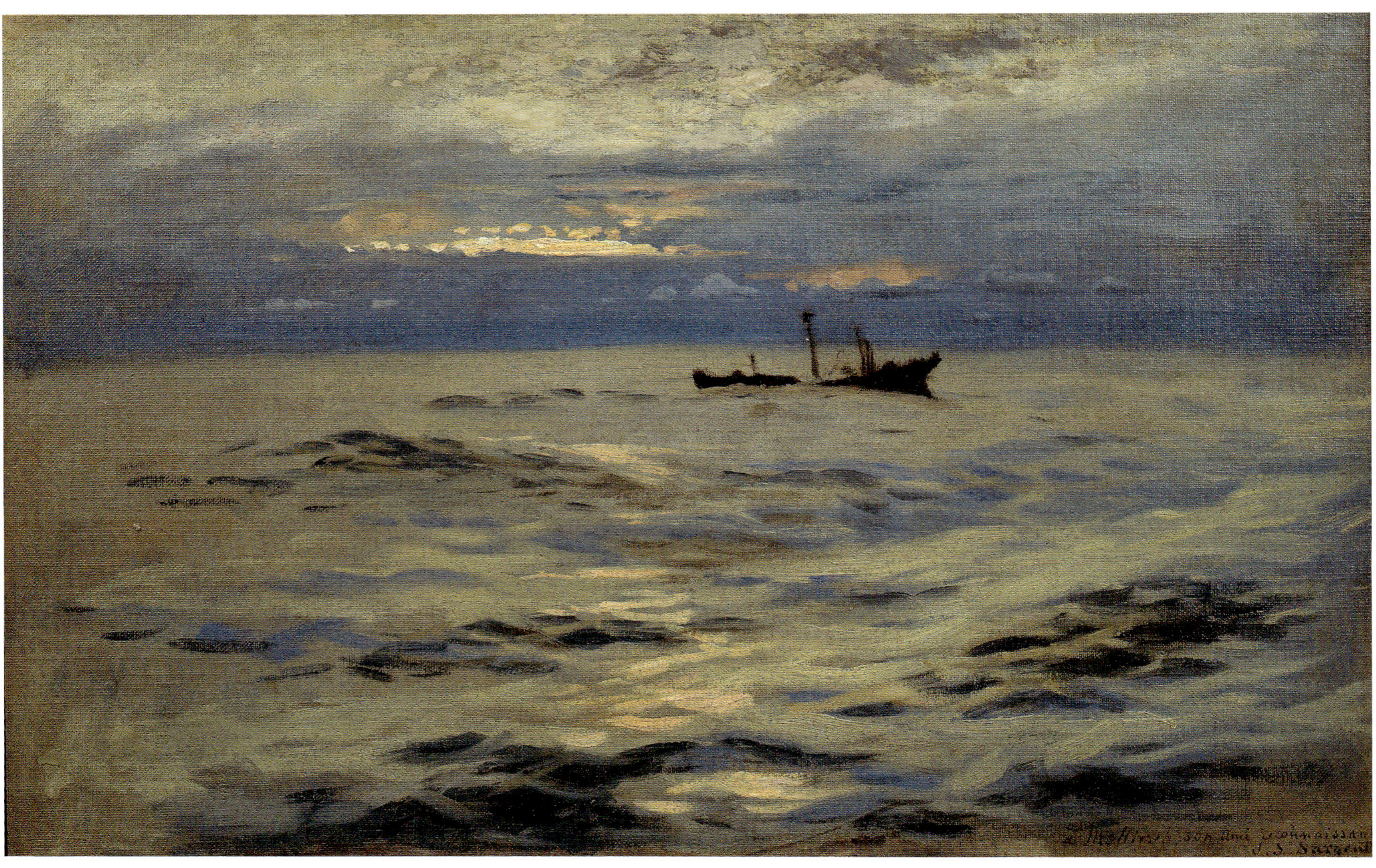

Fig. 53 *The Derelict*, *c.* 1876. Oil on canvas, 13¼ × 20 in (33.7 × 50.8 cm). Inscribed, lower right: *à M. Hirsch son ami reconnaissant/J.S. Sargent*. Private Collection. (Exhibition)

also the main subject of two other works by Sargent, *Mid-Ocean, Mid-Winter* and *Moonlight on Waves* (figs. 54, 55). The titles are posthumous and therefore not necessarily accurate as to season and time; both seem likely to have been inspired by Sargent's 1876 transatlantic crossings. The pencil drawing *Moonlight on Waves*, although smaller in size than the sketchbook pages of sailors and thus not necessarily part of the same book, may have been done aboard the ship, but *Mid-Ocean, Mid-Winter* seems to have been painted with a steady hand on land, or at least after the storm had passed.[15] It could be a preliminary study for *Atlantic Storm*, for its small size matches the scale of other preparatory works. *Mid-Ocean, Mid-Winter* and *Moonlight on Waves* show the sea alone; the presence of the steamer is evident only from its white wake and in the drawing, from the storm-petrels, small seabirds that frequently followed ships at sea. Standing on deck, looking back at the evidence of the ship's progress, travelers were often spell-bound, perhaps thinking of the passage in personal and psychological terms. As the French novelist Gustave Flaubert remarked, both seriously and facetiously, the sea had no bottom, and thus it gave rise to deep thoughts. Contemplating the vast emptiness and great power of the open ocean was to engage with the sublime, to reckon with the small role of man in the face of nature, and even to come to grips with mortality.[16]

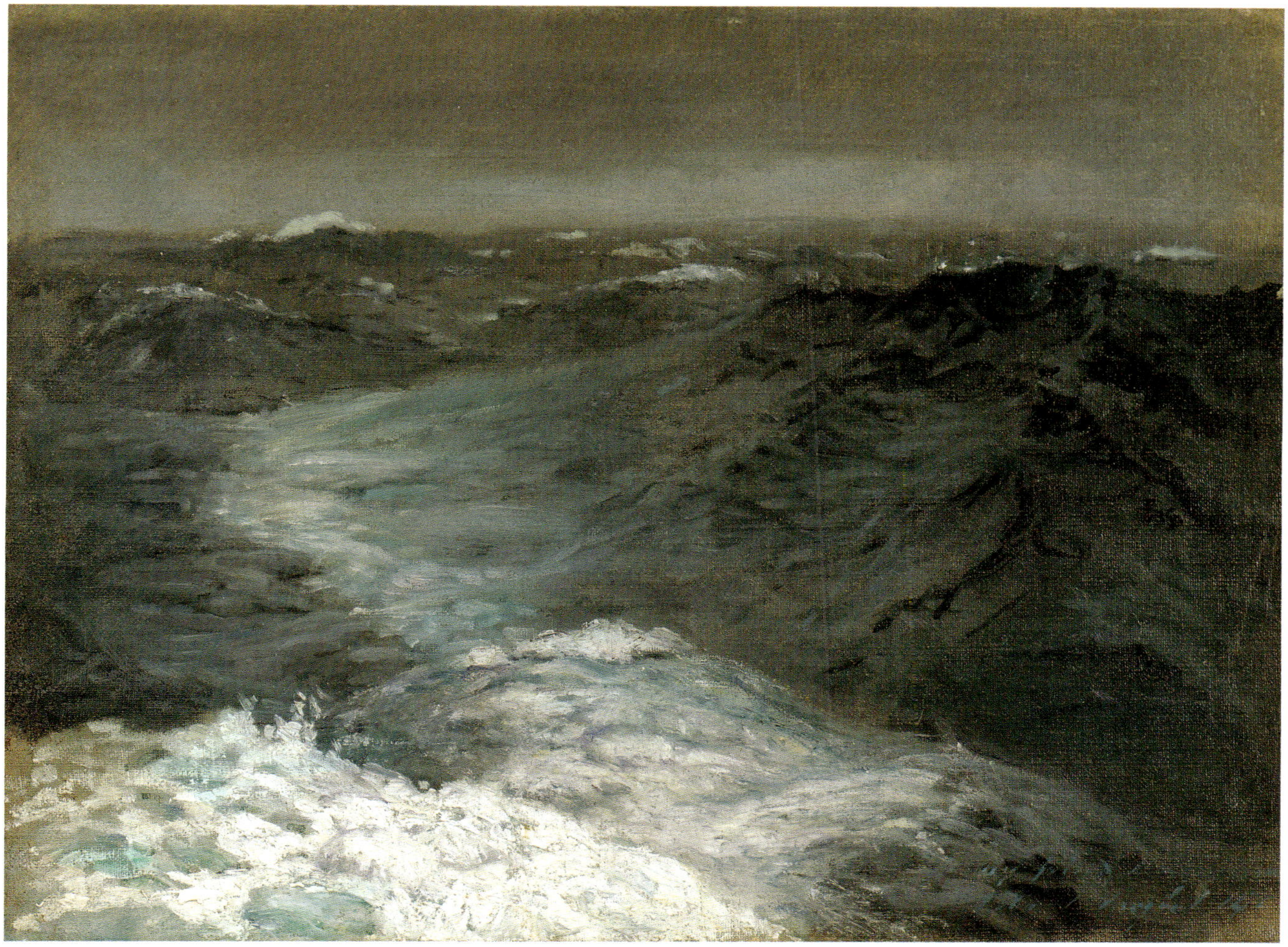

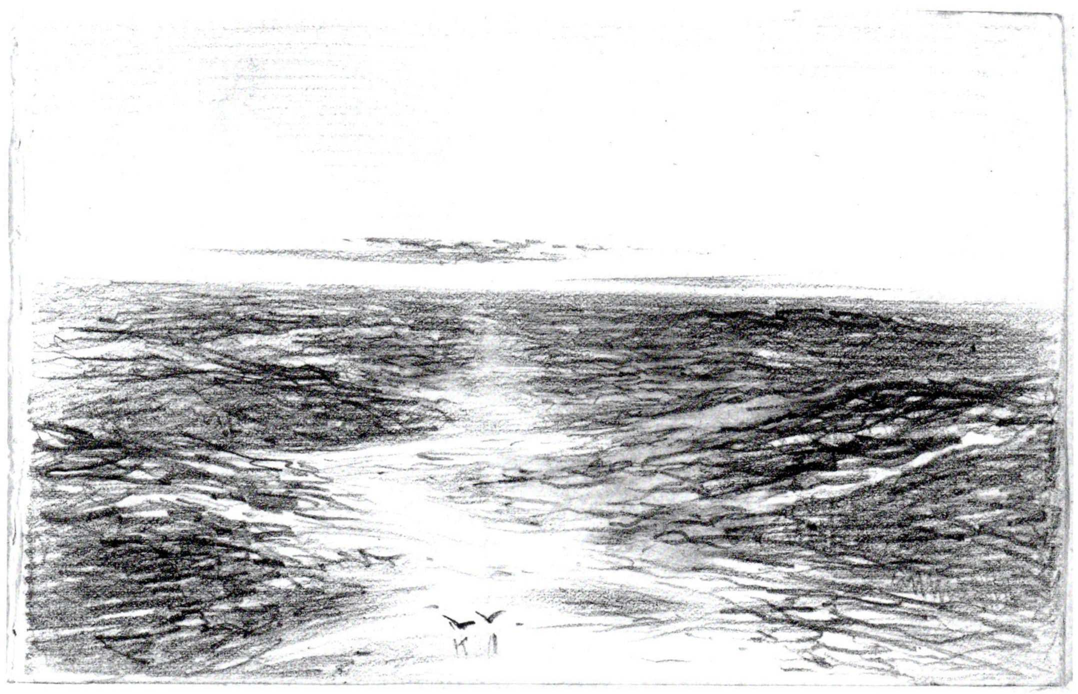

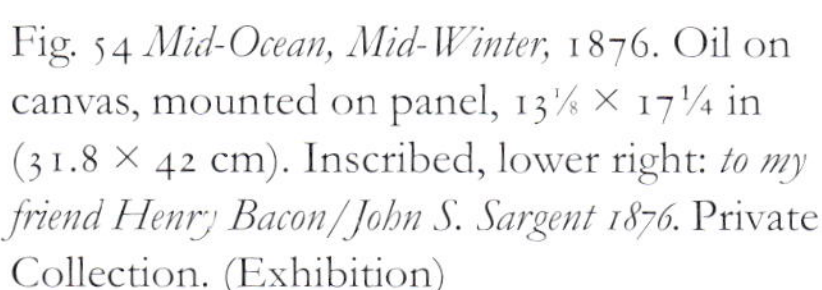

Fig. 54 *Mid-Ocean, Mid-Winter,* 1876. Oil on canvas, mounted on panel, 13⅛ × 17¼ in (31.8 × 42 cm). Inscribed, lower right: *to my friend Henry Bacon/John S. Sargent 1876.* Private Collection. (Exhibition)

Fig. 55 *Moonlight on Waves*, 1876. Graphite on paper, 3¾ × 5⅞ in (9.5 × 14.9 cm). In the John Singer Sargent Scrapbook (50.130.154). The Metropolitan Museum of Art. Gift of Mrs Francis Ormond, 1950. (50.130.154l) (Exhibition)

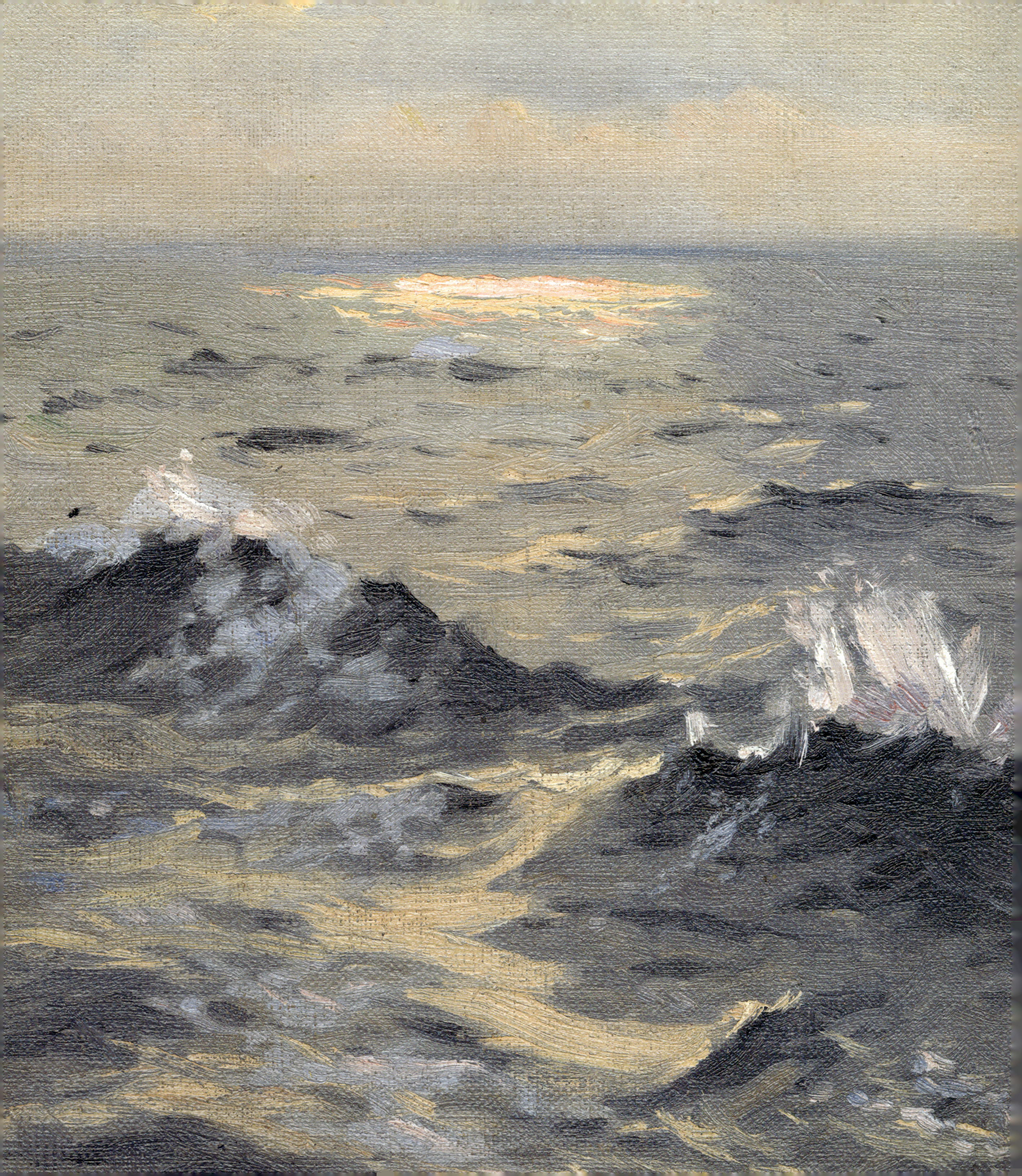

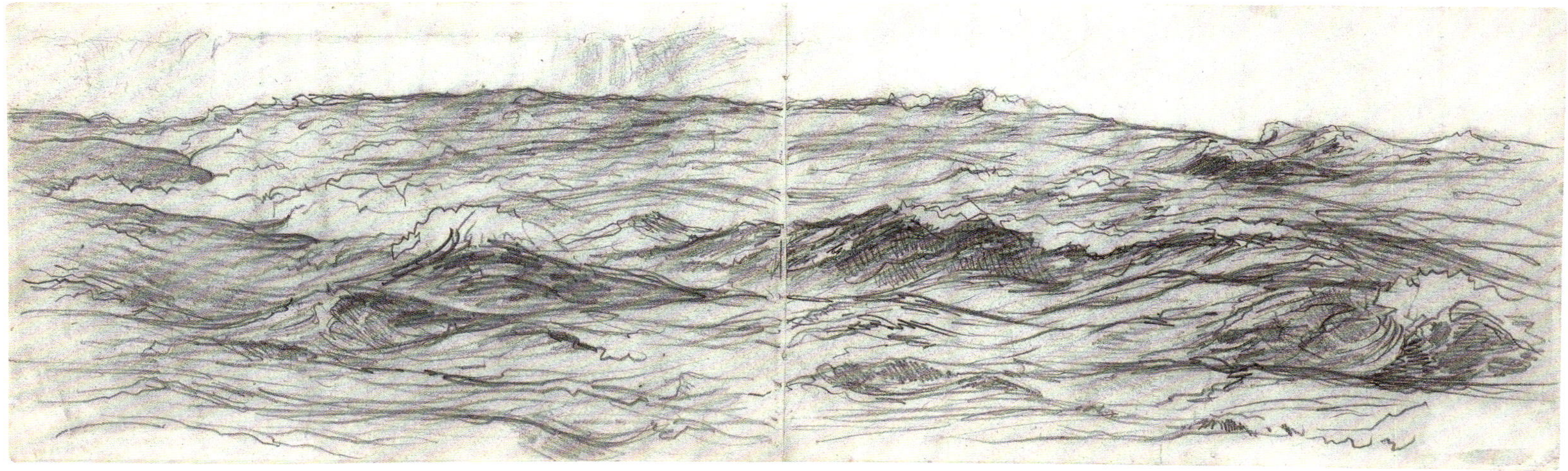

Fig. 57 *Wave*, 1876. Graphite on paper, 4 × 13½ in (10.1 × 34.2 cm). Inscribed lower right, on paper mount: *John S. Sargent*. Private Collection. (Exhibition)

While stormy seas had provided epic settings to artists for generations, their paintings most often included some reference to man's accomplishments or follies. Depictions of the sea alone, with no clear vantage point from a ship or the shore, were unusual. Lacking a clear narrative, seemingly empty of life, and devoid of human activity, the motion of the waves was a formal and abstract subject that would have seemed completely unfinished to most critical eyes in Sargent's day. Such subjects were suitable only as sketches, studies after nature that would be consulted in the studio when the painter turned his attention to creating a finished work suitable for display. It is not surprising that these paintings by Sargent seem never to have been exhibited until the twentieth century. At this early stage in his career, he was not yet ready to publicly abandon pictorial convention, and perhaps in an effort to make an acceptable work of art, he added the deck of the ship to his watery composition in *Atlantic Storm*, a larger painting that he might have considered a finished piece rather than a study.[17]

The second large canvas Sargent made, *Atlantic Sunset*, is much less unusual in its formal arrangement, with horizontal bands delineating sea and sky, and the dark shape of the distant ship providing some sense of scale (fig. 50). The painting is related to two smaller oils, *The Derelict* and *Seascape*, and a pencil drawing, *Wave* (figs. 53, 56, 57). All four scenes were conceived at sea, seemingly looking out over the side of a ship; none of them includes any detail of nearby deck or rigging, strand or shore; there is no evidence of solid footing for the viewer, who seems suspended above the waves. *Seascape*, a vertical oil painting, and *Wave*, an elongated horizontal drawing, convey the limitless expanse of water in all directions; no matter how the composition is framed, the sea has no beginning and no end. In both *Atlantic Sunset* and *The Derelict* an abandoned ship, broken and riding low in the water, anchors the view. The subject of a derelict craft was a melancholy one, providing evidence of man's failure against the elements and hinting at the possibility of similar danger for the onlookers who traveled the same seas. Derelicts were common and they were a significant navigational hazard, particularly at night, in the fog, or during a storm. "During the five years between 1887 and 1891," reported one historian, "not fewer

Facing page: Fig. 56 Detail of fig. 26, *Seascape*, *c.* 1876. Frank M. Gren "Annapolis Collection." (Exhibition)

than 957 derelict ships were reported to the Hydrographer at Washington … on average there were about twenty derelicts drifting in the North Atlantic at any instant."[18] These empty ships, wrecked by weather or fire and deserted by their crews, were carried along by the Gulf Stream. They could drift thousands of miles and they fueled the popular imagination with legends of abandoned treasure and of skeleton captains still sitting at finely appointed dinner tables.

In *Atlantic Sunset* Sargent was not interested in the narrative potential of the derelict ship but in the ephemeral effects of the fading sunlight on the clouds and the water. The sky and sea are defined with a narrow range of smoky gray blues, but it is the light that has captured the artist's attention. Using a broad brush, Sargent added loose strokes of pale yellow and peach-colored paint to the tops of the waves and the edges of the clouds. At the very top, singular jabs of salmon orange mark the last reflection of the sun's rays as it sets. Sargent's execution is remarkably free; the carefully rendered details of the rolling waves and the shafts of sunlight that are evident in the smaller sketches, *The Derelict* and *Seascape*, are loosened to the bare minimum in *Atlantic Sunset*. Instead of environmental accuracy, Sargent concentrated on the general effect of transient opalescence. If in *Atlantic Storm* Sargent added elements to make a more understandable narrative, in *Atlantic Sunset* he subtracted them, creating an image in which his own touch is one of the chief subjects of the painting. In its fluidity and sensitivity to color, it seems more akin to some of the most modern French art of the preceding decade.

Whether a metaphor for destruction or the location of a charming seaside holiday, marine imagery, particularly of the pleasurable variety, became increasingly popular in France after the mid-nineteenth century. With the development of the seaside resorts of the Normandy coast, easily reached by railway from the capital, fashionable and wealthy Parisians began to spend time at the shore, enjoying the cool breezes, bathing in the salt water, and observing the activities of the local workers that could be seen, from a distance, as timeless and picturesque. But no matter how many tourists crowded the beach, when one turned to the sea one was alone. That contemplative experience began to be recommended in the ever-increasing number of travel guides to the area. Those summer visitors, upon their return to Paris, became eager patrons for the seascapes and beach scenes being painted in a variety of artistic styles. The Impressionists, whose freely brushed canvases now seem to have been particularly suited to their casual subject, were particularly drawn to the theme. Their informal compositions echoed the freedoms of the modern traveler, reminding them of their holidays along the shore.[19]

If indeed Sargent attended the Impressionist exhibition in 1876, he would have seen Monet's *Beach at Sainte-Adresse* (1867, Art Institute of Chicago), one of a number of loosely painted beach scenes the French painter had made in Normandy some years earlier. Monet did not exhibit his painting for ten years after completing it, perhaps hoping for public opinion to catch up with the technical freedom of his work. In the same show, Berthe Morisot displayed a group of her paintings of ships in the harbor of the Isle of Wight, images so ephemeral and sketchy that she was singled out as one of the most radical of the painters represented in the exhibition. Ludovic Lepic, better known as a subject of Edgar Degas' work than as an artist in his own right, showed over twenty seascapes with such intriguing titles as *Effect of Fog at Sea*, *Moonlight at Sea*, and *Sun Effect (The Channel)*, but few of them have been located. Lepic's spare *Boats on the Beach at Berck* was one (fig. 58); it captures the mutable seaside environment in a carefully planned rhythmic composition with softly painted iridescent skies.

One might associate Sargent's loose touch and interest in fleeting atmospheric effects, so evident in *Atlantic Sunset*, with these modern works by the Impressionist circle. But one thing sets Sargent's canvases apart from those of most of these innovative French painters, even from Edouard Manet, whose marine paintings of the 1860s remain remarkable for their fresh vitality and spare and inventive compositions. Sargent was not painting the activities of the coast, but the open sea. Of all these artists, only Degas had ever crossed the Atlantic. During his journey in 1872 he, like so many other shipboard travelers, apparently ignored the ocean as much as he could and instead documented in a series of small sketches his fellow passengers—Englishmen with whom he complained he was unable to converse.[20] The images of Monet, Morisot, and Lepic are beach or harbor scenes, anchored visually to the shore and thus to the human experience, still traditional in their perspective. Manet's finished canvases are also about the activities of man; his ships are in port, or they sail together in a fishing fleet, or they engage in one of the oldest subjects of marine painting, a battle at sea.

The painter whose work had broken some of these conventions, and who was also a veteran of many voyages, was another American, James McNeill Whistler. Whistler, born in the United States, had first crossed the Atlantic as a child, when his mother took him and his siblings from New England to Russia, where her husband was employed as a civil engineer. Whistler returned to the United States when he was fifteen and went back to Europe six years later. He divided his time between Paris and London, sailing across the Channel on innumerable occasions, sometimes for a stay of only a few days. Early in 1866, he embarked for Chile, where he stayed for several months and then returned to England. Certainly the sea did not frighten him, and it became the subject of some of his own most inventive paintings.

Sargent was said to have met Whistler in the early 1870s; certainly he was aware of his art.[21] Sargent's familiarity with (and admiration for) the older painter's work is clearly evident in his own paintings, chiefly of Venice, but also in spare compositions like *Whitby Fishing Boats* (fig. 59), in which Sargent's banded composition and relatively thin veils of color recall Whistler's compositional strategies. Whistler had painted and etched ships and boats in the Thames beginning in the late 1850s; his first large-scale beach scene, *Alone with the Tide* (Wadsworth Atheneum, Hartford, Connecticut), was painted in Brittany in 1861. He turned his attention to the sea itself the following year with *Blue and Silver: Blue Wave, Biarritz* (1862, Hill-Stead Museum, Farmington, Connecticut). The insistently awkward naturalism and thick facture of

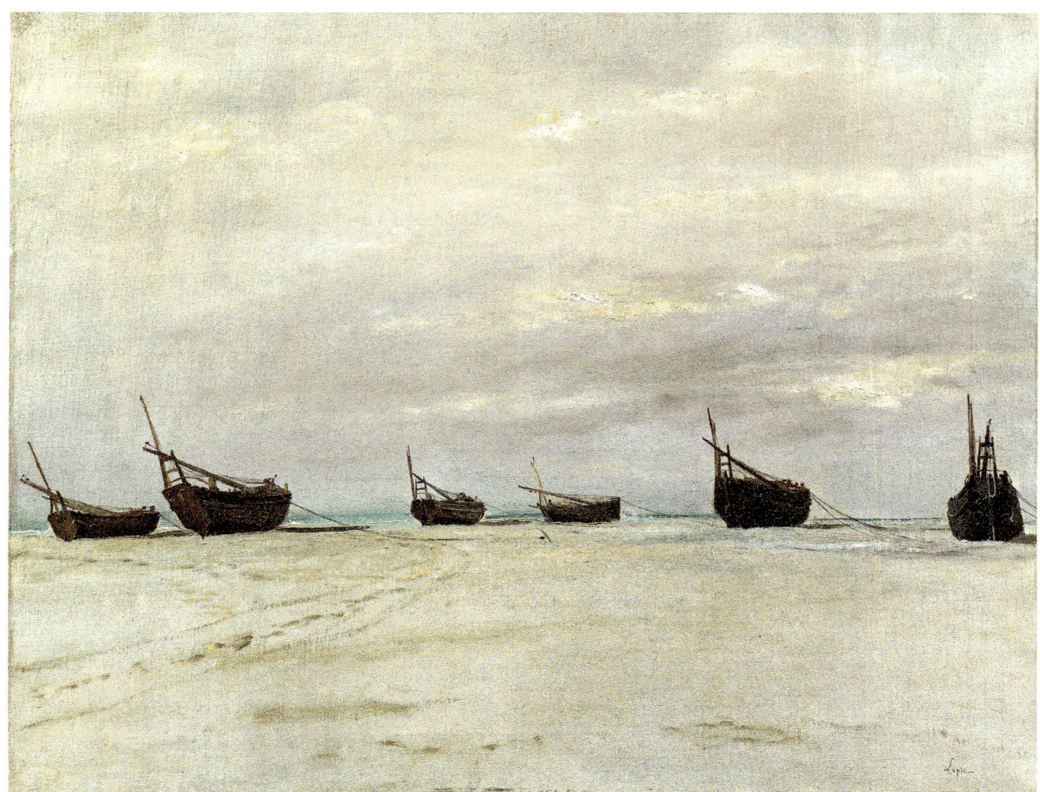

Fig. 58 Ludovic Lepic, *Boats on the Beach at Berck*, *c.* 1876. Oil on canvas, 30 × 40 in (76.2 × 101.6 cm). Fine Arts Museums of San Francisco, Museum purchase, Grover A. Magnin Bequest Fund, 1987.5.

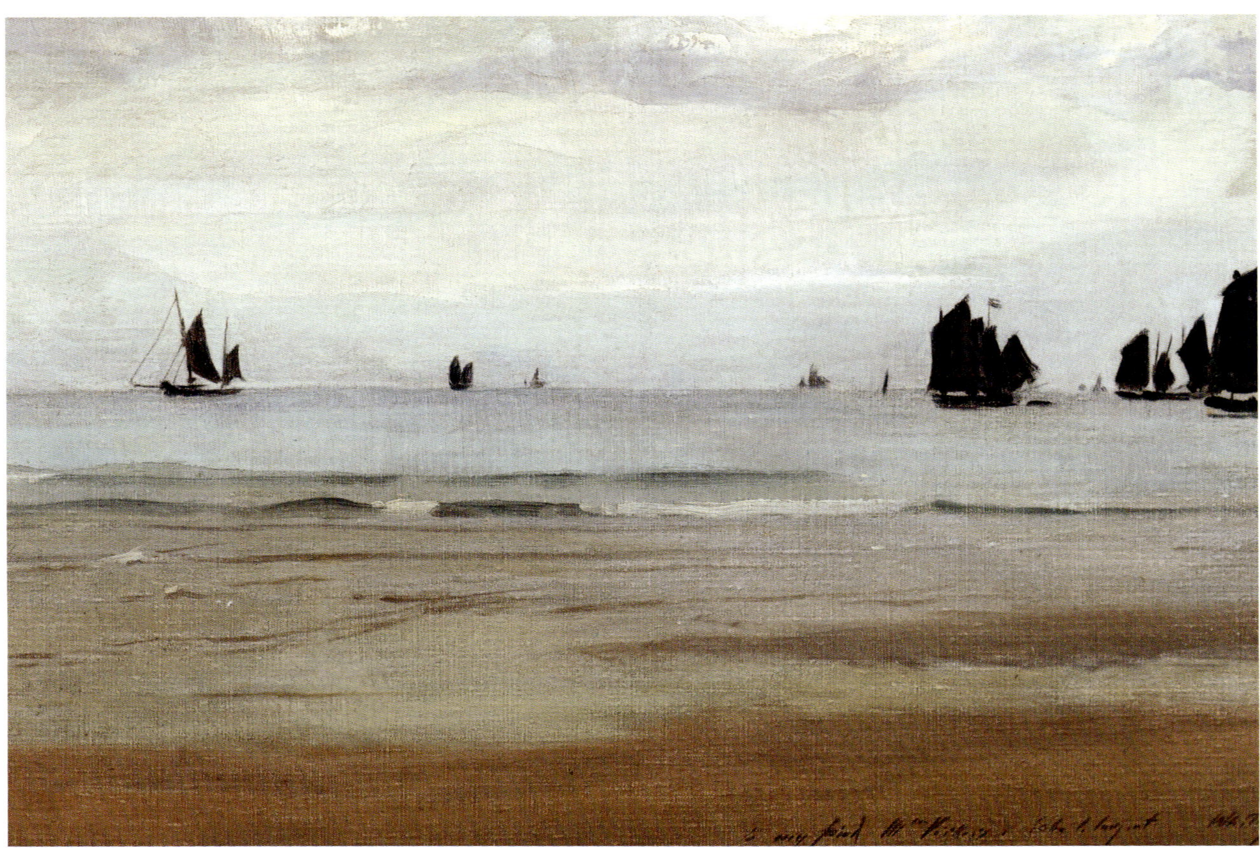

Fig. 59 *Whitby Fishing Boats*, 1884. Oil on canvas, 18½ × 27 in (47 × 68.6 cm). Inscribed, lower right: *to my friend Mrs Vickers, John S. Sargent Whitby*. Private Collection. (Exhibition, Washington and London only)

these coast scenes clearly allies Whistler's work with that of the French realist Gustave Courbet, whom he greatly admired and whose paintings of the sea Sargent would also have known. The respect was mutual, and Whistler and Courbet spent October and November of 1865 together on the Normandy coast at Trouville. There Whistler transformed his style, creating daringly empty and abstract compositions in which the patterns of line and color across the surface of the picture plane take precedence over the representation of the details of the natural world, for example, *Crepuscule in Opal* (fig. 60). Courbet also refined his seascapes, and many of the views of the shore he painted after 1865 seem lighter, fresher, and while still landlocked, more devoted to the contemplation of the infinite, as in *L'Immensité* (fig. 61). The interlude greatly affected Courbet, who ten years later, in exile during the last year of his life, wrote to Whistler in fond remembrance of the time when they had gone "bathing on a frozen beach" together and had painted "the sky, the sea, and the fish all the way to the horizon." Their reward, Courbet added, was "dreams and sky."[22]

Dreams and sky seem like the true subjects of Sargent's seascapes as well, as perhaps seascapes always are, but it is difficult to resist analyzing them in the context of this promising young painter's career. At the time of his transatlantic crossing in 1876 Sargent's artistic aspirations were yet to be fulfilled; he made these unusual pictures when he was still a student, with no public exhibitions to his name. In his studies in Paris he had concentrated on figure painting—the only reliable source of income for a painter other than teaching—and he worked hard to master the skills taught at the École des Beaux-Arts, soon making the human form his chief

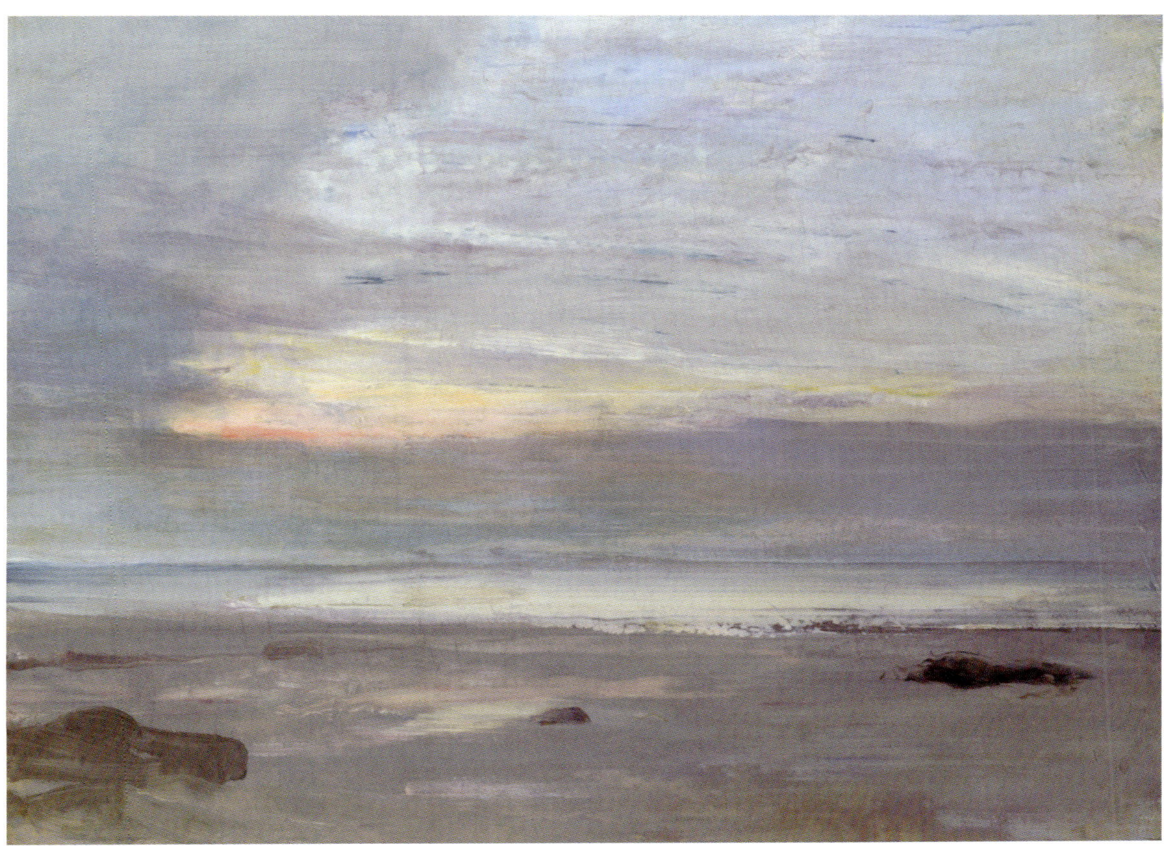

Fig. 60 James McNeill Whistler, *Crepuscule in Opal*, 1865. Oil on canvas, 13¾ × 18⅛ in (35 × 46 cm). Toledo Museum of Art, Gift of Florence Scott Libbey, 1923.20.

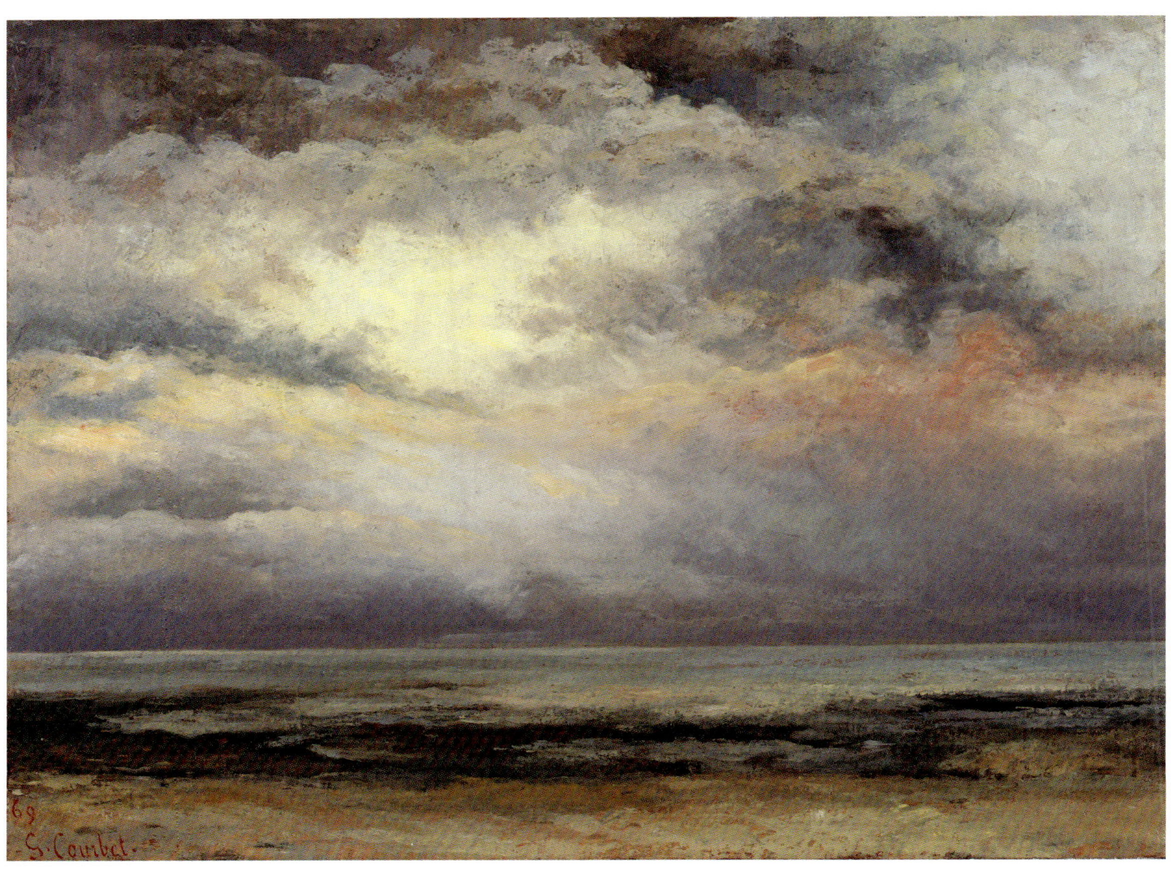

Fig. 61 Gustave Courbet, *L'Immensité*, 1869. Oil on canvas, 23⅝ × 32⅜ in (60 × 82.2 cm). Victoria & Albert Museum, London. Bequeathed by Constantine Alexander Ionides, CAI.59.

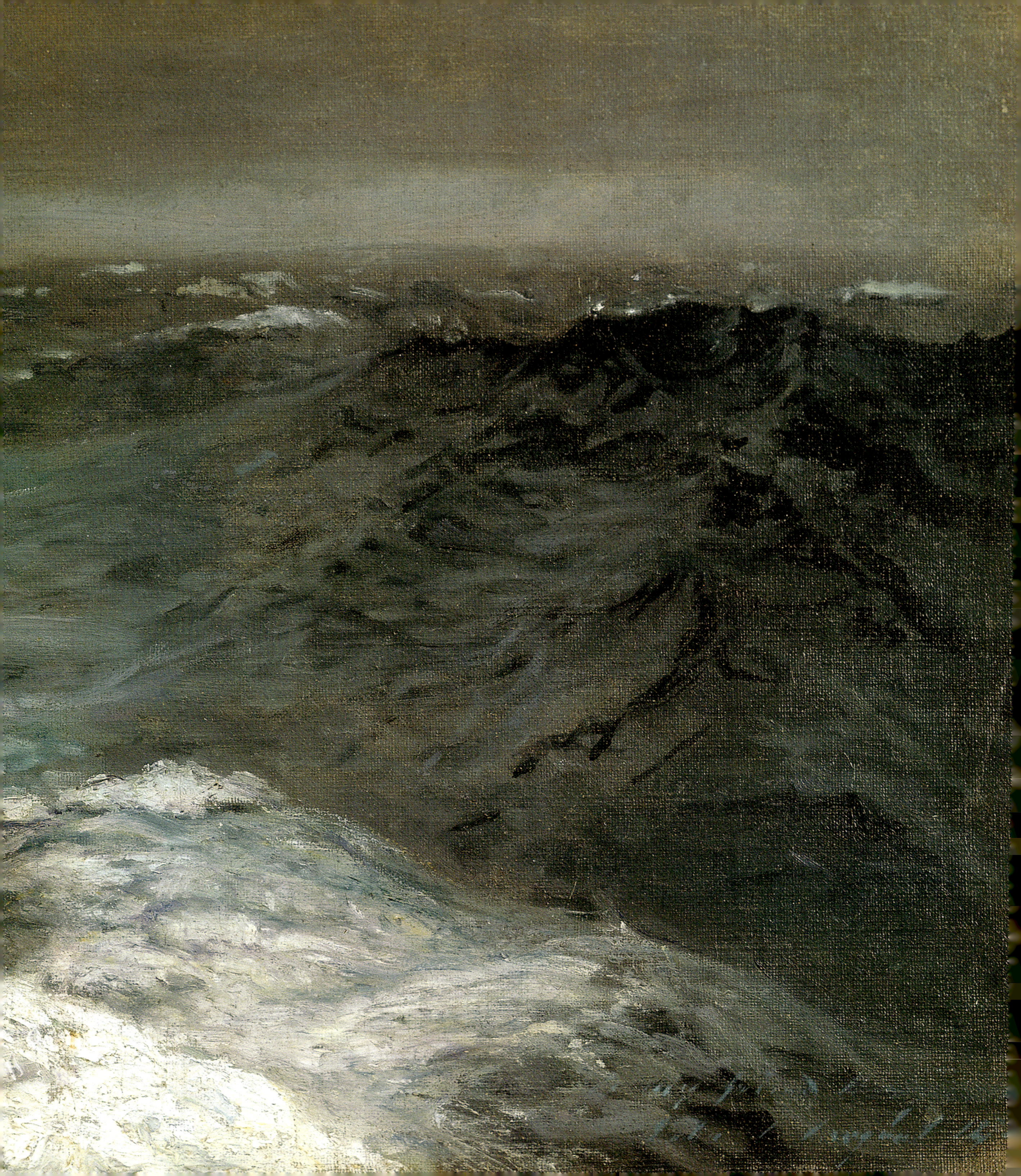

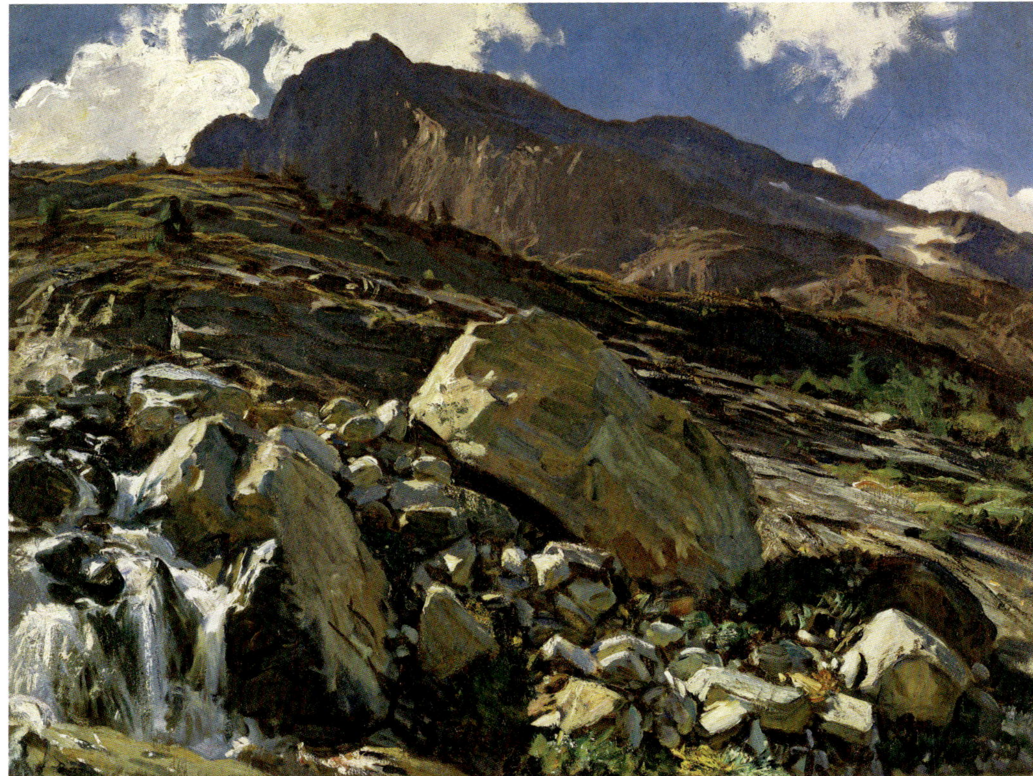

Fig. 63 *Simplon Pass*, 1911. Oil on canvas, 28½ × 36½ in (71.8 × 92.7 cm). Corcoran Gallery of Art, Washington, D.C. Bequest of James Parmelee, 41.22.

preoccupation. Nevertheless William Bouguereau, one of France's leading figure painters, already saw Sargent as a "clever youth" who was "on the wrong track," no doubt meaning that he was veering away from the traditional standards of the Academy.[23] Sargent's preference for painting with broad strokes of his brush, deliberately leaving behind the clear evidence of his own hand, link him to the more modern approach of the Impressionists, whose work he also saw and admired. But they too felt that he was on a different path. "He wasn't an Impressionist as we used the term," Monet later recalled.[24] Neither traditional nor avant-garde, Sargent would plot his own artistic course, combining the legacy of the old masters with an immediacy that spoke of his own modern age.

In 1887 Henry James would famously pronounce that "on the very threshold of [his] career" Sargent had "nothing more to learn."[25] This was already evident in his very earliest works, the seascapes with which he started his career. *Mid-Ocean, Mid-Winter* (see fig. 62), with its emphasis on surface design, the touch of the artist's hand, and direct engagement with natural forms, predicts the landscapes Sargent would paint some forty years later. *Simplon Pass* of 1911, for example, is a sea of stone (fig. 63). The mountainous ocean waves of *Mid-Ocean, Mid-Winter* have been replaced by actual mountain peaks, watery froth has become sun and snow. Both subjects are anonymous, undistinguished by any recognizable landmarks. It does not matter where they are; their appeal lies not in the identification of a singular national landmark, but in their stateless-ness, and through it, their universality. By studying his earliest paintings, one can already see the consistency of Sargent's talent and the independence of his vision.

Facing page: Fig. 62 Detail of fig. 54, *Mid-Ocean, Mid-Winter*, 1876. Private Collection. (Exhibition)

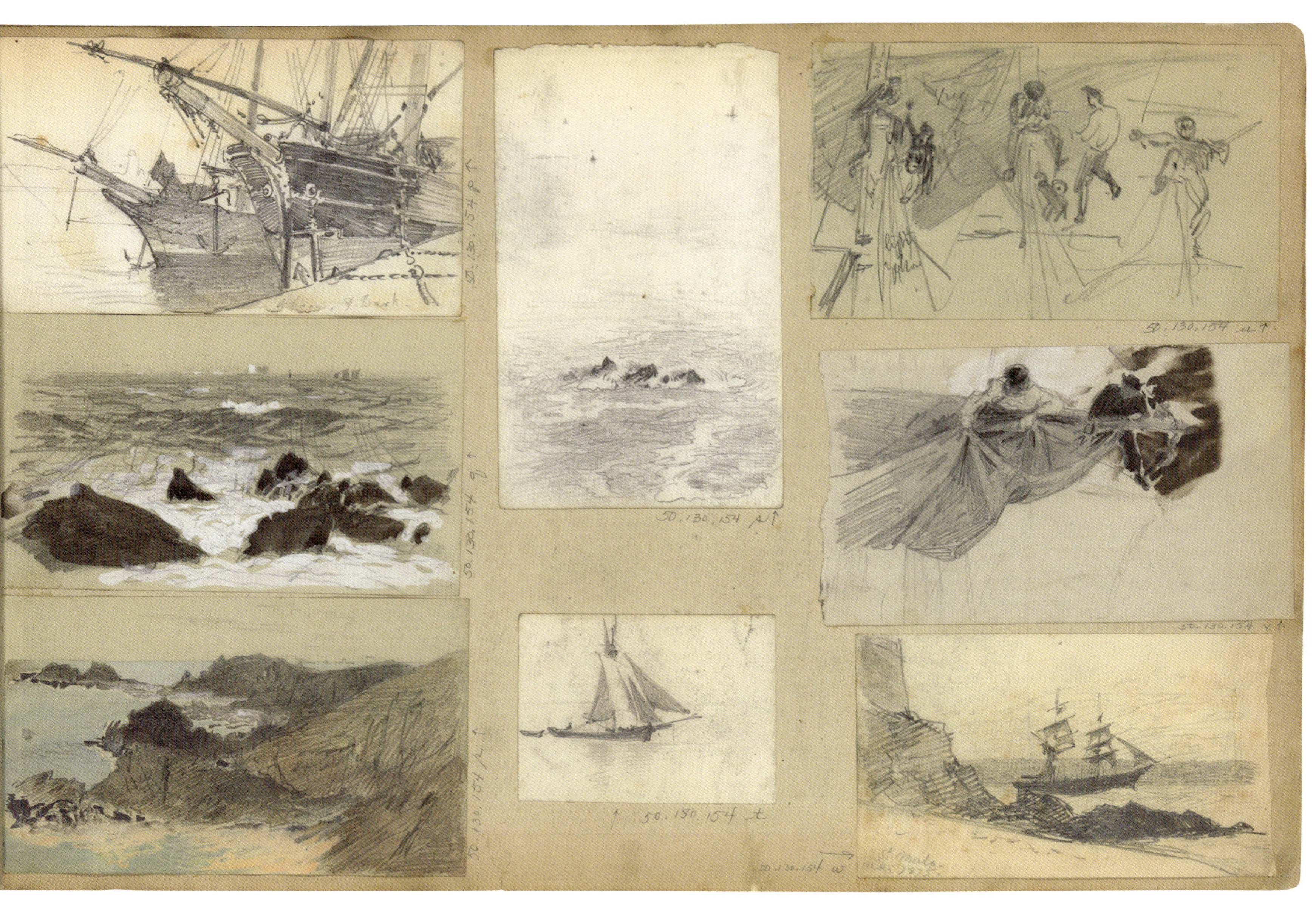

Fig. 64 View of p. 12 (recto), John Singer Sargent Scrapbook. The Metropolitan Museum of Art, Gift of Mrs Francis Ormond, 1950. (50.130.154) (Exhibition)

Sargent's Scrapbook of the 1870s

STEPHANIE L. HERDRICH

An important and little-studied scrapbook in the collection of The Metropolitan Museum of Art preserves a significant group of twenty-seven drawings and watercolors created by John Singer Sargent during trips to coastal regions in Normandy (1874) and Brittany (1875 and 1877), during his first two Atlantic crossings in 1876, and perhaps during visits to coastal Italy (1878) (fig. 64).[1] Twenty-three of these drawings represent marine and coastal subjects manifesting Sargent's fascination with recording effects of light, tonal relationships, the form and dynamism of water, and vignettes of life around the sea.

Sargent created the album between 1874, when he arrived in Paris to pursue his formal artistic training, and 1880. During this period, the artist gathered and inserted into the scrapbook a total of fifty-three of his own drawings and watercolors; more than 150 prints and commercial photographs of works of art, architecture, and travel destinations; and cartoons and illustrations clipped from contemporary periodicals. As he explored the possibilities of portraiture and genre painting in the late 1870s, the varied material he assembled in this volume provides a rare glimpse into the mind and method of the young artist. The scrapbook exemplifies his careful, exhaustive search for subjects and inspiration in the art of the past and the world around him as he made the transition from student to professional.[2]

By choosing to preserve his own drawings in a scrapbook and interspersing them with a diverse collection of ephemera, Sargent created a selective narrative of his interests during his student and early professional years. He omitted almost entirely from the book his academic and studio work as well as preparatory studies for his major exhibition pieces in favor of including the sketches he made on his summer holidays and copies after works of art.[3] As such, the scrapbook is not a chronological or comprehensive anthology, but rather a more personal and unique portrait of his taste and priorities.

Throughout his life Sargent was an indefatigable and dedicated draftsman. Encouraged by his parents, he avidly recorded the world around him from a young age. Anecdotes of his precocious talent were chronicled in his parents' letters to relatives back in the United States. In an 1861 letter to his mother, Dr Fitzwilliam Sargent noted that his son, then only five years old, had already established an enthusiasm for sketching: "Johnny is well and as fond as ever of drawing."[4] As the family traveled through Europe according to the seasons, Sargent's parents provided him with stimulating subjects and ample materials to pursue his interest; the young artist had filled no fewer than thirteen sketchbooks by the time he arrived in Paris

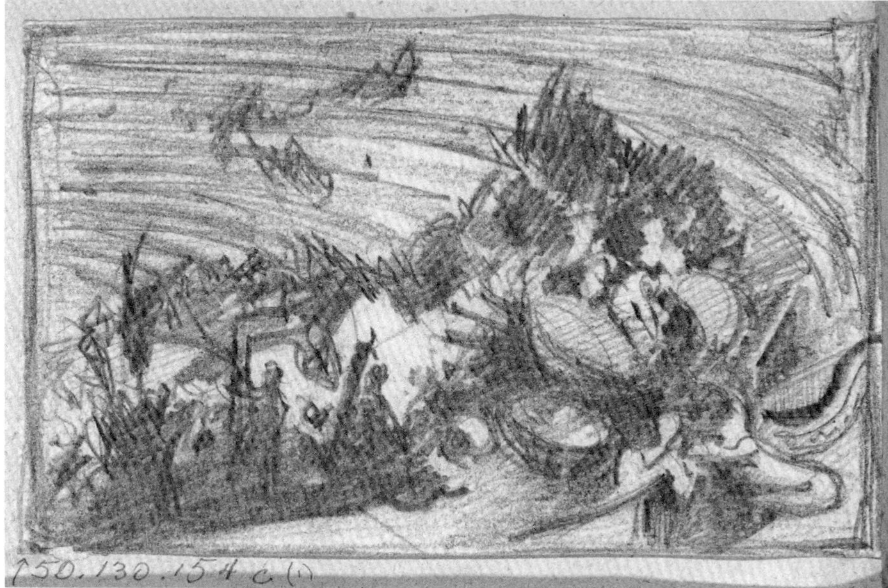

Fig. 65 Compositional study for *Rehearsal of the Pasdeloup Orchestra at the Cirque d'Hiver*, *c.* 1876–78. Graphite on paper, 3⅜ × 5⅜ in (8.6 × 13.7 cm). In the John Singer Sargent Scrapbook (50.130.154). The Metropolitan Museum of Art, Gift of Mrs Francis Ormond, 1950. (50.130.154c)

when he was eighteen years old.[5] In addition to these early sketchbooks, many informal drawings from the late 1860s and early 1870s are in the collections of The Metropolitan Museum of Art in New York and the Fogg Art Museum at Harvard University, two of the largest repositories of Sargent's works on paper.[6] These pre-1874 drawings and sketches reflect the artist's meticulous interest in recording the world around him and his broad technical ability as a draftsman.[7] Sargent continuously sketched the landscape, portraits of family members and friends, and art and artifacts across many eras of history.

The American painter Will H. Low documented Sargent's prolificacy and ability upon the latter's arrival in the studio of Carolus-Duran in 1874:

> [Sargent] made his appearance in the Atelier Carolus-Duran almost bashfully, bringing a great roll of canvases and papers, which unrolled displayed to the eyes of Carolus and his pupils gathered about him sketches and studies in various mediums, seeming the work of many years; (and John Singer Sargent was only seventeen) . . . an amazement to the class, and to the youth [Low] in particular a sensation that he has never forgotten.[8]

While the exact drawings that Sargent displayed in the studio are unidentified, his surviving efforts in the Fogg and the Metropolitan suggest that he had a vast inventory of accomplished works from which to choose and probably assembled a considerable portfolio for his interview.

Once Sargent settled in Paris and began his formal studies, the character and quantity of his graphic work evolved, as did his method for preserving it. His earlier preoccupation with recording picturesque landscape scenes and interesting vignettes yielded to more purposeful and selective drawing as part of his training. In between his morning painting lessons with Carolus-Duran and his supplemental evening sessions in the studio of Léon Bonnat, Sargent spent his afternoons honing his drawing skills in the École des Beaux-Arts atelier of Adolphe Yvon. There he most likely produced highly finished academic exercises, of which only a small number have been recorded.[9]

When Sargent drew for his own pleasure or interest, he continued to use small portable sketchbooks. Many of the fifty-three sketches and watercolors in the scrapbook bear evidence of having been removed from such sketchbooks and can be grouped by paper size and type. In several instances Sargent made notations next to drawings and continued sketches on the scrapbook's pages, therefore it is clear that he selected the sheets and assembled the volume himself.

By deciding to preserve his drawings in a scrapbook, Sargent sought a method of organizing, sorting, and editing works that were important to him. He privileged his marine drawings by including them in the volume while omitting all preparatory studies for completed, exhibited canvases, with two exceptions. These are a pair of sketches—fig. 65 is one—for *Rehearsal of*

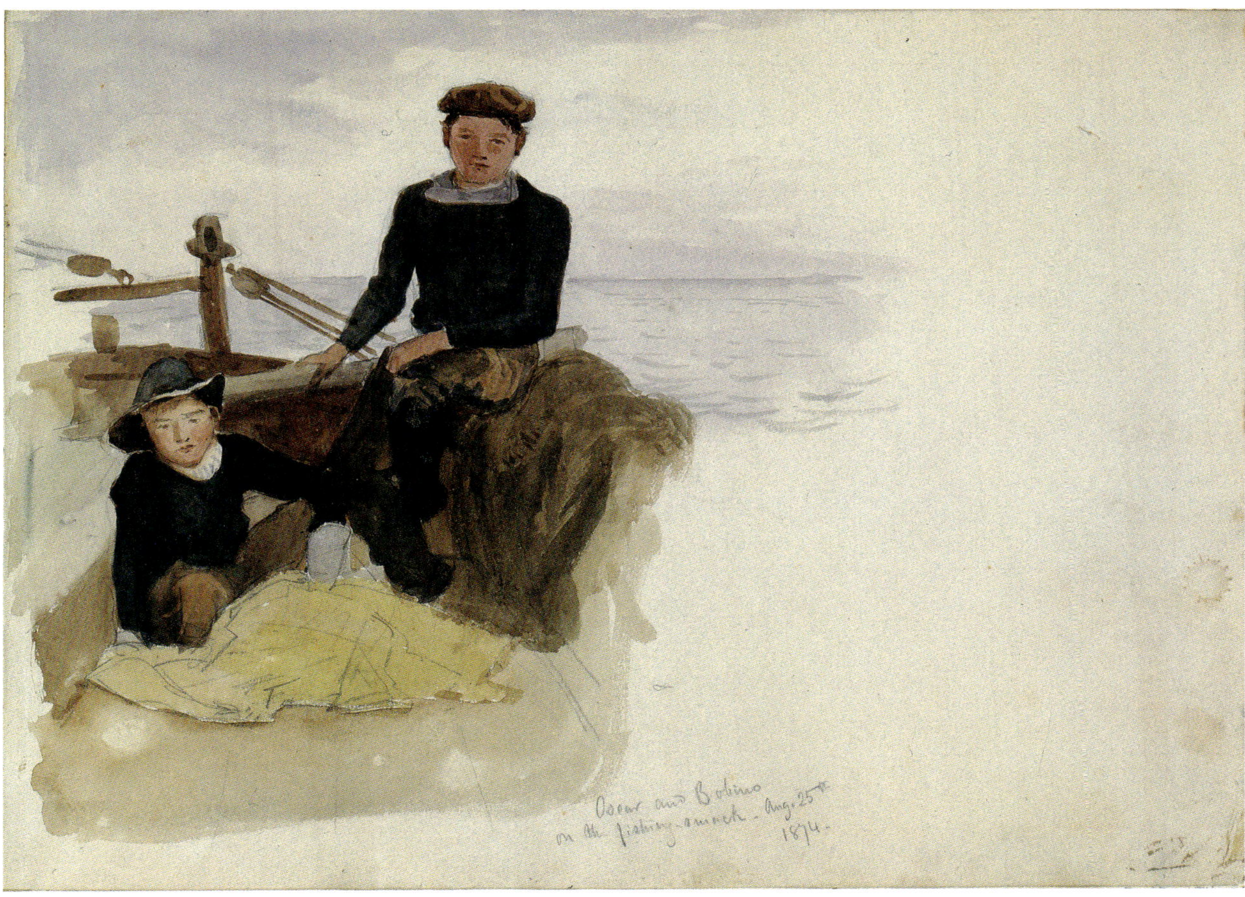

the Pasdeloup Orchestra at the Cirque d'Hiver (c. 1876–78, Museum of Fine Arts, Boston).[10] In making such decisions, the artist clearly distinguished this informal and personal work from his academic and professional output.

As Richard Ormond has discussed in the introduction, Sargent's attraction to the sea was embedded in his family's history. Although as a child the artist had spent many winters living on the French coast at Nice, his peripatetic family had the habit of traveling through more temperate Alpine regions during the summer months. His first summer at the seashore in 1874 corresponds to the beginning of his artistic training in Paris. For several successive summers, released from the ateliers and the École with newly advanced skills, Sargent returned to the shore or the sea. While his attention to and interest in the sea varied, several common themes emerge. Sargent often recorded characteristic vignettes of life around the sea as well as essential qualities of water in motion with an increasing interest in recording effects of light and tonal relations. Sargent's marine drawings in the scrapbook and related loose sheets characterize his developing graphic abilities and inform his later work.

For the summer of 1874 Sargent and his family settled at the tiny town of Beuzeval on the Calvados coast of Normandy. Although his father wrote to family friend George Bemis on 26 July of that year that "John is at work sketching every day," the artist included in the Metropolitan scrapbook only one work known to date from that summer.[11] Inscribed "Aug. 25th 1874," *Oscar and Bobino on the Fishing Smack* (fig. 66), a carefully composed watercolor of two

Fig. 66 *Oscar and Bobino on the Fishing Smack*, 1874. Watercolor and graphite on paper, 11⅞ × 16½ in (30.2 × 41.9 cm). Inscribed at lower center: *Oscar and Bobino / on the fishing smack. Aug. 25th / 1874.* In the John Singer Sargent Scrapbook (50.130.154). The Metropolitan Museum of Art, Gift of Mrs Francis Ormond, 1950. (50.130.154pp) (Exhibition)

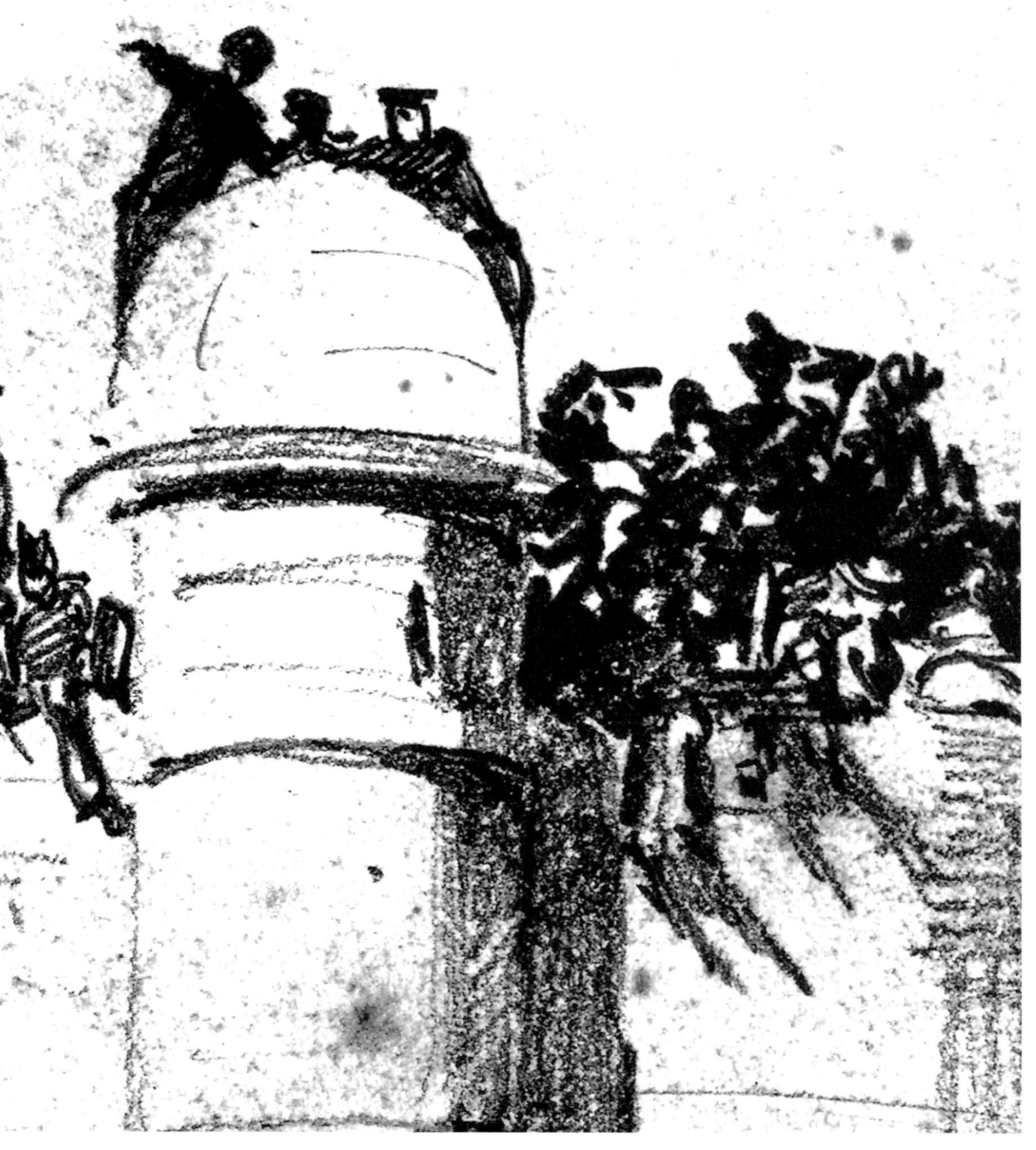

Fig. 67 Detail of fig. 69, *Ramparts at Saint-Malo—Yacht Race*, 1875. Corcoran Gallery of Art, Washington, D.C.. Gift of Miss Emily Sargent and Mrs Francis Ormond, sisters of the artist, 49.148c. (Exhibition)

young sailor boys, represents Sargent's youthful style. Broad, flat passages of watercolor are applied over a detailed sketch and the background water is represented conventionally rather than from observation. Within the scrapbook, *Oscar and Bobino* is a landmark against which to measure the artist's increasing technical ability.

Sargent and his family returned to the sea for the summer of 1875, renting a house in Dinard, a small town next to Saint-Énogat on the Breton coast. Having spent the academic year in Paris honing his considerable skills, the artist's sketches from this summer demonstrate his advancing talent. They also document his frequent peregrinations with his family. As Dr Sargent explained in a letter to Bemis, the family varied local wanderings with "a 'Constitutional,' or a prowl about the streets of St. Malo & St. Servan, on the opposite side of the bay; occasionally we make a cruise to some of the islands, or go up the Rance [river] to Dinan."[12] Sargent made the short trip from Saint-Énogat to Saint-Malo as early as May, according to the inscription on *Saint-Malo* (fig. 68), a quick sketch of a sailing vessel off the coast. He reveals a confident and bold technique in his rendering of the rock formations with dark, strong hatching. The artist's developing interest in representing tonal relations with varying shades of graphite is characteristic of his graphic work during this period.

A distinct group of thirteen sheets from a dismantled sketchbook further illuminates Sargent's interests during the summer of 1875. He affixed twelve of these sheets into the Metropolitan scrapbook; the thirteenth sheet, *Ramparts at Saint-Malo—Yacht Race* (fig. 69), is in the collection of the Corcoran Gallery of Art.[13] The group includes eight sheets of marine and coastal views, four sheets with rural and agricultural vignettes, and one sheet that combines the motifs. On the verso of *Boy and Girl Seated by Tree* (fig. 70), the artist made several quick studies of marine and rural figures, thus linking the two subjects (*Sailors and Reapers*, fig. 71).[14] This series of drawings from the summer of 1875 reveal that Sargent traveled from Saint-Énogat not only to nearby Saint-Malo but along the coast to Saint-Briac and inland to the rural town of Dol. The dating of the entire set is based on *La Pierre du Champ Dolent* (fig. 72), which is inscribed "Dol June '75." That drawing documents a distant view of a prehistoric stone monument near Dol, a small town about twenty-three kilometers southeast of Saint-Malo.

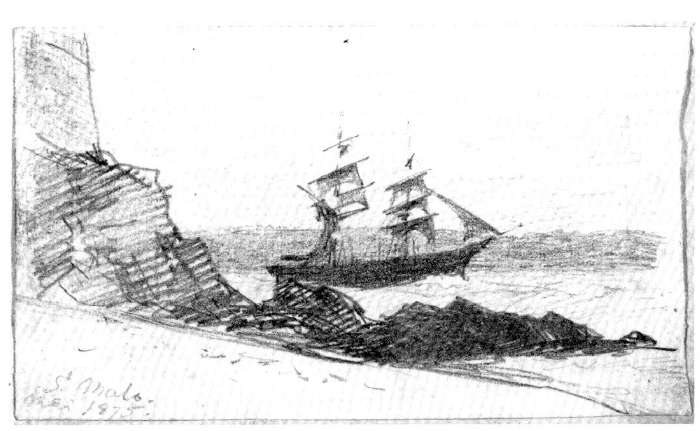

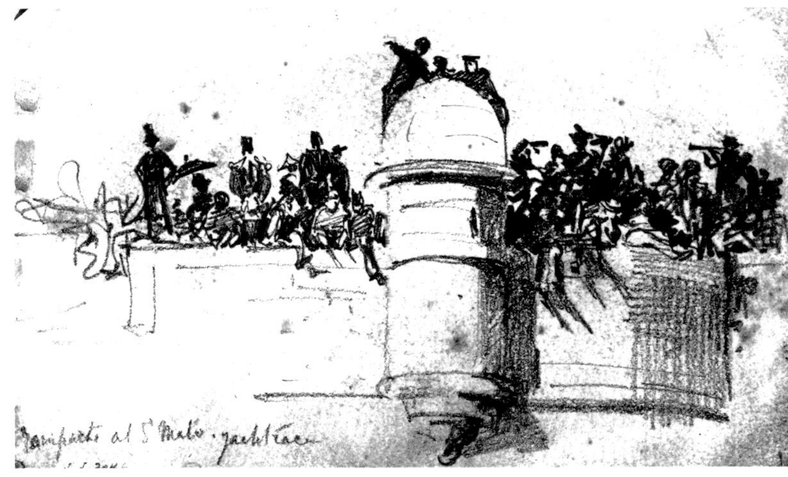

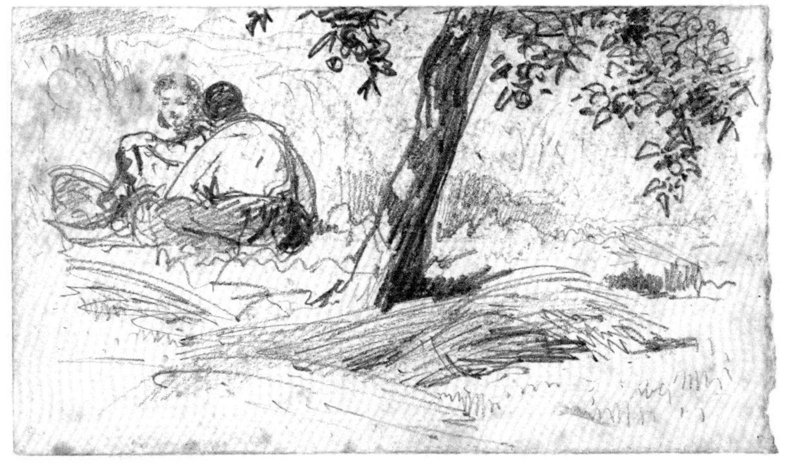

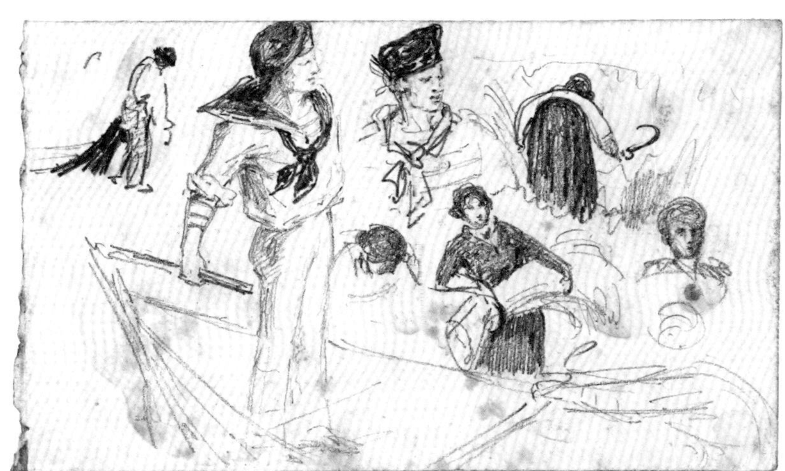

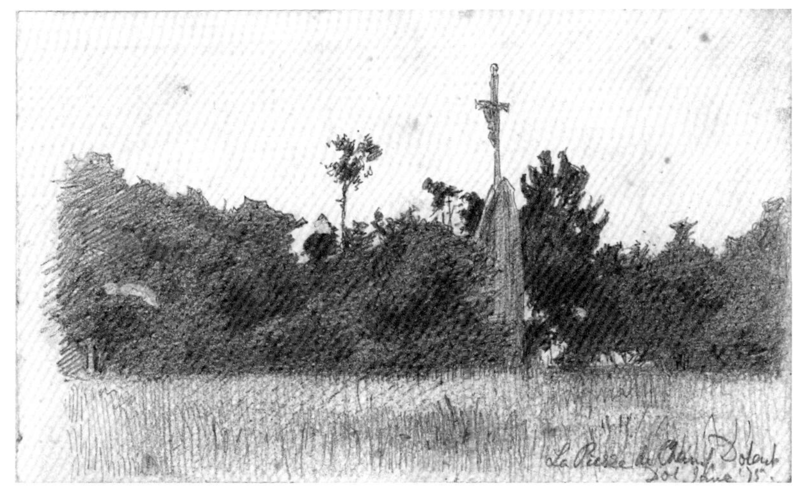

Fig. 68 *Saint-Malo*, 1875. Graphite on paper, $3\frac{1}{2} \times 5\frac{11}{16}$ in (8.9×14.4 cm). Inscribed, lower left: *S. Malo./Mai 1875*. In the John Singer Sargent Scrapbook (50.130.154). The Metropolitan Museum of Art, Gift of Mrs Francis Ormond, 1950. (50.130.154w) (Exhibition)

Fig. 69 *Ramparts at Saint-Malo – Yacht Race*, 1875. Graphite on paper, $3\frac{11}{16} \times 6\frac{1}{2}$ in (10×16.5 cm). Inscribed, lower left: Ramparts at S. Malo · yacht race. Corcoran Gallery of Art, Washington, D.C. Gift of Miss Emily Sargent and Mrs Francis Ormond, sisters of the artist, 49.148c. (Exhibition)

Fig. 70 *Boy and Girl Seated by Tree*, 1875. Graphite on paper, $3\frac{11}{16} \times 6\frac{1}{2}$ in (10×16.5 cm). From the John Singer Sargent Scrapbook (50.130.154). The Metropolitan Museum of Art, Gift of Mrs Francis Ormond, 1950. (50.130.154mm recto)

Fig. 71 *Sailors and Reapers*, 1875. Graphite on paper, $3\frac{11}{16} \times 6\frac{1}{2}$ in (10×16.5 cm). From the John Singer Sargent Scrapbook (50.130.154). The Metropolitan Museum of Art, Gift of Mrs Francis Ormond, 1950. (50.130.154mm verso) (Exhibition, Washington and London).

Fig. 72 *La Pierre du Champ Dolent*, 1875. Graphite on paper, $3\frac{11}{16} \times 6\frac{1}{2}$ in (10×16.5 cm). Inscribed, lower right: *La Pierre du Champ Dolent / Dol June '75*. In the John Singer Sargent Scrapbook (50.130.154). The Metropolitan Museum of Art, Gift of Mrs Francis Ormond, 1950. (50.130.154kk)

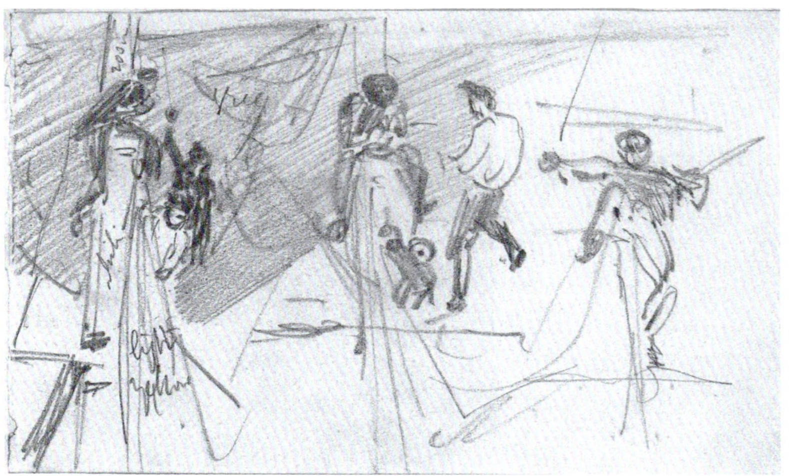

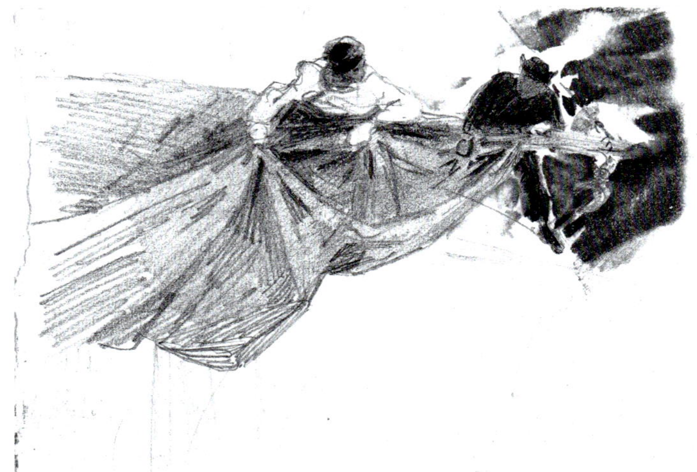

Fig. 73 *Sailors in Rigging of Ship*, 1875. Graphite on paper, $4 \times 6\frac{1}{2}$ in (10.2 × 16.5 cm). Inscribed at left: *grey/light yellow* [and other illegible color notations]. In the John Singer Sargent Scrapbook (50.130.154). The Metropolitan Museum of Art, Gift of Mrs Francis Ormond, 1950. (50.130.154u) (Exhibition)

Fig. 74 *Two Sailors Furling Sail*, 1875. Watercolor and graphite on paper, $3\frac{15}{16} \times 6\frac{9}{16}$ in (10 × 16.7 cm). In the John Singer Sargent Scrapbook (50.130.154). The Metropolitan Museum of Art, Gift of Mrs Francis Ormond, 1950. (50.130.154v) (Exhibition)

Fig. 75 *Boom of a Sailing Ship*, *c.*1875. Graphite and brown wash on paper, $6\frac{5}{16} \times 9\frac{1}{2}$ in (16.1 × 24.1 cm). Inscribed upper right: *8 a.* Harvard Art Museum, Fogg Art Museum, Gift of Mrs Francis Ormond, 1937.7.35.8.

Fig. 76 *Two Men in Ship's Rigging, Two Scenes with Sailboats*, 1875. Graphite on paper, $3\frac{15}{16} \times 6\frac{1}{2}$ in (10 × 16.5 cm). In the John Singer Sargent Scrapbook (50.130.154). The Metropolitan Museum of Art, Gift of Mrs Francis Ormond, 1950. (50.130.154jj) (Exhibition)

Fig. 77 *Schooner and Bark in Harbor*, 1875. Graphite on paper, $4 \times 6\frac{1}{2}$ in (10.2 × 16.5 cm). Inscribed at lower right: *Schooner & Bark*. In the John Singer Sargent Scrapbook (50.130.154). The Metropolitan Museum of Art, Gift of Mrs Francis Ormond, 1950. (50.130.154p) (Exhibition)

Facing page: Fig. 78 Detail of fig. 77, *Schooner and Bark in Harbor*, 1875

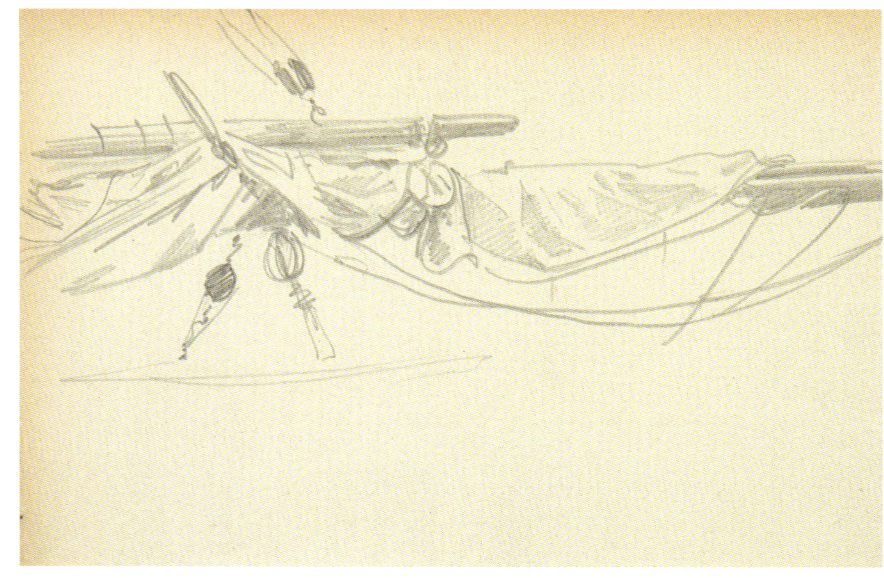

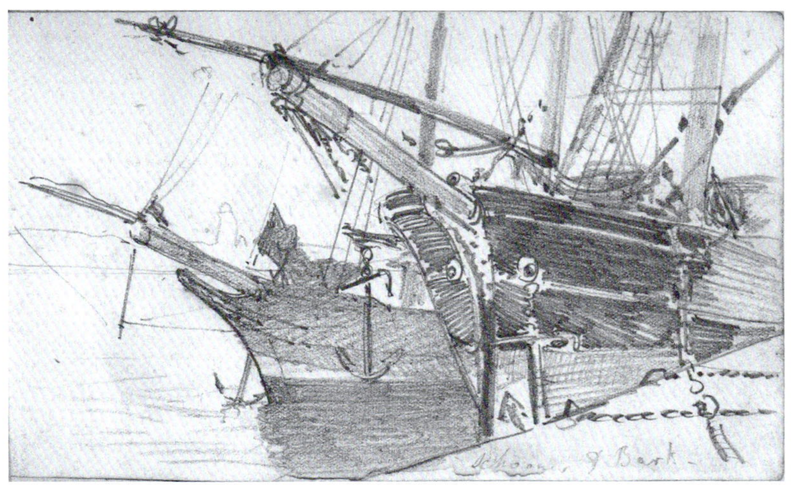

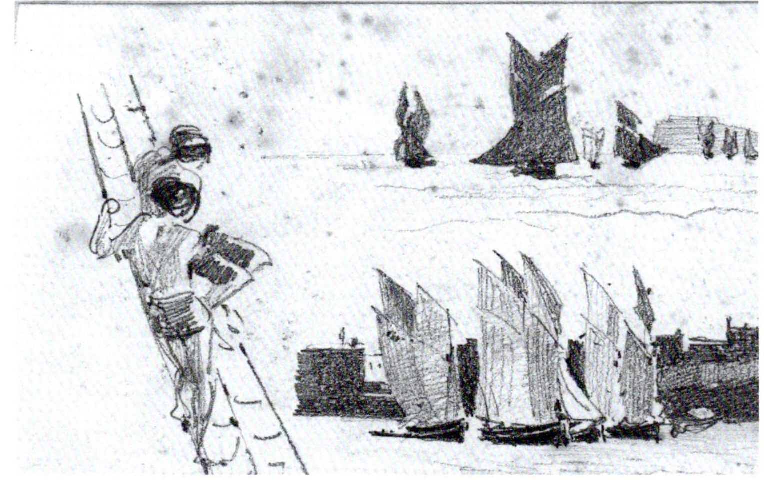

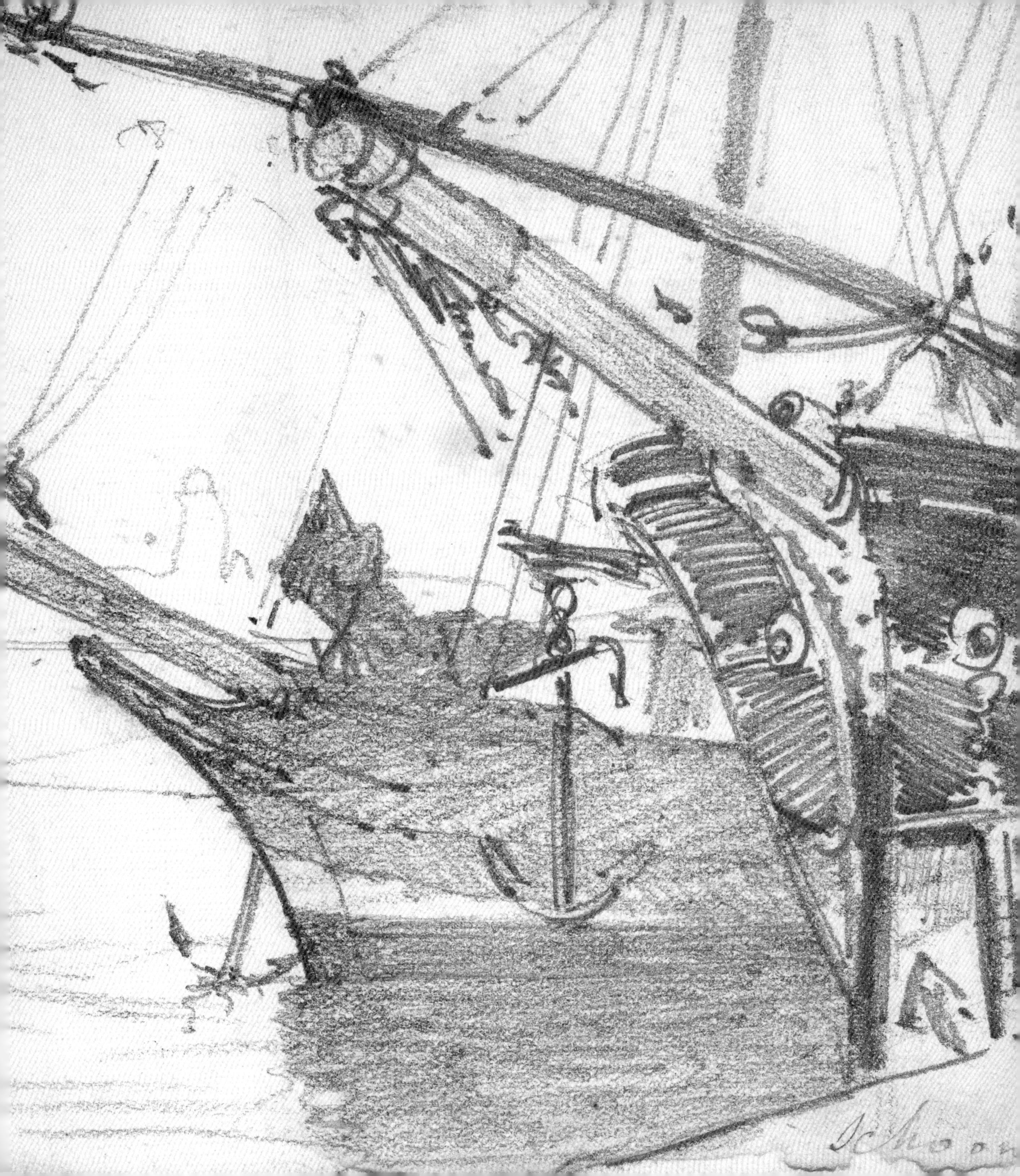

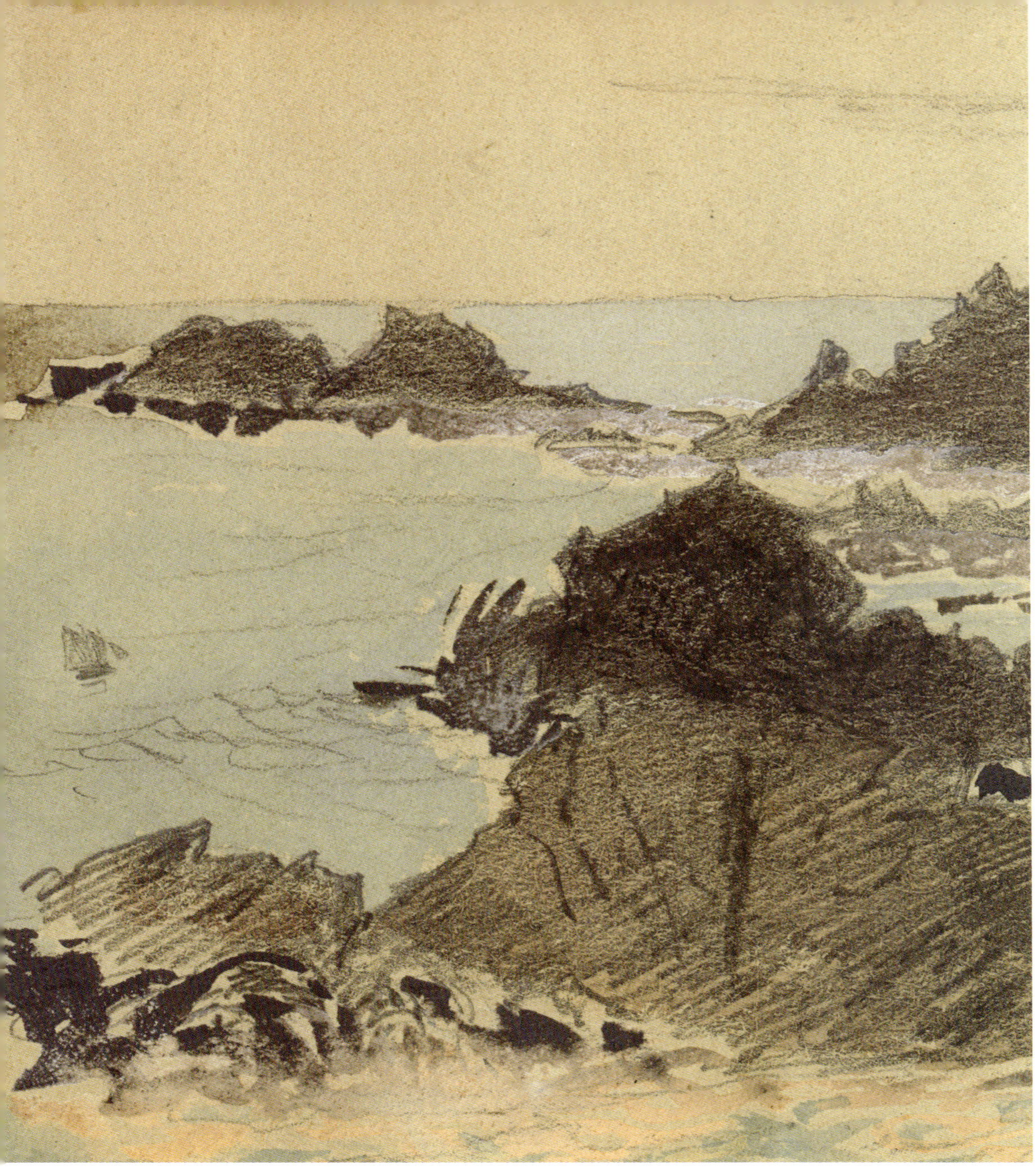

Fig. 79 Detail of fig. 83, *Rocky Coast*, 1875. In the John Singer Sargent Scrapbook (50.130.154). The Metropolitan Museum of Art, Gift of Mrs Francis Ormond, 1950. (50.130.154r) (Exhibition)

At Saint-Malo, Sargent recorded vignettes of the bustling harbor with particular attention paid to the activities of sailors. In *Sailors in Rigging of Ship* (fig. 73) he captured the dynamic figures with the briefest of sketches while adding notations about color and light. In *Two Sailors Furling Sail* (fig. 74) the artist paid close attention to the shadows and drape of the sails, accenting the sheet with dark, tonal passages of watercolor or ink. While he may or may not have intended such quick sketches to relate to a larger composition, his color notations across the sail and use of watercolor suggest a new attention to painterly concerns. *Two Men in Ship's Rigging, Two Scenes with Sailboats* (fig. 76) includes distant views of the crowded harbor—perhaps during the yacht race depicted in the Corcoran sheet, *Ramparts at Saint-Malo—Yacht Race*. Another loose sheet not in the scrapbook, *Boom of a Sailing Ship* (fig. 75), relates in subject and style to these drawings, although Sargent removed the human presence to concentrate on details of the ship's rigging and sail. In *Schooner and Bark in Harbor* (fig. 77), a depiction of an unidentified port in the Saint-Malo region, Sargent created a dynamic composition of diverging angles among the masts, nets, ropes, and riggings in his detailed study of the boats. This tangle of forms would become the subject of his later port scenes, including *Ships and Boats* (see fig. 38).

Sargent further revealed his interest in the region's rugged coastline and the movement of water in *Waves Breaking on Rocks* (fig. 80), *Coastal Scene* (fig. 81), and *Rocky Coast* (fig. 83). For the rough sea of the first drawing, he again combined graphite and watercolor, using white pigment to accent the breaking surf. After pasting this sheet into the scrapbook, he recorded detailed notes describing colors and relative tonal values on the scrapbook page opposite the drawing. In *Coastal Scene* the artist used an elevated vantage point to record subtle patterns of the water's surface as it flowed

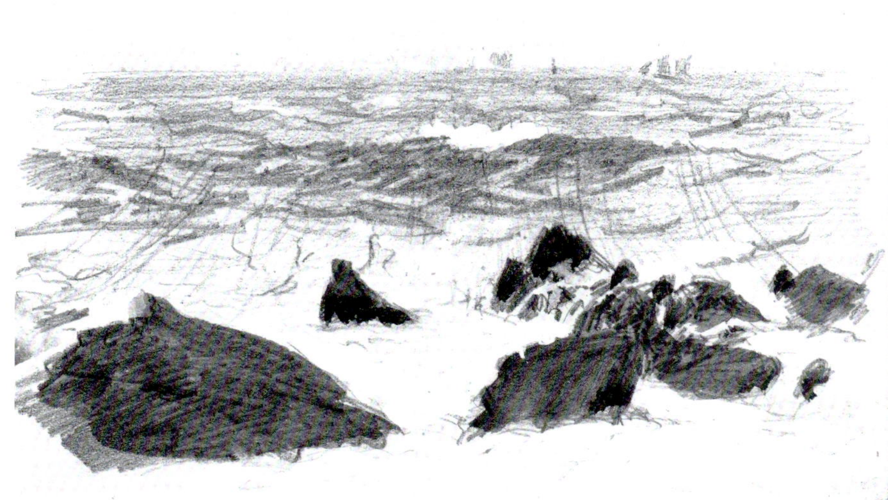

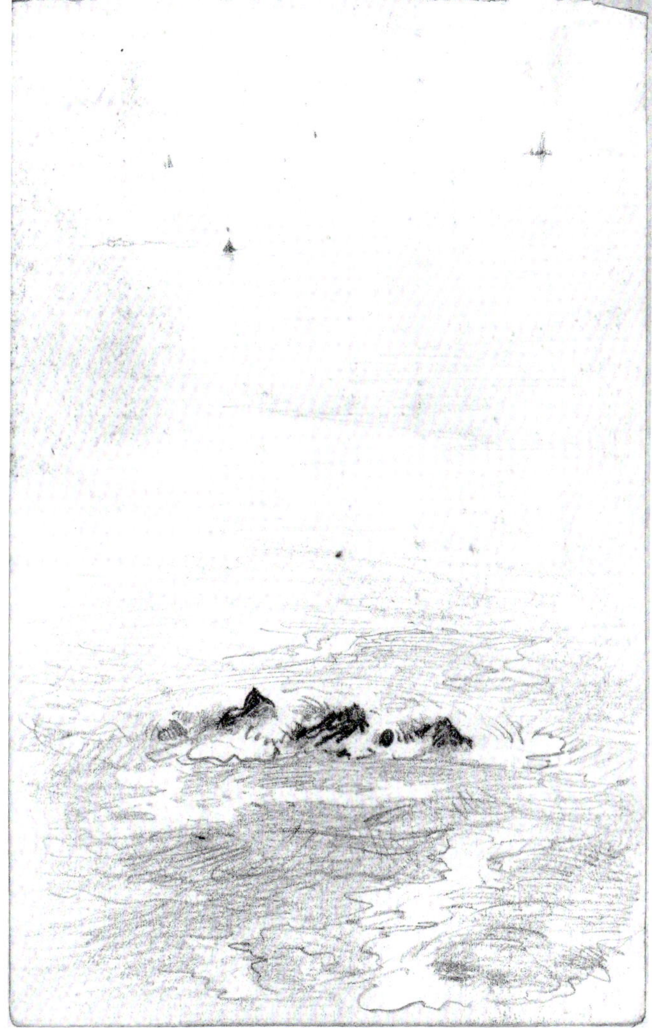

Fig. 80 *Waves Breaking on Rocks*, 1875. Watercolor and graphite on paper, 4 × 6½ in (10.2 × 16.5 cm). Inscribed on scrapbook page: *murky sky warm . water general / tone in foreground like sky. in distance / dark blue purple. Accents clear blue / green. foreground foam lightest value, / blue lilac & icegreen. rocks dark brown / darkest value: in rought streaks* [illegible] */ to marblings of foam lighter than water.* In the John Singer Sargent Scrapbook (50.130.154). The Metropolitan Museum of Art, Gift of Mrs Francis Ormond, 1950. (50.130.154q) (Exhibition)

Fig. 81 *Coastal Scene*, *c.* 1875. Graphite on paper, 6⅝ × 4 in (16.8 × 10.2 cm). In the John Singer Sargent Scrapbook (50.130.154). The Metropolitan Museum of Art, Gift of Mrs Francis Ormond, 1950. (50.130.154s) (Exhibition)

Fig. 82 Photograph of the site depicted in *Rocky Coast* (see fig. 83): view of La Pointe du Décollé from Le Rocher Napoléon, 2008. Photograph by Hervé Lambrecht, Cancale.

Fig. 83 *Rocky Coast*, 1875. Watercolor and graphite on paper, 4 × 6½ in (10.2 × 16.5 cm). In the John Singer Sargent Scrapbook (50.130.154). The Metropolitan Museum of Art, Gift of Mrs Francis Ormond, 1950. (50.130.154r) (Exhibition)

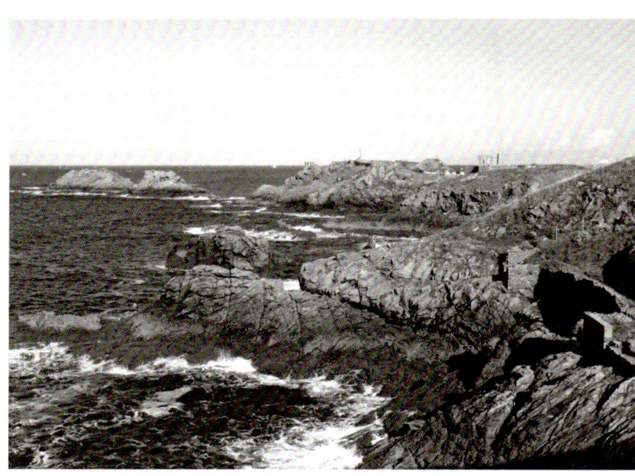

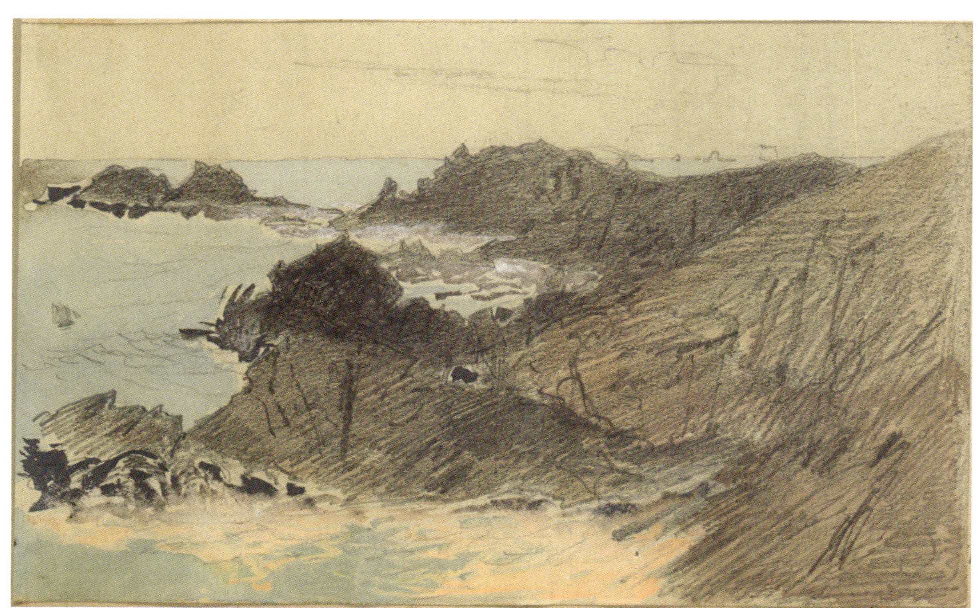

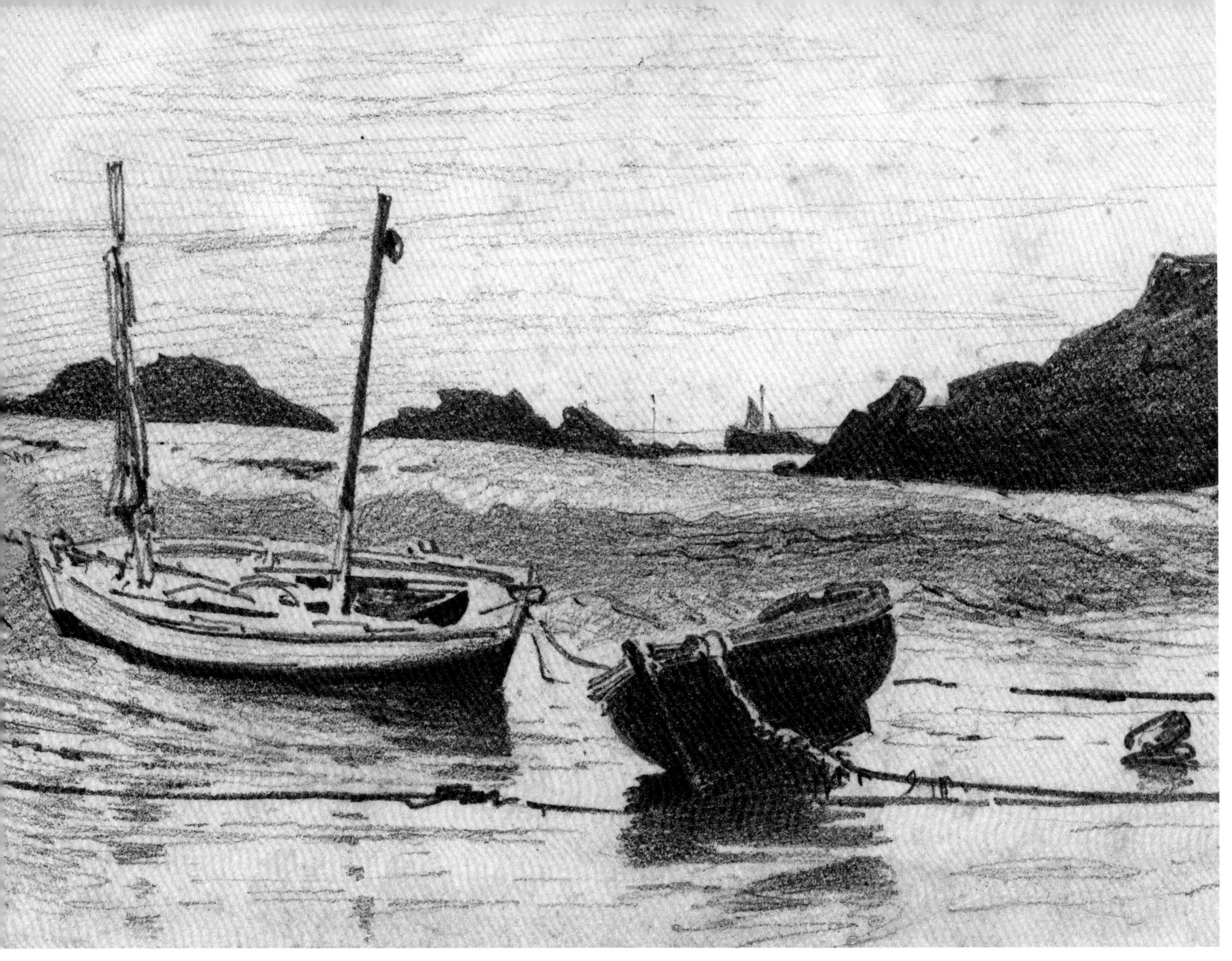

Fig. 84 Detail of fig. 87, *Two Small Boats Moored to Beach*, *c.* 1875. In the John Singer Sargent Scrapbook (50.130.154). The Metropolitan Museum of Art, Gift of Mrs Francis Ormond, 1950. (50.130.154hh) (Exhibition)

around the rock formation. He translated his interest in coastal scenes and studies of water into such paintings as *Seascape with Rocks* (see fig. 19) and *Seascape* (see fig. 26).

In *Rocky Coast* Sargent used a high and distant vantage point—specifically that at Le Rocher Napoléon in Saint-Lunaire, just west of Saint-Énogat—to depict the characteristic silhouette of La Pointe du Décollé to the right of islands off Saint-Malo in the background (fig. 82). He revealed the massive scale of the landscape by including a minuscule ship at the left center edge of the composition. He combined a confident graphic technique with flat passages of watercolor to create an unusually beautiful and subtly colored composition. He described the rugged landscape with broadly rendered, long, diagonal pencil strokes, which he covered with earth-brown watercolor wash, and added flat pencil passages of aqua pigment to suggest the

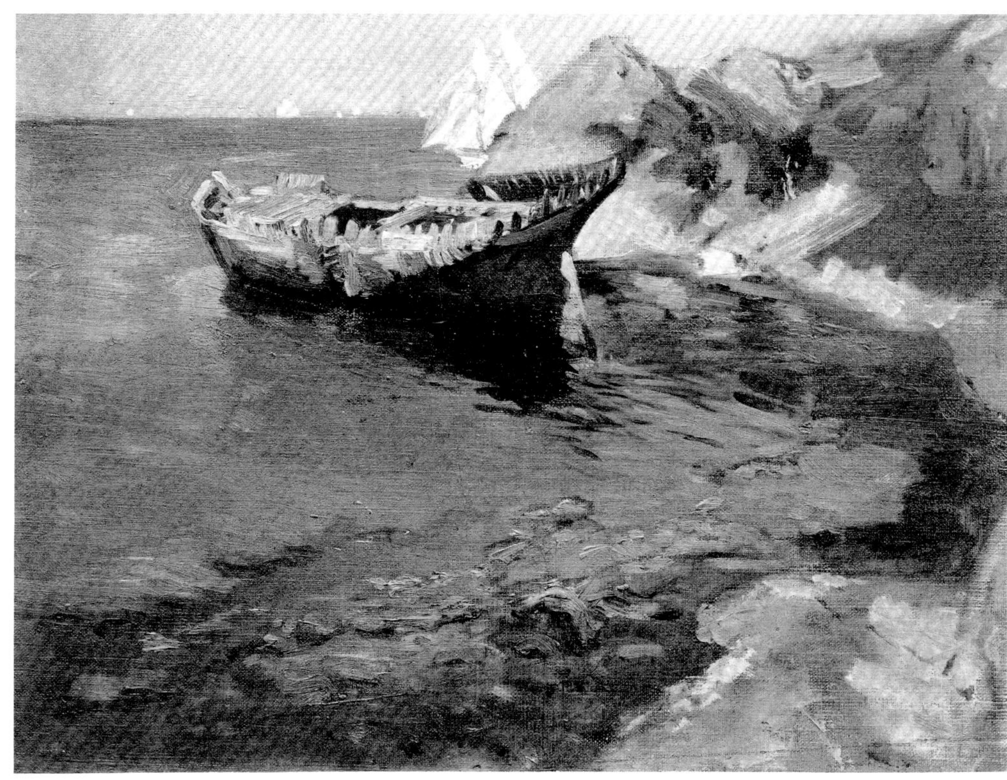

Fig. 85 *An Old Boat Stranded*, *c.* 1875. Oil on canvas, 13 × 16¾ in (33 × 42.5 cm). Untraced.

Fig. 87 *Two Small Boats Moored to Beach*, *c.* 1875. Graphite on paper, 3¹¹⁄₁₆ × 6½ in (10 × 16.5 cm). In the John Singer Sargent Scrapbook (50.130.154). The Metropolitan Museum of Art, Gift of Mrs Francis Ormond, 1950. (50.130.154hh) (Exhibition)

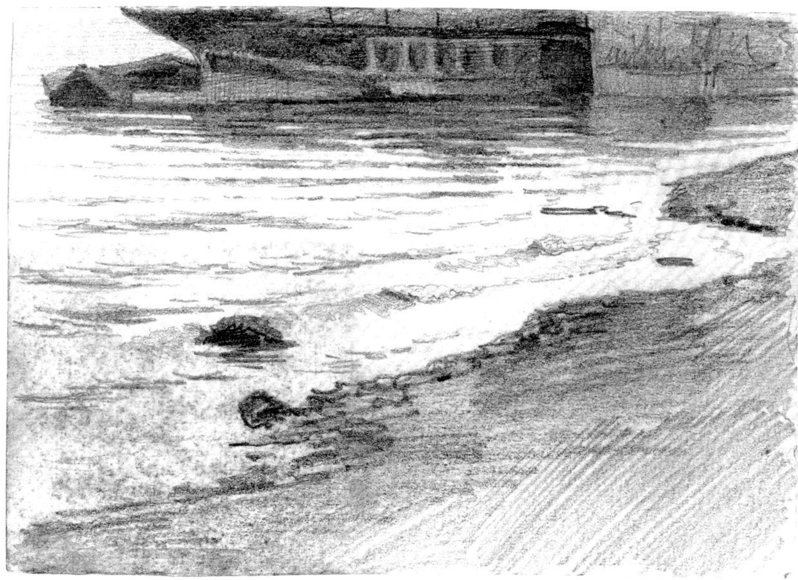

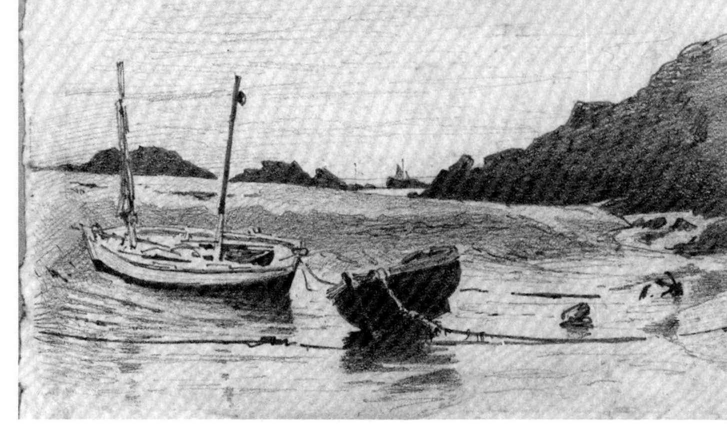

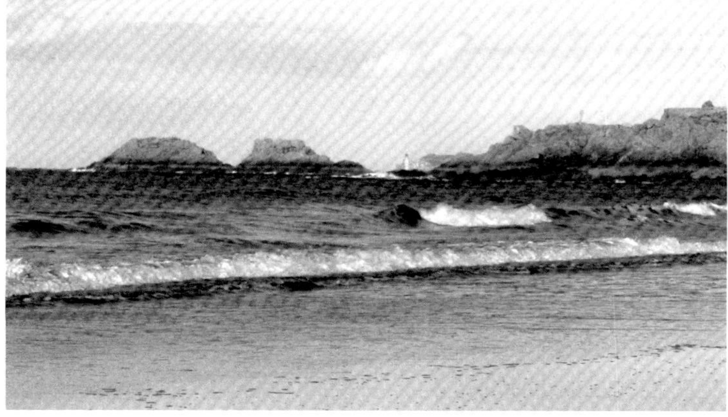

Fig. 86 *Water's Edge*, *c.* 1875. Graphite on paper, 5½ × 7½ in (14 × 19.1 cm). In the John Singer Sargent Scrapbook (50.130.154). The Metropolitan Museum of Art, Gift of Mrs Francis Ormond, 1950. (50.130.154nn) (Exhibition)

Fig. 88 Photograph of the site depicted in *Two Small Boats Moored to Beach* (see fig. 87): view of La Pointe du Décollé from the beach at Saint-Briac, 2008. Photograph by Hervé Lambrecht, Cancale.

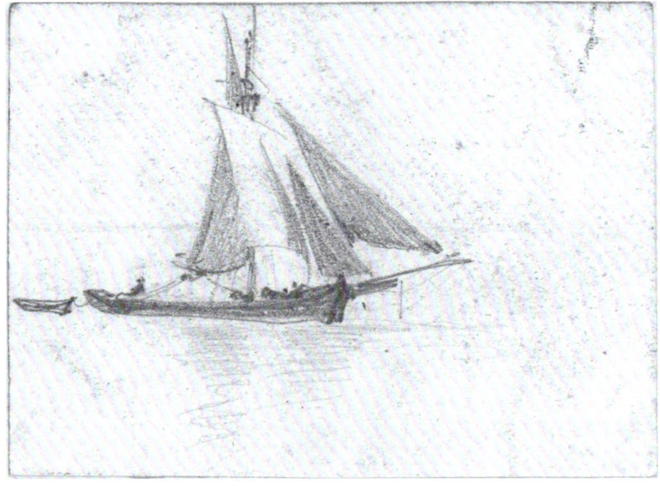

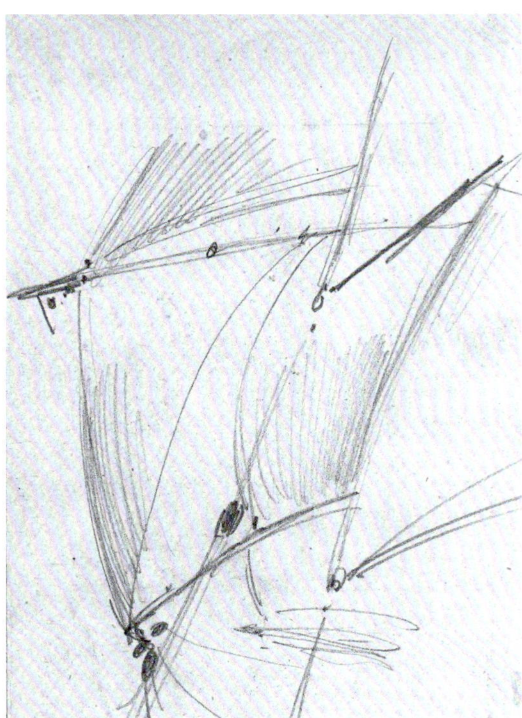

Fig. 89 *Sailboat Towing Dory*, *c.* 1875. Graphite on paper, 2 11/16 × 3 9/16 in (6.8 × 9 cm). In the John Singer Sargent Scrapbook (50.130.154). The Metropolitan Museum of Art, Gift of Mrs Francis Ormond, 1950. (50.130.154t) (Exhibition)

Fig. 90 *Sails*, *c.* 1875. Graphite on paper, 6¼ × 4¼ in (15.9 × 10.8 cm). In the John Singer Sargent Scrapbook (50.130.154). The Metropolitan Museum of Art, Gift of Mrs Francis Ormond, 1950. (50.130.154z) (Exhibition)

Fig. 91 *Fishermen with Nets*, *c.* 1875. Graphite on paper, 4 3/16 × 6 7/16 in (10.6 × 16.3 cm). The Metropolitan Museum of Art, Gift of Mrs Francis Ormond, 1950. (50.130.94) (Exhibition, Washington and London)

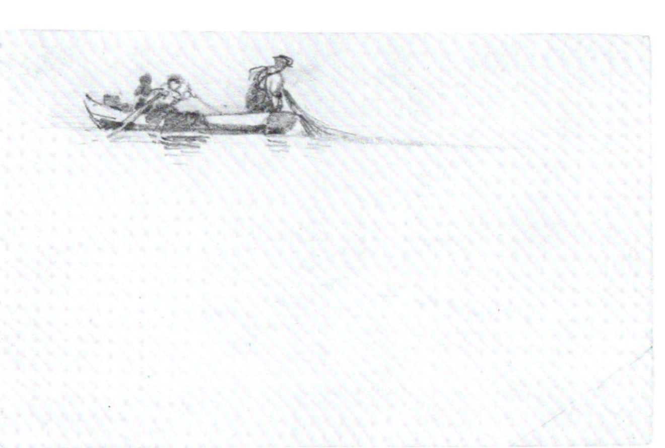

water. He applied pale peach watercolor to suggest the wet sand at the shoreline in the foreground and white accents to create atmospheric effect. The composition of a larger drawing, *Water's Edge* (fig. 86), combines Sargent's interest in boats and the coast and resonates with the unlocated painting *An Old Boat Stranded* (fig. 85). One drawing from the sketchbook, *Two Small Boats Moored to Beach* (fig. 87), also appears to be a view of the Pointe du Décollé, this time from the beach at Saint-Briac (fig. 88) about thirty kilometers west of Saint-Énogat.[15] In this detailed and highly finished drawing Sargent suggests the glassy surface of wet sand and rippling water against the boldly rendered rocky coast, using tonal variety to indicate depth and space.

Sargent's general interest in recording vignettes of life near the sea makes some of the drawings in the scrapbook difficult to date with precision. In the diminutive *Sailboat Towing Dory* (fig. 89) Sargent depicts a silhouette of a boat. In *Sails* (fig. 90) Sargent made a quick study of billowing sails and rigging. On the loose sheet *Fishermen with Nets* (fig. 91) Sargent depicted a fisherman in a small boat pulling up his net. By studying this vignette from a distance and placing it at the upper left corner of the sheet, he avoided a detailed rendering in favor of capturing a typical and picturesque scene of life along the coast. In such sketches, Sargent recorded characteristic details of these marine environments rather than producing specific studies for his formal compositions.

A related pair of drawings from 1876 in the scrapbook reveals how Sargent used drawing to generate a composition, translating sketches made on the beach in *Men Hauling Lifeboat Ashore* (fig. 92) into the more finished studio composition *Men Hauling Boat onto Beach* (fig. 93). In *Men Hauling Lifeboat Ashore* he painted in watercolor and sketched two versions of the same scene across two pages of a sketchbook. In the watercolor segment at left, the artist broadly suggested with a dark

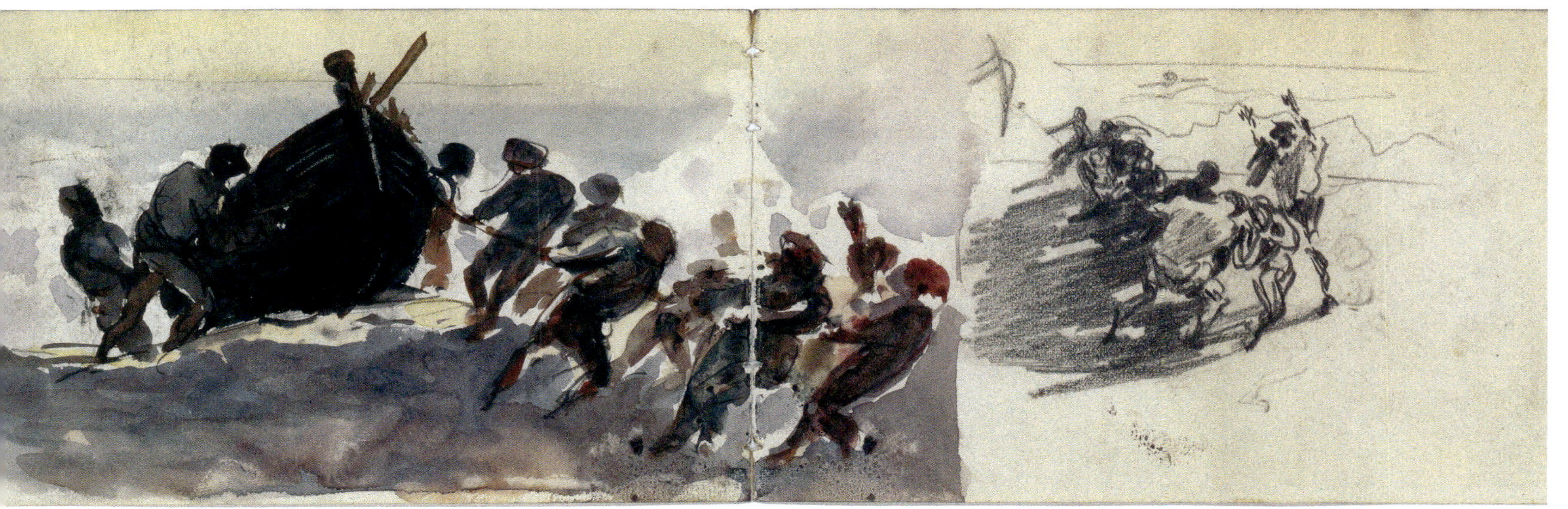

Fig. 92 *Men Hauling Lifeboat Ashore*, 1876. Watercolor and graphite on paper, 3¾ × 11¾ in (9.5 × 29.8 cm). From the John Singer Sargent Scrapbook (50.130.154). The Metropolitan Museum of Art, Gift of Mrs Francis Ormond, 1950. (50.130.154n recto) (Exhibition, Washington and Houston)

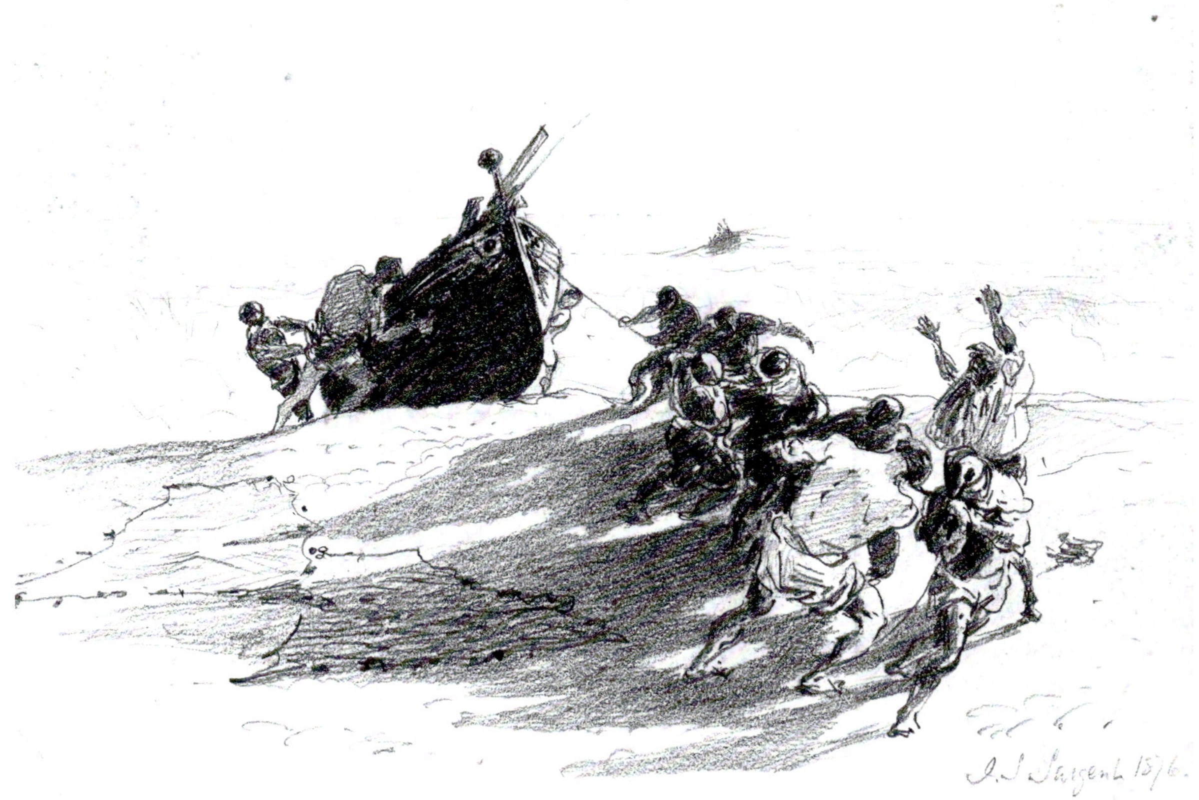

Fig. 93 *Men Hauling Boat onto Beach*, 1876. Graphite on paper, 6⅝ × 9¾ in (16.8 × 24.8 cm). Inscribed at lower right: *J.S. Sargent 1876*. In the John Singer Sargent Scrapbook (50.130.154). The Metropolitan Museum of Art, Gift of Mrs Francis Ormond, 1950. (50.130.154o) (Exhibition)

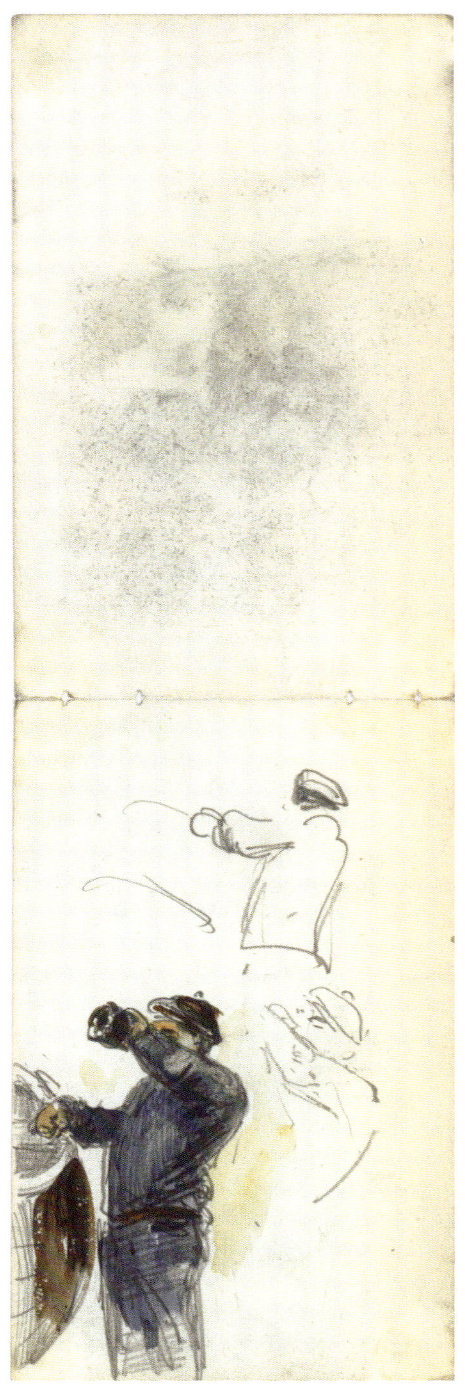

Fig. 94 *Sailor*, 1876. Watercolor and graphite on paper, 11¾ × 3¾ in (29.8 × 9.5 cm). From the John Singer Sargent Scrapbook (50.130.154). The Metropolitan Museum of Art, Gift of Mrs Francis Ormond, 1950. (50.130.154n verso) (Exhibition, Washington and Houston)

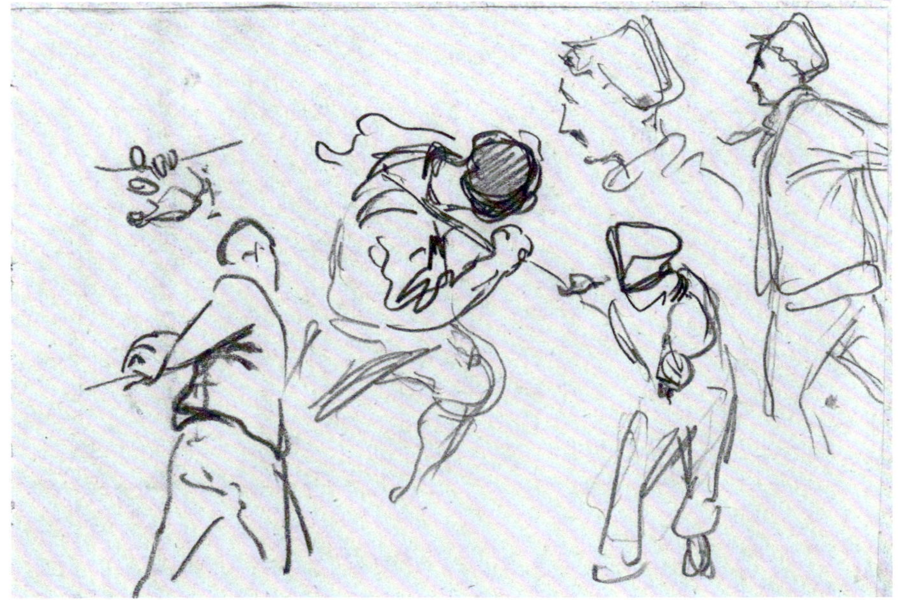

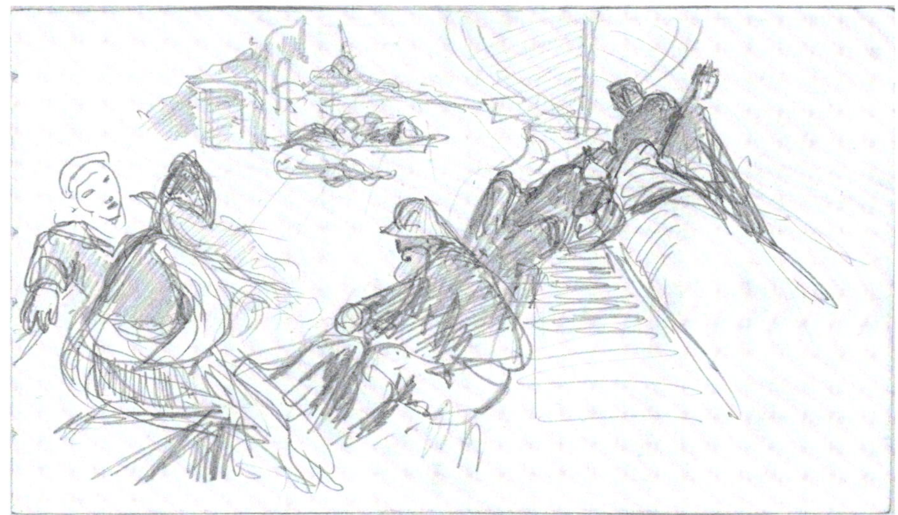

Fig. 95 *Men Pulling Ropes*, *c.* 1876. Graphite on paper, 4⁵⁄₁₆ × 6¼ in (11 × 15.9 cm). In the John Singer Sargent Scrapbook (50.130.154). The Metropolitan Museum of Art, Gift of Mrs Francis Ormond, 1950. (50.130.154aa) (Exhibition)

Fig. 96 *Sailors Relaxing on Deck*, 1876. Graphite on paper, 4⁵⁄₁₆ × 7¼ in (11 × 18.4 cm). In the John Singer Sargent Scrapbook (50.130.154). The Metropolitan Museum of Art, Gift of Mrs Francis Ormond, 1950. (50.130.154x) (Exhibition)

palette the various movements of the sailors as they work to pull the boat up the steep shoreline. At right he quickly sketched the scene in graphite with bold assuredness and strong shadows, accentuating the bare back of the near figure as well as the dynamic gesture of the man with raised arms at right. He also altered his viewpoint, compressing the composition. When this sheet was removed from the scrapbook, additional

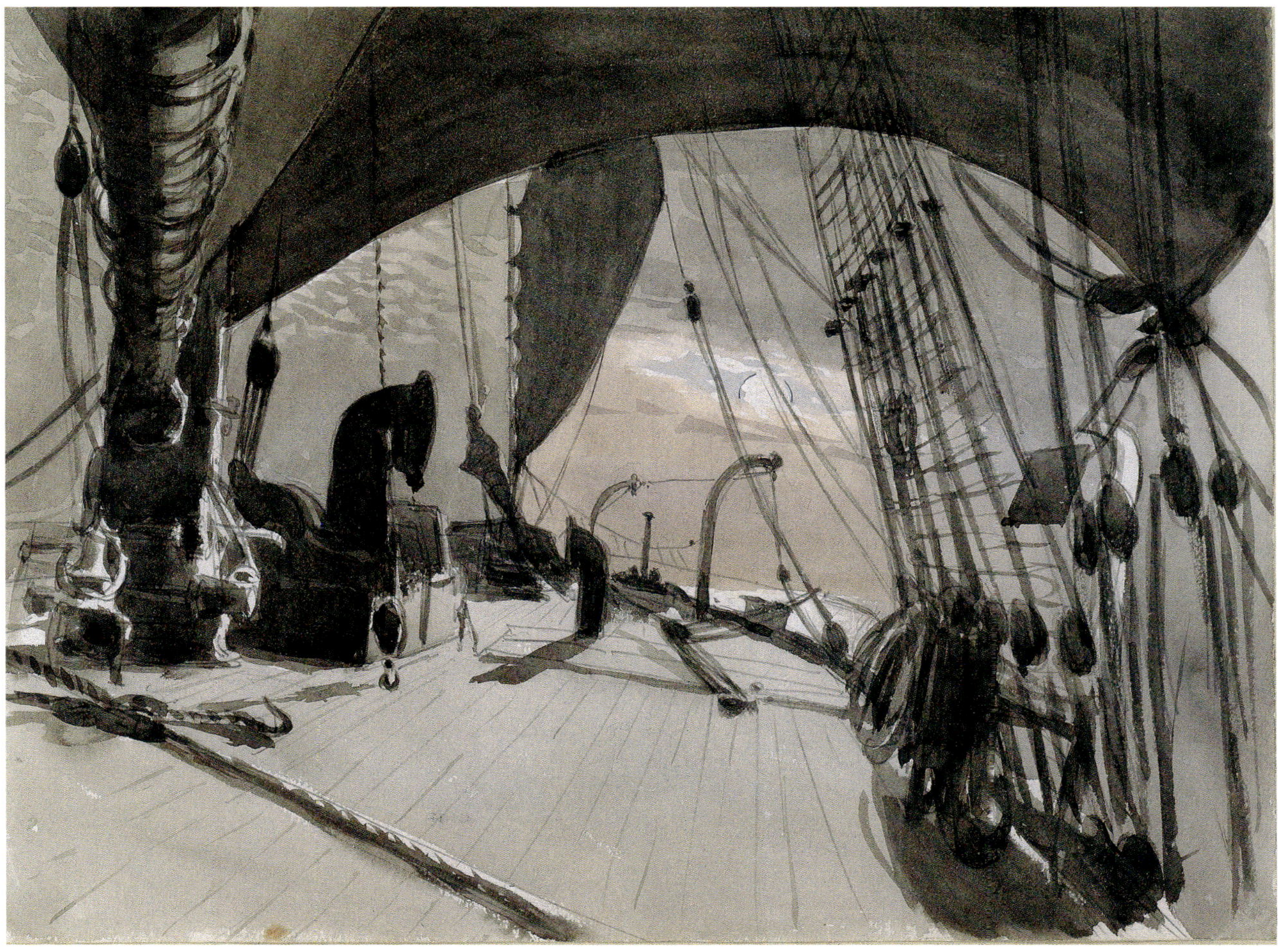

studies of a sailor drinking were revealed (fig. 94). Sargent quickly sketched the form in graphite twice, before working up a third more complete version in watercolor.

The larger graphite study, *Men Hauling Boat onto Beach*, is a more finished rendering of the scene in the double image. Sargent took a near vantage point and created more detailed studies of the two figures in the foreground. He probably saw in this subject an opportunity to represent the human figure in a variety of attitudes and motions, and from different angles. He altered the composition from the first recorded impression to the more detailed drawing in order to emphasize this interest. Sargent signed and dated the sheet "1876," suggesting his intention to create a more formal composition. The drawing *Men Pulling Ropes* (fig. 95), in which the artist made multiple studies of figures in action, may relate to the subject of the two aforementioned works.

In 1876, Sargent made his first transatlantic voyage to the United States, setting sail from Liverpool in May on the Cunard liner *Abyssinia* and returning from New York in October aboard the *SS Algeria*. Given the long days at sea, it is hardly surprising that he passed time creating a series of six drawings (figs. 96, 102–104, 107, 108) and a watercolor (fig. 97) that he preserved in his scrapbook, as well as six loose drawings (figs. 98–101, 105, 106). On these sheets he recorded carefully observed details of the ships, vignettes of life during the passages, and views of the ocean. He often indicated varying light and weather

Fig. 97 *Deck of Ship in Moonlight*, 1876. Watercolor and graphite on paper, 9 × 11¾ in (22.9 × 29.8 cm). From the John Singer Sargent Scrapbook (50.130.154). The Metropolitan Museum of Art, Gift of Mrs Francis Ormond, 1950. (50.130.154bb) (Exhibition, Washington and Houston)

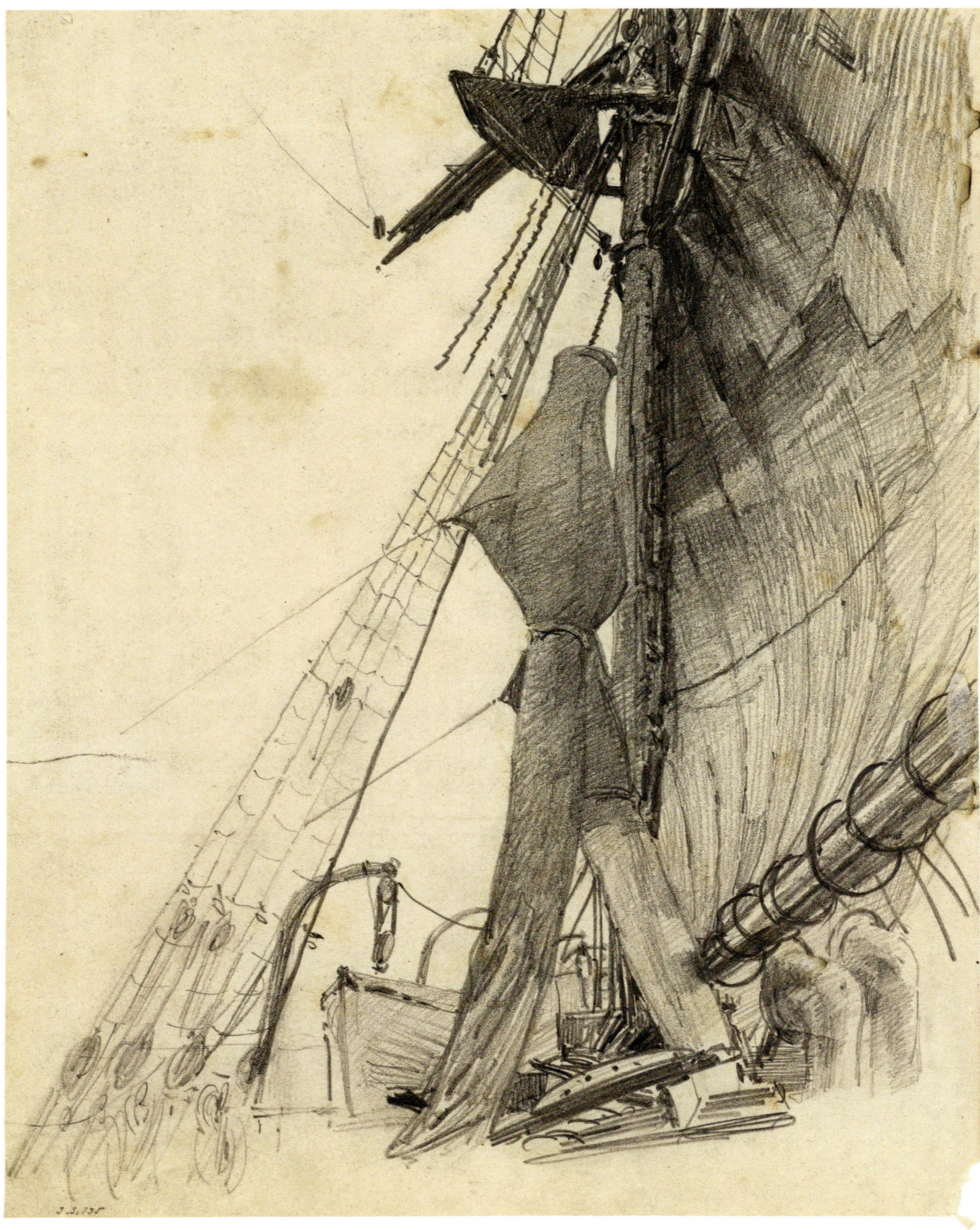

Fig. 98 *Sketch of Sail and Rigging*, *c.* 1876. Graphite on paper, 11 7/16 × 8 7/8 in (29 × 22.5 cm). Museum of Fine Arts, Boston, Gift of Miss Emily Sargent and Mrs. Violet Ormond in memory of their brother John Singer Sargent, 28.957. (Exhibition)

conditions, even documenting a dramatic storm that occurred during his return to Europe. Many of the motifs captured in the sketches would reappear in the oil paintings from the journey.

Three loose sheets in the Museum of Fine Arts, Boston, evidence Sargent's study of ship decks and rigs. In *Sketch of Sail and Rigging* (fig. 98), he presented a meticulously drawn and shaded view of a deck, sails, masts, and rigging from a low vantage point to suggest their impressive scale. He carefully observed the mechanics of a sail as it attaches to a boom in the near view, *Sketch of Tackle on Spar* (fig. 99). These drawings informed the settings of his oils from the trips, such as *The Artist's Mother Aboard Ship* (fig. 27) and *The Cook's Boy* (fig. 28). An anchor resting on a deck is the subject of another focused view, the detailed *Sketch of Man with Anchor* (fig. 100). In this unusual image, Sargent drew a minuscule figure on the deck—perhaps a witty commentary on the size of the anchor when studied close at hand. Anchors also appear, less prominently, in two other sketches of decks (figs. 101 and 107). In the loose sheet *Scene on a Ship Deck* (fig. 101), the anchor is seen at a greater distance than in the Boston sheet. As a

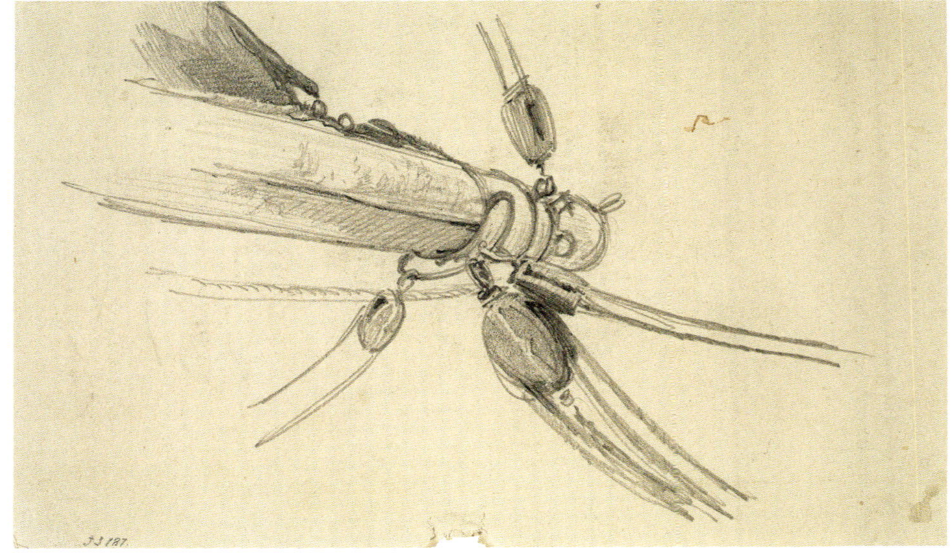

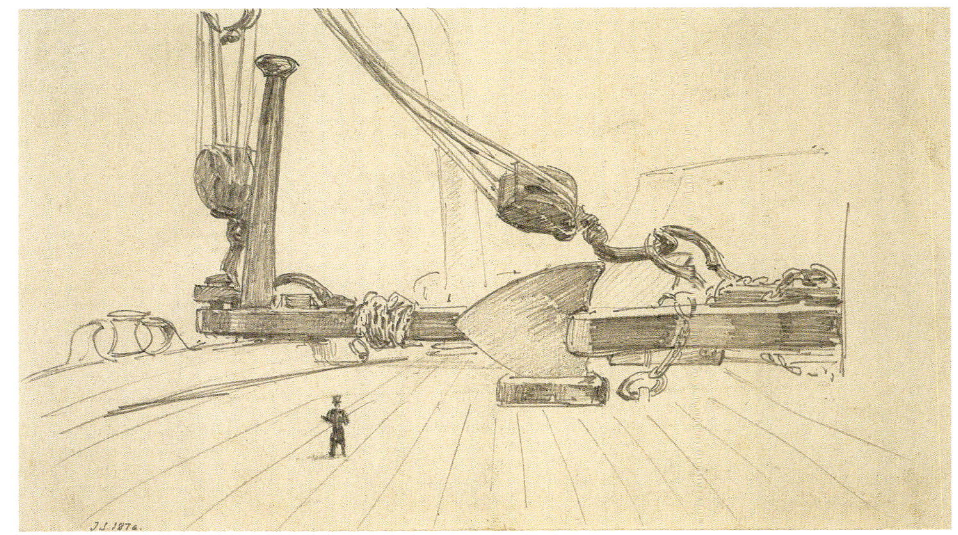

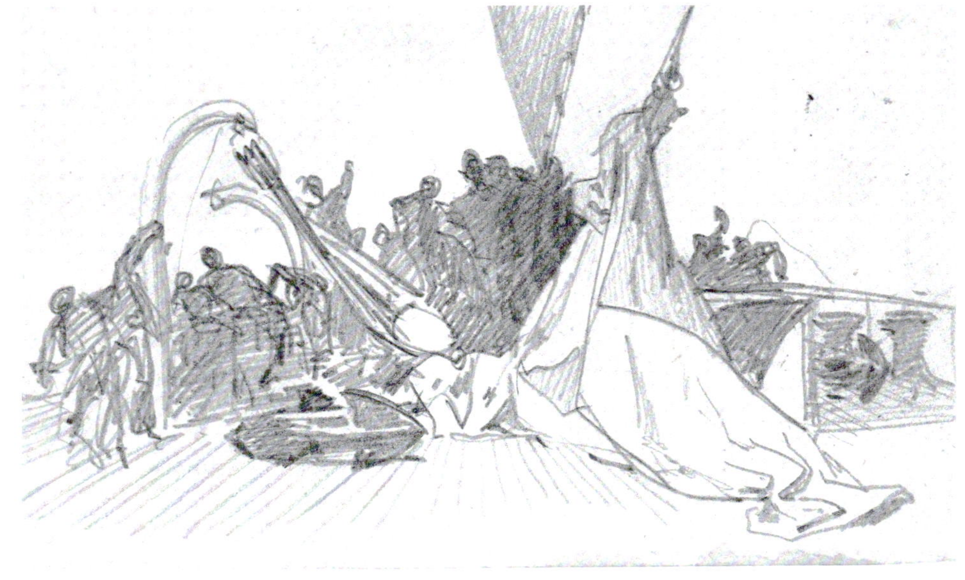

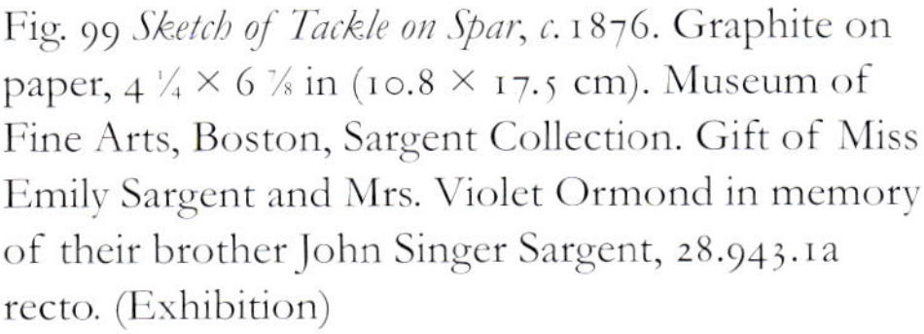

Fig. 99 *Sketch of Tackle on Spar*, *c.* 1876. Graphite on paper, 4 1/4 × 6 7/8 in (10.8 × 17.5 cm). Museum of Fine Arts, Boston, Sargent Collection. Gift of Miss Emily Sargent and Mrs. Violet Ormond in memory of their brother John Singer Sargent, 28.943.1a recto. (Exhibition)

Fig. 100 *Sketch of Man with Anchor*, 1876. Graphite on paper, 4 5/16 × 7 1/16 in (11 × 18 cm). Inscribed, lower left: *J.S.* 1876. Museum of Fine Arts, Boston, Sargent Collection. Gift of Miss Emily Sargent and Mrs. Violet Ormond in memory of their brother John Singer Sargent, 28.943.2. (Exhibition)

Fig. 101 *Scene on a Ship Deck*, 1876. Graphite on paper, 4 × 6 3/4 in (10.2 × 17.1 cm). Harvard Art Museum, Fogg Art Museum, Gift of Mrs Francis Ormond, 1937, 1937.8.79. (Exhibition)

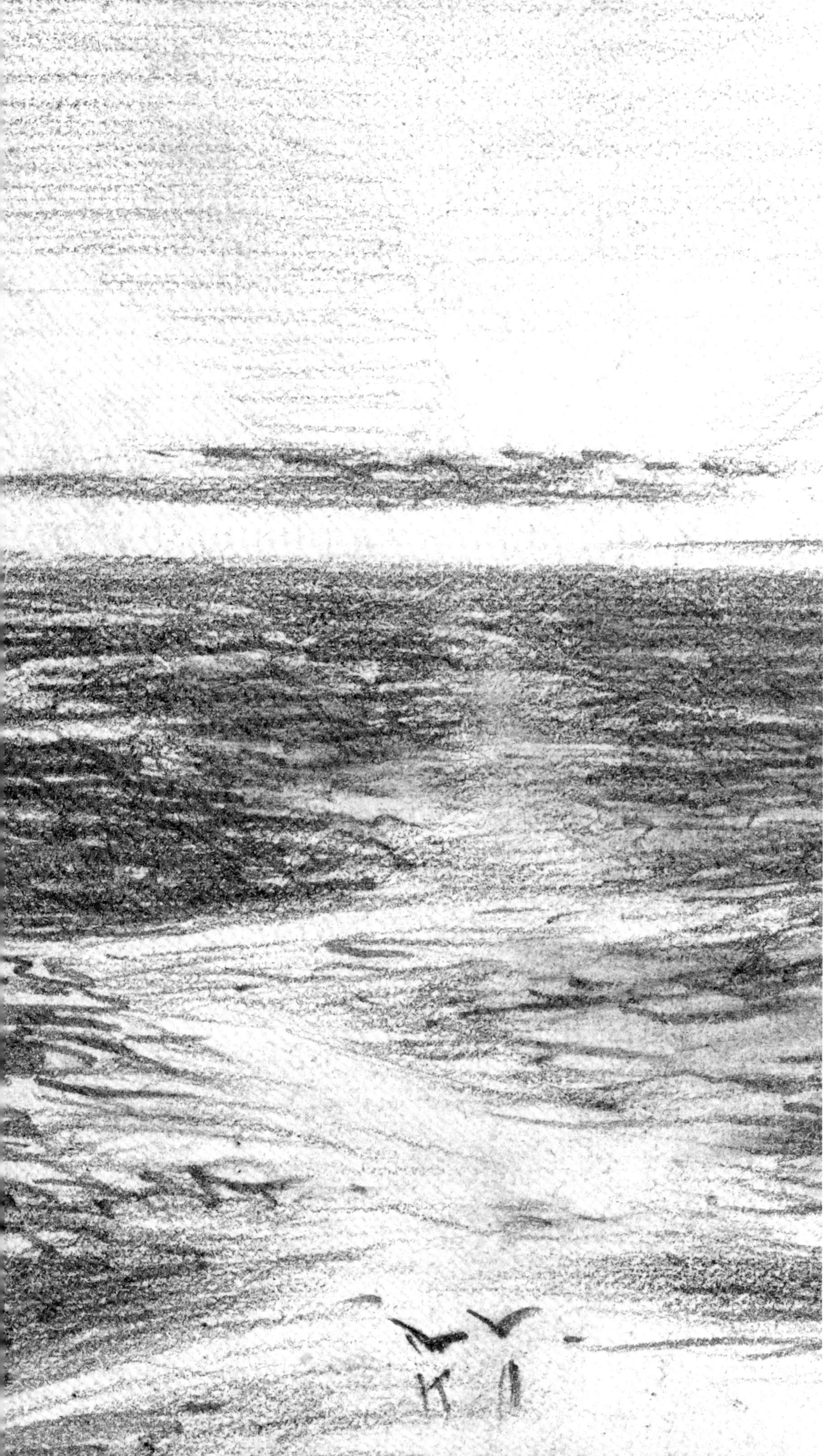

result, it appears far less imposing and is in scale with the silhouetted figures leaning over the deck's rails, their attention apparently focused on something nearby.

Careful studies of the ship's decks and lifeboats would also figure in oil paintings from the journeys, such as *Atlantic Storm* (fig. 51) and *The Artist's Mother Aboard Ship*. Among these is *Lifeboats on Davits* (fig. 104); after pasting it into the scrapbook, Sargent carefully transcribed detailed color notations with relative tonal values onto the page beneath the drawing. Additional notes are scattered across the sketchbook page, suggesting that Sargent intended to later create a painting of the scene. A related, similarly annotated loose drawing is *Boat Deck* (fig. 105), which shows a calm sea. An equally tranquil sea provided Sargent the opportunity to create a pencil and watercolor view of the empty stillness of the moonlit deck at night (fig. 97), as well as detailed portrayals of sleeping sailors like *Men Sleeping on Deck of Ship* (fig. 107) and *Sailors on Deck of Ship* (fig. 108).

In stark contrast to these quieter scenes are Sargent's records of sailors' and passengers' activities during rough weather. In *Sailors on Sloping Deck* (fig. 103) Sargent recorded the precipitous tilt of the ship in violent seas and created a dynamic composition balancing the sloping angle of the deck with the swelling waves to the right. He conveyed the movements of the sailors tugging lines with quick, agile strokes of his pencil. Also in unsettled weather conditions the artist executed the loose sheet *Woman Looking out to Sea* (fig. 106), studying the windswept dress and scarf of the subject —possibly his sister Emily—against the churning waves beyond, while barely rendering the ship's deck. A similarly hooded and draped figure appears in *Sailors Relaxing on Deck* (fig. 96) and appears as the subject of the oil *The Artist's Mother Aboard Ship* (fig. 27).

Sargent was also preoccupied with the movement of the ocean. In *Moonlight on*

Facing page: Fig. 102 Detail of fig. 55, *Moonlight on Waves*, 1876. In the John Singer Sargent Scrapbook (50.130.154). The Metropolitan Museum of Art, Gift of Mrs Francis Ormond, 1950. (50.130.154l) (Exhibition)

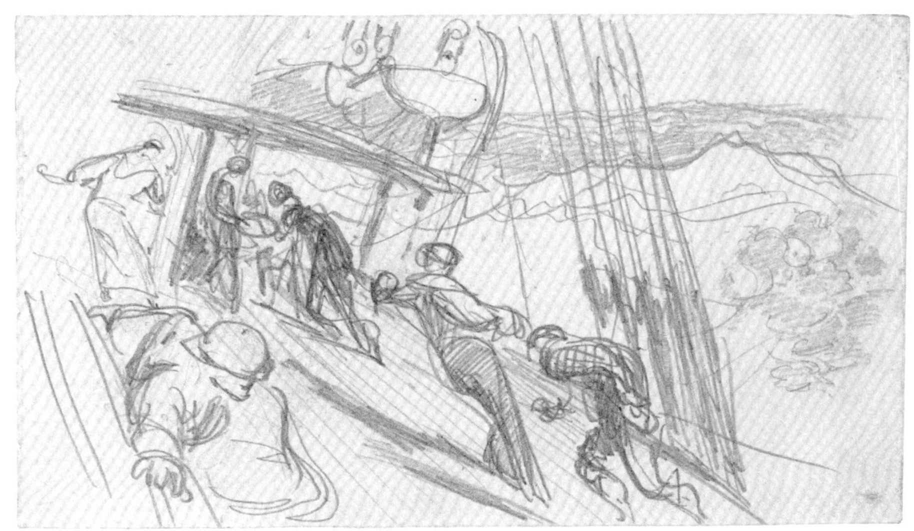

Fig. 103 *Sailors on Sloping Deck*, 1876. Graphite on paper, $4\frac{5}{16} \times 7\frac{1}{4}$ in (11 × 18.4 cm). In the John Singer Sargent Scrapbook (50.130.154). The Metropolitan Museum of Art, Gift of Mrs Francis Ormond, 1950. (50.130.154i) (Exhibition)

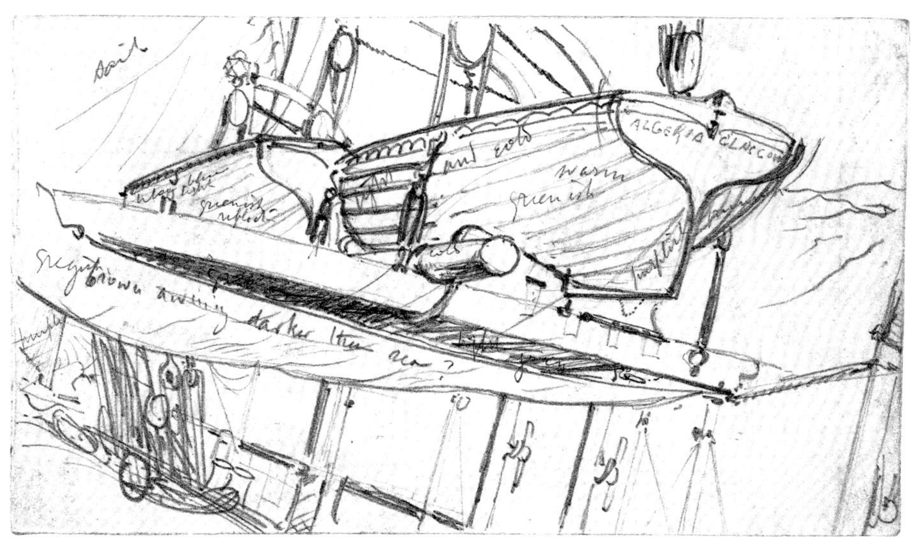

Fig. 104 *Lifeboats on Davits*, 1876. Graphite on paper, $4\frac{5}{16} \times 7\frac{1}{4}$ in (11 × 18.4 cm). Inscribed on back of lifeboat: *ALGERIA GLASGOW*; [color notations across the sheet]. Inscribed beneath the drawing (on the scrapbook page): *sea deep blue darker than shade in boats. foam colder than boats; / close by, [marblings?] of light green. .immense spreading surf thick cold white / deck lighter than sea, where wet, rich brown with purple – shade of boats / lighter than sea; very varied in tone. dark accents at top and / bottom. sail very dark brownish purple shade* In the John Singer Sargent Scrapbook (50.130.154). The Metropolitan Museum of Art, Gift of Mrs Francis Ormond, 1950. (50.130.154j) (Exhibition)

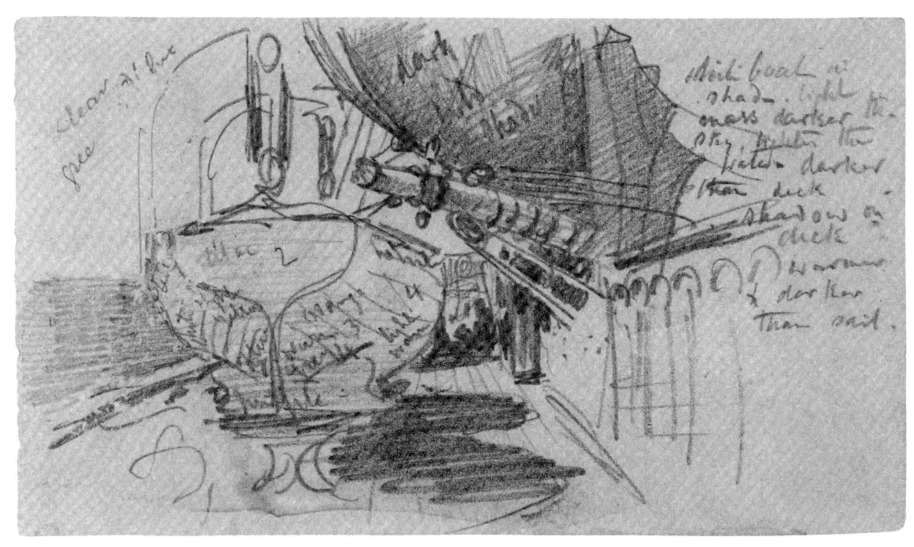

Fig. 105 *Boat Deck*, 1876. Graphite on paper, $3\frac{11}{16} \times 6\frac{11}{16}$ in (10.1 × 17 cm). Inscribed at right center: *whole boat in shadow. Light / mass darker than / sky lighter than / water. darker / than deck / shadow on / deck / warmer / to darker / than sail.* [also other scattered color notations on lifeboat] The Metropolitan Museum of Art, Gift of Mrs Francis Ormond, 1950. (50.130.90) (Exhibition, Washington and Houston)

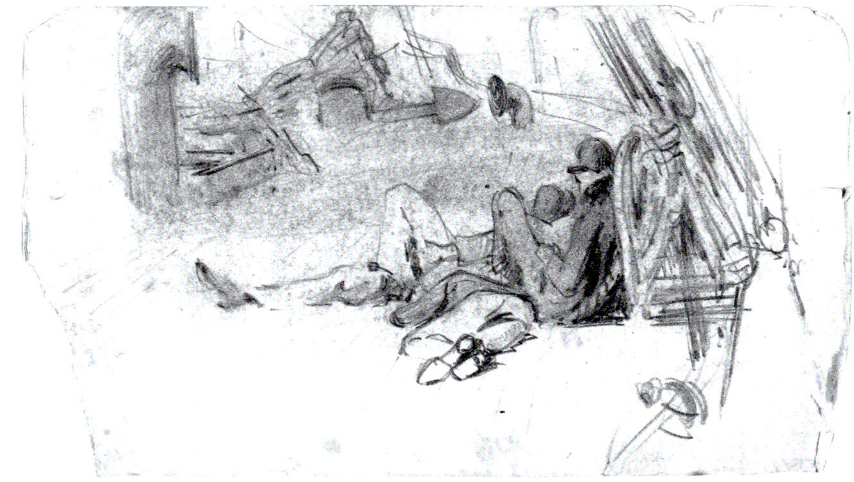

Fig. 106 *Woman Looking Out to Sea*, 1876. Graphite on paper, 7⁵⁄₁₆ × 4³⁄₁₆ in (18.5 × 10.7 cm). The Metropolitan Museum of Art, Gift of Mrs Francis Ormond, 1950. (50.130.140c) (Exhibition, Washington and Houston)

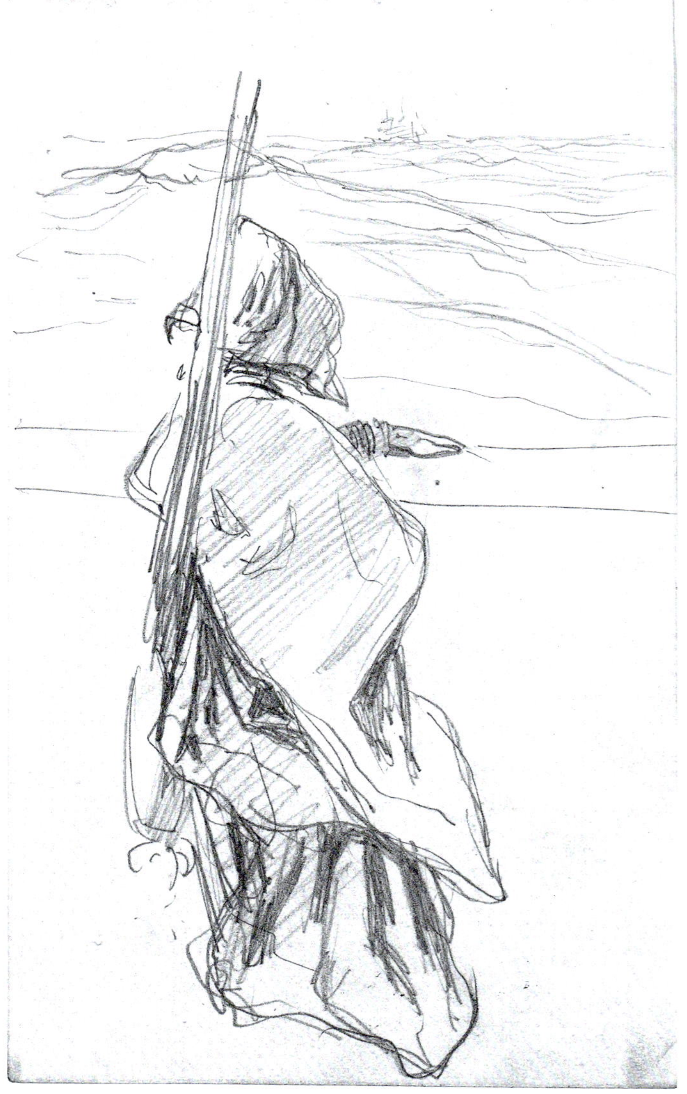

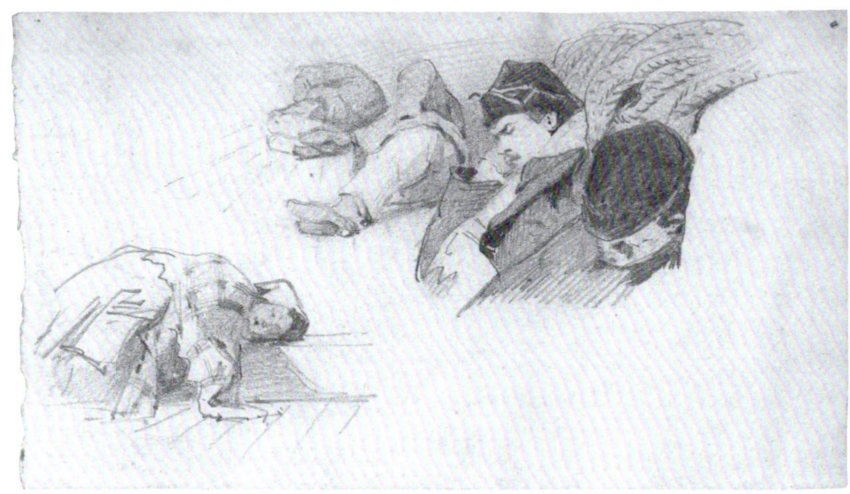

Fig. 107 *Men Sleeping on Deck of Ship*, 1876. Graphite on paper, 4 × 6¾ in (10.2 × 17.1 cm). In the John Singer Sargent Scrapbook (50.130.154). The Metropolitan Museum of Art, Gift of Mrs Francis Ormond, 1950. (50.130.154k) (Exhibition)

Fig. 108 *Sailors on Deck of Ship*, 1876. Graphite on paper, 4 × 6⅝ in (10.2 × 16.8 cm). In the John Singer Sargent Scrapbook (50.130.154). The Metropolitan Museum of Art, Gift of Mrs Francis Ormond, 1950. (50.130.154m) (Exhibition)

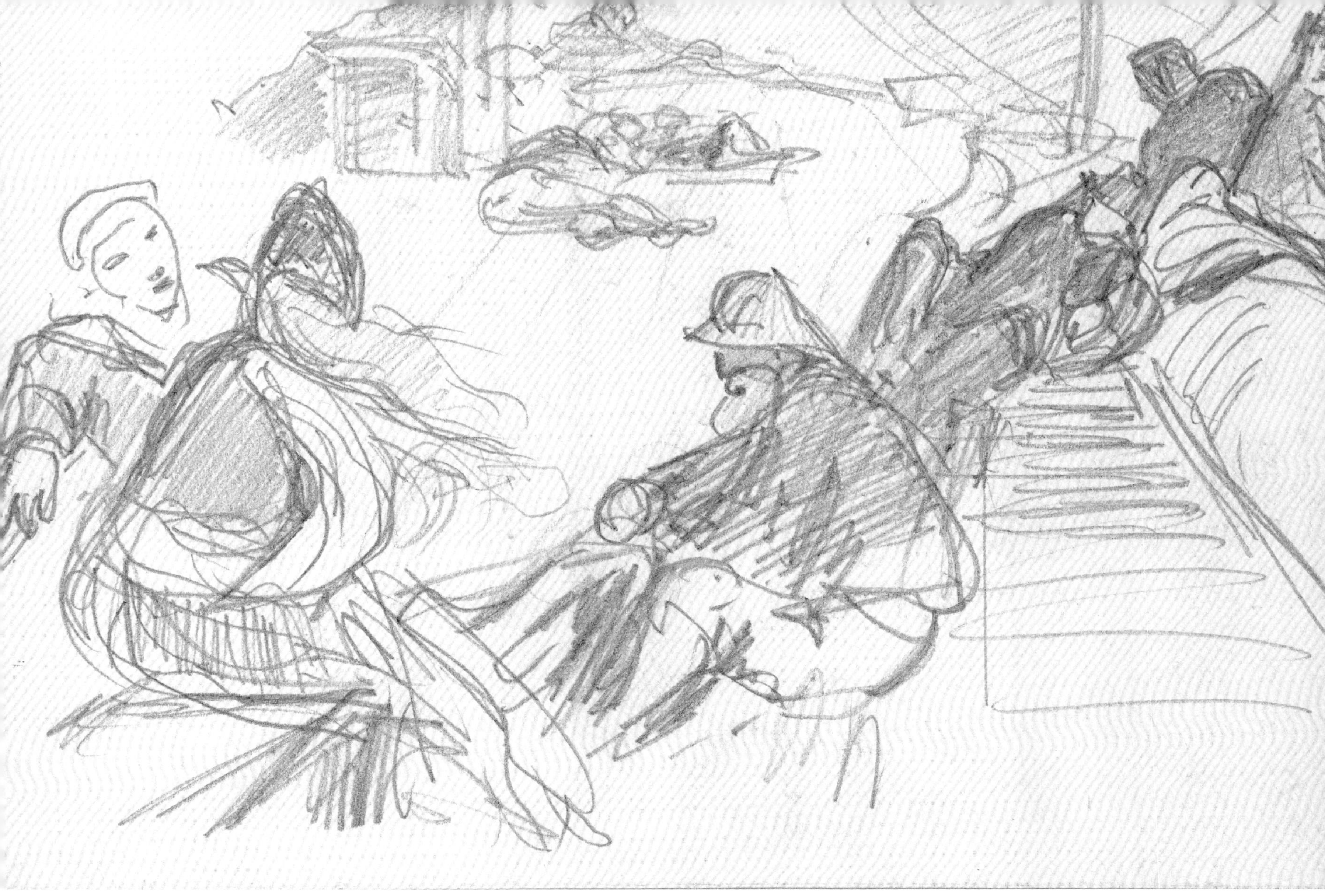

Waves (fig. 55; detail fig. 102), the artist suggested subtle light effects and the rolling motion of water in a ship's wake with an accomplished graphic technique. He addressed similar artistic challenges in his renderings of the stormy sea shown in the oil paintings *Mid-Ocean, Mid-Winter* (fig. 54) and the highly dramatic *Atlantic Storm* (fig. 51). While he could not have painted on deck in such conditions, he did capture the dynamic circumstances in his sketchbook.[16]

Two additional loose sheets relate to the drawings of this period, although they defy exact dating. *Sailboat Deck with Figures* (fig. 110) and *Cattle in Stern of a Boat* (fig. 111) demonstrate Sargent's interest in nautical subjects and his concern with recording the movement of boats through the water. The boat in *Sailboat Deck with Figures* could represent a type of coastal ferry or freight boat on which he may have traveled between different towns. On the verso of the sheet, the artist transcribed the lyrics to an old sea song, "Rosemary Lane." In *Cattle in Stern of Boat*, he studied the ship's prow, filled with bovine passengers, as it breaks through the rough waters.

Although Sargent returned to the sea during the summers of 1877 (Brittany) and 1878 (Italy), it is difficult to link any of the drawings in the scrapbook directly to these sojourns. Occupied with creating

Fig. 109 Detail of fig. 96, *Sailors Relaxing on Deck*, 1876. In the John Singer Sargent Scrapbook (50.130.154). The Metropolitan Museum of Art, Gift of Mrs Francis Ormond, 1950. (50.130.154x) (Exhibition)

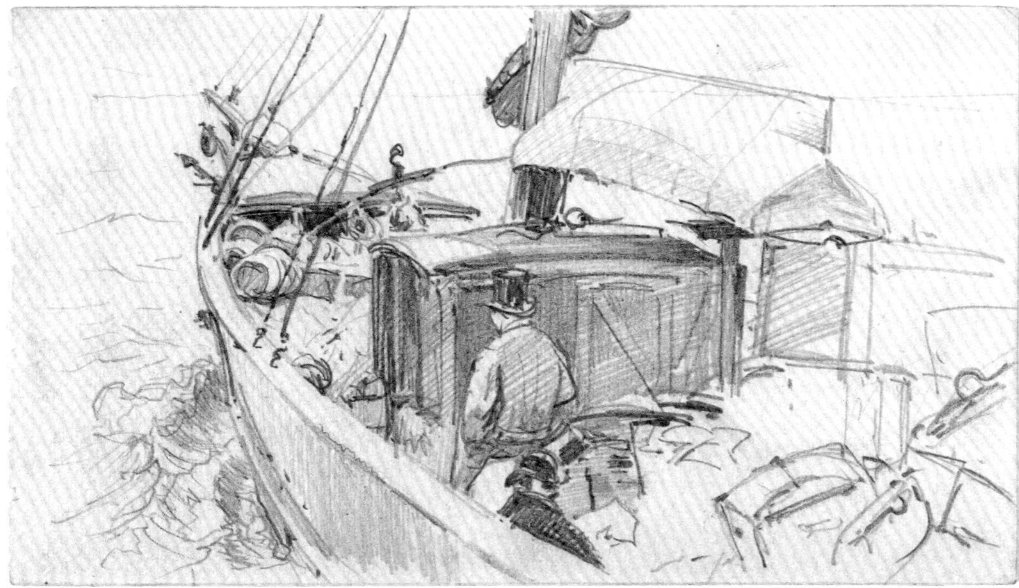

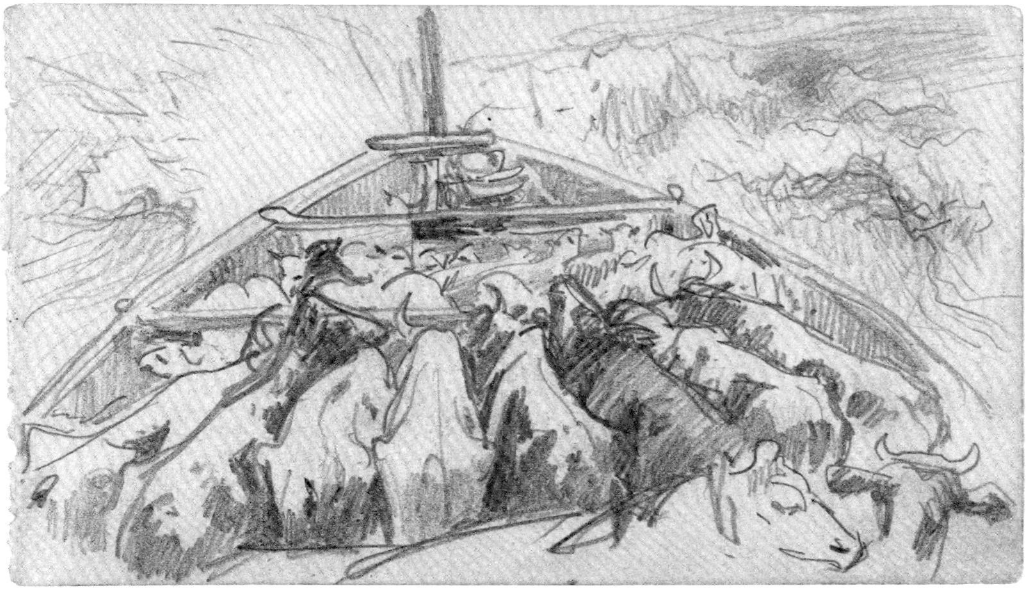

Fig. 110 *Sailboat Deck with Figures*, 1876. Graphite on paper, 4 3/16 × 7 3/16 in (10.7 × 18.2 cm). The Metropolitan Museum of Art, Gift of Mrs Francis Ormond, 1950. (50.130.140a) (Exhibition, Washington and London)

Fig. 111 *Cattle in Stern of a Boat*, *c.* 1876. Graphite on paper, 3 15/16 × 6 11/16 in (10 × 17.2 cm). The Metropolitan Museum of Art, Gift of Mrs Francis Ormond, 1950. (50.130.91) (Exhibition, Washington and London)

exhibition works such as *En Route pour la pêche* (see fig. 8), and *Neapolitan Children Bathing* (see fig. 31), Sargent increasingly worked in oil and kept his preparatory works separate from his more personal sketches. A group of three drawings not included in the scrapbook may date from these summers: *Two Men in Boats* (fig. 112), *Oarsman* (fig. 113), and *Two Men in Boat* (fig. 114).

As a group, Sargent's marine drawings reveal his developing skills as a draftsman as well as his use of drawing to record vignettes and to study essential characteristics of elements that would figure in his paintings. He increasingly used drawing to record tonal values and relationships, creating aides mémoires for later paintings. His subjects and interests overlapped during several summers, and many of the themes he explored in the 1870s would endure in his œuvre. The artist's interest in rendering water and capturing its motion would reappear in later images of Venice, the Italian Lakes, and the Val d'Aosta, Italy.

By removing his marine drawings from their original context within sketchbooks and choosing to save them in a scrapbook, Sargent made them part of a larger and more complex narrative in which his interest in copying and collecting images played a vital role. The artist had copied works of art and architecture since early childhood, a practice that he continued in the 1870s during his technical training.[17] Although Carolus-Duran insisted that his pupils study the paintings of Diego Velázquez, he also encouraged them to mine art history for other potential role models. As H. Barbara Weinberg has noted, "Sargent . . . adopted his teacher's belief in the efficacy of establishing a personal dialogue with the past, choosing mentors other than the great Spaniard if their lessons seemed apt."[18]

In the scrapbook, Sargent included seventeen drawings and watercolors after diverse works from all eras of art history and across many media. He copied painting,

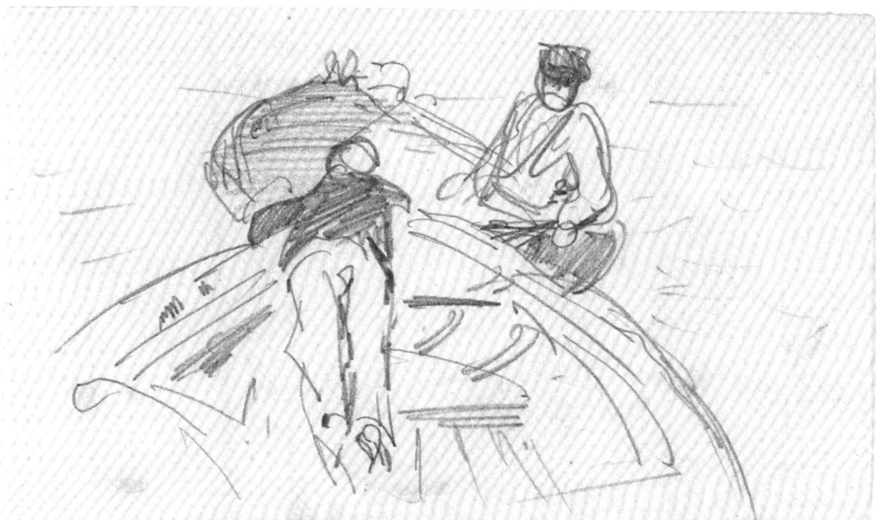

Fig. 112 *Two Men in Boats*, *c.* 1877–78. Graphite on paper, 3⁹⁄₁₆ × 5¹³⁄₁₆ in (9 × 14.8 cm). The Metropolitan Museum of Art, Gift of Mrs Francis Ormond, 1950. (50.130.98 recto) (Exhibition, Washington and Houston)

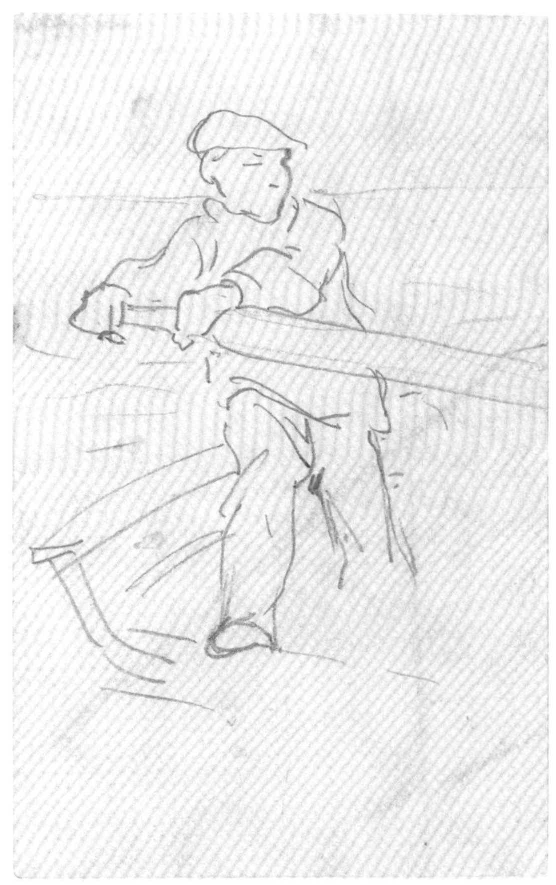

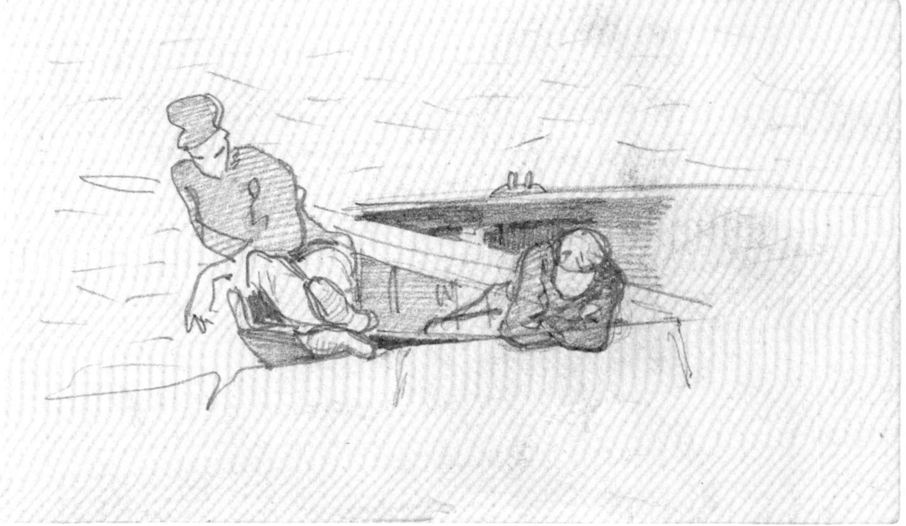

Fig. 113 *Oarsman*, *c.* 1877–78. Graphite on paper, 5¹³⁄₁₆ × 3⁹⁄₁₆ in (15 × 9 cm). The Metropolitan Museum of Art, Gift of Mrs Francis Ormond, 1950. (50.130.104) (Exhibition, Washington and London)

Fig. 114 *Two Men in Boat*, *c.* 1877–78. Graphite and gray pencil on paper, 3⁹⁄₁₆ × 5¹³⁄₁₆ in (9 × 14.8 cm). The Metropolitan Museum of Art, Gift of Mrs Francis Ormond, 1950. (50.130.99) (Exhibition, Washington and London)

sculpture, and architecture from ancient Greece and Rome and contemporary France. He found inspiration in the sculpture of Michelangelo, the paintings of Tintoretto, the rustic peasants of Jean-François Millet, and the formal compositions of Nicolas Poussin. On several sheets he traced Egyptian motifs directly from a book.[19]

Sargent came of age as an artist when reproductions of works of art were increasingly available as prints in illustrated magazines and as commercial photographs. His avid copying and collecting activities were deeply intertwined, and he included approximately 150 prints, lithographs and photographs in the scrapbook. From an early moment, the artist and his family participated in the increasingly popular activity of collecting commercial photographs. As photography historian Elizabeth Anne McCauley has noted, by the 1860s collectors of commercial photographs had increasingly larger inventories from which to choose and the images "were no longer sold just as luxury goods mounted on bristol boards with engraved gold trim and lettering."[20]

Sargent's early efforts at collecting photographic reproductions in scrapbooks are recorded in a letter to his friend Ben del Castillo. In May 1869 the thirteen-year-old wrote: "Ma gave me a large album of white Roman binding to stick photographs in, and I have stuck in about 60 of Rome and a great many of Naples. I have a good many old Greek and Roman poets, and I am trying to get the first Caesars, I will get some photographs of the Museum at Munich, where there are some very beautiful statues."[21] The whereabouts of this album are unknown.[22] In 1871 Sargent wrote to his friend Violet Paget (Vernon Lee) that "Papa has come home . . . He has brought me 50 or 60 beautiful and interesting photographs of all the principal towns and ruins of Sicily so that on looking at them we almost feel as if we had been there. There are a few of some beautiful statues and bas reliefs."[23] For the peripatetic young artist, the collecting of such materials served as a memory of places visited and sites seen, but it also manifested contemporary educational values. Writers promoted the exercise of scrapbook making as a means of developing taste and discrimination, especially in children. In 1880 journalist Jessie E. Ringwalt encouraged mothers to help their children make scrapbooks. "Through these experiments," Ringwalt wrote, "the taste will be developed, sometimes with great rapidity, and the child will soon show a greatly improved choice and skill."[24]

In the 1870s Sargent enlisted his friends in other cities in collecting photographs. Once he had obtained these photographs, he used them to develop his knowledge of the art of the past. In August 1873 he acknowledged Violet Paget's help in procuring a photograph of an unidentified sculpture, writing "Many thanks also for the photo of that great bust."[25] In the long paragraph that followed, Sargent elaborated on his careful study of the distinguishing features of Greek statuary as well as the figures of Tintoretto and Paolo Veronese. In letters to his cousin Mrs Elizabeth Austin, who also sent him photographs, Sargent suggested how his copying and collecting efforts overlapped. "I thank you very much for your kind letter and for your kindness in taking the trouble to get me these photographs," he wrote in 1874, "I am sorry to hear that the magnificent Tintoretto has not been photographed, for I remember it as being very fine, but I must content myself with a little outline of the principal female figure in one of my Dresden Sketch-books."[26] As an aide mémoire for art he had already studied, Sargent embraced the use of photographs and seemed to prefer them over his own drawings. He collected photographs when he could, but copying was an acceptable substitute.

Sargent amassed an impressive collection of images. While a complete inventory of these reproductions is beyond the scope of this essay, a few observations may be made. Sargent gathered images of paintings, drawings, decorative sculpture, architectural details, and monuments in locales that were familiar to him in Italy and Spain. Sargent included only one nautical subject, a print after *Calais Pier* by J.M.W. Turner, an artist he deeply admired (see fig. 115 and p. 19). This port scene showing boats tossed in a stormy sea combines his interest in ships and the dynamic movement of water as evidenced in his own drawings. The influence of the artist's childhood in Italy is suggested in several photographs and prints after the Italian masters Michelangelo and Raphael. His interest in the exotic is represented in two watercolors by Mariano Fortuny, *Le Marchand de Tapis* (1870, Museu Montserrat, Barcelona) and *Chef Kabyle dans la mosquée de Tangier* (location unknown), an important inspiration for Sargent's *Fumée d'ambre gris* (see fig. 119).

By far the largest group of reproductions included in the scrapbook seem to have been acquired by Sargent as souvenirs during his trip to Spain and Morocco in 1879–80. At least twenty-two photographs in the scrapbook bear the mark of J. [Jean] Laurent (1816–92), a well-known French-born commercial photographer who began systematically recording the art and monuments of Spain during the 1860s. An 1873 inventory of his studio numbered some 6,350 negatives representing the paintings and monuments of Spain and Portugal. Although Laurent operated a storefront in Paris on the rue Richelieu from the late 1860s, Sargent probably purchased the Spanish images in Madrid.[27] These include architectural details of the Alhambra as well as numerous paintings by Velázquez and other masters in the Prado. The scrapbook also includes photographs (by unidentified studios) of other works of art throughout Europe, scenic postcards of North Africa, and *cartes de visite* of Moroccans in exotic dress. By gathering

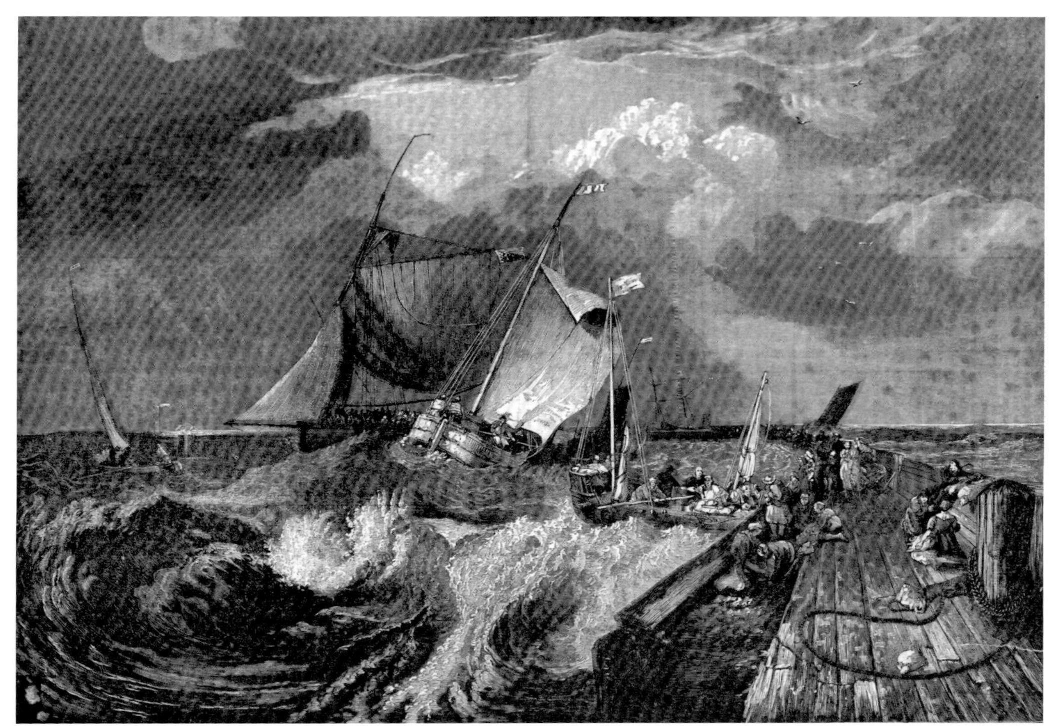

Fig. 115 Print after J.M.W. Turner, *Calais Pier*, *c.* 1803. National Gallery, London. P. 4 recto in the John Singer Sargent Scrapbook (50.130.154). The Metropolitan Museum of Art, Gift of Mrs Francis Ormond, 1950.

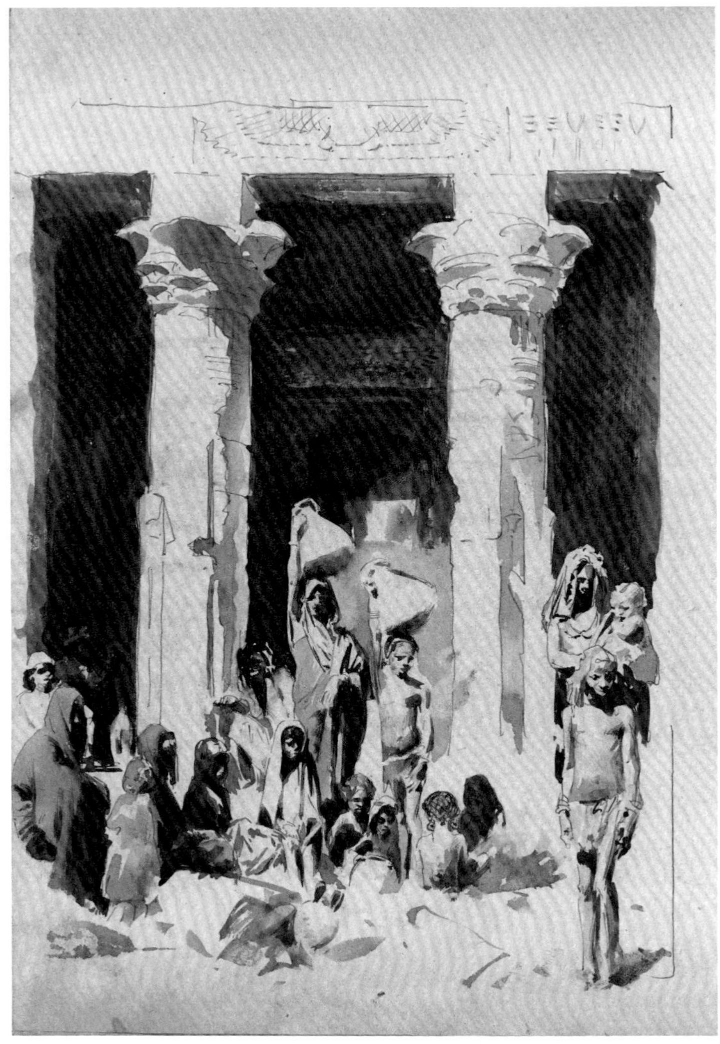

Fig. 116 *Nubians in front of the Temple of Dendur* (after J. Pascal Sébah, Turkish, 1838–90), *c.* 1880. In the John Singer Sargent Scrapbook (50.130.154). The Metropolitan Museum of Art, Gift of Mrs Francis Ormond, 1950. (50.130.154cc)

Fig. 117 George du Maurier (1834–1896), *Music at Home*, from *Punch*, vol. LXXIV, p. 30, 26 January 1878. P. 39 verso in the John Singer Sargent Scrapbook (50.130.154). The Metropolitan Museum of Art, Gift of Mrs Francis Ormond, 1950.

Fig. 118 George du Maurier (1834–1896), *A Linguistic Opportunity*, from *Punch*, vol. LXXIII, p. 114, 15 September 1877. P. 40 recto in the John Singer Sargent Scrapbook (50.130.154). The Metropolitan Museum of Art, Gift of Mrs Francis Ormond, 1950.

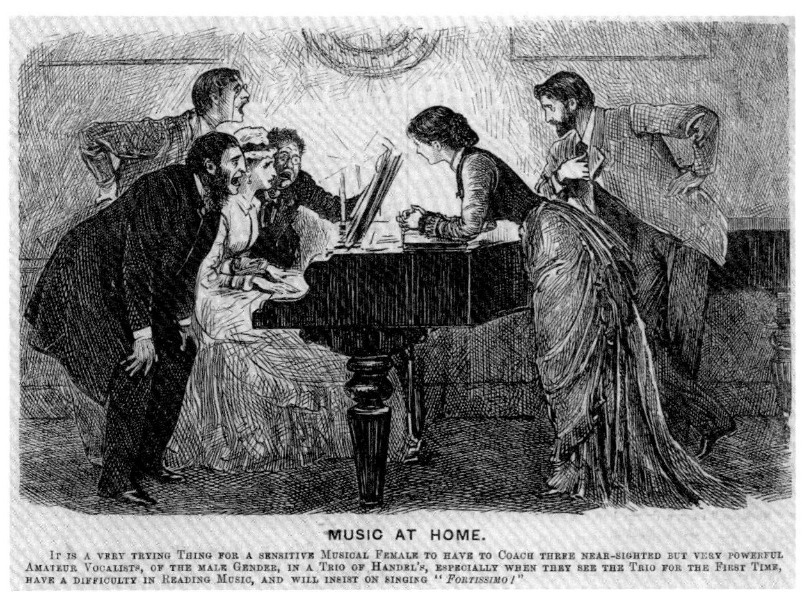

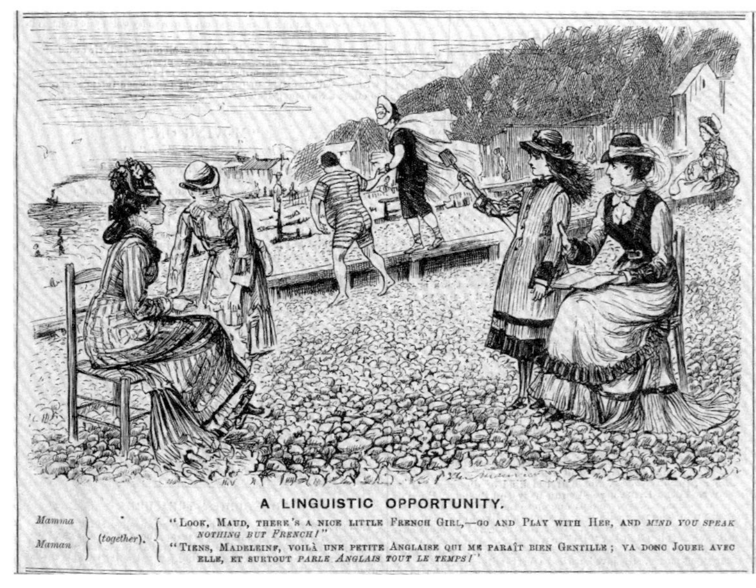

and collecting images of exotic types, landscapes, and architectural details during his trip to Spain and Morocco, the artist built a vocabulary for his later subject pictures such as *Fumée d'ambre gris* (see fig. 119). Sargent even included in the scrapbook a drawing after a photograph by Turkish photographer J. Pascal Sébah, *Nubians in front of the Temple of Dendur* (fig. 116).[28]

One final group of material, underscoring the personal and quirky nature of scrapbooks, is a collection of cartoons by the well-known illustrator-turned-novelist George du Maurier (1824–96). Sargent, a great admirer of the English illustrators, was introduced to du Maurier by the latter's close friend Henry James.[29] Sargent, who probably appreciated the older artist's gentle, ironic humor mocking the manners and mores of British society, filled pages 39 through 44 of the scrapbook with cartoons published between about 1873 and 1879 in the British magazine *Punch, or the London Charivari*.[30] He included several cartoons from du Maurier's *Music at Home* (fig. 117) series. The illustrator's satires of the pitfalls of amateur musicians may have amused Sargent, a talented pianist who often performed for his friends. Du Maurier's *A Linguistic Opportunity* (fig. 118), showing a French and English child on holiday at the seashore being encouraged to practice the other's language, could have been a scene from Sargent's own peripatetic childhood.

Above all, Sargent probably admired du Maurier's delicate and accomplished drawings which were greatly esteemed during the period. In 1883 James penned a lengthy assessment of the illustrator's work, noting that the drawings could be appreciated for their own merit: "The wealth of execution was sometimes out of proportion to the jest beneath the cut; the joke might be as much or as little of a joke as one would; the picture was, at any rate, before all things a picture."[31] In conclusion, James asserted of du Maurier's drawings, "[n]o English artistic work in these latter

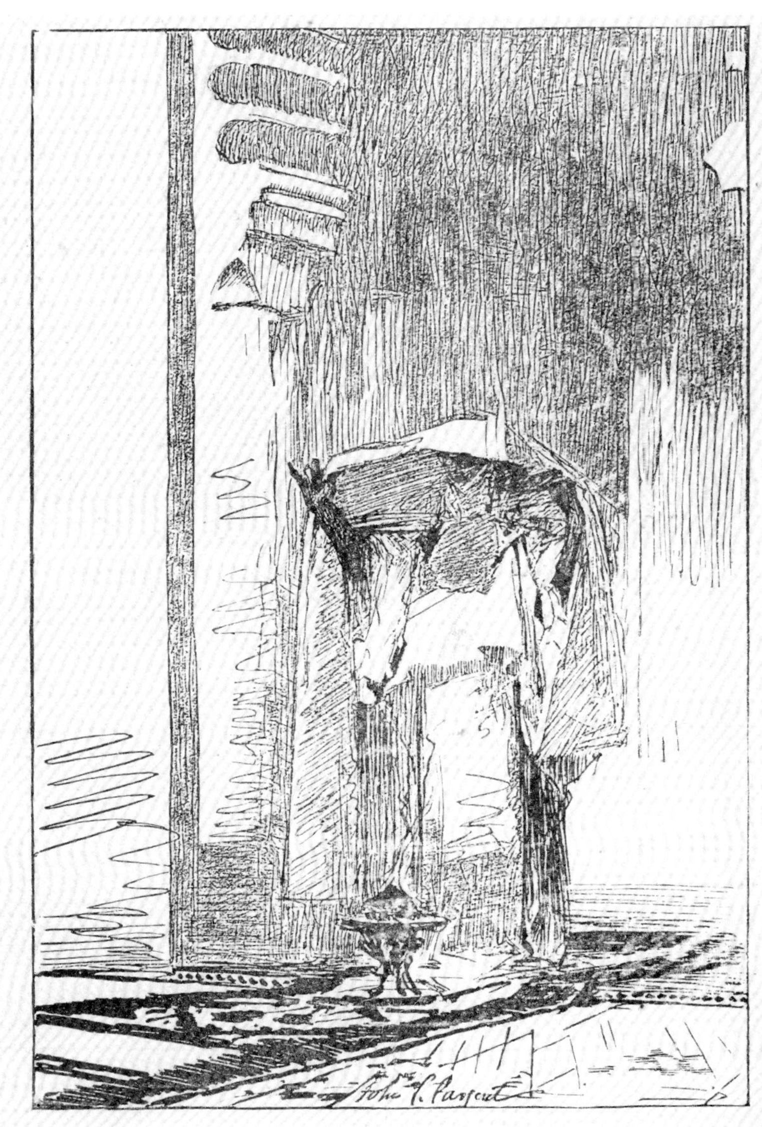

Fig. 119 Reproduction of Sargent's oil *Fumée d'ambre gris* (1880, Sterling and Francine Clark Art Institute, Williamstown, Massachusetts). P. 60 verso in the John Singer Sargent Scrapbook (50.130.154). The Metropolitan Museum of Art, Gift of Mrs Francis Ormond, 1950.

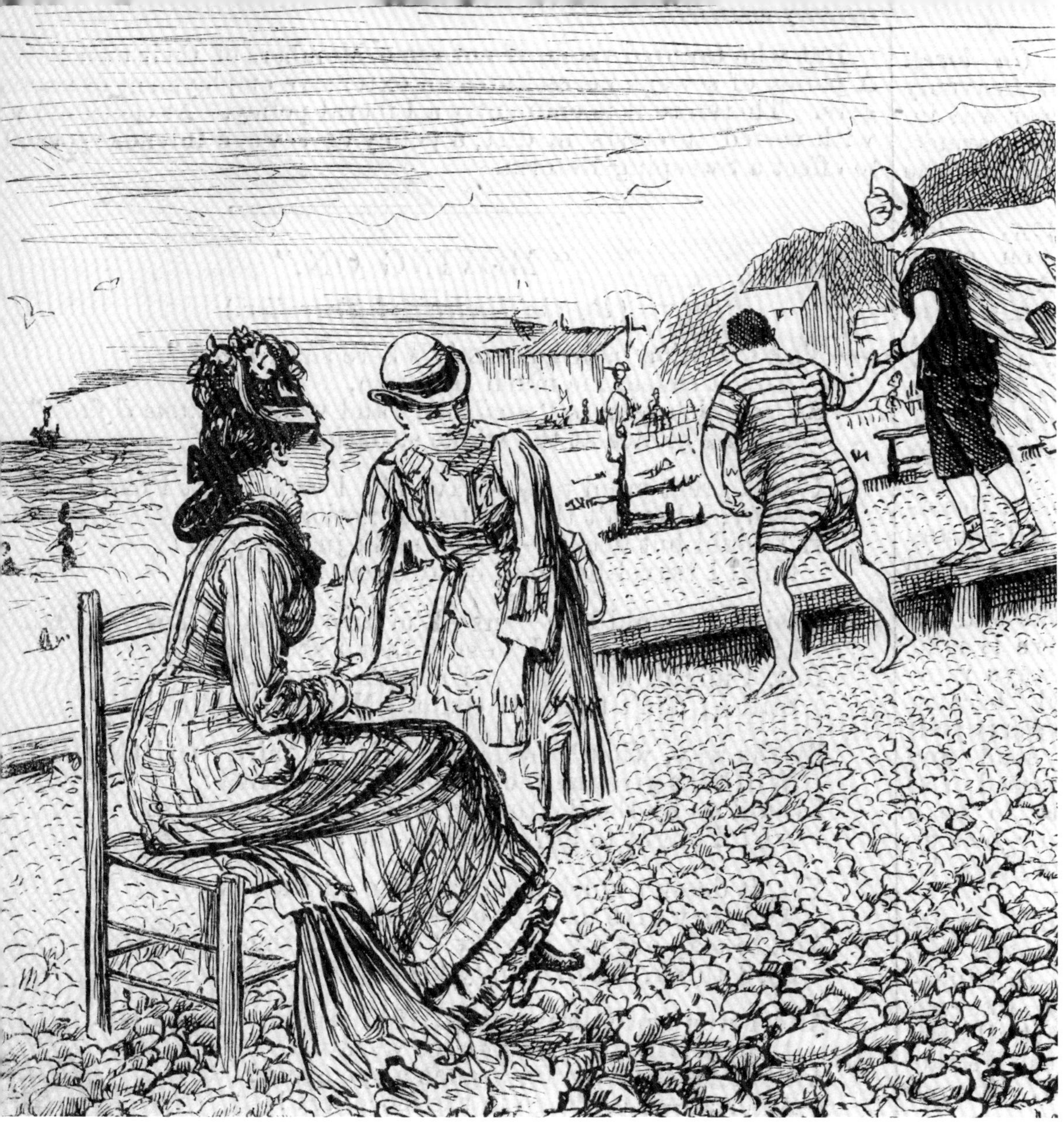

Fig. 120 Detail of fig. 118, George du Maurier (1834–1896), *A Linguistic Opportunity*, 1877. P. 40 recto in the John Singer Sargent Scrapbook (50.130.154). The Metropolitan Museum of Art. Gift of Mrs Francis Ormond, 1950.

years has, in our opinion, been more exquisite in quality."[32]

By using an album to collect, organize, and preserve drawings, Sargent was following a time-honored tradition dating back to the Renaissance when artist and critic Giorgio Vasari had encouraged the practice of gathering drawings in albums as an educational tool.[33] By storing ephemera for future reference and enjoyment, Sargent participated in the relatively modern phenomenon of scrapbooking. In his conflation of artistic tradition and modern fad, the artist created a unique source book that he must have intended to turn and return to for ideas and inspiration.

By the mid-nineteenth century, scrapbook making was an established phenomenon. Advances in color-printing technology and commercial photography accounted for the proliferation of printed ephemera. Contemporary periodicals and publications lamented the fleeting quality and large volume of such materials while extolling the virtues of preserving choice bits in scrapbooks for later viewing. In 1892 a writer for *Harper's Monthly* wondered, "must we all go to making scrap-books in order to preserve the good things that fly on the leaves on the winged press?"[34] Significantly, the creation of a scrapbook implies that the material gathered will be not only preserved but referred to again. In 1879 a writer for *Harper's Bazaar* compared reviewing one's scrapbook with a journey, exclaiming, "[t]hen ten minutes with one's scrapbook are like a voyage, a scientific convocation, an evening with the poets—any form of recreation that the tired mind desires—and the shabby home-made cyclopedia becomes the freshest book in the library."[35]

As Sargent's habit of collecting images overlapped with his compulsive tendency to sketch and record the world around him, a scrapbook must have seemed like an ideal method to preserve choice material. Since the vast quantity of clippings assembled by the artist in the album pertains to works of art and architecture, it seems that he may have intended the book to be a sort of personal reference museum or an idiosyncratic textbook of art history. By prominently including his marine drawings in the scrapbook, he established his desire to be able to return to them later and endowed them with a privileged position in his œuvre.

Contemporary scrapbook makers realized the personal nature of their creations. As one writer acknowledged in 1875, "by looking through a book which another has read and marked, or by inspecting a museum of selections which he has thrown into a scrapbook, we may somewhat minutely read the person's character, though we have never seen him."[36] Sargent's scrapbook reveals his interests and inspirations at a particular and significant moment in his life—the beginning of his professional career. One of the latest datable clippings in the album is a reproduction of his 1880 painting, *Fumée d'ambre gris* (fig. 119). For such a young and unestablished artist to have a work reproduced was a momentous occurrence.[37] As such, he preserved the image among his very personal collection of works by great masters. It is ironic that, for Sargent, having his painting reproduced as ephemera must have seemed a measure of his artistic achievement.

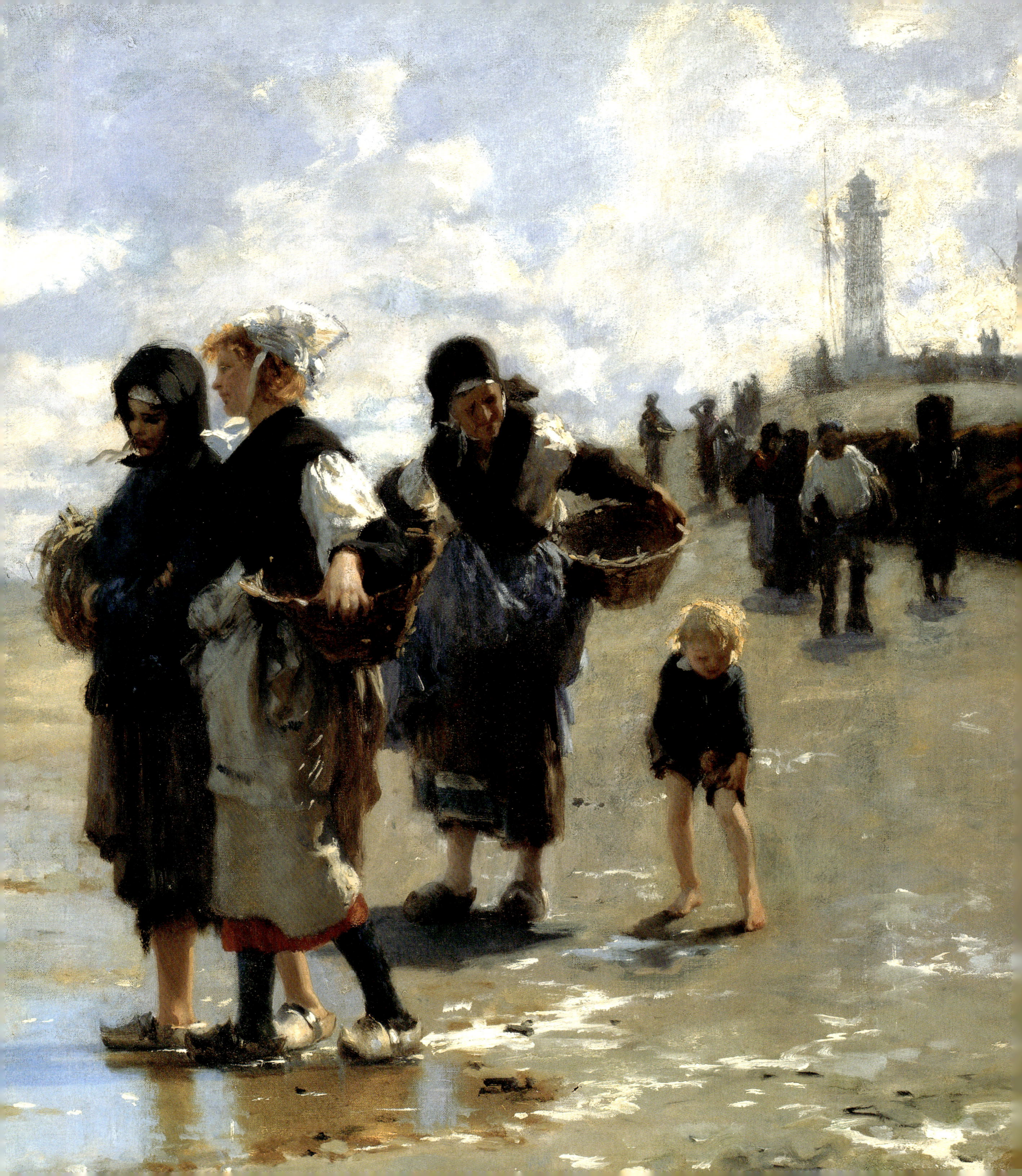

Testing the Waters: Sargent and Cancale

SARAH CASH

In the spring of 1878 the young John Singer Sargent announced his arrival on the burgeoning international art scene in a deliberate and unusual manner, choosing to exhibit his first two subject pictures—and at that depicting the same subject—in rapid succession, one on each side of the Atlantic. For his first work shown in the United States he submitted *Fishing for Oysters at Cancale* (fig. 122; now in the Museum of Fine Arts, Boston) to the inaugural exhibition of the newly formed Society of American Artists (SAA) in New York City, held at the Kurtz Gallery from 6 March to 5 April. *En Route pour la pêche* (fig. 123; in the collection of the Corcoran Gallery of Art, Washington), nearly twice the size of its companion painting, was Sargent's second submission to the prestigious Paris Salon, which opened on 25 May and closed on 19 August. Similar in composition and general appearance—though different in finish and detail—the two paintings present a picturesque view of women and children setting out to gather fruits of the sea at low tide in the small Breton fishing town of Cancale. While the impression conveyed is one of freshness and facile execution, the canvases resulted from an extensive, methodical endeavor. No fewer than twelve preparatory and related works in oil and pencil begun or produced wholly in Brittany in the summer of 1877 culminated, over the ensuing months in the artist's Paris studio, in the two exhibition pictures. These sparkling performances, created by an artist of just twenty-two, prefigured Sargent's legendary and prodigious œuvre.

Expanding on past discussions of this seminal body of work, which until recently have focused primarily on the Boston and Corcoran canvases, this essay will investigate in depth Sargent's choice of subject, title, style, and exhibition venue for the two paintings.[1] By attempting to reconstruct the artist's experience and working methods in Cancale and Paris, it will probe his artistic and market intentions when producing his first large body of work devoted to one subject.

In late June of 1877 Sargent embarked on an extended painting trip, journeying 250 miles west of Paris to Cancale, in northern Brittany.[2] The artist planned the expedition carefully and, as we now know, with a very specific purpose in mind: to prepare for the development, upon return to his studio at summer's end, of one or more paintings that he could exhibit publicly the following spring. He must have planned, at least, to submit an entry to the annual Salon exhibition in order to build on his successful debut there the previous year. By 5 June he "expect[ed] to spend some time at Cancale," wrote his sister Emily, "where he has to go to make studies."[3] Sargent remained there until about 20 August, making the

Facing page: Fig. 121 Detail of fig. 123, *En Route pour la pêche (Setting Out to Fish)*, 1878. Corcoran Gallery of Art, Washington, D.C., Museum Purchase, Gallery Fund, 17.2. (Exhibition)

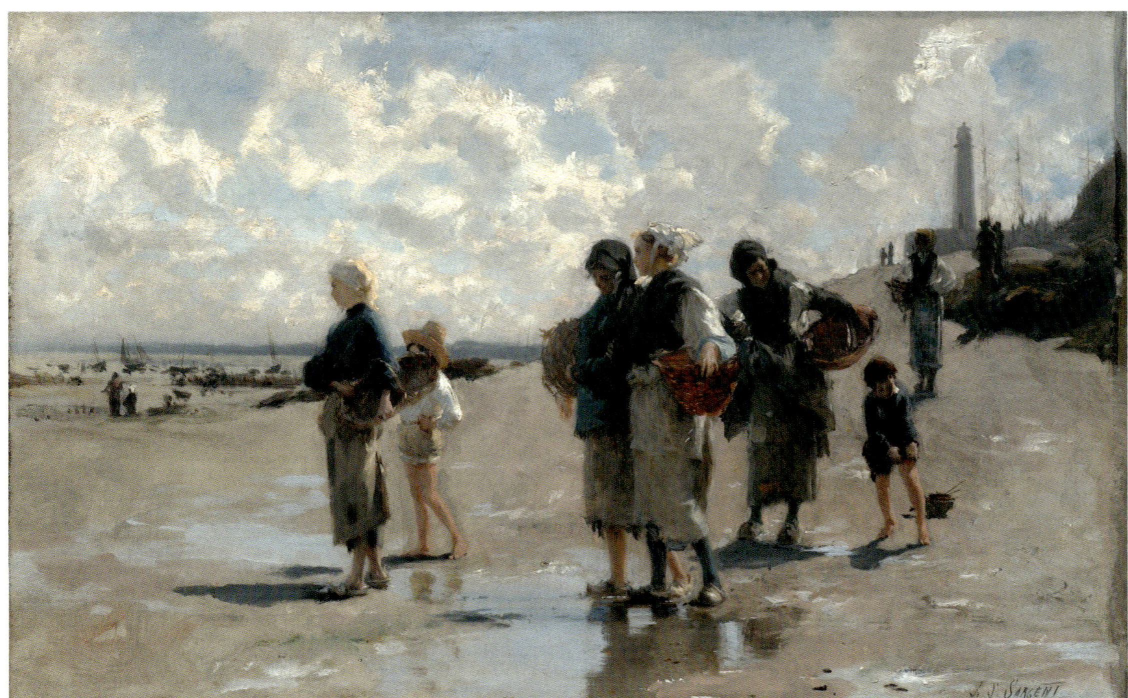

Fig. 122 *Fishing for Oysters at Cancale*, 1877–78. Oil on canvas, 16⅛ × 24 in (41 × 61 cm). Inscribed, lower right: *J. S. SARGENT / PARIS.* Museum of Fine Arts, Boston. Gift of Miss Mary Appleton, 35.708. (Exhibition)

Fig. 123 *En Route pour la pêche (Setting Out to Fish)*, 1878. Oil on canvas, 31⅛ × 48⅜ in (78.8 × 122.8 cm). Inscribed, lower right: *JOHN S. SARGENT. / PARIS 1878.* Corcoran Gallery of Art, Washington, D.C., Museum Purchase, Gallery Fund, 17.2. (Exhibition)

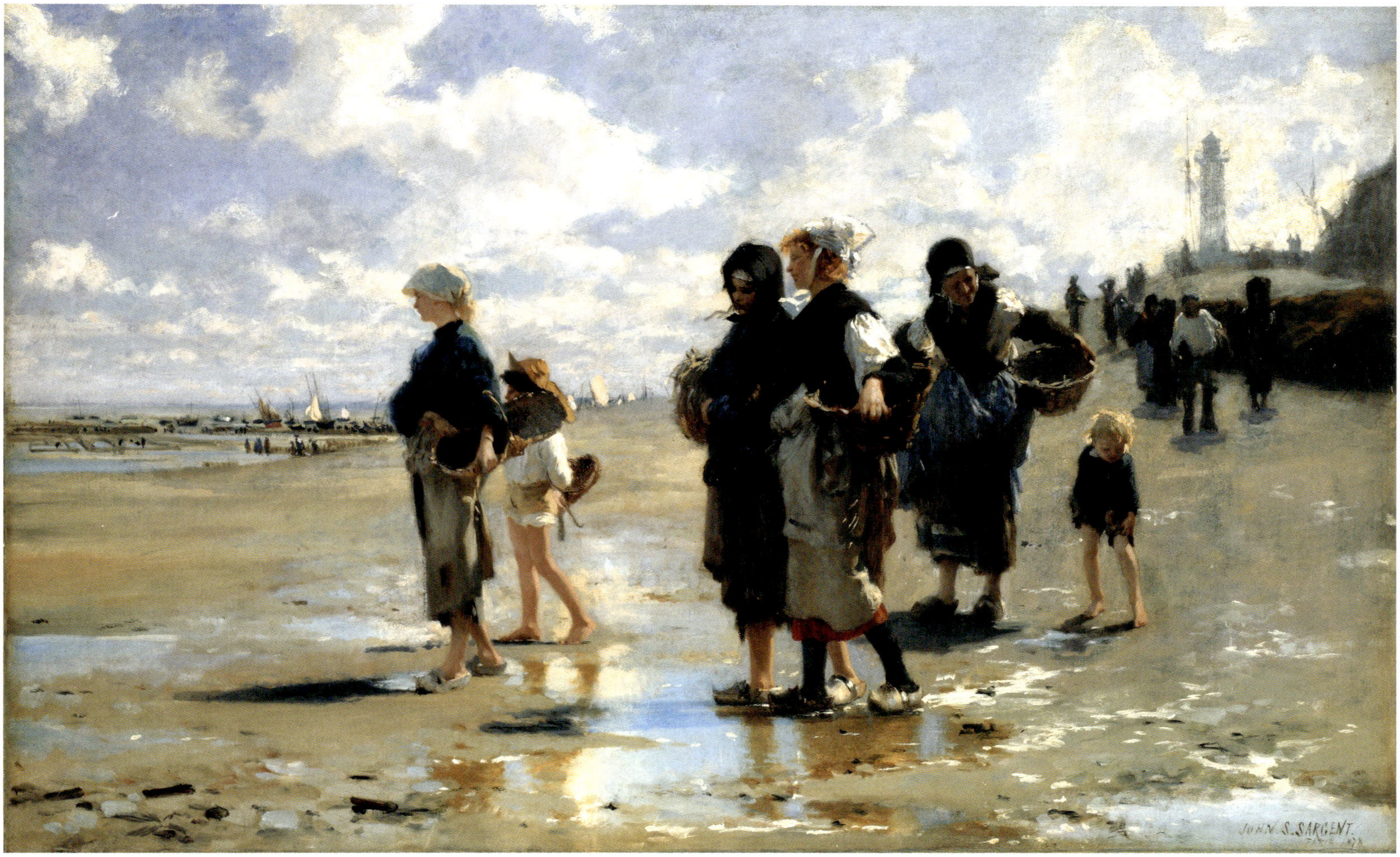

two-month extended sketching and painting trip his longest to date spent in one place.[4] Moreover, he undertook it without the customary company (or distraction) of his peripatetic family, who remained in Paris, traveling instead with his fellow art student, Eugène Lachaise (1857–1925). These factors alone constituted an important artistic milestone and signaled a step toward the independence of professional life. The large body of work that Sargent produced on the trip underscores his ambitious goals.

The artist had had multiple opportunities to consider picturesque Cancale, on Brittany's northern Emerald Coast, as a painting venue. He may have made a note of the town, or perhaps even passed through or near it, during a visit to nearby Saint-Énogat and surrounding areas with his family during the summer of 1875.[5] He surely was aware of the town's reputation, since ancient times, for superb and plentiful oysters; it had long been recognized in Europe and elsewhere, in his father's words, as "the famous oyster garden of France."[6] Oyster harvesting in Cancale, a tourist attraction in Sargent's time as now, was then performed on specific days of the year. Cancalaise men traveling in fleets, or *caravanes*, of flat-bottomed sailboats unique to the Bay of Mont-Saint-Michel called *bisquines*, would dredge enormous amounts of oysters from the bay (fig. 124). After the *bisquines* dumped their loads into the harbor, Cancalaise women and children would purge the catch of empty shells, starfish, algae, and rocks (fig. 125). They would then place the oysters in wooden and stone structures (*parcs*) for further cleaning, sorting by size, counting, and the preparation of orders before hauling them to shore for sale or shipment. The dramatic processions of departing or returning *caravanes* and of peasants engaged in such shoreline pursuits were as picturesque as the surroundings in which they were undertaken. Although the working town of Cancale was not a major destination for artists of the era, who generally preferred

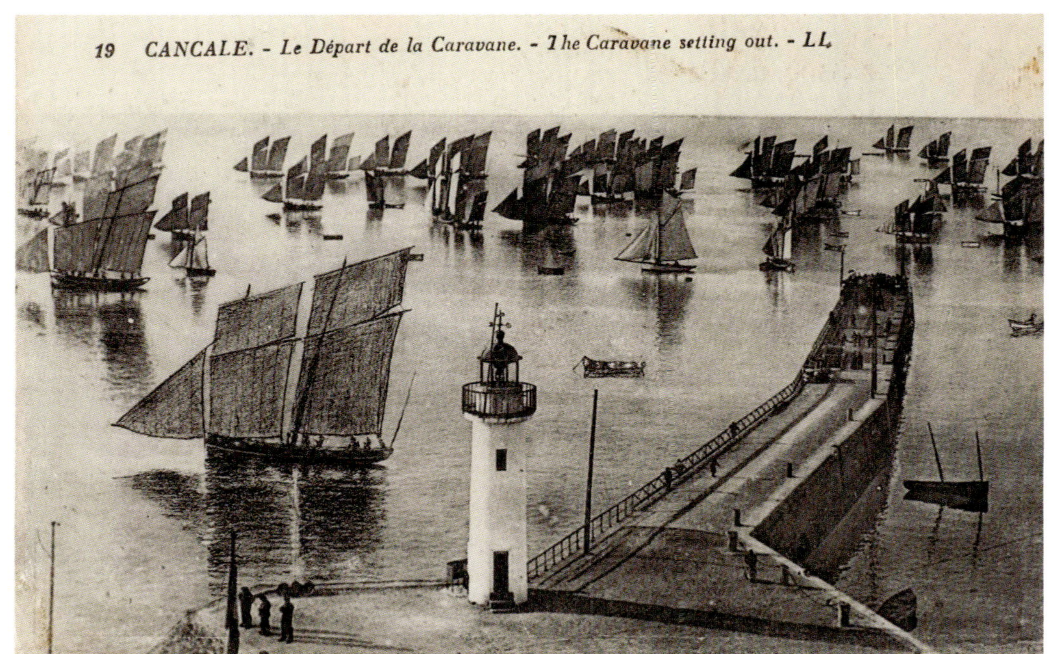

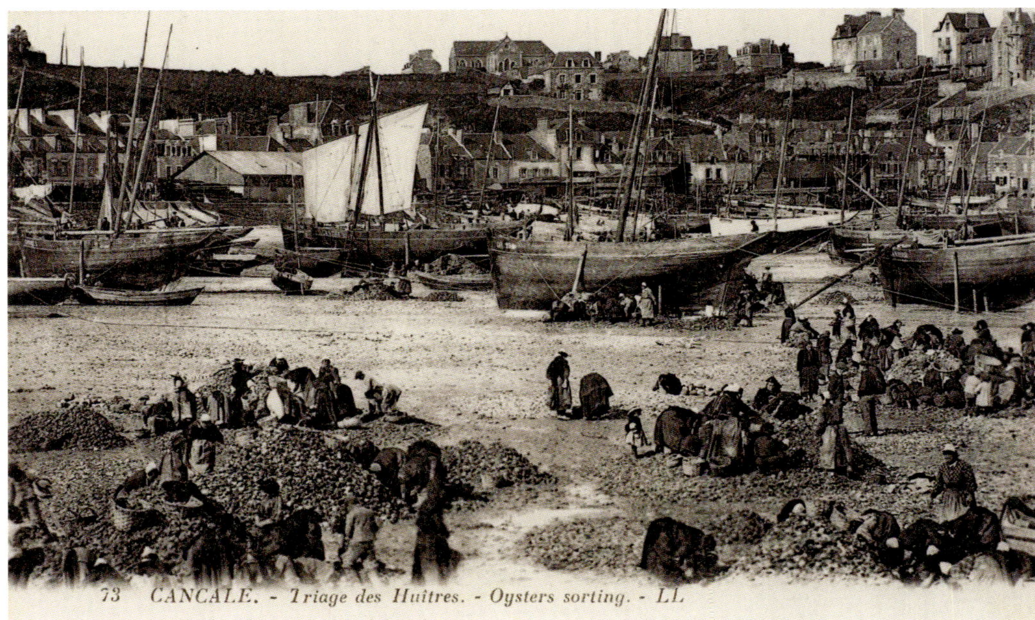

Fig. 124 Postcard showing the Departure of the Caravane at Cancale, *c.*1900–1910. Collection of John McCabe, www.oysters.us.

Fig. 125 Postcard showing oyster sorting, Cancale, *c.*1900–1910. Collection of John McCabe, www.oysters.us.

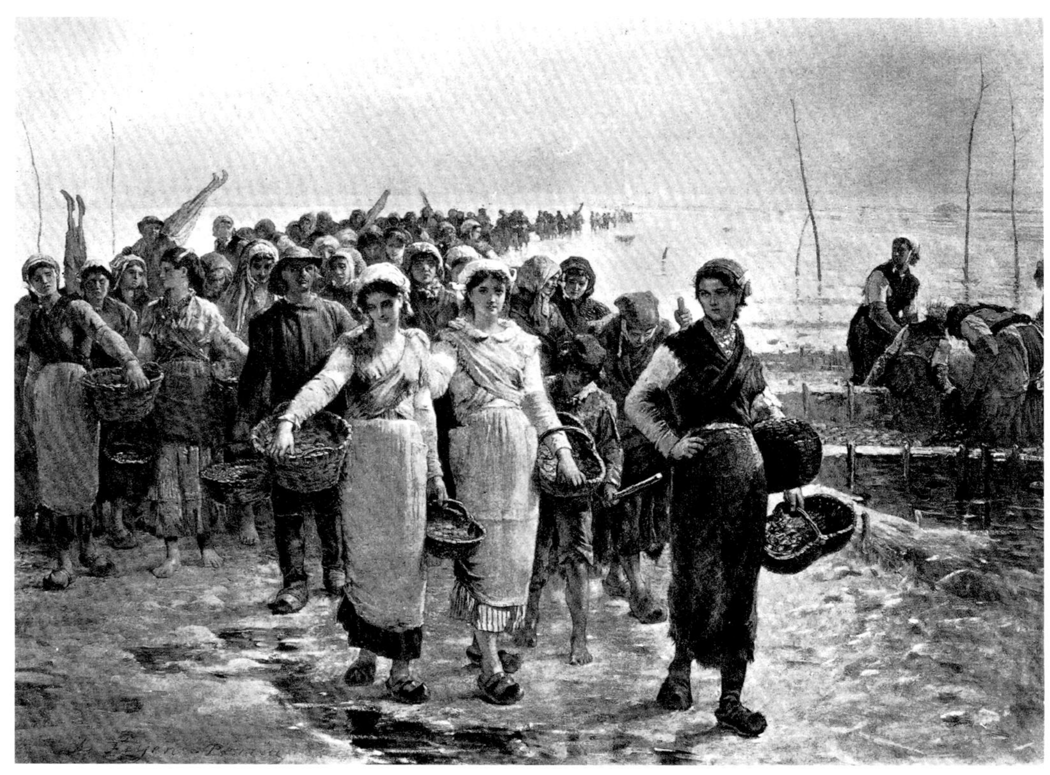

Fig. 126 François-Nicolas-Augustin Feyen-Perrin (1826–1888), *Retour de la pêche aux huîtres par les grandes marées à Cancale (Return of the oyster fishers at Cancale)*, *c.* 1874. Oil on canvas, 58⅞ × 78¾ in (149 × 200 cm). Formerly Musée du Luxembourg, Paris. Untraced.

resorts such as Pont-Aven, at the Salon Sargent may have seen paintings by several artists depicting Cancale's fishing and oystering activities. Most notably, the French brothers Eugène Feyen (1815?–1908) and François-Nicolas-Augustin Feyen-Perrin (1826–1888) made something of a specialty of the latter subject. As Richard Ormond has noted, Sargent may well have seen Eugène Feyen's scene of oyster gatherers, *Les Glaneuses de la mer* (1872, French Senate), in the Salon of 1872, or his younger brother's entry into the 1874 Salon, the imposing *Retour de la pêche aux huîtres par les grandes marées à Cancale* (fig. 126); each was purchased from its respective Salon for the Musée du Luxembourg, an honor that no doubt received considerable attention. The few other artists exhibiting Cancale fishing views included Karl-Pierre Daubigny (1846–1886), Marie-Auguste Flameng (1843–1893), and Émile-Louis Vernier (1829–1887), each of whom submitted two such scenes to Salons between 1874 and 1877.[7] Oystering and fishing subjects proved quite popular among painters of Sargent's time, when canvases depicting peasants engaged in any manner of agricultural or market activity held great nostalgic appeal for an increasingly urban French public.[8]

Little in Sargent's past, however, could have prepared him for his experience upon arrival in the small town. A first view from his coach or boat ride from the Saint-Malo train station, just nine miles west, would have revealed the graceful topography of Cancale (fig. 127). There, the refined upper town, *la bourge*, where grand homes of wealthy boat owners surround the market square, gives way to the curving port below, *la houle*, populated by fisherfolk. A long day's journey would have been rewarded, at the Hôtel de l'Europe (now Hôtel la Mère Champlain), with a view of the active shoreline and the vast Bay of Mont-Saint-Michel beyond.[9] In the other direction, at the northeast edge of the port, Sargent would have discovered a granite lighthouse,

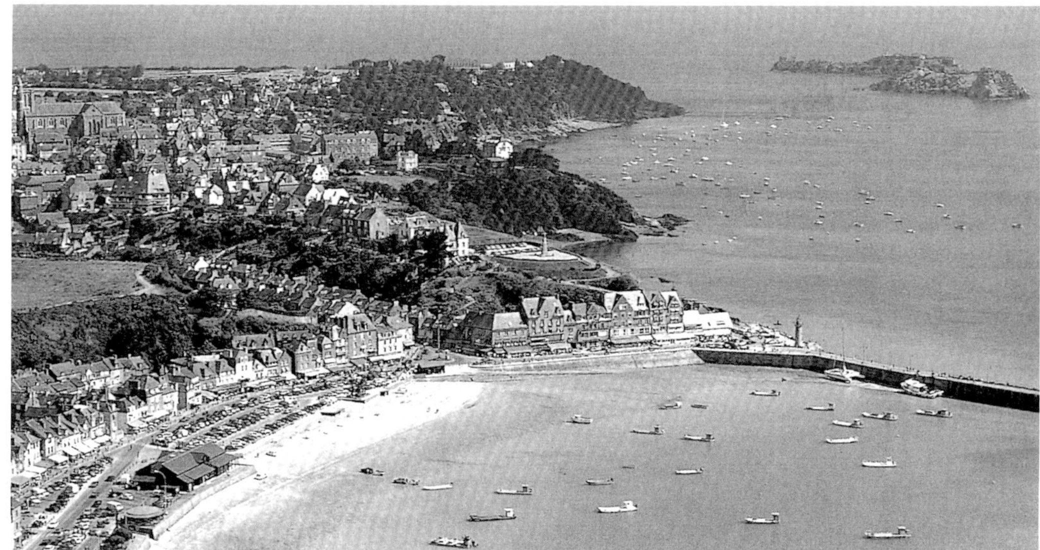

Fig. 127 Postcard with aerial view of Cancale (showing upper and lower town). John Singer Sargent Catalogue Raisonné Archive.

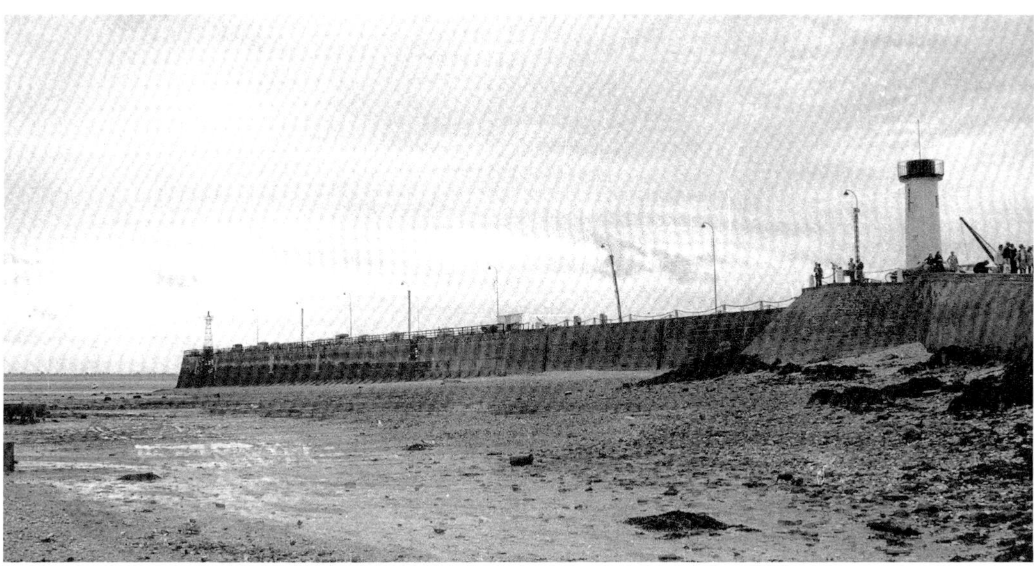

Fig. 128 Photograph of the beach at Cancale, with lighthouse and quay, *c.* 1971. John Singer Sargent Catalogue Raisonné Archive. This is roughly the view depicted in *Fishing for Oysters at Cancale* and *En Route pour la pêche*; the lighthouse was there in Sargent's time, but not the long jetty.

built in 1863, from which a quay and short jetty, known as La Fenêtre, led down to the water; the scene is much the same today, though with a second lighthouse at the tip of a longer jetty. The slipway leading to a broad beach on the other side of this barrier from the port would provide Sargent with his vantage point (fig. 128) for *En Route pour la pêche* and *Fishing for Oysters at Cancale*.

Nature's grandeur would have been surpassed only by that of her awe-inspiring changes; while exploring the port, Sargent and Lachaise would have absorbed the remarkable sights and sounds of the area's dramatic tides. With the greatest tidal mean range in Europe and one of the largest in the world, waters can rise fifty feet from their lowest level.[10] Accordingly, the intertidal zone is vast; high tide meets the edge of the lower town before receding up to six miles in some locations, giving way to vast stretches of muddy seashore.[11] Occupying a liminal space between land and sea, Cancale was the perfect spot for Sargent—the memories of his recent seaside and transatlantic journeys still fresh—to prepare intensively for the first subject pictures of his career.

Assuming that he was aware of the village's reputation as an "oyster garden" and of at least some contemporary depictions of Cancale fishing subjects, Sargent must have been somewhat disappointed to find that peasants intent on harvesting oysters were nowhere to be seen. Whether dredged by boat or harvested from *parcs*,

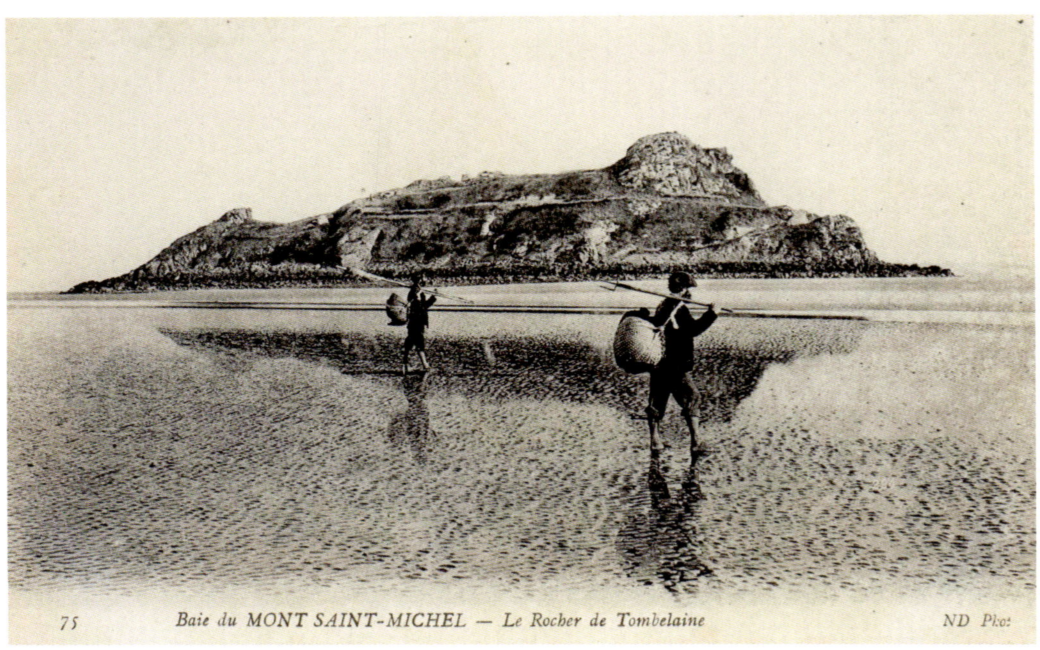

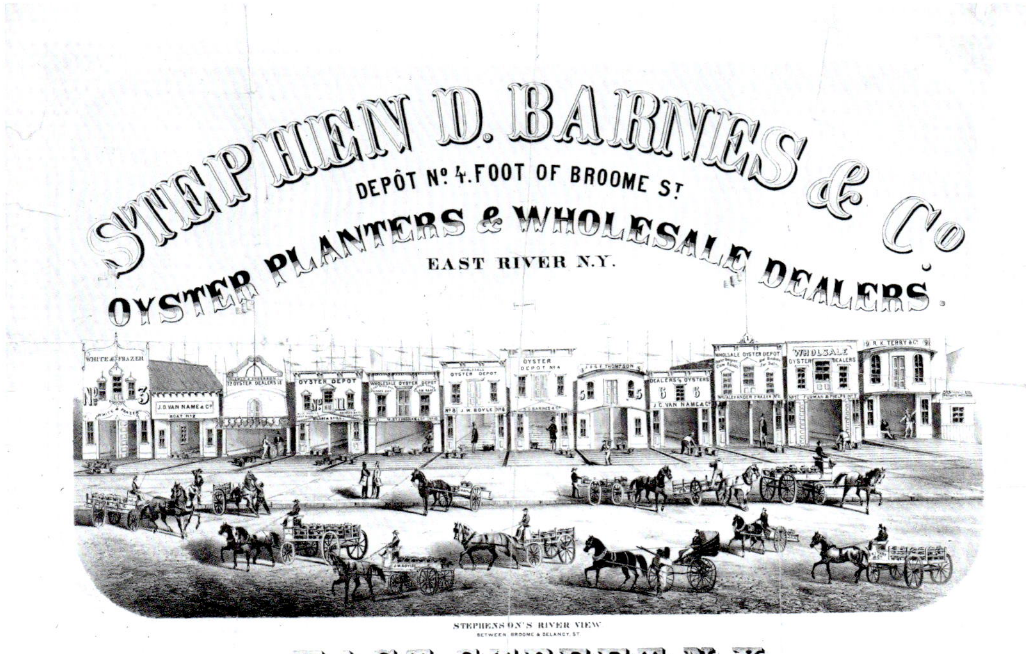

Fig. 129 Postcard of men fishing on foot in the exposed tide-flats near Mont-Saint-Michel, *c.*1900–1910. Collection of John McCabe, www.oysters.us.

Fig. 130 Probably W. Stephenson and Co., New York, publisher, *Stephenson's River View: Stephen D. Barnes & Co.*, *c.* 1854–56, lithograph. 17 ½ x 24 in. (44 x 61 cm). Collection of The New-York Historical Society. Bella C. Landauer Collection of Business and Advertising Ephemera.

the collection of oysters and, by extension, their sale, was strictly prohibited in Cancale (and elsewhere in France) by order of the government during the summer months, precisely the time of Sargent's visit.[12] These centuries-old regulations were intended to protect the oyster population, weakened and not prime for eating during their egg-laying season, and were also important in mitigating the effects of long-standing overfishing.

As quickly as Sargent realized that he would have to alter his artistic plans for the summer, he must have recognized that there was no dearth of shoreline activity to observe and sketch in preparation for his exhibition pictures. During these non-harvest months, women were tasked with cleaning out the beds, repositioning any oysters moved around by the tides, and repairing the *parcs*.[13] Moreover, although oysters are the most famous product of Cancale, other fruits of the sea are plentiful there. The artist would have seen women and children, and perhaps a few older men not away on summer fishing expeditions, foraging for the makings of their dinner when low tide exposed vast public tidelands (fig. 129). They would have found shrimp, clams, mussels, crabs, sea snails, scallops, small fish, seaweed, and possibly the occasional oyster, all either washed up on shore or trapped in pools left by the receding tide such as those seen in Sargent's finished paintings.[14]

It is this precise subject that Sargent described in his title for the Corcoran picture when he showed it at the Salon of 1878.[15] *En Route pour la pêche*, translated as "Setting Out to Fish," emphasizes the path or procession toward fishing, most likely on foot, or *la pêche à pied*. Although he undoubtedly had planned to create for the Salon a painting of peasants setting out for, or returning from, fishing for oysters, or *la pêche aux huîtres*, the artist ultimately must have been pleased that his submission's subject and title differed markedly from those of artists like the Feyen brothers.[16] His congenial group of well-scrubbed peasants, meandering along the shore against a glistening backdrop of summer weather, stands in stark contrast to the brothers' somber portrayals of masses of women returning weary from the physically demanding pursuit of cleaning and hauling oysters.

For his display of the smaller painting in his first-ever American exhibition, the artist chose a title carefully calculated to appeal to a vastly different audience. *Fishing for Oysters at Cancale* would have held special meaning for the viewers he was especially eager to impress. For during the second half of the nineteenth century New York was the epicenter of America's oyster-mania, a fact that could not have escaped Sargent during his 1876 visit to nearby Philadelphia and Newport, cities also caught up in the craze.[17] Inexpensive and ubiquitous, the bivalves were the most popular seafood in the country; the United States was their largest producer worldwide before dire overfishing culminated late in the century. Articles in the popular press provided detailed descriptions of the various types of oysters and how they were harvested; inventoried the vast numbers procured, shipped, and consumed; marveled at the speed at which shuckers could work; and offered recipes for roasting, broiling, and stewing oysters, which often comprised two dinners a week for the average American family.[18] Visitors to the SAA's inaugural exhibition surely would have appreciated in the painting's title not only the reference to oysters but also to their best-known European source, Cancale. In all things oyster-related, New York may well have seen itself during this period as the American counterpart of the Breton port (figs. 130, 131). New York led the country's export of the bivalve, shipping, for example, 76 million to England annually by 1882;[19] it boasted oyster cellars on nearly every street corner, advertised by red muslin balloons; it was home to vast floating wholesale oyster markets along the Hudson and East rivers,

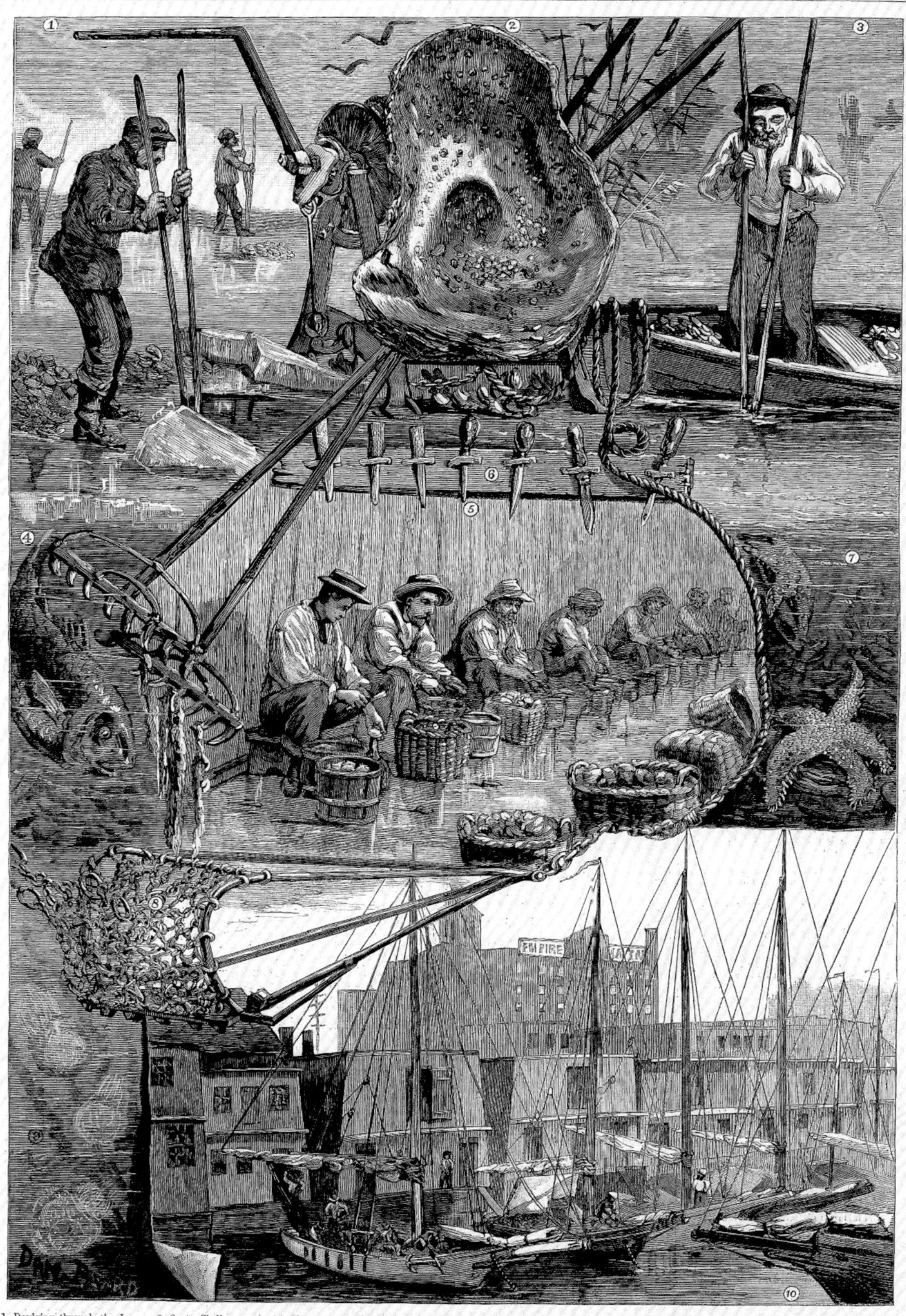
584 HARPER'S WEEKLY. VOLUME XXVI., NO. 1343.

1. Dredging through the Ice. 2. Oyster-Shell covered with Young. 3. Dredging from a Boat. 4. Drum-Fish. 5. Opening Oysters for Export. 6. Oyster Knives. 7. Star-Fish. 8. Dredge. 9. Young Oysters. 10. Oyster Sloops at foot of West Tenth Street.

OPENING OF THE OYSTER SEASON.—Drawn by Dan. Beard.—[See Page 582.]

Fig. 131 Daniel Beard, print of the oyster industry in *Harper's Weekly* (September 16, 1882), p. 584.

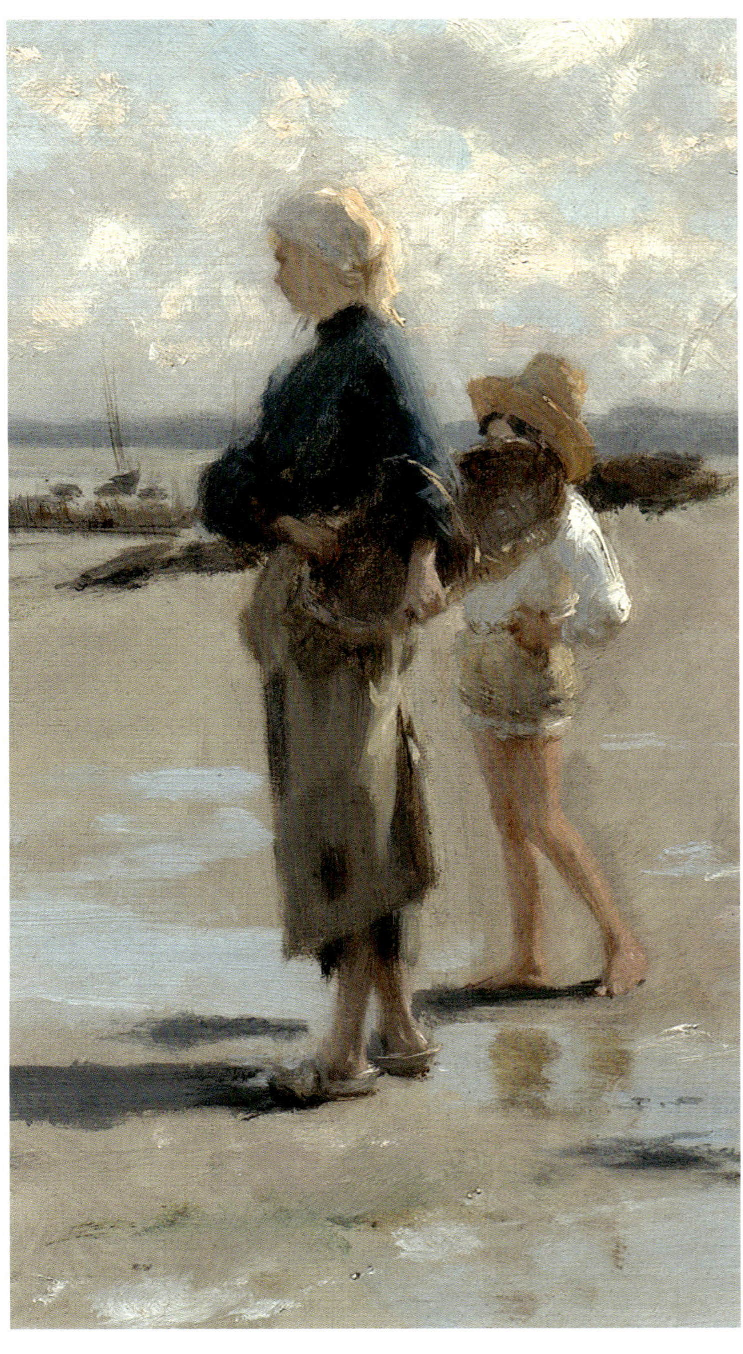

Fig. 132 Detail of fig. 123, *En Route pour la pêche (Setting Out to Fish)*, 1878. Corcoran Gallery of Art, Washington, D.C., Museum Purchase, Gallery Fund, 17.2. (Exhibition)

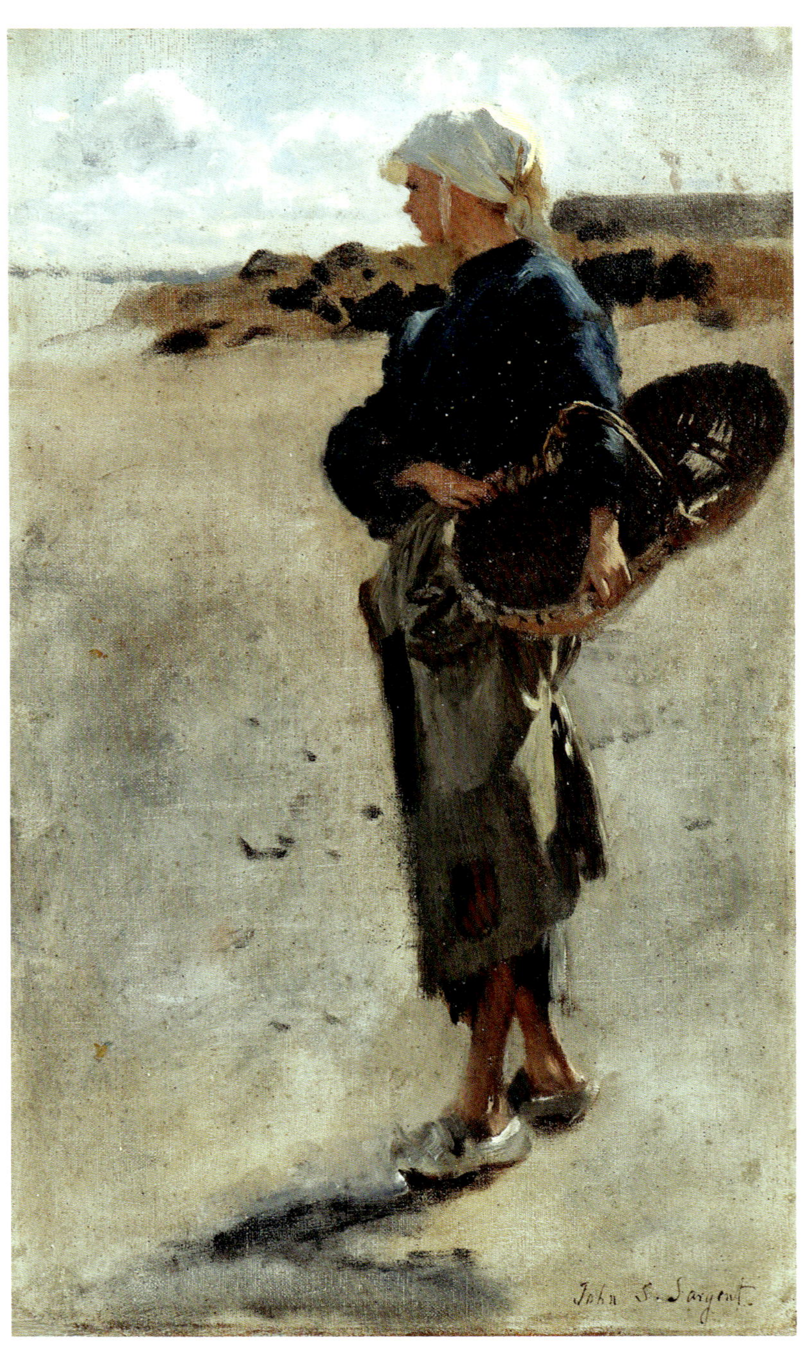

Fig. 133 *Breton Girl with a Basket,* study for *En Route pour la pêche* and *Fishing for Oysters at Cancale*, 1877. Oil on canvas, 19 × 11½ in (48.3 × 29.2 cm). Inscribed, lower right: *John S. Sargent.* Terra Foundation for American Art, Daniel J. Terra Collection, Chicago, 1999.129. (Exhibition)

comprised of highly ornamented two-story barges (see fig. 129); and it pioneered the cultivation of oysters after the destruction of their natural beds.[20] Sargent's deliberate titling of his two exhibition submissions perfectly aligns with the artist's well-documented campaign to advance his reputation on both sides of the Atlantic at this early and crucial point in his career.[21]

Sargent's known output of eleven preparatory sketches for the two exhibition pictures, the closely related canvas *Fisherwomen Returning* (fig. 150), and four works not directly related to the theme of the fishing excursion make it clear that he was pleased to have chosen Cancale as his summer destination.[22] The preliminary sketches include a plein air compositional sketch (fig. 145) and five figure studies in oil (figs. 133, 137, 140, 141, 143), which in turn appear to derive from a group of five pencil drawings (figs. 134, 135, 138, 142, 144). Their freshness of handling and close interrelationships suggest that all were executed on site in Cancale; as his father, Fitzwilliam, wrote to his sister Anna Maria on 20 August, the artist had "been busy in making drawings and sketches of the fishermen and fisherwomen, for pictures."[23] While no letters from Sargent's own hand survive from the trip, one from his sister Emily to Violet Paget of 29 July 1877 provides the most detail about the journey, and allows that the artist's first month was filled with challenges:

> He has had a good deal of rainy and cloudy weather at Cancale, which has interfered a great deal with his work, so he may be detained longer than he expected. He has great difficulty in finding people willing to pose, the married women never will, and they dislike their children to be painted, and the young girls rarely will consent. When he does find anyone willing, the crowd around him is so great, that he cannot work, so he has to make friends with

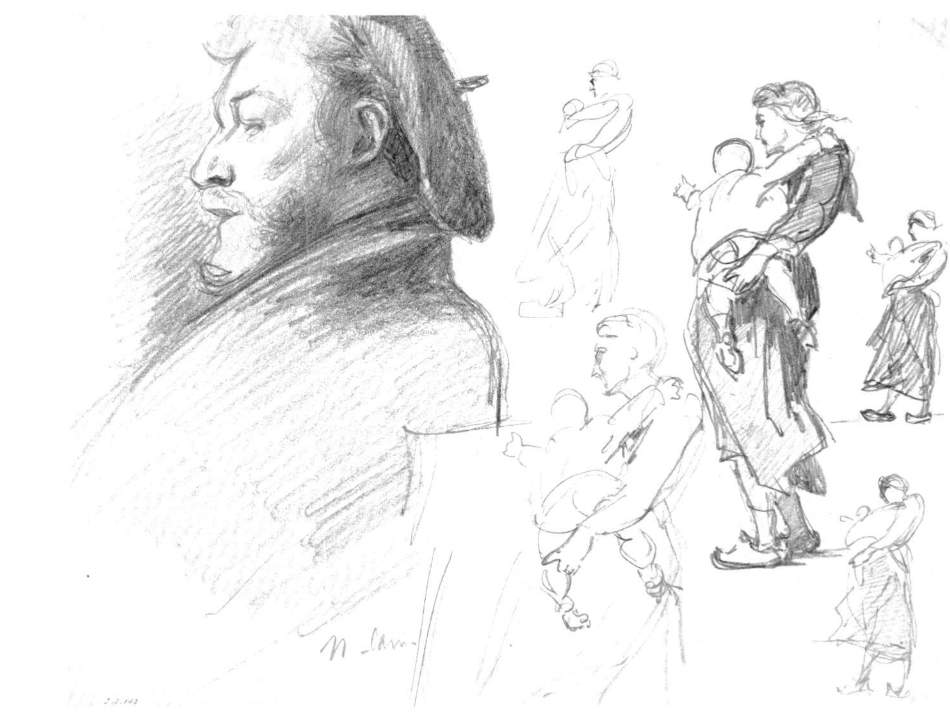

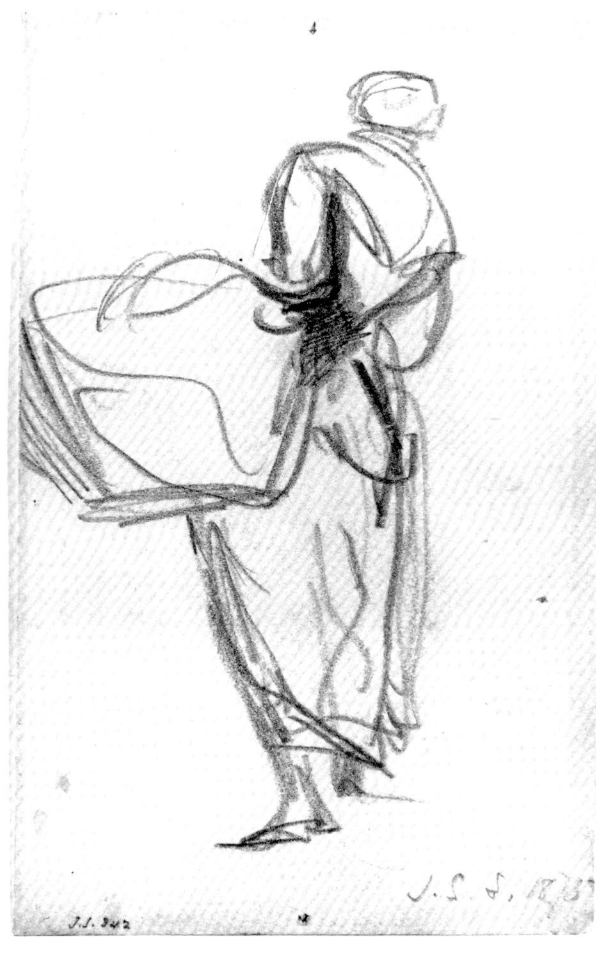

Fig. 134 *Portrait of Neville Cain and Study of Mother and Child*, 1877. Graphite on paper, 8⅞ × 11 in (22.6 × 27.9 cm). Harvard Art Museum, Fogg Art Museum, Gift of Miss Emily Sargent and Mrs Francis Ormond, in memory of their brother, John Singer Sargent, 1931.97. (Exhibition)

Fig. 135 *Woman with Basket*, 1877. Graphite on paper, 5⅝ × 3⁷⁄₁₆ in (14.3 × 8.7 cm). Inscribed, bottom right: *J.S.S. 1875*. The Metropolitan Museum of Art, Gift of Mrs Francis Ormond, 1950. (50.30.92) (Exhibition, Washington and Houston)

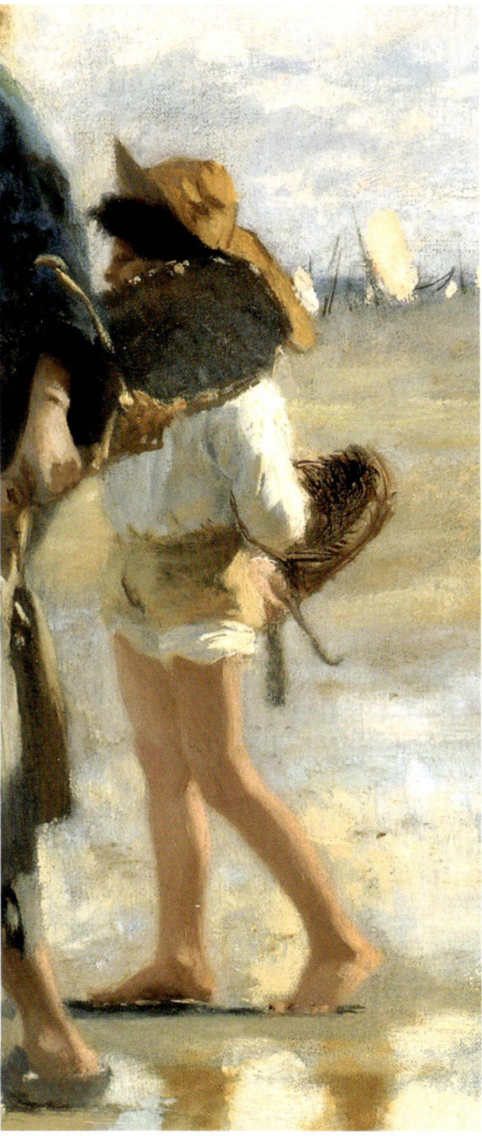

Fig. 136 Detail of fig. 123, *En Route pour la pêche (Setting Out to Fish)*, 1878. Corcoran Gallery of Art, Washington, D.C., Museum Purchase, Gallery Fund, 17.2. (Exhibition)

some old woman, and get her to let him paint in her court. An old French artist who has been going to Cancale for the last fifteen years, is at the same and only Hôtel there, and even he finds the same difficulty as John does, in spite of his age & experience. When he first went there, he says they were all willing to pose, but now they are so independent that a much higher price will not tempt them.[24]

As Richard Ormond has noted, the "old French artist" may well have been one of the Feyen brothers whose paintings of oyster gatherers had earned some renown in Paris.[25]

After transporting the entire group of studies back to his Paris studio in late August, Sargent populated the Boston and Corcoran canvases with selected large and small elements from each preparatory work. Such an orchestration of on-site oil studies into one or more studio compositions was consistent not only with Sargent's training under Carolus-Duran, but also with his working methods at this time in his career.[26] A close consideration of the many preliminary works and their relationships to the completed paintings suggests sequences of execution. Beginning at the left of the Boston and Corcoran canvases, we can trace the lead fisherwoman in a white cap (*coiffe*), blue jersey, and light skirt, who holds a basket on her left hip, back to one of the four oil studies in the Terra collection (figs. 132, 133). This study appears to derive from a sheet in the Fogg Art Museum of lightly sketched vignettes mostly describing a woman in Breton dress and clogs (*sabots*), seen in profile and balancing a child also on the left hip (fig. 134). A more emphatic and freely handled drawing of a woman with her back to the viewer holding a large basket on the same hip (fig. 135), in The Metropolitan Museum of Art, may have served as another antecedent for the Terra collection figure.[27]

The young boy paired with the lead figure in the exhibition pictures appears to be based directly on a second oil sketch in the Terra collection (fig. 137). This, in turn, likely followed a graphite study of a boy in a striped jersey and beret in the collection of The Metropolitan Museum of Art (fig. 138) that is similar in handling to the Fogg drawing just mentioned (see fig. 134). In

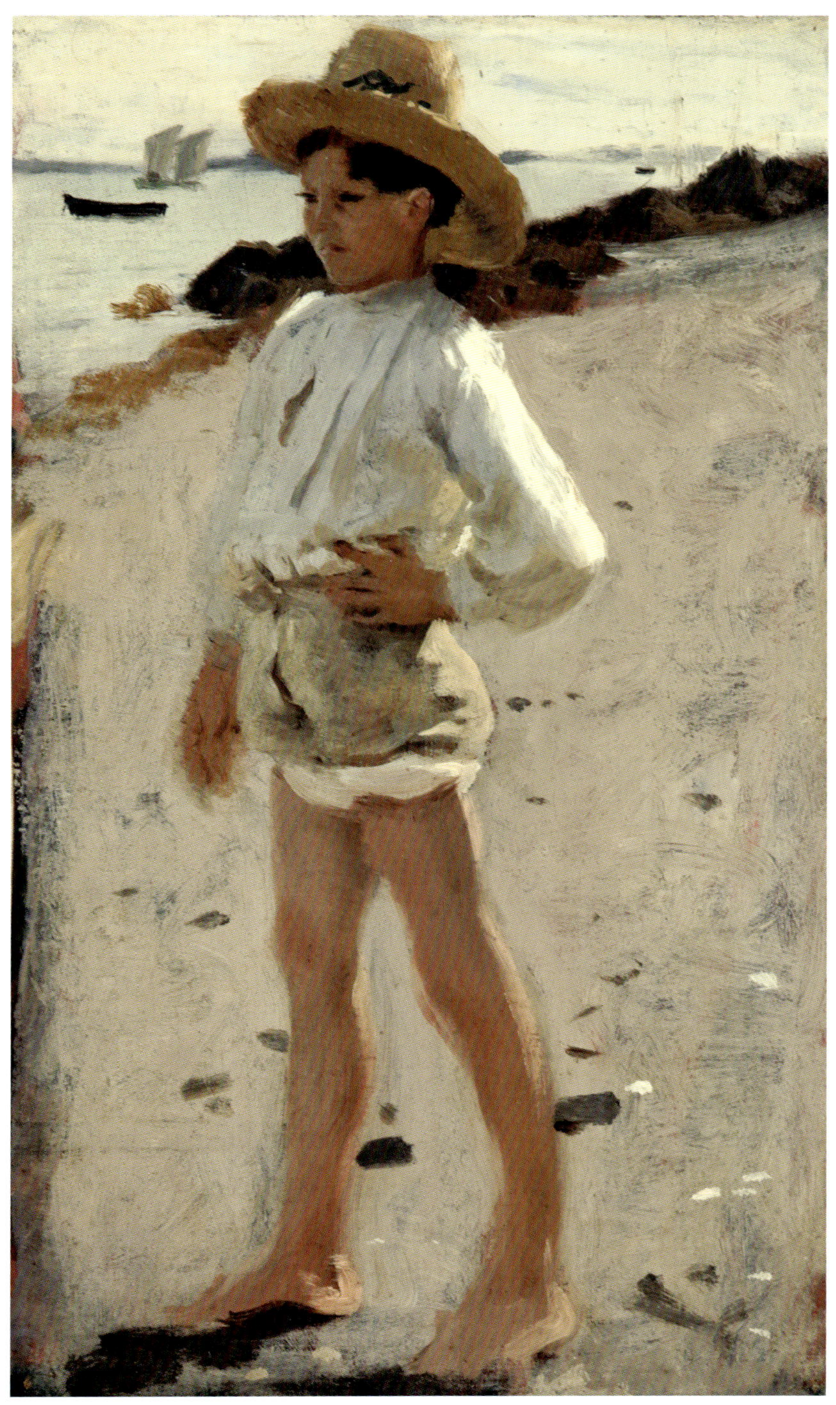

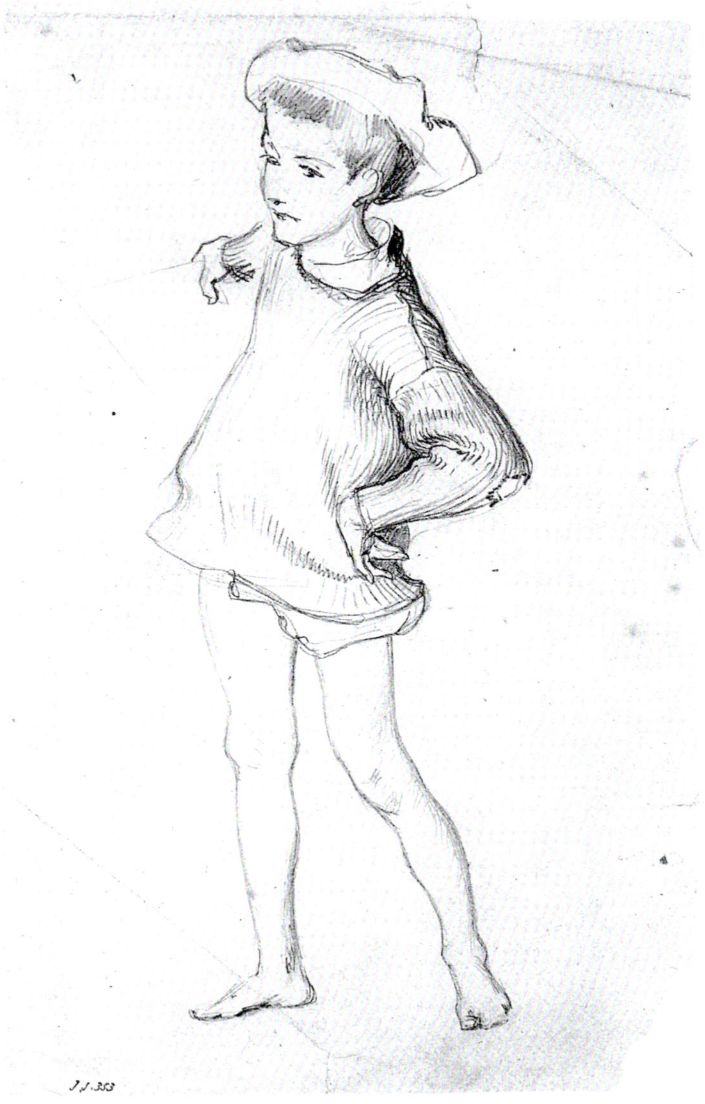

Fig. 137 *Young Boy on the Beach,* study for *En Route pour la pêche* and *Fishing for Oysters at Cancale*, 1877. Oil on canvas, 17¼ × 10¼ in (43.8 × 26 cm). Terra Foundation for American Art, Daniel J. Terra Collection, Chicago, 1999.132. (Exhibition)

Fig. 138 *Child*, study for *En Route pour la pêche* and *Fishing for Oysters at Cancale*, 1877. Graphite on paper, 8¼ × 5 in (21 × 12.7 cm). Inscribed, lower left: *J.S. 353*. The Metropolitan Museum of Art, Gift of Mrs Francis Ormond, 1950. (50.130.114) (Exhibition, Washington and Houston)

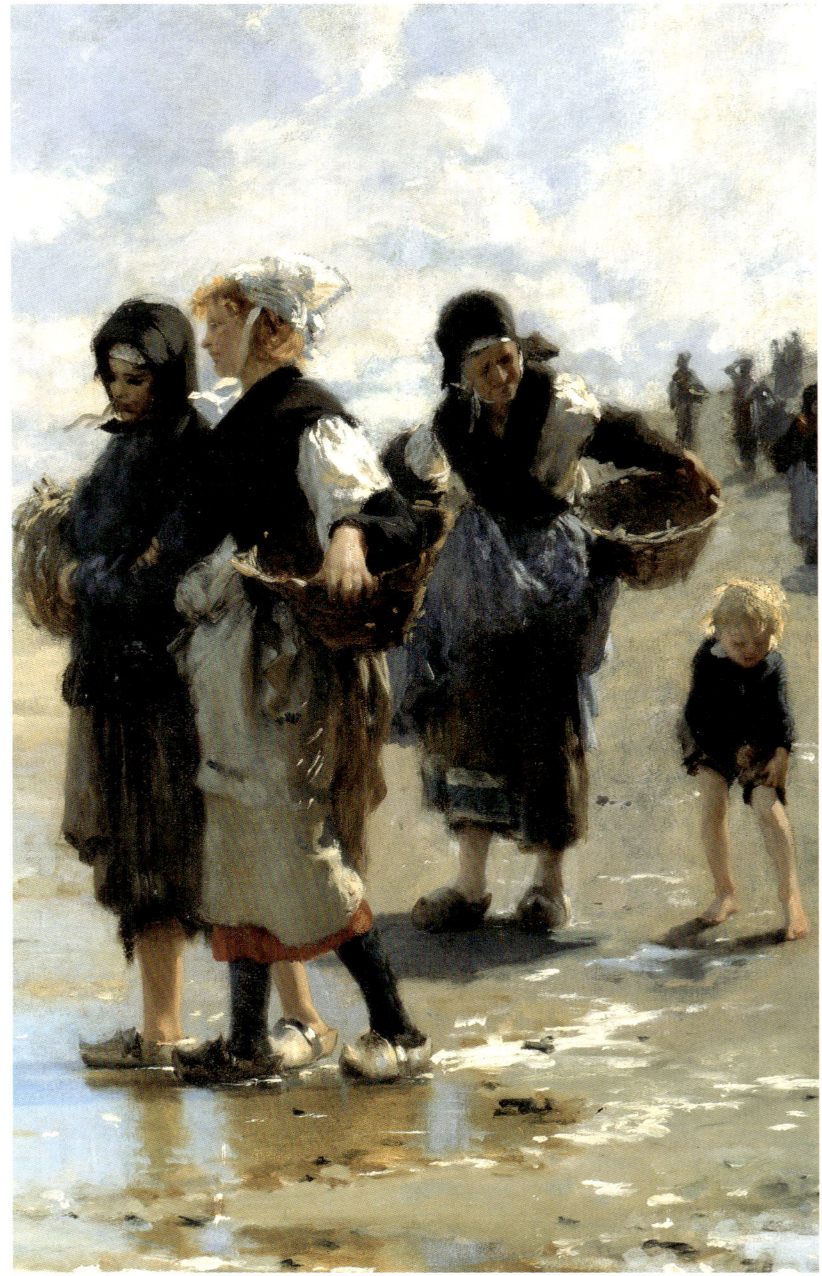

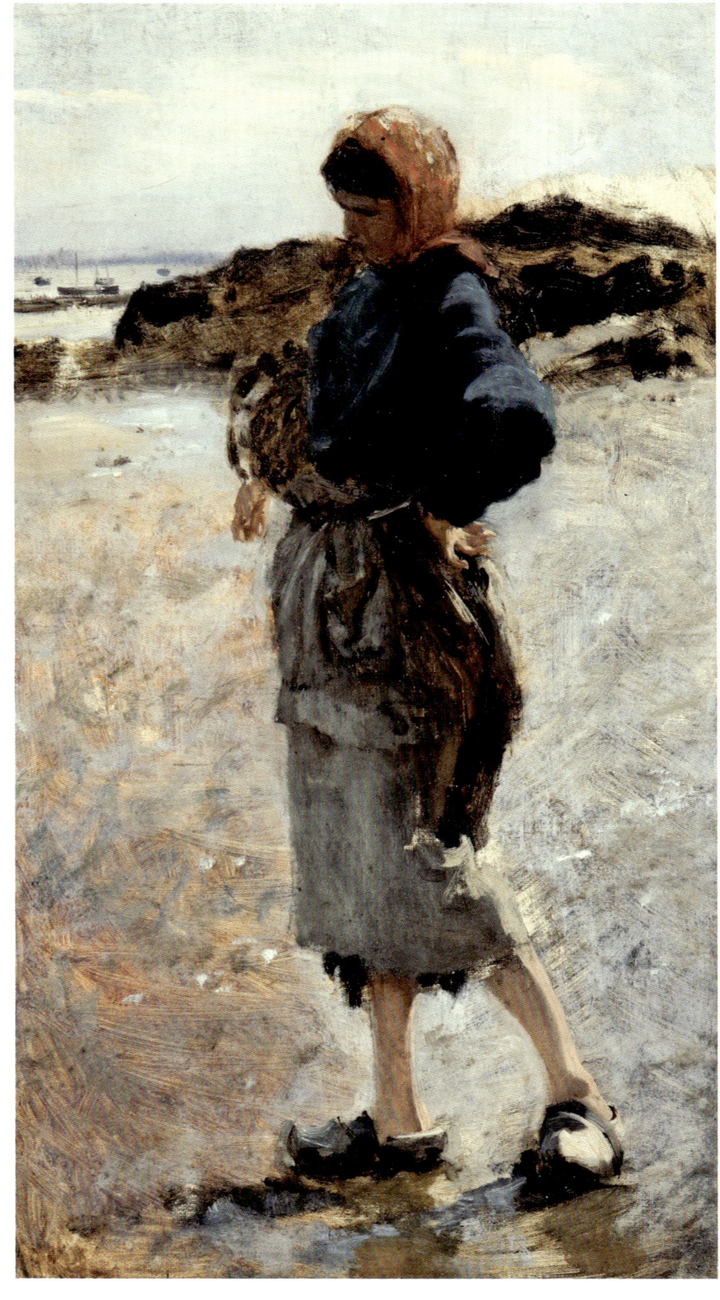

Fig. 139 Detail of fig. 123, *En Route pour la pêche (Setting Out to Fish)*, 1878. Corcoran Gallery of Art, Washington, D.C., Museum Purchase, Gallery Fund, 17.2. (Exhibition)

Fig. 140 *Girl on the Beach*, study for *En Route pour la pêche* and *Fishing for Oysters at Cancale*, 1877. Oil on canvas, 19 × 11½ in (48.3 × 29.2 cm). Terra Foundation for American Art, Daniel J. Terra Collection, Chicago, 1999.131. (Exhibition)

the Metropolitan sheet the boy's left hand rests on his hip with palm facing outward (as it does in the Corcoran work), and he grasps an invisible object at the end of his outstretched right arm. However, four details align the boy in the Terra study more closely to his counterpart in the Boston canvas, suggesting that Sargent placed him in this work before the Corcoran one: in each the boy's face turns slightly toward the viewer, and in each he sports short hair, points his left hand forward on his hip, and does not carry a basket.

The third figure from the left in the finished paintings, a woman with a blue jersey, light skirt, dark headscarf, and a basket on her right hip, has her origins in a third Terra oil (figs. 139, 140), this time not related to a known pencil sketch. Although details of her costume and pose vary from

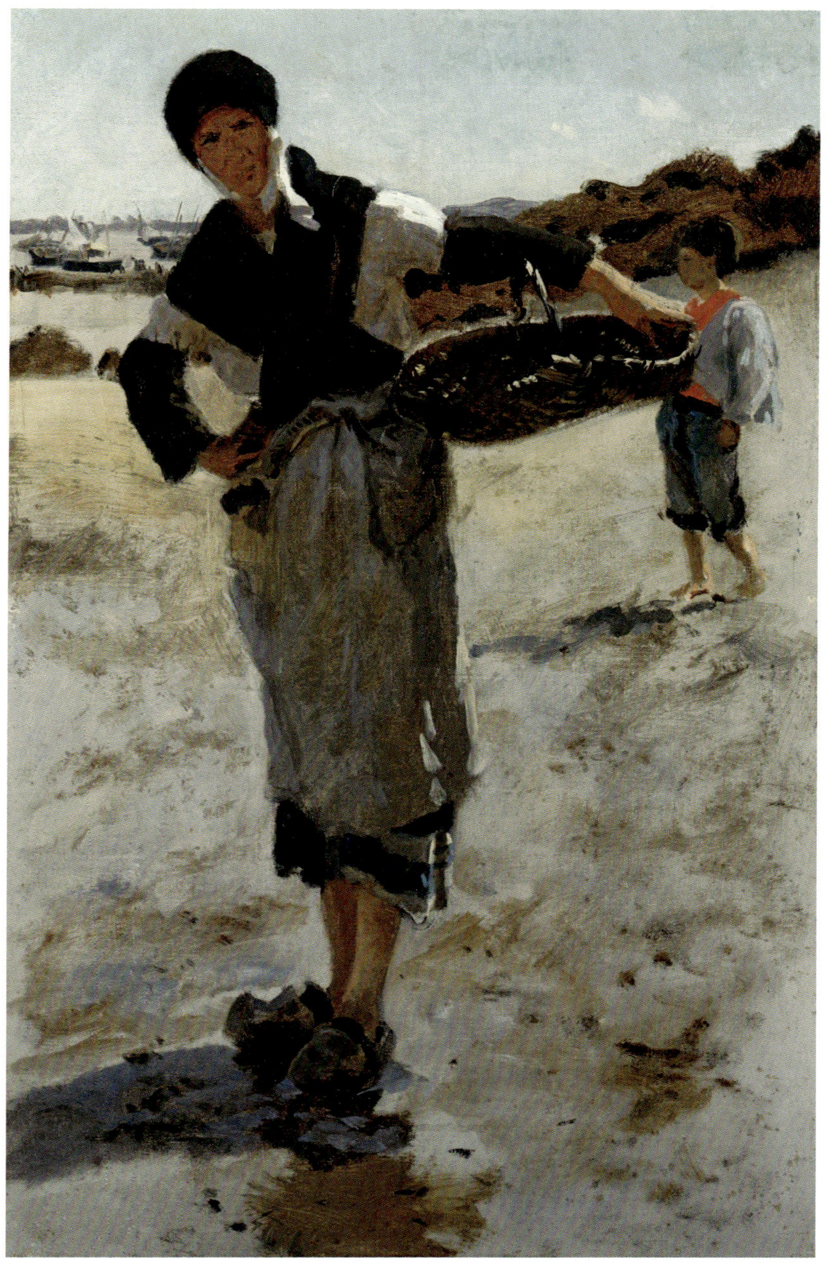

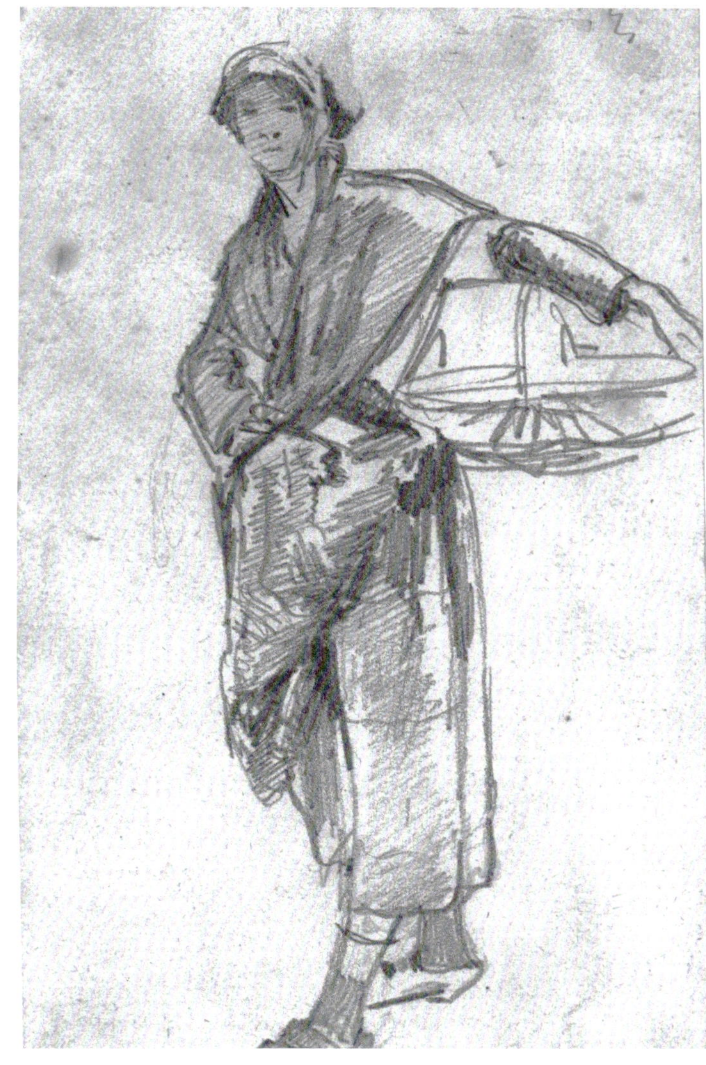

study to completed paintings—in the study, where she wears a red headscarf, her left hand rests on her hip rather than crossing her waist in the larger works—her legs and feet are similarly positioned in all three canvases. Again, details shared only by the Terra study and the Boston canvas suggest that this figure was placed in the latter painting first and in *En Route pour la pêche* second: in the Terra study and Boston painting her glance is slightly more downcast than in the Washington painting, and her right hand dangles down past the ragged edge of her basket.

While there are no extant preliminary works for the next figure in the completed works—the central, red-headed woman—nor for the young boy at the far right, the woman between them appears to derive from a fourth Terra oil sketch (fig. 141). The

Fig. 141 *Breton Woman with a Basket,* study for *En Route pour la pêche* and *Fishing for Oysters at Cancale,* 1877. Oil on canvas, 18½ × 11¾ in (47 × 29.8 cm). Terra Foundation for American Art, Daniel J. Terra Collection, Chicago, 1996.53. (Exhibition)

Fig. 142 *Woman Carrying Basket,* study for *En Route pour la pêche* and *Fishing for Oysters at Cancale,* 1877. Graphite on paper, 5⅞ × 3½ in (14.9 × 9 cm). Harvard Art Museum, Fogg Art Museum, Gift of Miss Emily Sargent and Mrs Francis Ormond, in memory of their brother, John Singer Sargent, 1931.87.B. (Exhibition)

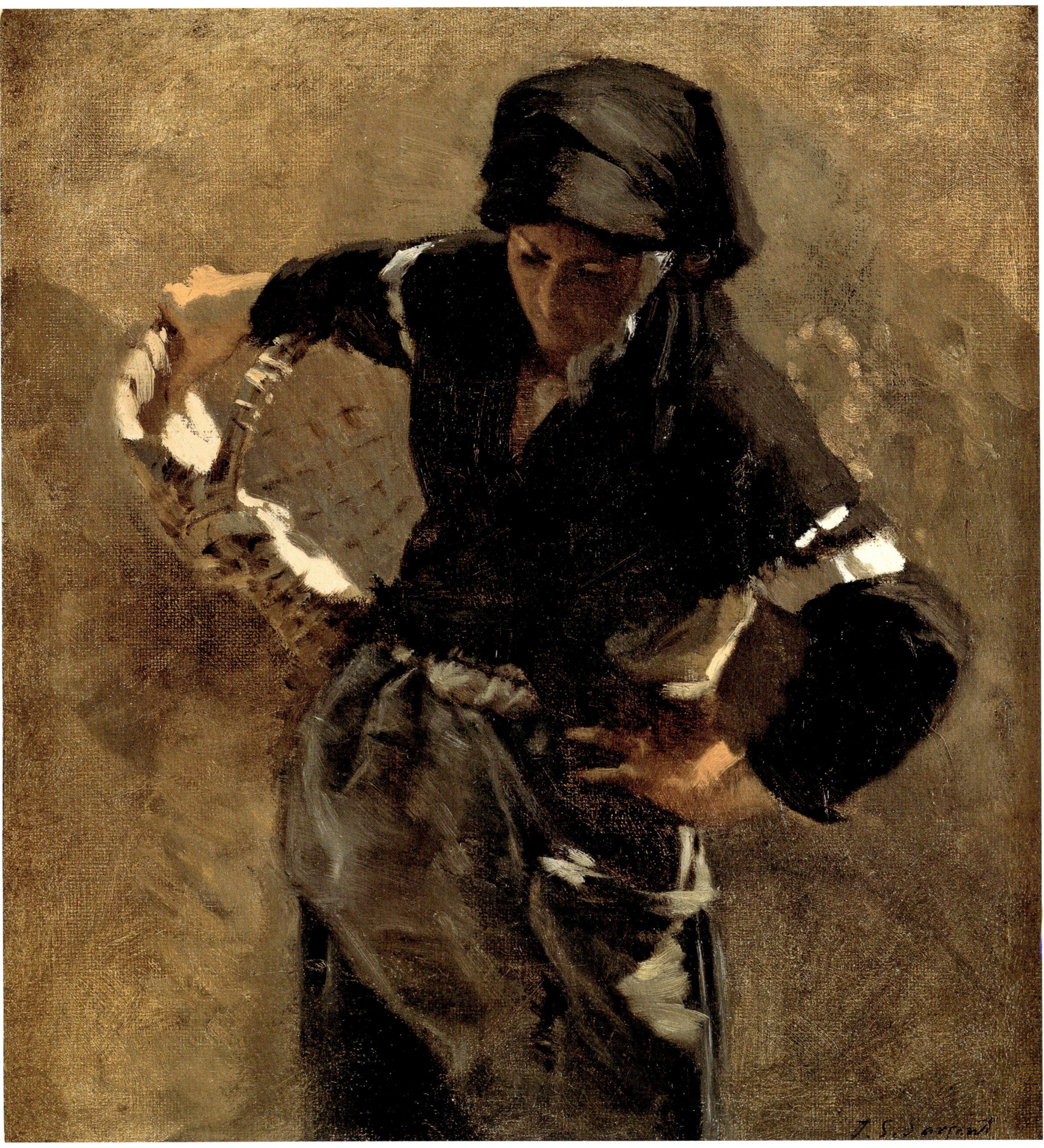

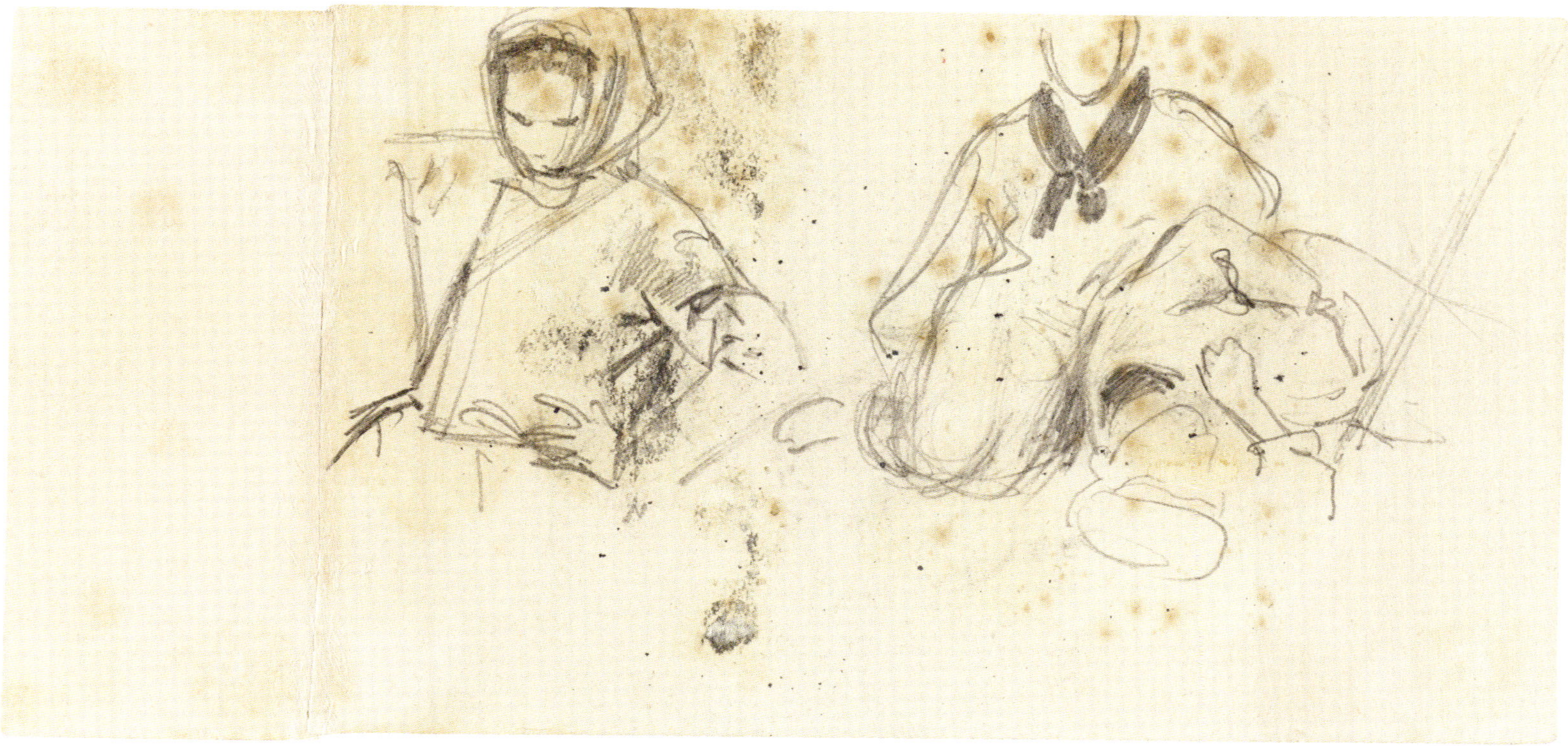

Fig. 144 *Sketch of a woman*, verso of fig. 156 *Reclining Figures*, 1877. Graphite on paper, 3 9/16 × 7½ in (9 × 19.1 cm). Philadelphia Museum of Art: Gift of Miss Emily Sargent and Mrs Francis Ormond, 1931, 1931–14–18a. (Exhibition)

woman in each finished canvas, like the one in the study, leans slightly to her right at the waist while resting a basket on her left hip, and wears a dark *marinière*, or shawl, crossed over the torso. This, in turn, is layered over a light-colored blouse whose foresleeves are wrapped in dark fabric, perhaps intended to protect or warm the arms while foraging in salty waters.[28] From here, though, the figure of this woman in the two finished paintings diverges, each version picking up a detail from the oil sketch. The blue-and-white striped underskirt in the study reappears in the Corcoran canvas, but the melon-shaped basket, which reappears at a different angle in the Boston picture, becomes a deep one in the Corcoran painting. This oil study also has a very closely related counterpart in a pencil sketch in the Fogg Art Museum (fig. 142). Although the woman in the drawing stands more erect than the figure in the oil study and in the finished paintings, where she looks down at the young boy rolling his trousers, details of her costume and pose are quite close to those in the oils. Her swagged overskirt, for example, appears in all four works, albeit changed from white in the Terra work to blue in the finished canvases.

A fifth and final known figure study in oil in a private collection (fig. 143) bears no close resemblance to any of the figures in the finished canvases, nor does its nearly square format, higher vantage point, and lack of landscape background relate it to directly to them or to the four Terra sketches.[29] However, the woman's downcast glance and her clothing are similar to those of the figure in the Terra study just discussed (whose pose she mirrors) and may represent a rejected idea for the general appearance of the central, red-headed woman.[30] Like three of the Terra oils, this canvas relates closely to a drawing. The model's dress and pose mimic those in a sketch of a woman recently revealed on the verso of a sheet in the Philadelphia Museum of Art (fig. 144).

The thinly painted and schematic, often dabbed handling of the four Terra oils—as well as their somewhat muted

Fig. 143 Study for *En Route pour la pêche* and *Fishing for Oysters at Cancale*, 1877. Oil on canvas, 11½ × 10½ in (29.2 × 26.7 cm). Inscribed, upper left: *to my friend Rotch, souvenir of / John S. Sargent* and bottom right (probably not in the artist's hand): *J.S. Sargent.* Private Collection. (Exhibition, Washington only)

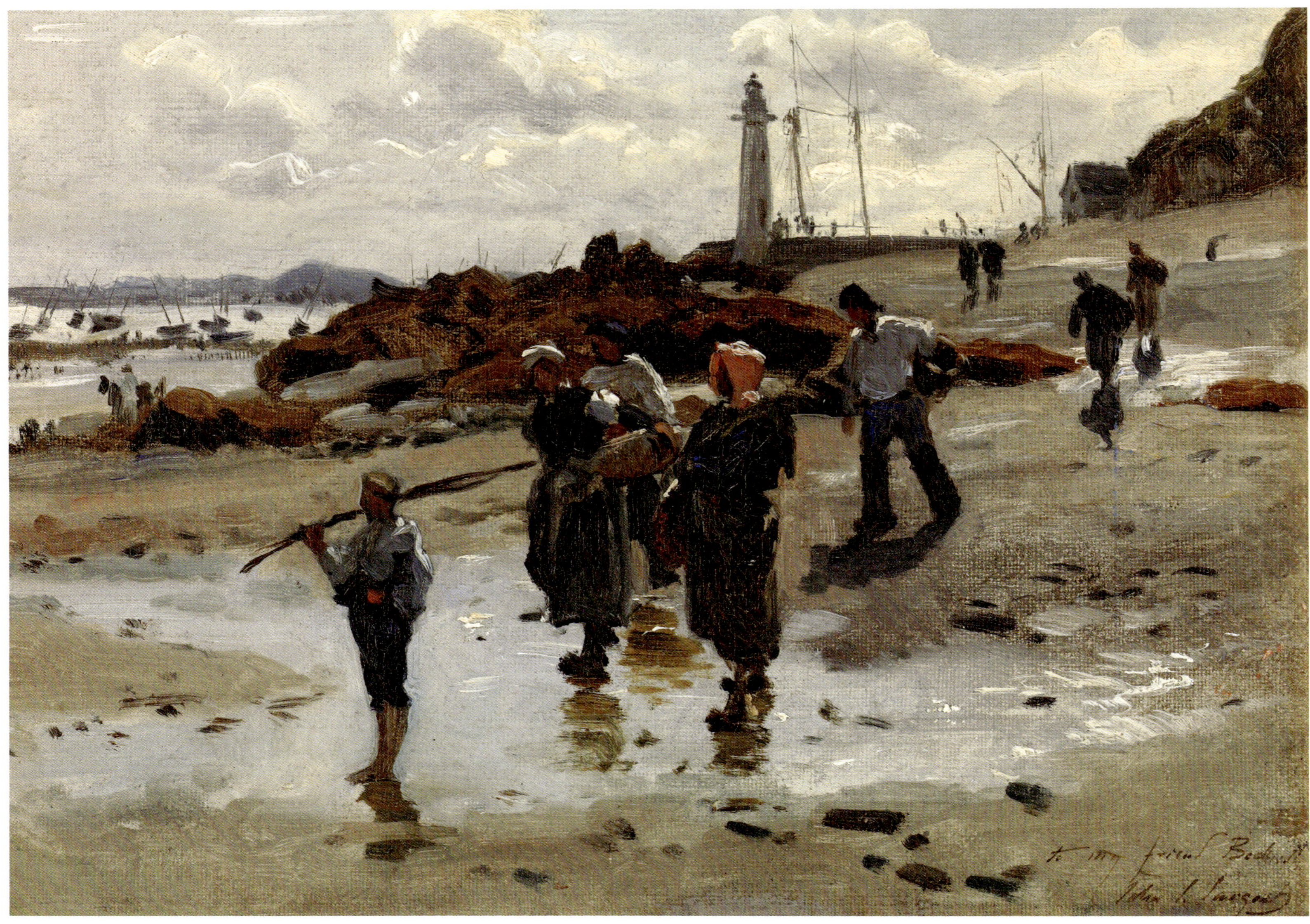

Figs. 145, 146 Sketch for *En Route pour la pêche* and *Fishing for Oysters at Cancale* (detail opposite), 1877. Oil on canvas, 8¾ × 11½ in (22.2 × 29.2 cm). Inscribed, lower right: *to my friend Beckwith/John S. Sargent*. Private Collection. (Exhibition)

palette— relate them to a small, undated plein air canvas inscribed to the artist's friend J. Carroll Beckwith (fig. 145). Sharing the Terra sketches' rocky backgrounds punctuated by sailboats, the Beckwith work was brushed from a vantage point further to the left (north) than that of the sketches, but still to the right (south) of the view shown in the Boston and Corcoran paintings. This oil surely records the scene that inspired Sargent's composition for the pair, depicting the same site but a more naturalistic grouping of figures, which are quickly blocked in and show no facial detail. They move down the sloping beach armed with fishing gear, apparently preparing to gather ingredients for the evening's meal. A small boy dressed in short or rolled-up pants and a toque-style hat carries a fishing pole or shrimp net, leading a group of two women and two men through tidal pools; they are followed, further up on the banks, by two more pairs of figures.

Details of pose, costume, and palette link several of the figures in the compositional sketch to those in the Terra oils and the exhibition pictures. For example, in all three aspects—save for her white cap—the woman holding a basket on her left hip relates closely to the figure in the final Terra oil discussed (fig. 141), and thus to the woman fifth from left in the finished canvases. Similarly, in her salmon-colored head scarf, blue jersey, and tan skirt, the woman at right in the sketch is closely linked to the Terra study depicting the woman in a red head scarf (fig. 140), and, by extension, to the figure third from the left in the completed paintings. The white-shirted man in waders leaning to his right and holding a basket on his left hip just behind the central group appears again in the Corcoran painting, where he carries nets under each arm, their weight apparently causing him to lean further to his right. The pose, clothing, and pole of the boy in the compositional sketch differentiate him from his counterparts in the Terra oil (fig. 137)

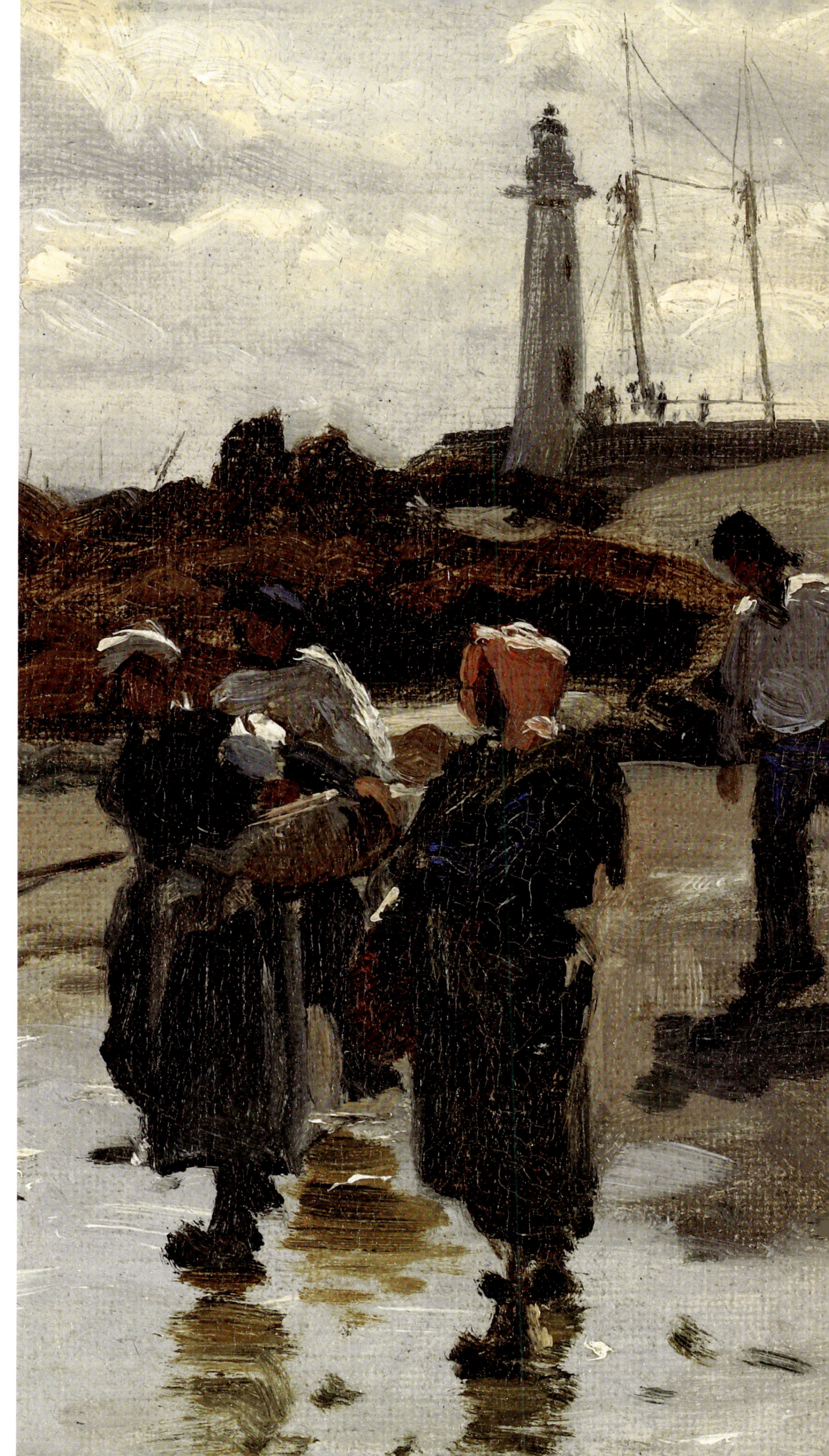

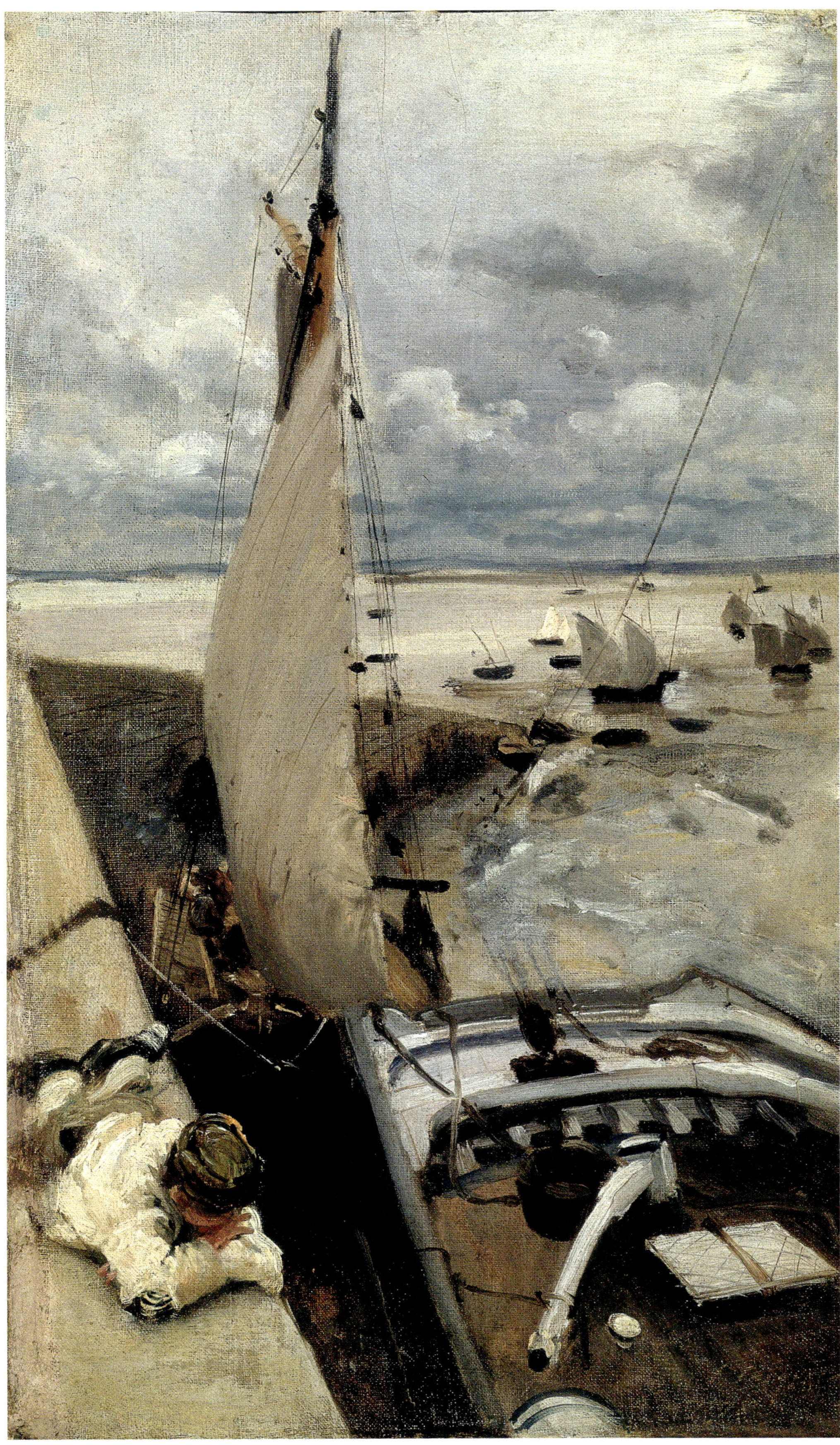

and the completed canvases; however, his toque, light shirt, and short pants suggest he may have served as Sargent's model for the boy reclining in a daydream in *Low Tide at Cancale Harbor* (fig. 147). Indeed, the latter work shares the warm tonal palette of the Beckwith sketch, as well as its handling, particularly in the naturalistically rendered sky.

Precisely how, when, and in what sequence Sargent proceeded from the plein air pencil and oil sketches to completing his two studio pictures is unknown. In the context of academic practice, the smaller size of *Fishing for Oysters at Cancale* and its closer relationship to two of the four Terra studies would suggest that the artist began work on it first (perhaps even in Cancale), either as a preparatory sketch for, or preliminary version of, the larger Corcoran work.[31] In such a scenario he then would have decided to repurpose the Boston canvas after sculptor Augustus Saint-Gaudens alerted him, in early October, to plans for the SAA exhibition the following spring.[32] However, Sargent may have had reason to eschew traditional procedure in favor of a more unconventional approach, as he did in works such as *A Capriote* (1878), the first version of which is somewhat more tightly executed and detailed than the subsequent two.[33] For example, since he apparently traveled to Cancale specifically to prepare his second Salon submission, he may well have set right to work on the larger canvas immediately after returning to Paris in late August, only beginning work on the smaller one after pledging to submit to the SAA show. In either situation, by the time Sargent wrote to his friend Gus Case in November or December that he was preparing the Boston painting for submission to the SAA exhibition, to open in March 1878 (just over two months before the Salon), he must have been working on the two exhibition pictures side by side.[34]

Newly discovered technical information about the relationships among the figures in the Chicago, Boston, and Corcoran works adds further intrigue to an analysis of the artist's working methods. For example, when an image of the Boston canvas is doubled in size and electronically superimposed on a photograph of the Corcoran painting, the contours of each of the three pairs of figures match precisely from one image to the other (fig. 148). However, the figures' contours only match when they are overlaid in pairs.[35]

The coincidences within and among the works just mentioned are too great to definitively conclude that Sargent could have so precisely enlarged the figure contours only by eye. Such enlargements may be effected through the use of grids, but no tick or grid lines—or indications of graphite underdrawing—have been detected in either painting.[36] This suggests the possibility that the artist may have employed a mechanical enlarging tool in use during this period such as the magic lantern, which could project slides onto surfaces where he could have sketched or blocked in figures using earth pigment washes, later altering their details.[37] The presence of a dark border, comprised of a thin wash of bluish-black paint, at the top, bottom, and right edges of the Boston canvas—and the corresponding presence of a thinly painted border at the left, bottom, and right edges of the Washington image—may have served as registration marks in such an enlargement process. Within such a scenario are three options: the artist may have projected an image of the Boston canvas onto the Corcoran one; he may have done the reverse, reducing the scale of the Corcoran image; or he may have projected a now lost image on both canvases.

It was at precisely this time in his life that Sargent developed an avid interest in photography by assembling a collection of numerous examples of the medium (see pp. 82–85). Not only did he include photographs of various works of art and architecture in his scrapbook preserved in the Metropolitan Museum of Art, he began to have his paintings photographed. Soon after completing his 1877 portrait of Fanny Watts (Philadelphia Museum of Art), he had it photographed in the studio of Auguste Perichet, which, at 52 rue de Notre-Dame-des-Champs, was located just doors from his own.[38] Likewise, Sargent's 1878 portrait of Édouard Pailleron (Musée d'Orsay) is the earliest of several of his works photographed by the Paris firm of Adolfe Braun (1811–1877), which specialized in documenting works of art.[39] A photograph of *Capri Peasant—Study* (1878, private collection) is contained in an undated scrapbook that belonged to Sargent, now in the library of The Metropolitan Museum of Art.[40] By 1880, the artist was sharing photographs of his paintings with ease, writing to Vernon Lee on 9 July that he would send her a photograph "of a little picture [he] perpetrated in Tangiers."[41]

It is also possible that Sargent saw a photographic enlargement device in the fall of 1877, if one were employed when he and Beckwith began assisting Carolus-Duran with the ceiling decoration for the Palais du Luxembourg. During this early period when the artist was gaining confidence and

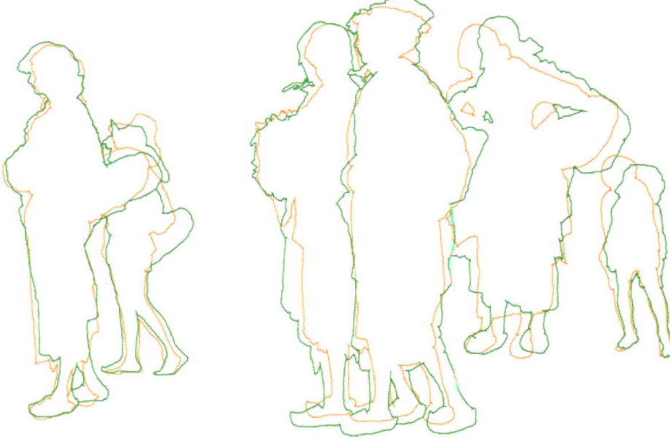

Fig. 148 Photoshop image showing outlines of figures in *Fishing for Oysters at Cancale* (in orange, enlarged by 100%) and laid over green outlines of figures in *En Route pour la pêche*.

Fig. 147 *Low Tide at Cancale Harbor*, 1878. Oil on canvas, 19⅛ × 11⅛ in (48.6 × 28.3 cm). Inscribed, lower right: [?] *Sargent/1878*. Museum of Fine Arts, Boston, Zoe Oliver Sherman Collection, 22.646. (Exhibition)

exploring a variety of media and methods, the use of mechanical enlargement cannot be rejected, nor without proper documentation can it be confirmed. This possibility, considered with the complex yet not entirely resolved relationships among the Cancale works, suggests intriguing avenues for further exploration. Such an investigation would be enriched by a close study of Sargent's multiples of four other paintings during the 1878–79 period: three paintings of a Capri girl in olive trees (1878), three oils of a dancing Capri girl on a rooftop (1878), two of the Luxembourg Gardens (1879), and two of the rehearsal of the Pasdeloup Orchestra (*c.* 1879).[42]

Whatever Sargent's process and timeline for creating his exhibition paintings, a close analysis reveals that he planned each work's distinctive style just as he would select its title: in accordance with his venue choice. Sargent knew, for example, that the SAA's membership was comprised of younger, mostly European-trained American artists who set out to challenge the conservative tendencies and restrictive exhibition policies of the National Academy of Design. Aware of the Society's acceptance and promotion of a breadth of painting styles, in contrast to the Academy's restrictive stance favoring traditional subjects and tight brushwork, Sargent surely saw the ideal opportunity to exhibit a fresh, relatively loosely painted scene. Moreover, not only was his participation in the SAA exhibition prearranged, but he surely anticipated that the relatively small display at the Kurtz Gallery (ultimately 124 works) would allow each work to receive some degree of attention.

The differences that distinguish the artist's SAA submission from his Salon entry were carefully calculated in order to appeal to New York and Paris audiences and critics respectively. In order to have a painting accepted—and noticed—as one of thousands of works shown at the staid and highly regulated annual Salon exhibition opening on 25 May, Sargent knew that he would have to do two things. Not only would he have to enter a larger version of the fishing picture, he would have to execute it as formally and as tightly brushed as his training with Carolus-Duran would allow in order that it conform with the Salon's accepted standards of finish. Having accomplished these tasks, he also rendered the Corcoran canvas more weighty and formal than its smaller counterpart, the processional nature of the group emphasized by the larger size of its figures in proportion to the picture plane. Its saturated, brilliant palette, emphasizing sunlight, atmosphere, and the reflections of the white clouds on the tide pools, contrasts with the more tonal hues of the Boston picture. The more tightly handled paint defines many elements with greater detail, such as the figures' faces, the seaweed-covered rocks at right, the kelp scattered on the shoreline, the oyster beds in the left middle ground, and the ships' masts.

Sargent's market-driven choice of titles and styles for *Fishing for Oysters at Cancale* and *En Route pour la pêche* had the desired results, for both elicited positive reviews. By far the greater notice, however, was accorded the former picture. This may have been due, in part, to its appealing subject and title, but this is not borne out in print by the critics, who instead responded enthusiastically to the painting's formal qualities and character. Nearly every writer noted the painting's small size and unfinished, sketch-like nature. A reviewer for the *Nation* praised it as "one of the best studies of flashing daylight ever made by an American artist";[43] another, for the New York *Herald*, called it "one of the most charming little pictures in the gallery . . . delightfully suggestive."[44] Five days later the same *Herald* critic commended it similarly but continued, "we could only ask for a little more finish . . . enough to more sharply define the forms."[45] A writer for the Boston *Daily Advertiser* who wrote extensively on the subject of studies praised the painting, describing it as a "little picture" and noting that "[n]early every painting [in the exhibition] is a study."[46] Prominent art critic Clarence Cook—while not impartial to the SAA, at whose formation he was present—wrote that when compared to some large canvases in the exhibition, small works such as the "magical" *Fishing for Oysters at Cancale* allowed the "[t]he visitor . . . to perceive at last that big canvases do not always make big pictures . . . In memory's picture gallery these little pieces loom up large."[47] In an 1879 review, one of several praising the canvas more than a year after the closing of the SAA exhibition, *Fishing for Oysters at Cancale* was still being commended for its sketch-like nature.[48] The critic for the New York *Evening Mail* found the painting "[d]ecidedly one of the best pictures in the collection . . . an admirable composition and specimen of color."[49]

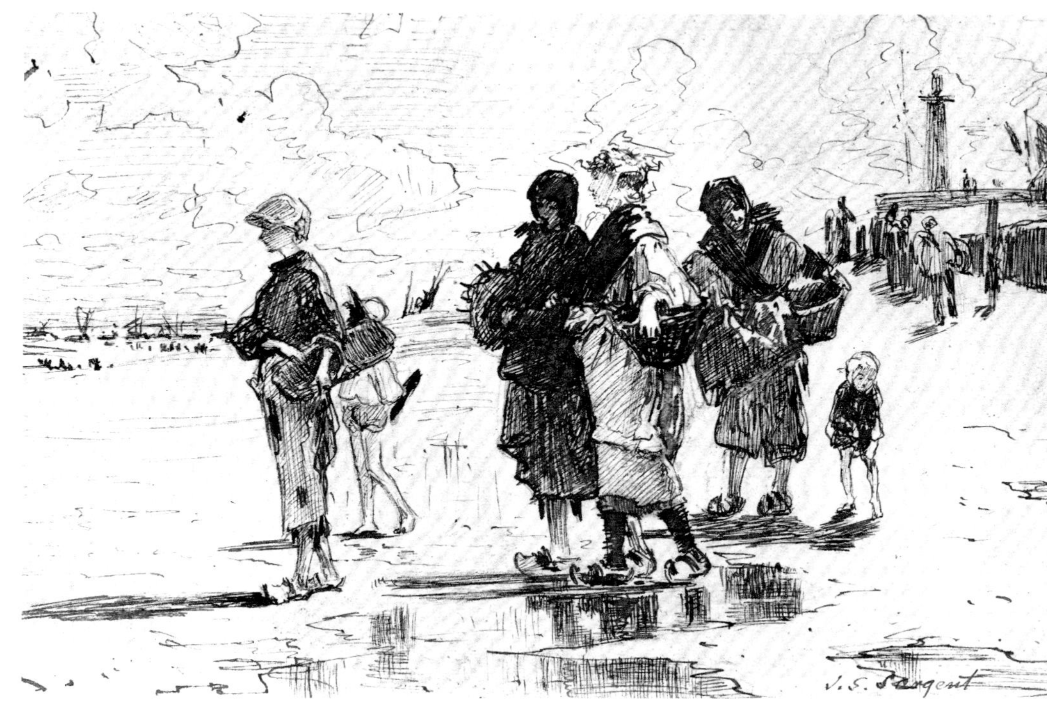

Fig. 149 Sketch after *En Route pour la pêche (Setting Out to Fish)*, 1878. Pen and ink and graphite on paper, 4½ × 7 in (11.4 × 17.8 cm). Corcoran Gallery of Art, Washington, D.C. Gift of Irving Moskovitz, 1976.57. (Exhibition). Reproduced as an engraving in Roger Ballu, "Le Salon de 1878: Deuxième et Dernier Article," *Gazette des Beaux-Arts* 18, no. 1 (July 1878, p. 179). Inscribed lower left: *PAR YVES & BARRET. SC.*; inscribed lower right: *J.S. Sargent*. This volume is also included in the exhibition, courtesy of Virginia Commonwealth University, James Branch Cabell Library, Special Collections & Archives.

While thirteen reviews of the first SAA exhibition mentioned *Fishing for Oysters at Cancale*, *En Route pour la pêche* garnered only one critical mention during its showing at the Salon, albeit a lengthy and positive one in the prestigious *Gazette des Beaux-Arts*.[50] Roger Ballu's prose did not differ significantly from that of the New York critics. He praised Sargent's free, broad brushwork as well as the effects of sunlight on the wet sand relieved by the reflections of the blue sky in the tide pools. He paid the artist a further compliment by commissioning him to execute a drawing after the Corcoran canvas, to be reproduced in the article (fig. 149).

Buoyed by critical praise, Sargent had further reason to be satisfied with the results of his careful plans for the execution, titling, and exhibition of the two Cancale paintings. For even before the SAA and Salon exhibitions closed their doors, each painting had found a patron, marking the first two sales of the young artist's career.[51] *Fishing for Oysters at Cancale* sold to the prominent Hudson River School painter and SAA founding member Samuel Colman (1832–1920), who apparently drew lots with another artist to purchase the painting.[52] The older artist remarked that he bought the painting to "key myself up with. I am afraid that I may fall below just such a standard, and I wish to have it hanging in my studio to reproach me whenever I do."[53] *En Route pour la pêche* sold during the Salon to Sargent family friend Rear Admiral Augustus Ludlow Case (1812–1893), who had retired to Newport just three years before from a long and distinguished naval career.[54] While we only know that Case "liked the picture," his devotion to a life of the sea cannot be discounted as a motive for the purchase, thereby suggesting a parallel with the artist's own maritime heritage and its influence on his artistic pursuits of the 1870s.[55]

Although studies for the two exhibition pictures comprise most of the known works Sargent produced in Cancale, four other canvases and one drawing associated with the village merit attention here. Most closely linked to the Boston and Corcoran paintings

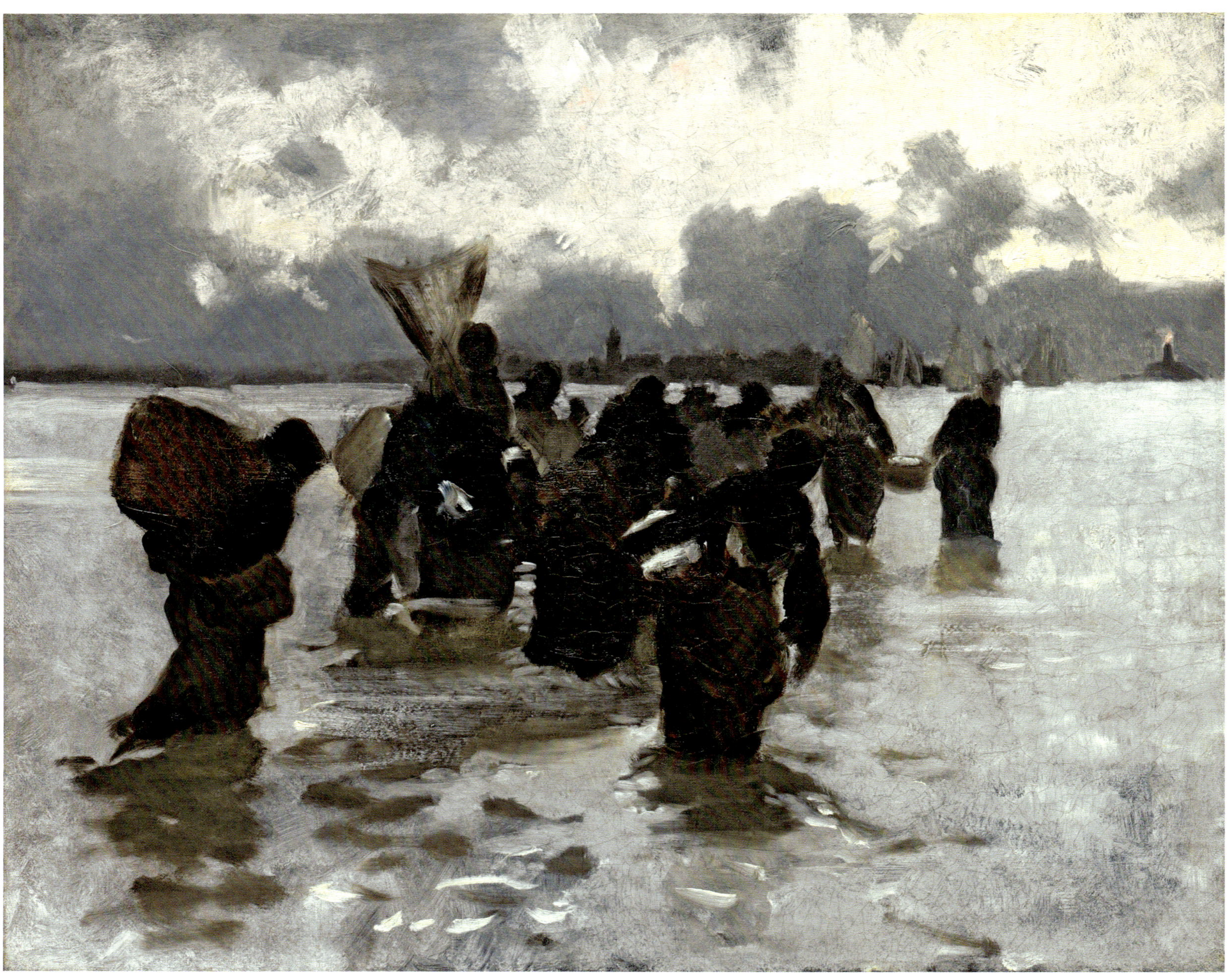

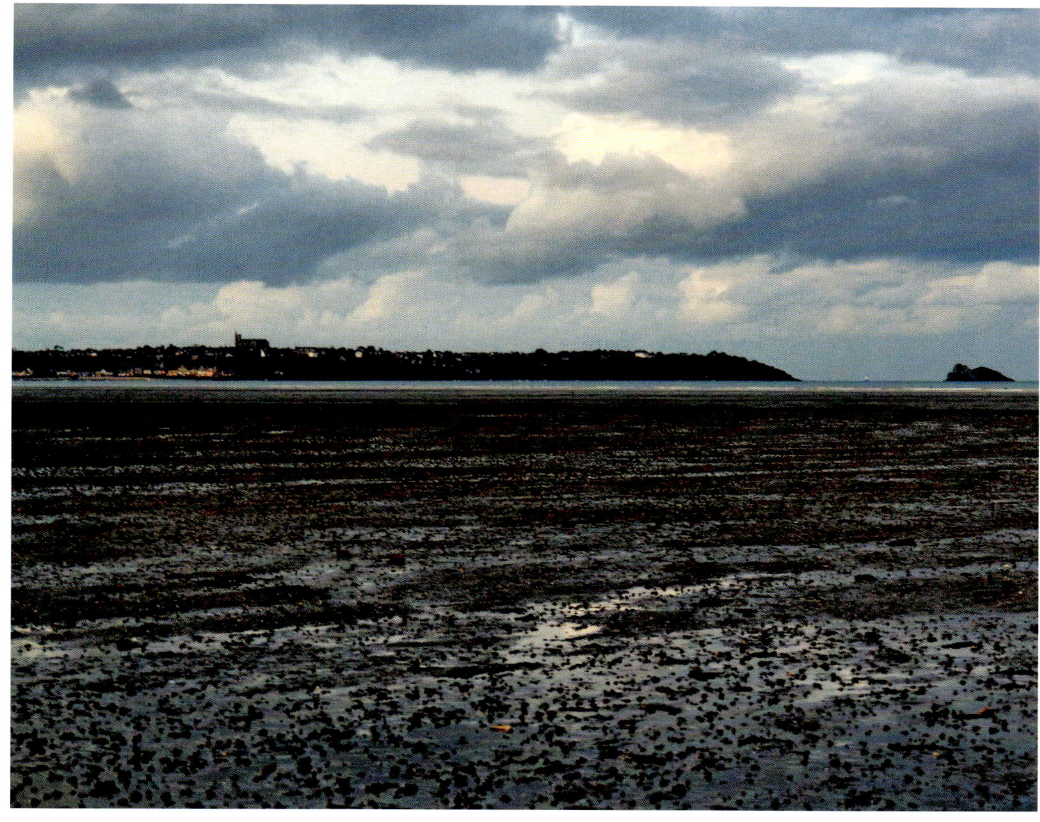

Fig. 150 *Fisherwomen Returning*, 1877. Oil on canvas, 19⅝ × 24⅛ in (49.8 × 61.4 cm). The Nelson-Atkins Museum of Art, Kansas City, Missouri. Gift of Mr and Mrs Louis Sosland, F77–36/1. (Exhibition)

Fig. 151 Photograph of the site depicted in *Fisherwomen Returning*: view of Cancale and the Pointe de la Chaîne across the Bay of Mont-Saint-Michel, 2008. Photograph by Hervé Lambrecht, Cancale.

is an oil now known as *Fisherwomen Returning* in the Nelson-Atkins Museum of Art (fig. 150).[56] Like them it describes a group of figures carrying baskets, suggesting some kind of fishing activity, but there the similarity ends. A much larger group of figures than in the two exhibition paintings moves through shallow water, returning to shore at dusk; not only has it become too dark to work, it was strictly forbidden to fish after sunset.[57] The black, huddled figures, one holding a shrimp net, strain against the weight of their laden baskets and are silhouetted against the lighter water below an unsettled sky. On the horizon lies the town of Cancale, dominated by the spire of its eighteenth-century church, Église Saint-Méen, and to its right (northeast) the Pointe de la Chaîne. Sargent appears to have taken liberties with geography and painted Le Herpin, the lighthouse built in 1876 on the further north Pointe du Grouin, on the nearby Rocher de Cancale, where no lighthouse existed (fig. 151). It is impossible to see Le Herpin appearing above the Rocher de Cancale from any vantage point near Sargent's; moreover, at twenty-four meters high, the lighthouse is fourteen meters shorter than the Rocher de Cancale.[58] Having traveled south of Cancale, Sargent located a vantage point from which to create the distant view somewhere between the

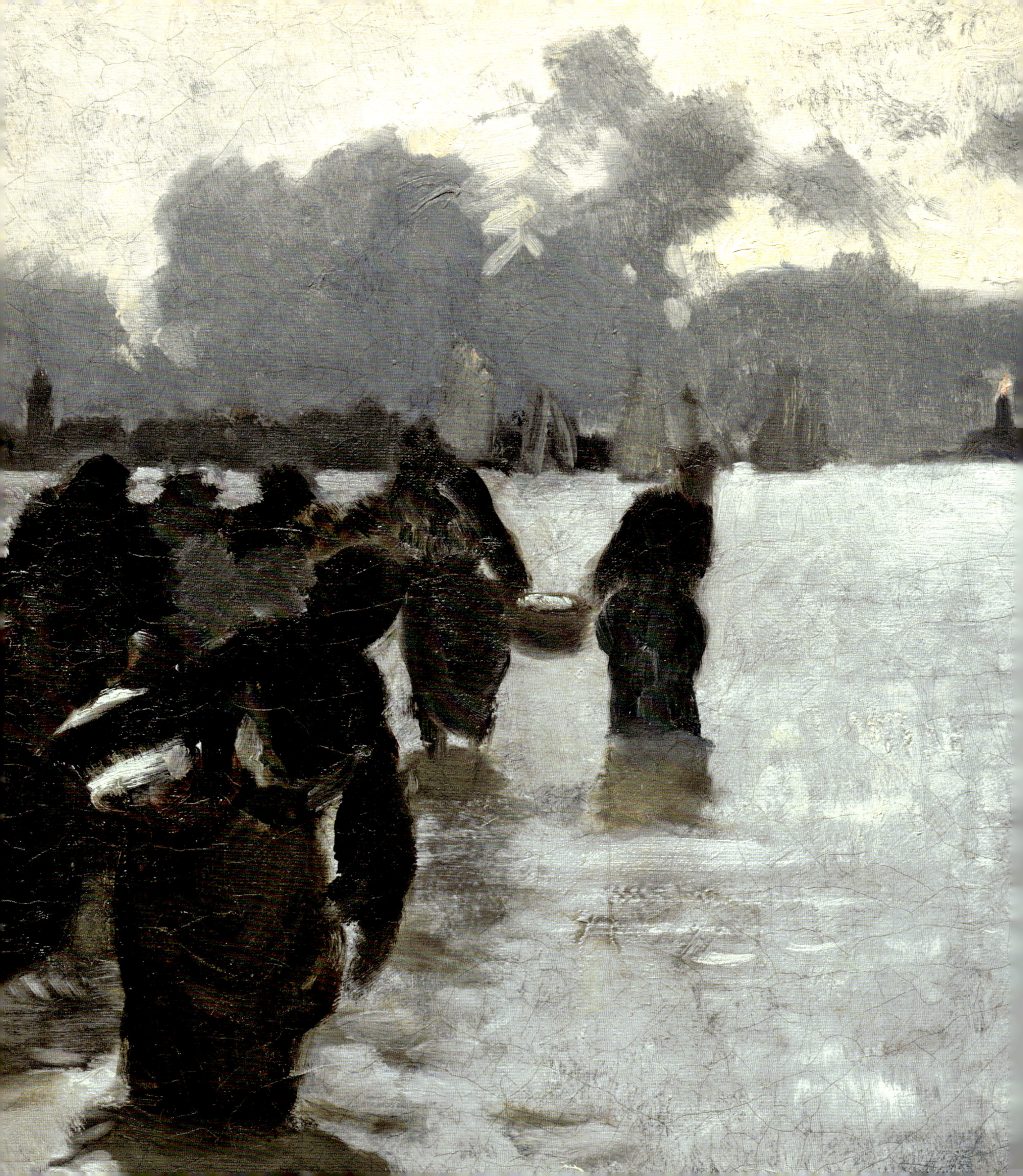

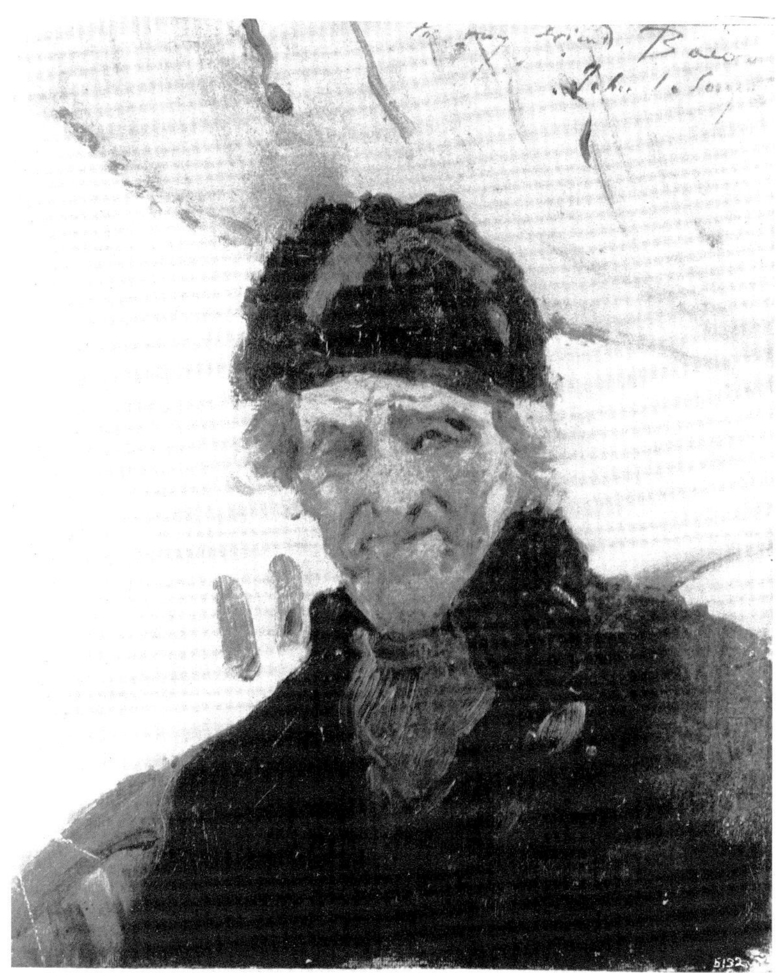

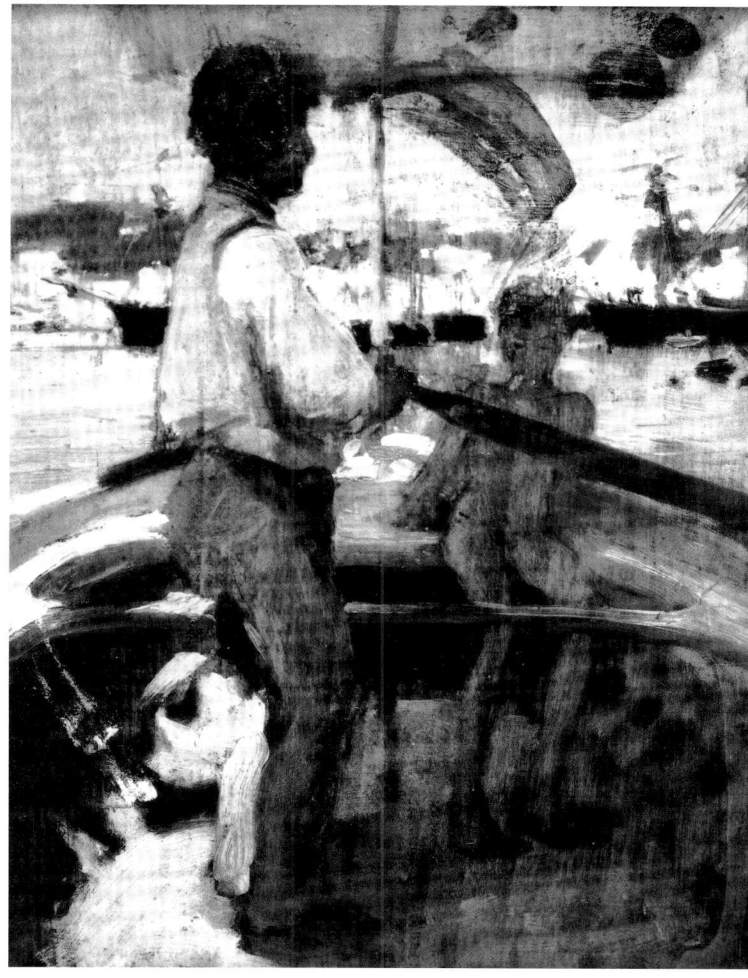

small beach of Le Porcon and a village to its north, Saint-Benoît des Ondes. The naturalistic appearance of the figures, topographical features, and sky, along with Sargent's free brushwork, suggest that he painted the work largely, if not wholly, on site. As the subject and the character of the painting differ so vastly from those of *En Route pour la pêche* and *Fishing for Oysters at Cancale*, it is difficult to determine where in the sequence of Cancale works it was executed. Its similarity in size to the latter work raises the possibility that Sargent first conceived them as pendant studies, but the great stylistic difference argues against that suggestion.[59]

Three more oils and a drawing from the Cancale trip underscore Sargent's close observation of the villagers, their lives of hardship, and their picturesque surroundings. Two unlocated oil sketches, apparently completed on site, depict a sailor with wizened features in the stern of his boat (fig. 153) and a man and boy in a boat (fig. 154). Although the latter panel shares the feel, handling, and general subject of the former, aspects of the image are difficult to reconcile with Sargent's other Cancale subject matter: the figure of the boy is unclothed, and the man rowing the vessel is standing.[60] *Low Tide at Cancale Harbor* (fig. 155), which depicts a boy reclining on the

Fig. 153 *The Brittany Boatman*, *c.* 1877. Oil on panel, 13½ × 10¼ in (34.3 × 26 cm). Inscribed, upper right: *to my friend Bacon/John S. Sargent*. Untraced.

Fig. 154 *Man and Boy in a Boat*, *c.* 1877. Oil on panel, 13½ × 10¼ in (34.5 × 26 cm). Untraced.

Facing page: Fig. 152 Detail of fig. 150, *Fisherwomen Returning*, 1877. The Nelson-Atkins Museum of Art, Kansas City, Missouri. Gift of Mr and Mrs Louis Sosland, F77–36/1. (Exhibition)

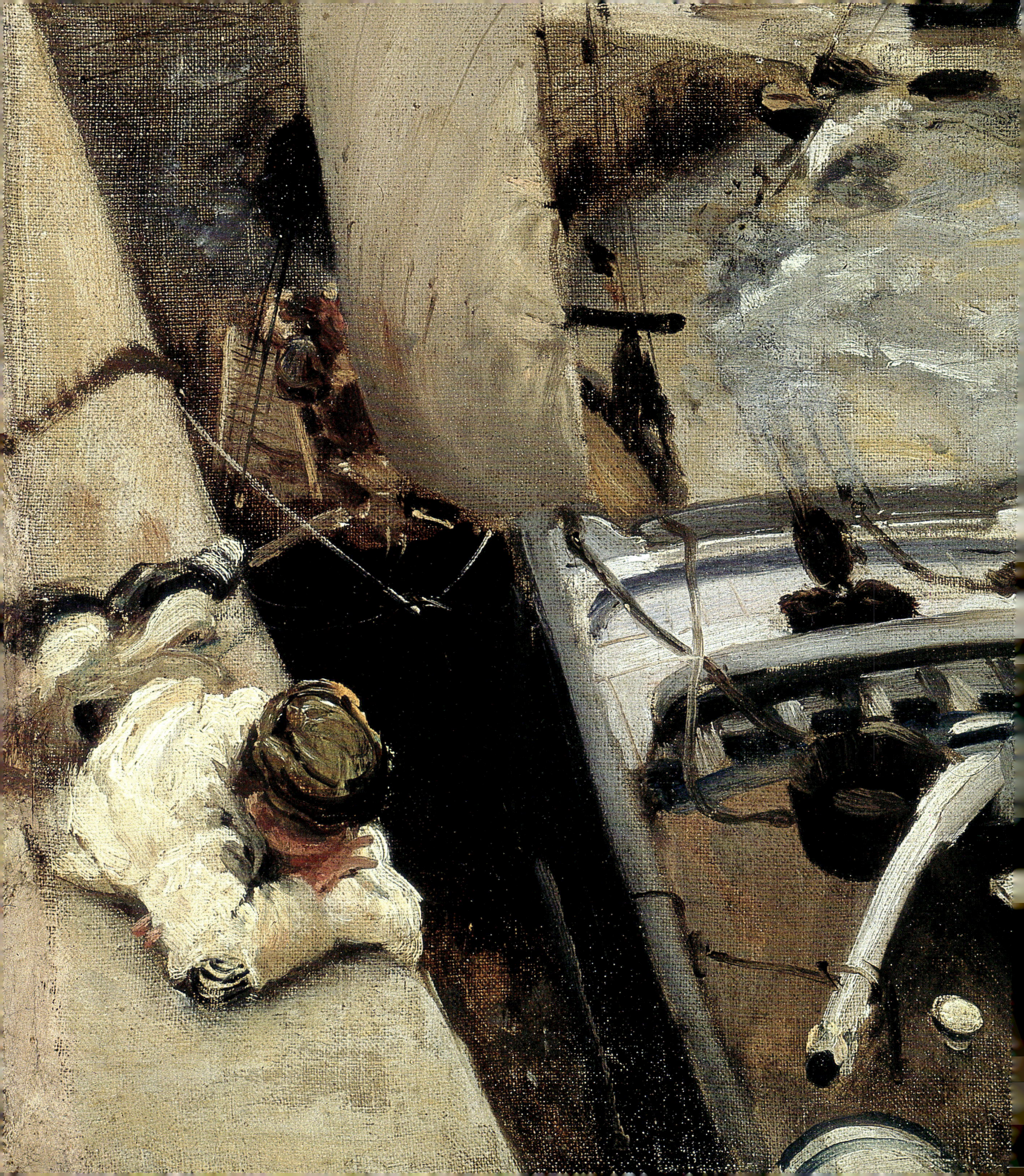

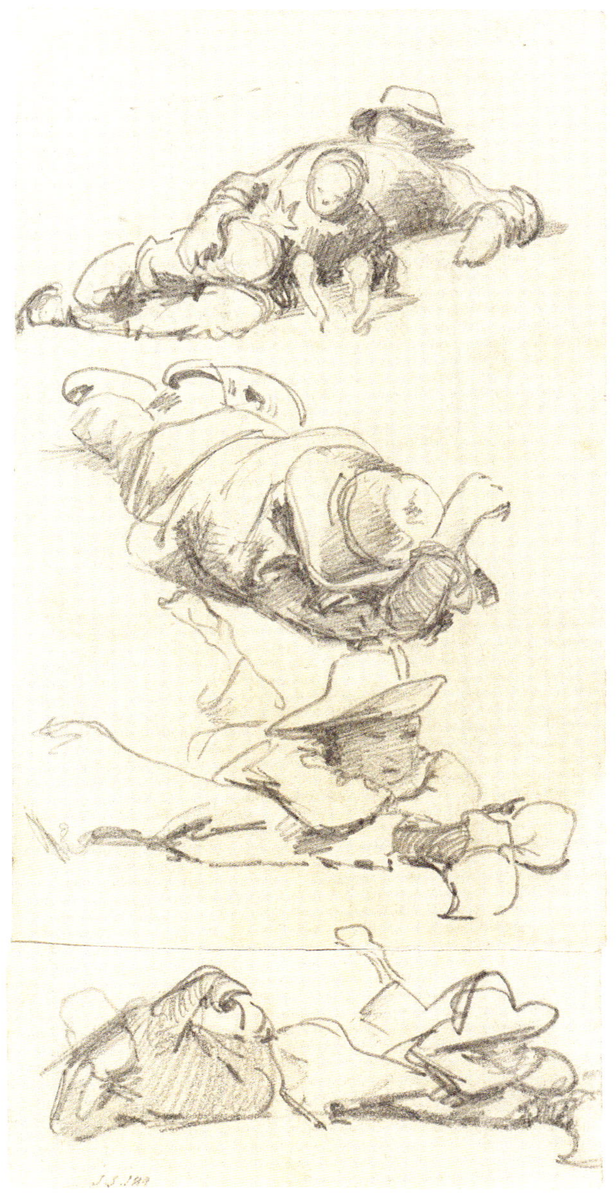

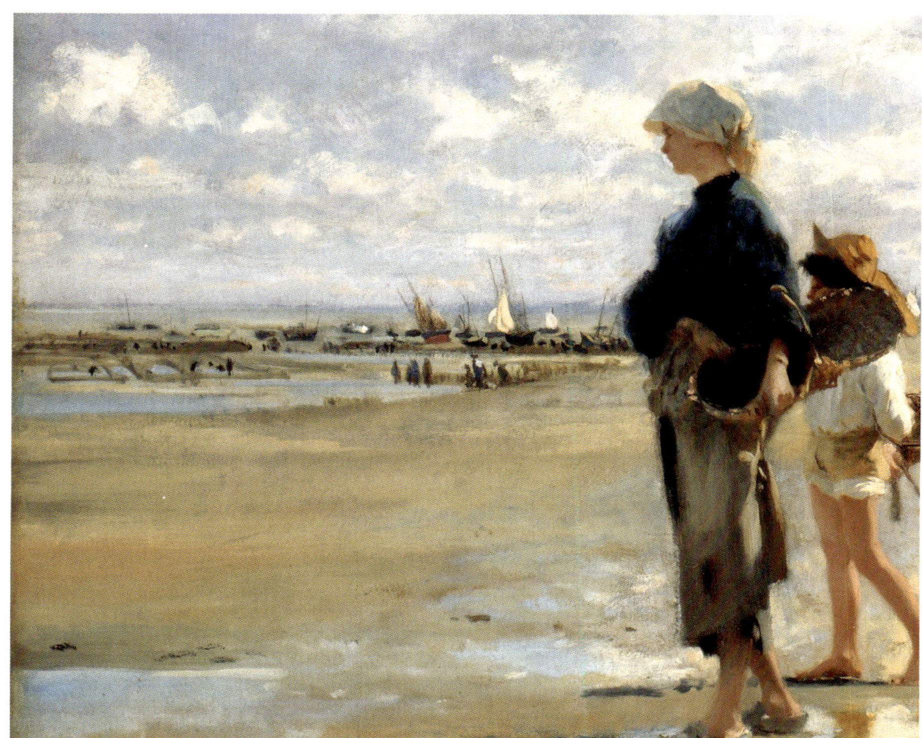

Fig. 156 *Reclining Figures*, 1877. Graphite on paper, 7½ × 3%₁₆ in (19.1 × 9 cm). Inscribed, lower left: *J.S.189*. Philadelphia Museum of Art: Gift of Miss Emily Sargent and Mrs Francis Ormond, 1931, 1931–14–18a. (Exhibition)

Fig. 157 Detail of fig. 123, *En Route pour la pêche (Setting Out to Fish)*, 1878. Corcoran Gallery of Art, Washington, D.C., Museum Purchase, Gallery Fund, 17.2. (Exhibition)

quay seen in the distance of the Boston and Corcoran paintings (figs. 122, 123), presents a foil to those two canvases in nearly every respect: its emphatically tonal palette, describing a dead low tide and a threatening sky; the elevated vantage point and dramatic perspective, emphasized by the sharp diagonal and horizontal lines cutting the vertical composition; and the figure, resting before or after his shoreline duties. The boy may have his source in a sheet of sketches in the Philadelphia Museum of Art (fig. 156). In the drawing the general pose and foreshortening of the second figure from the top, together with the sideways position of his legs (perhaps occasioned by his unwieldy *sabots*), link him to the boy in the painting, while the straw hat suggests that Sargent may have engaged the same Cancalais model who appears in the Terra sketch (fig. 137) and the two exhibition pictures.

Facing page: Fig. 155 Detail of fig. 147, *Low Tide at Cancale Harbor*, 1878. Museum of Fine Arts, Boston, Zoe Oliver Sherman Collection, 22.646. (Exhibition)

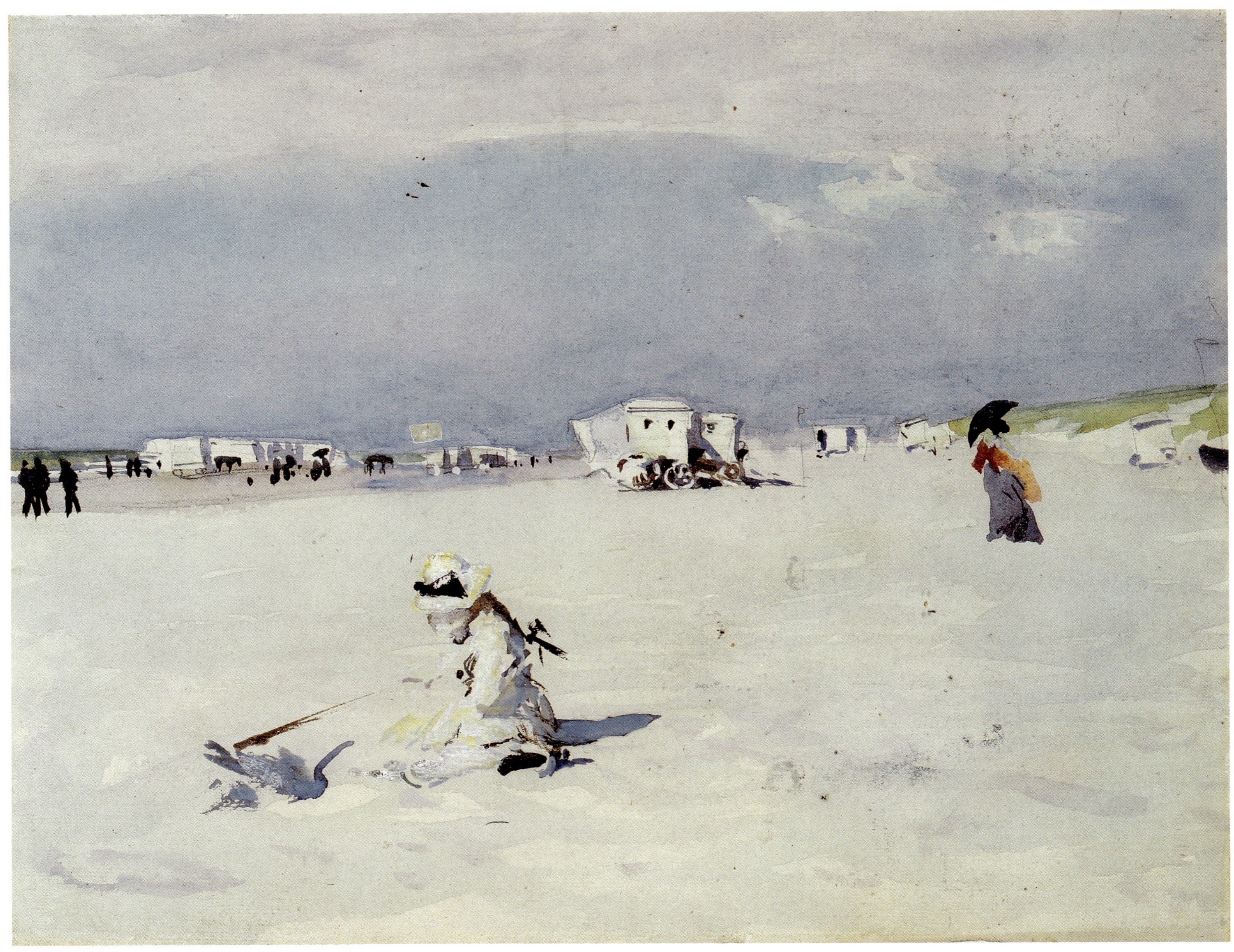

Fig. 158 *On the Sands*, *c.* 1877. Watercolor on paper, 8⅞ × 11¾ in (22.5 × 29.8 cm). Private Collection. (Exhibition)

A final work surely dating to the summer of 1877 appears altogether different in subject and style from the pictures heretofore discussed. Depicting an unidentified locale in Brittany, the small watercolor *On the Sands* (fig. 158) in a private collection shows a young girl at play in the foreground of a beach resort, identified by its bathing carriages and the elegantly clad woman with parasol in the middle ground. The painting's refined subject and bright, delicate style recalls the work of some of Sargent's contemporaries such as Eugène Boudin. However, its composition and detail link it to the two completed Cancale beach scenes. In each of the three works the artist boldly gives half of the picture plane over to the void of the sky, and each shows his staccato use of small, black, vertical and horizontal brushstrokes to suggest distant figures and details.

From June 1877 to early spring 1878 Sargent encountered a significant number of firsts as a newly professional artist. For the first time he spent an extended period away from his family; produced a large body of work devoted to one locale; synthesized a complex cycle of pencil and oil studies into finished canvases; and probably experimented with one or more transfer or enlargement methods. He prepared for his first subject pictures; his first American exhibition; his first nearly concurrent exhibitions on both sides of the Atlantic; and what would be not only his first substantive and international critical reception, but also his first sales. During this time Sargent experienced a period of focused and often experimental creativity. The painter revealed his youthful resilience when faced with unexpected turns of events. Upon arriving in Cancale to discover that it was not oyster-gathering season, he changed his course accordingly; he persisted in sketching models and views despite inclement weather; and back in Paris during the course of the fall, when offered the opportunity to show a painting at the Society of American Artists the following spring, he swiftly set to work preparing for that exhibition a canvas that he may have begun as a sketch for his Salon picture. This multi-layered blend of embracing new challenges, transforming changes into opportunities in a flexible yet calculated manner, and, in the end, creating remarkably assured and highly successful paintings, was a brilliant and auspicious harbinger of Sargent's nascent career.

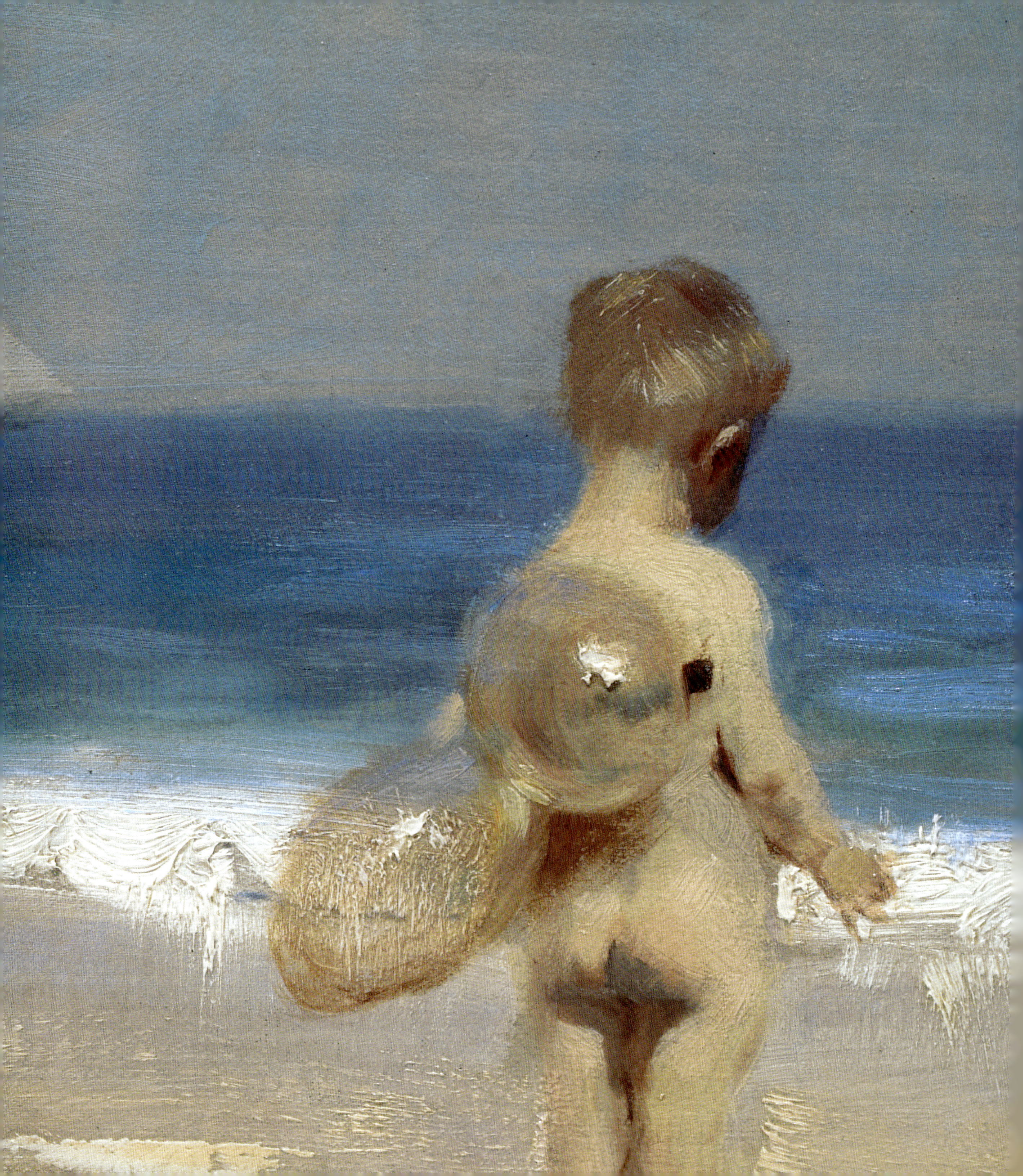

Bladders and Blue Shadows: "Neapolitan Children Bathing"

MARC SIMPSON

John Singer Sargent visited the Bay of Naples several times in his life, but the first and only real working trip he took there was in the summer of 1878. We have the transcription of a letter, several caricatures of him from other hands, the memoirs of friends, and roughly thirty works—among them some of the most memorable in the œuvre—as records of his stay.[1] The letter, written before 10 August from Capri and addressed to his friend Ben del Castillo, reveals a young man traveling alone, missing his Parisian friends, yet enjoying nonetheless his time in the Mediterranean south. He shares his adventures with bravado and playful exaggeration:

> If it were not for one German staying at the Marina, I should be absolutely without society and he is in love and cannot talk about anything but his sweetheart's moral irreproachability. We are going over to Sorrento in a day or two to visit her, and I have agreed to keep her husband's interest riveted to Vesuvius, Baiae, Pozzuoli and other places along the distant opposite shore.
>
> Naples is simply superb and I spent a delightful week there. Of course it was very hot, and one generally feels used up. It is a fact that in Naples they eke out their wine with spirits and drugs, so that a glass of wine and water at a meal will make a man feel drunk. I had to take bad beer in order not to feel good-for-nothing. I could not sleep at night. In the afternoon I would smoke a cigarette in an armchair or on my bed and at five o'clock wake up suddenly from a deep sleep of several hours. Then lie awake all night and quarrel with mosquitoes, fleas and all imaginable beasts. I am frightfully bitten from head to foot. Otherwise Italy is all that one can dream for beauty and charm.
>
> It is however true that the "Vandalia" is at Naples. Cap. Robson was very polite and asked me to lunch on board on Tuesday, but at lunch time I was sailing past the Vandalia's bows in the Capri market boat, packed in with a lot of vegetables and fruit. . . .[2]
>
> I am painting away very hard and shall be here a long time.[3]

Sargent stayed on Capri well into October. By November he was with his family in Nice.

Of the paintings from the stay only two canvases and seven panels show the sea, and so concern us here.[4] Of those, the only painting with a significant public life in the nineteenth century is the small picture now in the collection of the Sterling and Francine Clark Art Institute, *Neapolitan Children Bathing* (fig. 160). This was shown first at the National Academy of Design in New York in the annual exhibition of 1879.[5]

Facing page: Fig. 159 Detail of fig. 160, *Neapolitan Children Bathing*, 1879. Sterling and Francine Clark Art Institute, Williamstown, Massachusetts, 1955.852. (Exhibition)

On this inaugural appearance, *Neapolitan Children Bathing* prompted the critic for the New York *Herald* to call it "one of the most attractive pictures in the collection . . . a sparkling little work, full of air and sunlight . . . remarkable for good drawing and simple modeling . . . a remarkably clever bit of work."[6] In the intervening 130 years commentators have continually reaffirmed that initial enthusiasm. Apart from reiterating the canvas's directness and immediacy of impression, and to marvel anew at Sargent's skill in transcribing the visual world, there seems little to add to the critical encomiums and the specific documentary data recently assembled about the picture.[7]

It might prove worthwhile, however, to examine *Neapolitan Children Bathing* in light of the more general assumptions we make about realist pictures of the nineteenth century, especially ones as effective and compelling as this. Perhaps the most basic, yet often unexamined, assumption about a picture of this ilk concerns its origins. What prompted Sargent to make *Neapolitan Children Bathing*? Four of the simplest answers to that question—those that I propose to raise here—would imagine the work as a response to the wonders of the outside world; as an evolved end of a studio process; as a commercial answer to a patron; or as part of a dialogue with the works of other artists. Articulated separately, these notions highlight distinct sets of artistic priorities and an equally diverse series of achievements. Together they may help us to wonder anew at the revelations embodied within the small canvas.

Perhaps the most appealing image of the painting's origin is to think of Sargent, in the summer of 1878, wandering along the Neapolitan shoreline and, struck by a glimpse of four young boys on the sand, setting up his easel to capture the moment with all the freshness of the scene's informality and the vigor of his youthful, burgeoning virtuosity. This would explain the potent sensation of sun and heat that the picture conveys, of light within the canvas so bright that we almost want to squint. It likewise affirms the candid poses and attitudes of the four boys—one, the littlest, aware of the painter but the others apparently oblivious and unconcerned at being observed.

The way in which Sargent has painted the scene—seemingly random and summary sweeps of white across the beach, softly brushed blue and purple shadows, the impasto of the breaking wave, extraordinary threads of lemon yellow beneath the just cresting wave to the right—seems to betray enlightened observation and manual spontaneity on the painter's part. The yacht in the distance and, offshore, just to the right of the boy with the water wings, a swimmer's wet head, appear as happy coincidences rather than narrative elements of a planned composition. Sargent portrays the boys—three overlapping, indecorous (one with his lower legs and feet extending beyond the picture frame)—on their nondescript bit of hot beach in a fashion that epitomizes what we might call a snapshot aesthetic, capturing a slice of life common to wherever sun, sand, and little boys coexist. Not just the handling and the subject but the scale, too, of *Neapolitan Children Bathing*, a scant eleven by sixteen inches, suggests it is a sketch.[8]

In this scenario we can imagine Sargent, just twenty-two, retreating from the bustle of his Parisian life and heading south—to Italy, his native land. Sargent doubtless felt that he was due a vacation: during the fall of 1877 he had worked in both the École des Beaux-Arts and the atelier of Carolus-Duran, with whom he was collaborating on a major commission for a ceiling in the Palais du Luxembourg. In March 1878 he had put *Fishing for Oysters at Cancale* (see fig. 122) on exhibition in New York City as his first attempt to show in the United States, and not only was it reviewed favorably but it sold to a well-established artist, Samuel

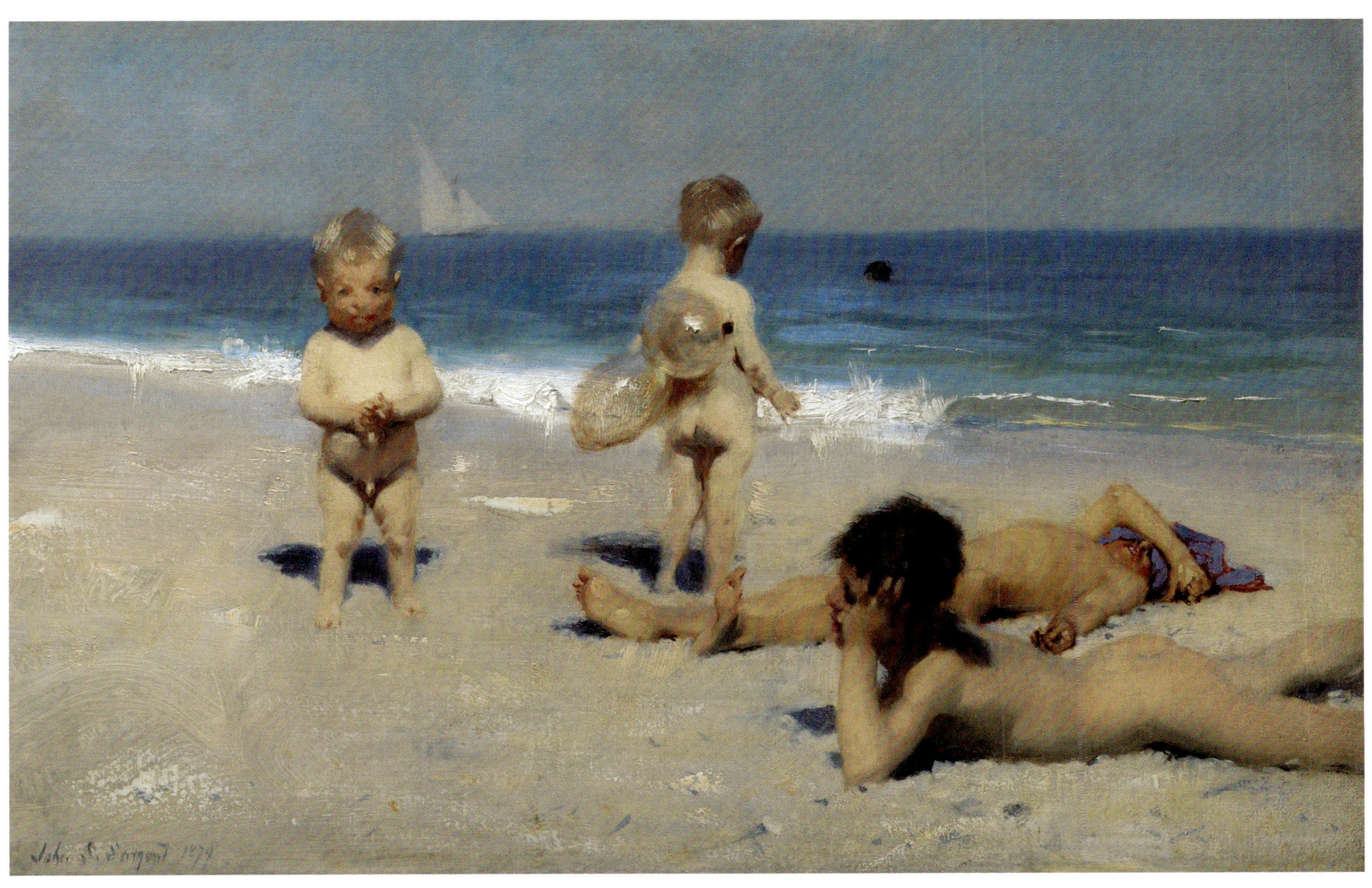

Fig. 160 *Neapolitan Children Bathing*, 1879. Oil on canvas, $10\frac{9}{16} \times 16\frac{3}{16}$ in (16.8 × 41.1 cm). Inscribed, lower left: *John S. Sargent 1879*. Sterling and Francine Clark Art Institute, Williamstown, Massachusetts, 1955.852. (Exhibition)

Colman. The next month a more carefully worked view of the fisherfolk showed at the Salon, and it too sold (see fig. 123). Meanwhile a portrait that Sargent had shown at the Salon of 1877 was well received at the Paris Exposition universelle of 1878. And, most significant of all, Carolus-Duran declared Sargent's apprenticeship complete by agreeing to sit as the subject for a major portrait.[9] So when, in late July, the young American headed to Italy, a few days of spontaneous sketching would be in order. And what could provide a more joyous, challenging subject to sketch than children on a hot sandy beach?

It was as a study or sketch that many of the picture's first viewers understood the work. In 1879, when the hierarchy of painting was much disputed and degrees of finish were an issue for artist, critic, and patron, writers applied these terms consistently to *Neapolitan Children Bathing*: "little seaside study," "a torn leaf from his album . . . [A] very lovely study," "a looser sketch than either of the three or four which he has so far sent to us from Paris."[10] Commentators from later decades, too, responded comparably: "the captivating little sketch of children on the seashore" (1902); "in the best tradition of *plein air* painting" (1970).[11] Most recently the authors of the catalogue raisonné referred to the enthusiasm New York critics felt "when the sketch was exhibited there in 1879."[12]

One must not hold the authors to this usage too literally. Both "sketch" and "study," however—words used by art writers for over a century of responses to the canvas—imply a painter seated before his subject, responding directly and earnestly to the scene before him. This is, for many, the sensation the picture generates, so true, so "very natural, home-like, and out-of-doorsy"[13] is it.

This truth effect—the impression that the painter is recording precisely what he sees before him—follows what few comments we have about Sargent's act of painting. One friend recounted seeing the painter outdoors in the mid-1880s:

> He was accustomed to emerge, carrying a large easel, to advance a little way into the open, and then suddenly to plant himself down nowhere in particular . . . His object was to acquire the habit of reproducing whatever met his vision without the slightest previous "arrangement" of detail, the painter's business being, not to pick and choose, but to render the effect before him, whatever it may be.[14]

And so Sargent's actions, 130 years of critical and scholarly writing about the picture, and, most crucially, *Neapolitan Children Bathing* itself—its subject, its scale, its bravura technique, its bright color and dazzled lack of focus—all combine to testify that, indeed, the work originated on the Neapolitan strand as Sargent walked there one day in the summer of 1878.

There are, however, complications in this view of *Neapolitan Children Bathing*. First, in the lower left corner Sargent has written "John S. Sargent 1879." In 1879 Sargent was not in Naples or its environs. He had left the region no later than October 1878, spending over a month with his family in Nice before returning to Paris by early December.[15] It is possible, of course, that Sargent painted the work in Italy but finished it in Paris in 1879 or, alternatively, signed and dated it only when he sold it (to an American named George Millar Williamson).[16] Another curious element of the inscription is that it includes no place name. All but two of the genre scenes that Sargent intended for sale or exhibition between 1878 and 1880 include that piece of information.[17] Moreover, of the six larger canvases he painted of Caprese subjects, three bear the inscription "Capri," as do two smaller works on panel or board.[18] The date and the choice not to inscribe a place on a canvas that was soon sold or exhibited become, in this context, anomalous.

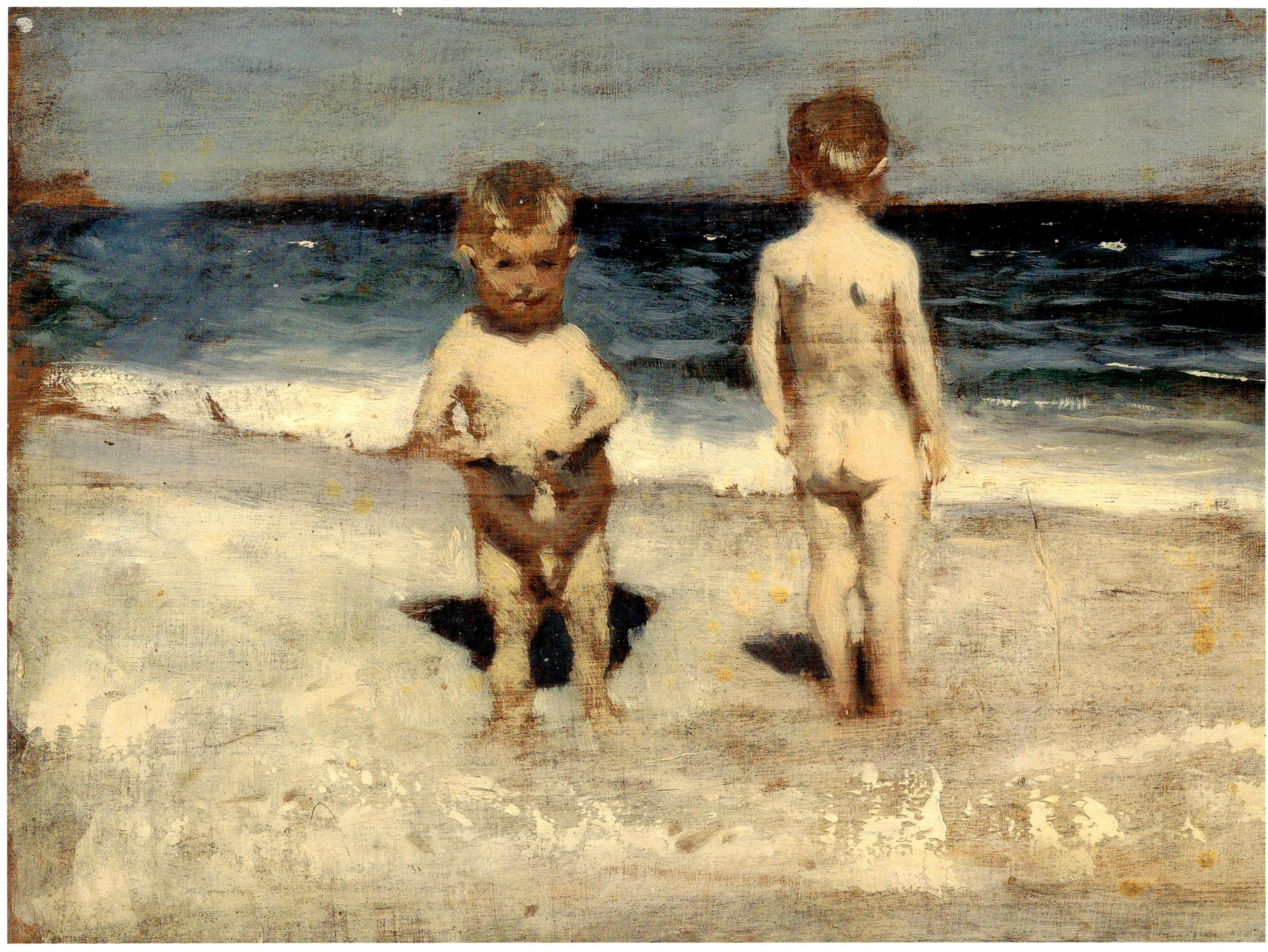

Fig. 161 *Two Boys on a Beach, Naples*, 1878. Oil on panel, 10 × 13½ in (25.4 × 34.3 cm). Private Collection. (Exhibition)

In addition to the curious aspects of the inscription, there are six seaside panels by Sargent showing boys lounging on the shore, three of which relate directly to the canvas. These, too, complicate the notion of *Neapolitan Children Bathing* being a study from life. The six are all oil on mahogany panel, and they give every evidence of having been painted outdoors. Their form and support are precisely what artists of the era used while away from home, traveling

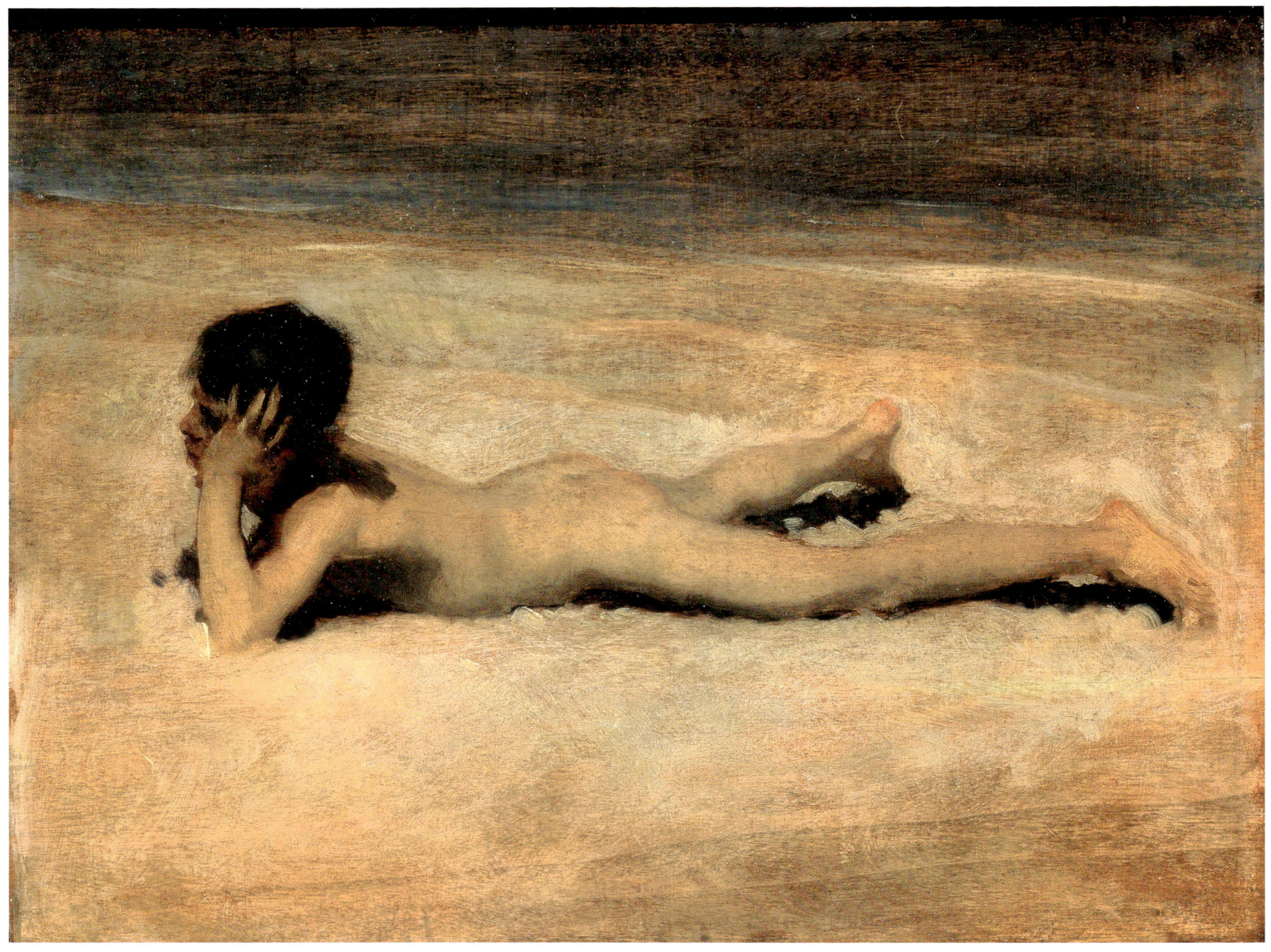

Fig. 162 *A Nude Boy on a Beach*, 1878. Oil on panel, 10½ × 13¹³⁄₁₆ in (26.8 × 35.1 cm). Tate, London. Bequeathed by John Tillotson, 1984. (Exhibition)

and having to pack up before their sketches' surfaces were entirely dry. The thin, commonly sized panels could be fitted into a slotted box, thus held apart and movable without fear of their rubbing against, or sticking to, one another.[19] All share a thin, apparently quick technique.

Sargent treated these six panels, too, as many artists treated their field studies: as working materials to be kept, or as trades or gifts with other painters and intimate friends who would understand the particular beauties and sensibilities of the plein air study. Three of the panels were in the artist's estate at his death in 1925 (*Two Boys on a Beach, Naples* [fig. 161]; *A Nude Boy on a Beach* [fig. 162]; and *Nude Boy on Sands* [fig. 163]); one was a gift to his Parisian friend the Finnish painter Albert Edelfelt (*Two Boys on a Beach with Boats* [fig. 165]); and the fifth he gave to his friend and collaborator the poet Alma Strettell (*Beach at Capri* [fig. 166]). Only *Boy on the Beach* (fig. 172) was apparently early out in the wider world through some as yet unknown transaction.[20]

If these are indeed individual figure studies done in the open air, then what is their relation to *Neapolitan Children Bathing*? *Two Boys on a Beach, Naples* shows the same two standing figures, more coarsely and quickly done, with the painter setting the scene of beach and breaking wave at a comparable diagonal. Sargent has spread bright paint with a palette knife in the panel's foreground, catching the notion of sunlight reflecting off sand, mimicking the breaking wave in vivacious brushwork (albeit less exuberantly so than on the canvas). The taller boy turns his back directly to us, holds his arm to his side, and plants his legs more solidly than in the canvas. In the panel he does not wear water wings. Likewise the younger child manifests minor differences from the boy in *Neapolitan Children Bathing*—thinner arms, more closely set eyes, a strangely elongated torso, and a relatively smaller head. Both of the boys lying down in *Neapolitan Children Bathing* seem to have

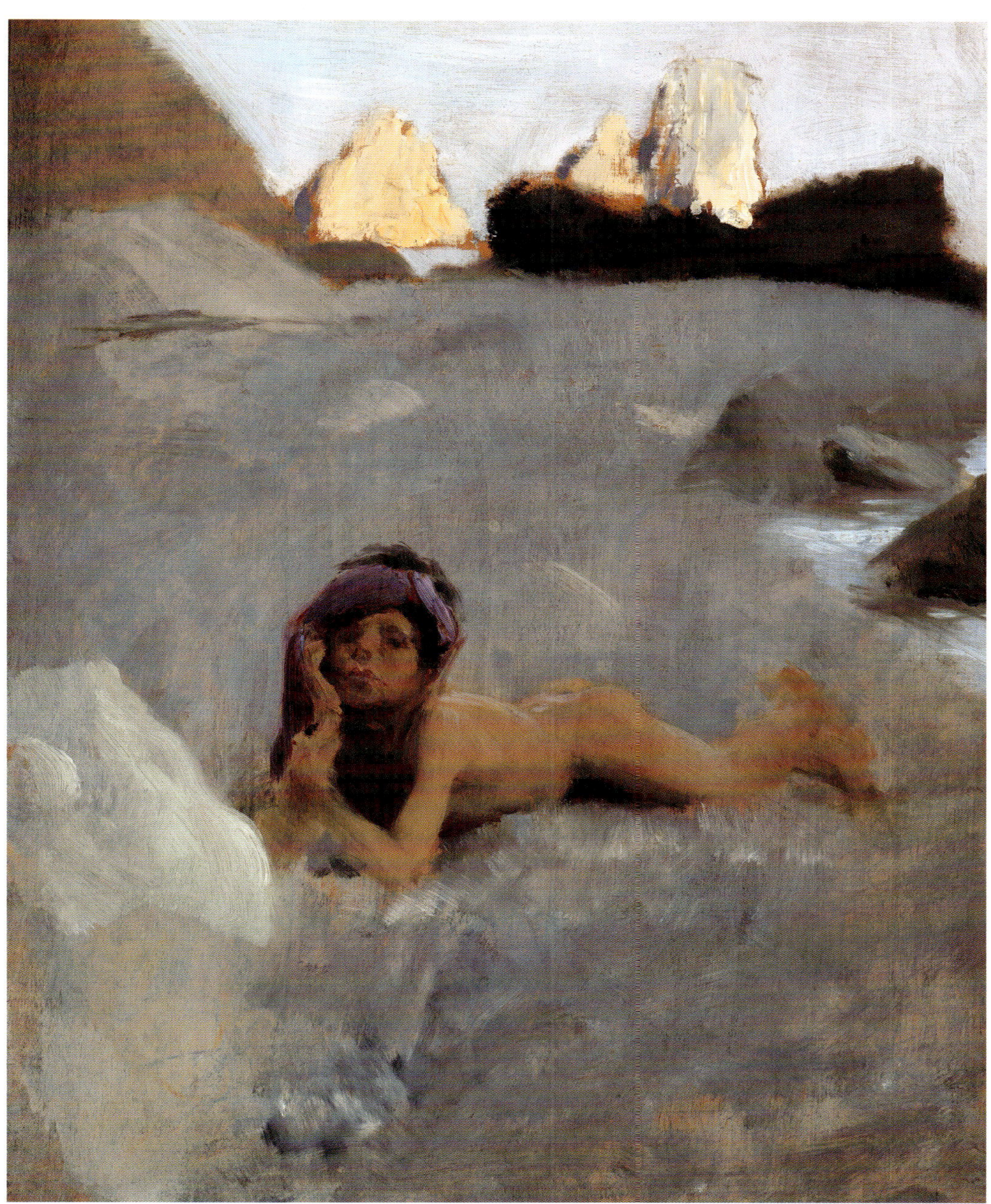

Fig. 163 *Nude Boy on Sands*, 1878. Oil on panel, 13 × 10 in (33 × 25.3 cm). Private Collection. (Exhibition)

Facing page: Fig. 164 Detail of fig. 160, *Neapolitan Children Bathing*, 1879. Sterling and Francine Clark Art Institute, Williamstown, Massachusetts, 1955.852. (Exhibition)

their original versions in the panels too: we see the foremost in *A Nude Boy on a Beach* (fig. 162), with ever so slight difference in hairline and the cast of shadow; note how delicately in this sketch Sargent has used the grain of the panel to surround the boy, suggesting shore and sand. While the splay of the feet and the position of the outstretched arm of the figure in *Boy on the Beach* (fig. 172) are different than in *Neapolitan Children Bathing*, it seems clear that the figure with the purple towel in the larger picture derives from this one, although there is no trace of sea on the panel. The likelihood of Sargent twice coming upon these four boys in such comparable poses, and recording them once on the three small panels and then again all four together on the canvas, is slim.

The preceding paragraph belabors the obvious. Presented with the four paintings, most art historians would assert, rightly, I believe, that the panels precede the canvas and record sights that Sargent then combined and modified when composing the larger painting. "Composing" is the operative word. *Neapolitan Children Bathing*, despite seeming to be a sketch or study of a real scene faithfully depicted, becomes in this view a fictional construction that evolved through a series of choices Sargent made as he developed the picture on canvas. We gain a sense of this composite character, perhaps, in the subtly unsettling scale of the pairs of boys, the two younger seeming disproportionately large in relation to the more mature figures lying on the sand. This notion of an assembled scene is a radically different account of the picture's origins than that evoked by the casual sense of it as, itself, a study or sketch.

The purple cloth that is so striking an element of the scene in *Neapolitan Children Bathing* points to yet a further complication. The cloth is, thanks to Sargent's manner of laying the blue-purple paint almost to the edges of the rose-colored underpaint, the most obviously outlined object in sight, the purple-red vibrating and calling attention to itself in a work that is otherwise a marvel of softened, three-dimensional forms. The cloth recurs in two further Capri panels. In one of those, *Nude Boy on Sands* (see fig. 163), the boy might well be the same as in *Boy on the Beach* (see fig. 172); both figures project a sly insouciance in spite of the one having most of his face covered. If the same boy, the two panels show distinctly different settings: one is nondescript while *Nude Boy on Sands* depicts the cool shade of Capri's Marina Piccola with the Faraglioni rocks, sunstruck, in the background. Sargent shows this same site, looking in the opposite direction, in the panel he gave to his friend Edelfelt (see fig. 165).[21] In this two clothed boys lie utterly relaxed, face down, on the sand. The purple cloth lies crumpled beside them. We see them from a greater height and distance than in any other of the panels. Sargent accentuates the bright warmth of the sunlight by showing boats and rocks in the distance, where the small patches of intense darkness indicating shadow act as balm to the scene's glare.

Beach at Capri (see fig. 166) also seems to have strong contrast of light and shade as its formal theme, the shadowed flesh of the boy and toddler being suggested by the dark color and grain of the panel and merely augmented by Sargent's addition of oil paint. Boats—beached, moored, and under sail—animate the middle ground and distance.

If these six panels form the repertoire of figures, poses, props, and setting that Sargent chose from to construct *Neapolitan Children Bathing*, it becomes worthwhile to consider what he omitted in making the larger picture: all the clothed boys, the materials of an active marina, any trace of a cooling shadow, and the recognizable site of Capri. These omissions all favor the general over the specific. Even in the title of the canvas—"Neapolitan" instead of "Capriote"—he moves to the broader term.

What does Sargent add? None of the surviving source panels shows any motif that would become the swimmer, the fifth

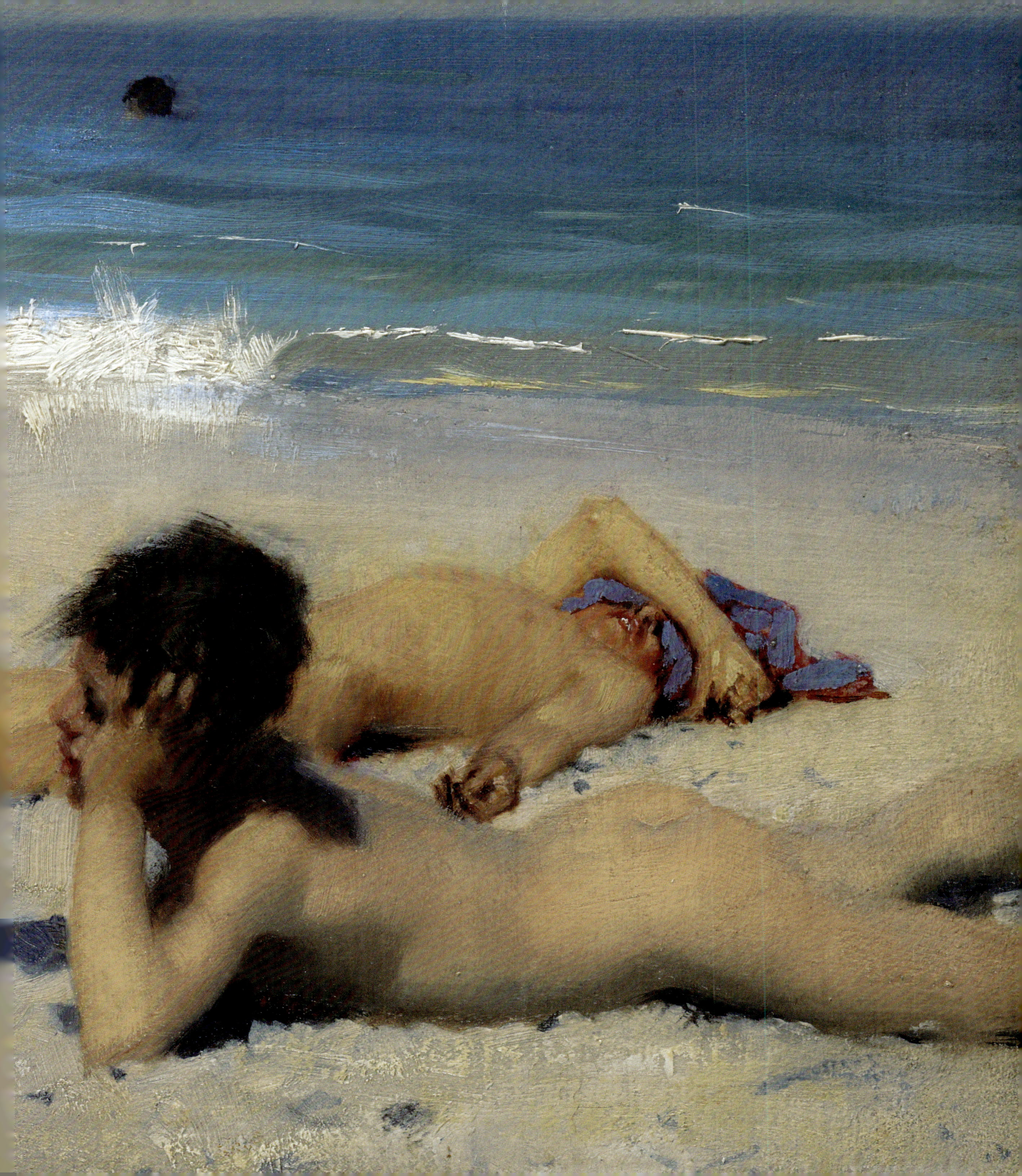

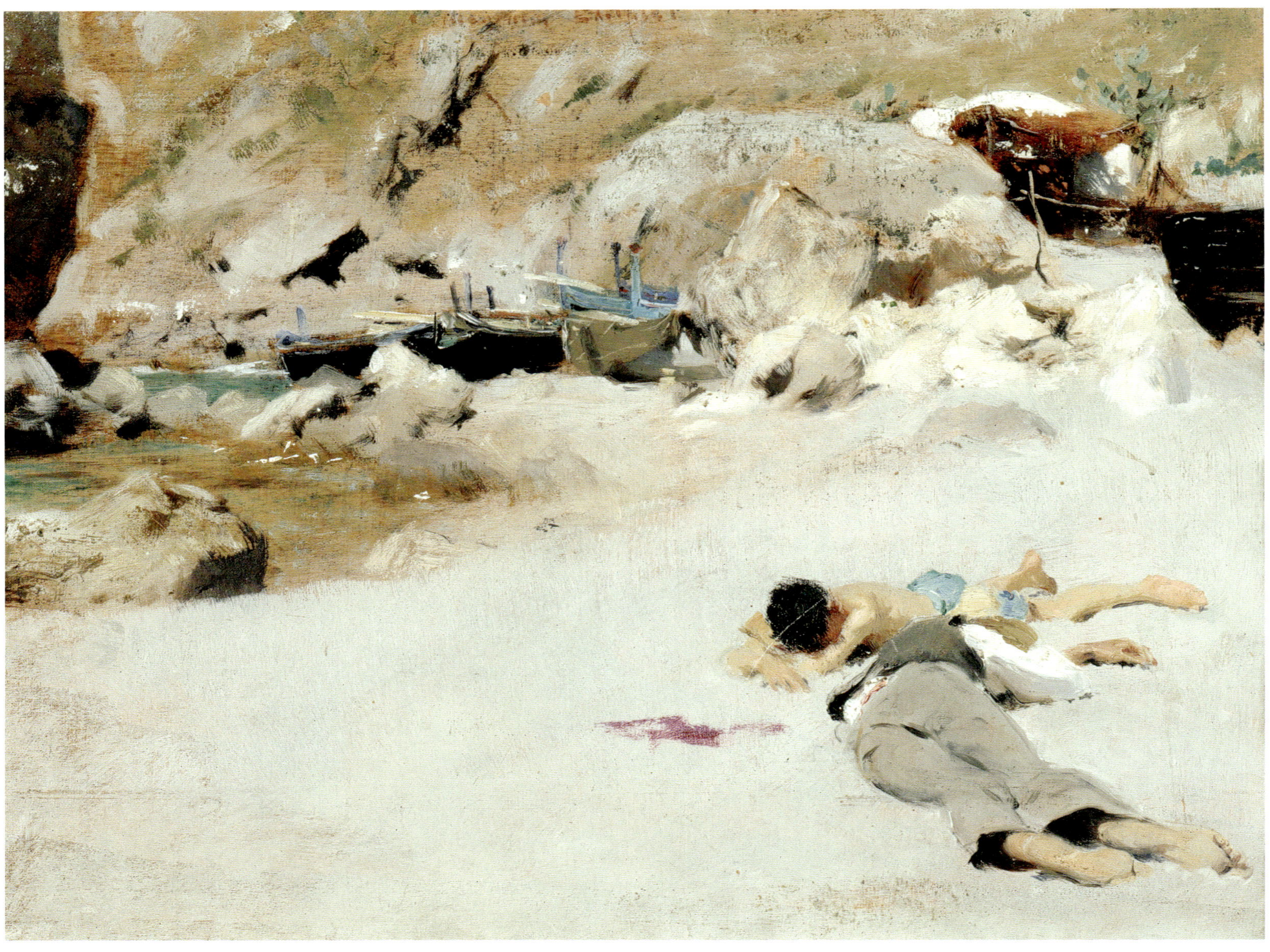

Fig. 165 *Two Boys on a Beach with Boats*, 1878. Oil on panel, 10 × 13¾ in (25.3 × 35 cm). Inscribed, upper left: *à mon ami Edelfelt John S. Sargent*. The Society of Swedish Literature in Finland. (Exhibition)

boy in *Neapolitan Children Bathing*, head surging through the water in the distance. Nor do they contain anything like the water wings now sported by the taller standing boy. These are a particularly pregnant addition. The earliest writers about the picture took note of them, aptly, since they glisten at the center of the canvas. The critic for the *Art Journal* looked too quickly at the picture and thought the boys were "playing on the seashore with great transparent balls, very likely sunfish."[22] Others, however, read the water wings aright as "a make-shift life-saving apparatus formed of two bladders" and urged that visitors to the exhibition appreciate, as "a remarkably clever bit of work . . . the painting of the semi-transparent air bags which the boy with his back to us has fastened to his shoulders as life preservers."[23] To at least one critic, the water wings made the boy wearing them the most notable of the group, in spite of his face being turned from us: "The chubby little fellows, and one particularly who has two bladders, shining with water and giving out shell-like reflections, attached to his

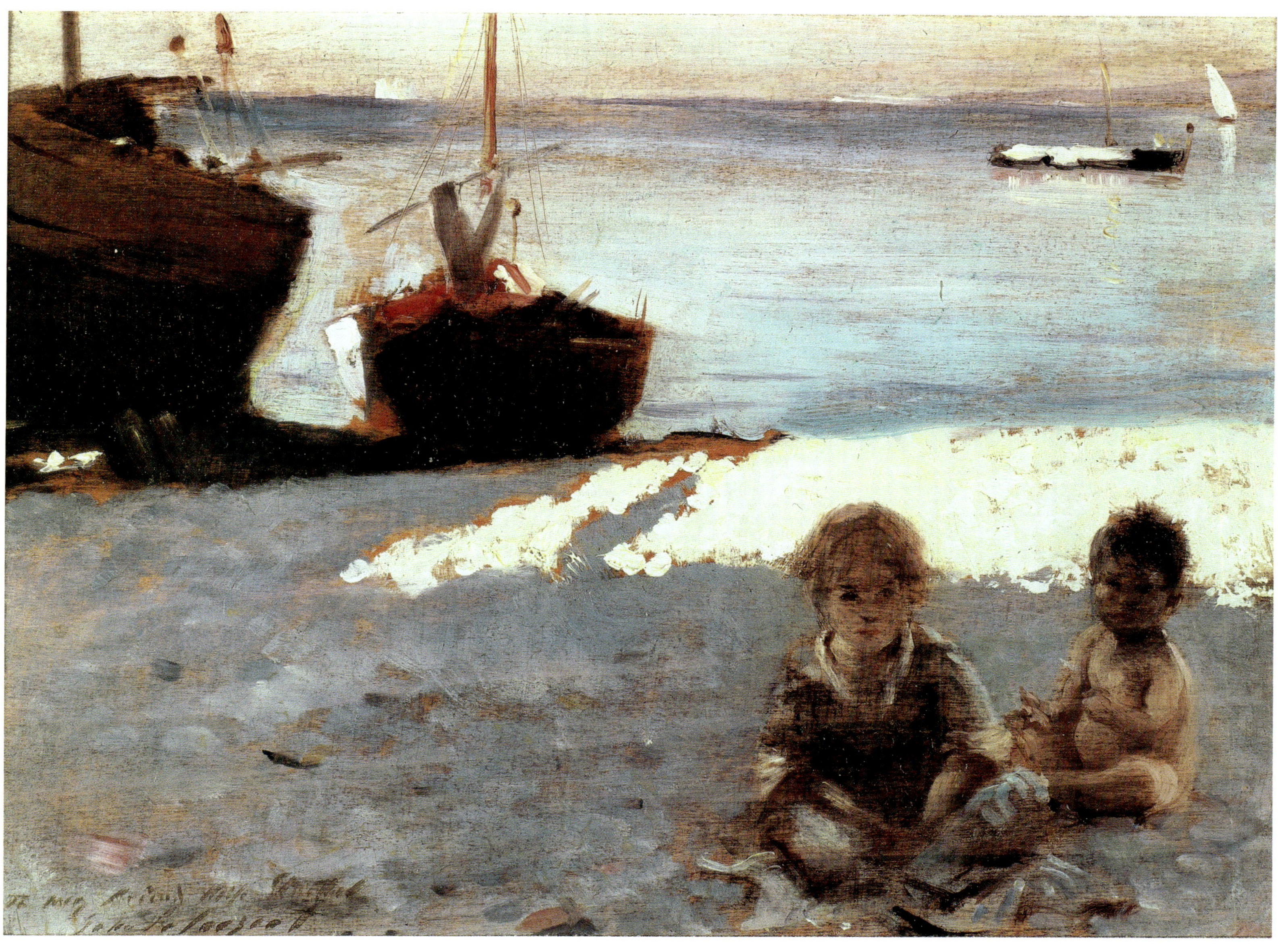

shoulders, are made to look like young cupids."[24]

For some critics the orbs' nacreous beauty was too extreme: "though Veronese would hardly have made them better, he would have subordinated them, nor let them play so chief a part."[25] Perhaps, however, Sargent conjured the water wings and chose not to subdue them for a purpose. They are apparently late additions to the composition; they lie on top of the breaking wave, the one to the left being a thin wash of golden brown over the high impasto of the foaming water (whereas he painted the wave up to either side of the boy's body). Further, by virtue of the firm shape and dark color of the band beneath the boy's arm, Sargent established a strong contrast with all the surrounding golden glow to draw the viewer's eye to the water wings. These—their whimsy and their beauty—shift the identity of the boy wearing them from a native Caprese urchin at home in the elements to an identity more akin with the presumed viewer's, "civilized" and needing protection from the surrounding

Fig. 166 *Beach at Capri*, 1878. Oil on panel, 10¼ × 13¾ in (26.2 × 35 cm). Inscribed, lower left: *To my friend Miss Strettel [sic] / John S. Sargent.* Fine Arts Museums of San Francisco, Bequest of Frederick J. Hellman to the California Palace of the Legion of Honor, 1965.32. (Exhibition)

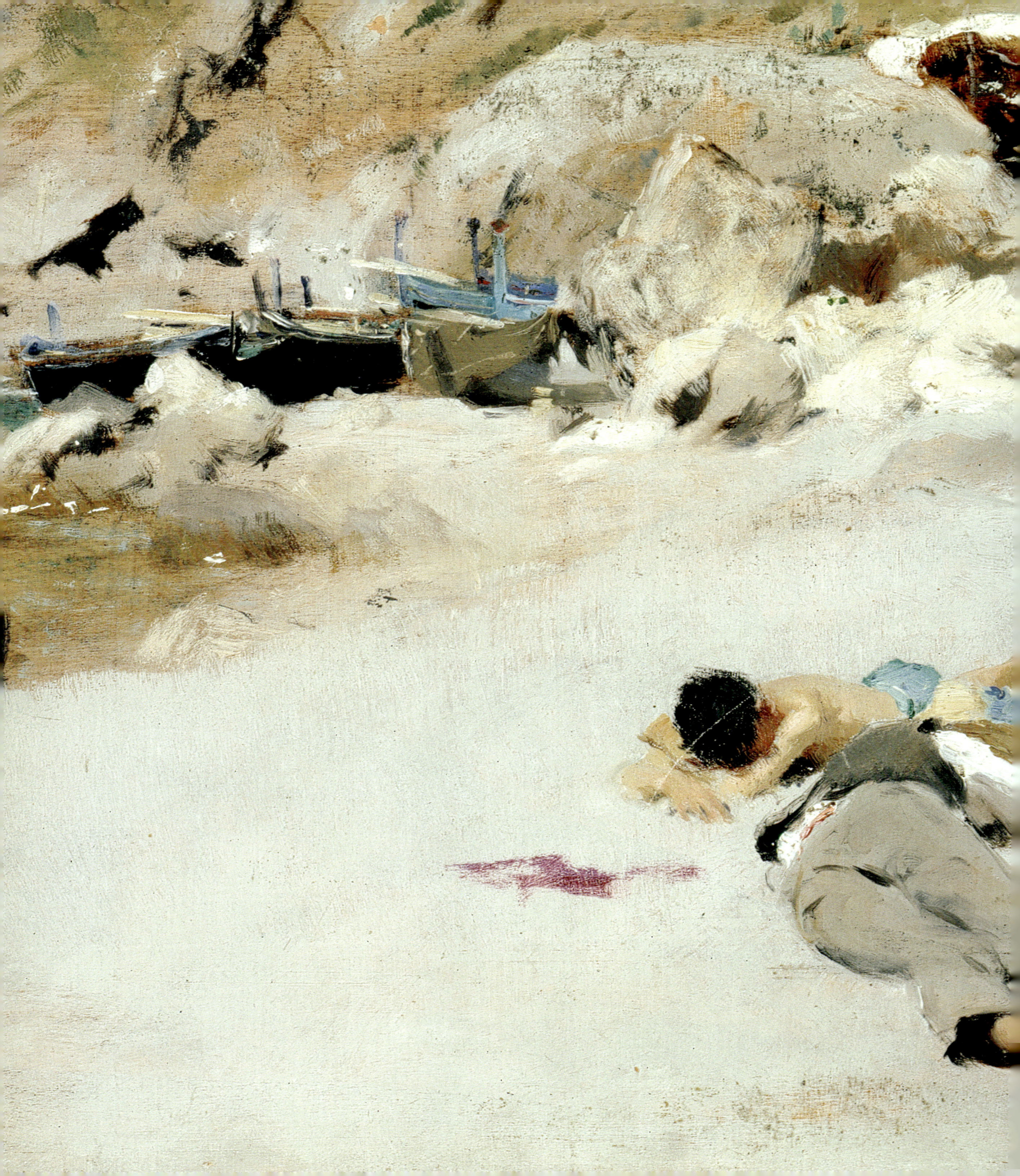

environment. The blondness of the two standing boys—and one of the boys in *Beach at Capri*, too, is light-haired—coupled with the water wings, introduces the potential of class and national distinctions into the scene, prompting some viewers to discriminate between those boys who belong to the island and those who are foreign. At least one critic in 1879 distinguished among them on the basis of complexion, invoking the "bronze and ivory cupids strewed like shells along the golden sands."[26]

Thus far we have touched upon two complementary accounts of the origins of *Neapolitan Children Bathing*, one beginning solely with the picture itself, which indicates that the picture illustrates a scene Sargent encountered while visiting the Bay of Naples in the summer of 1878. The second, arising from a consideration of the picture in conjunction with six of the other paintings that Sargent made during his stay there, indicates that it was a construct of Sargent's imagination, fabricated by combining and modifying those elements from his on-site studies that most pleased him into a coherent whole. The canvas is thus a fictive thing, with Sargent creating rather than documenting a scene.

This second interpretation allows for the possibility that the work was assembled after Sargent had left the island. It thus permits the inscribed date—1879—to be understood as appropriate to, and part of, its likely Parisian creative process. It also explains the unusual lack of a place name on the front of the painting, as if Sargent recognized that by identifying it with "Paris," some of the picture's Caprese magic, its compelling taken-from-nature aspect, would be lost.

We might call on another documentary element, however, in imagining yet a third origin of *Neapolitan Children Bathing*. While most of the affirmative responses that the painting inspired while at the National Academy of Design confined themselves to description and aesthetic evaluation of the picture,[27] the one written by Edward Strahan (pseudonym for Earl Shinn, a Philadelphia-born, Paris-trained painter-turned-critic) devoted barely two sentences to the canvas. Instead, he focused on the painter's biography and general talents and, citing *Neapolitan Children Bathing* in particular, provided the origins of his professional career:

> One of the most delightful, golden, happy accidental hits in the exhibition is John S. Sargent's "Neapolitan Children Bathing" (431). It is a looser sketch than either of the three or four which he has so far sent to us from Paris . . . [Mr. Sargent] is a thoroughly accomplished cosmopolitan. He comprehends music scientifically, reads all literatures with avidity, and paints better than his professor, Duran. Connected to his contribution to the academy there is a simple ballad-like story which may be worth the telling. It reminds us some how of our lost Couture's narrative of the quiet little elderly gentleman who sought his studio as color-grinder, and, after having cleaned the master's brushes and imbibed his critical opinions for several months, turned out to be a millionaire picture-collector from Rouen.[28] Mr. Sargent's visitor was not so disguised a character, but he too was an elderly, modest man, and he was little. He called on the young painter-amateur in Paris just after the latter's "Cancalaises" had made some sensation at the Salon, and remarked that he had picked out the canvas as to his liking, and though not rich, would like a smaller but similar one if the artist could be tempted with a certain genteel price which was named. Sargent, who had never had an order in his life, and had never figured before the world as a professional, took care to express no surprise or joy. He said quietly that he would furnish something or other for the money, and on the visitor's departure tore away to his friends, proclaimed the splendor of the

Facing page: Fig. 167 Detail of fig. 165, *Two Boys on a Beach with Boats*, 1878. The Society of Swedish Literature in Finland. (Exhibition)

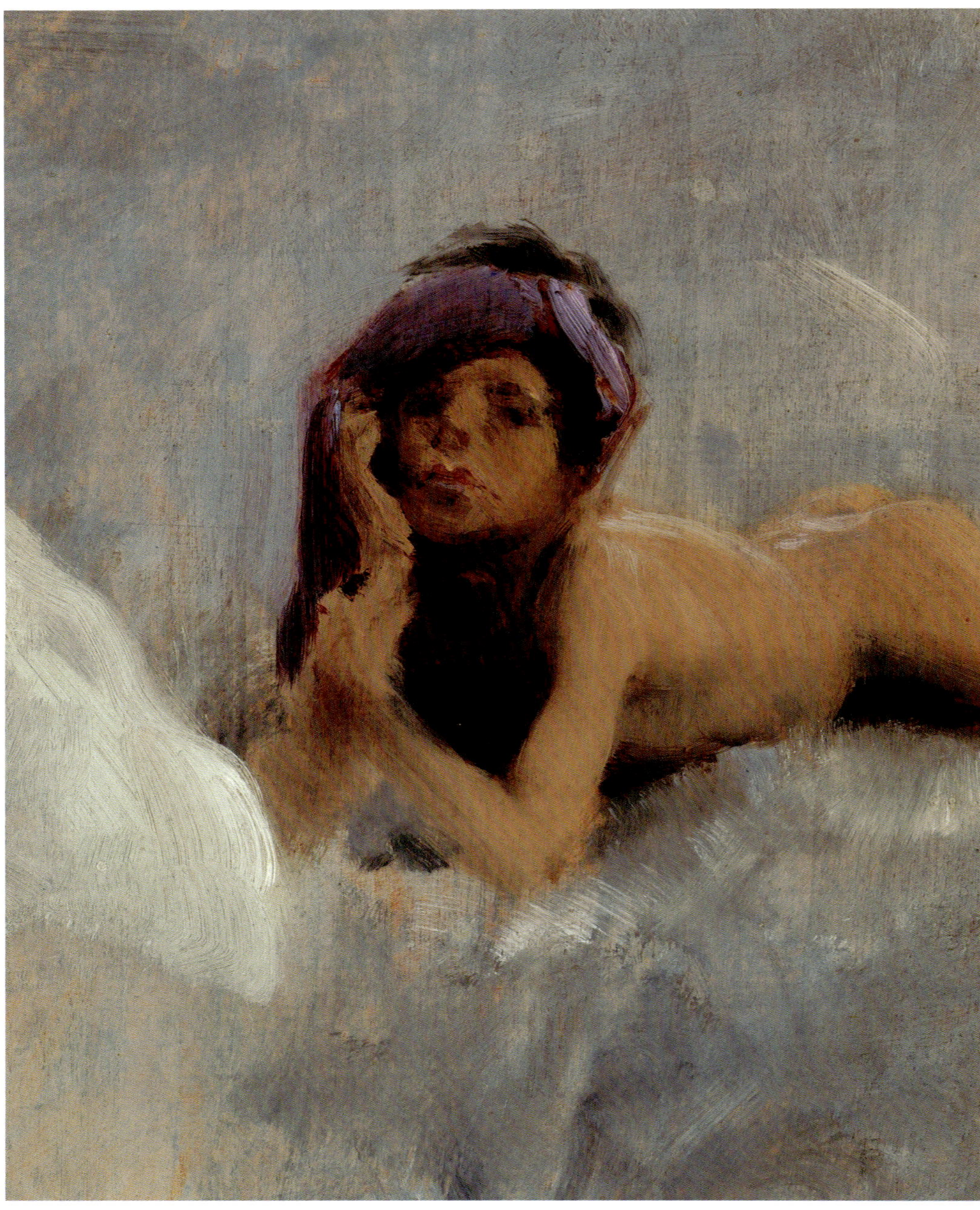

Fig. 168 Detail of fig. 163, *Nude Boy on Sands*, 1878. Private Collection. (Exhibition)

> order he had got, and spent most of the price in a crowded American orgy. When the picture was applied for, for this exhibition, the messenger was directed to one of those hopeless addresses far beyond the ends of the most endless streets in Brooklyn, to attain which street-cars fail and cabs are a mockery. There, in a suburban wilderness, in a small house, he found the small Paris visitor hugging the solitary picture. Instead of being an art-patron with a collection, he was simply a man who had fallen in love with an artist's work and concluded to treat himself. So the "Children Bathing" went to a Brooklyn art-lover who had perhaps never bought a picture and never did again. And a young painter's vocation was settled; for Sargent determined to become a professional painter.[29]

Let us examine Shinn's words, which include non-public knowledge that lends them authority.

The owner of record when *Neapolitan Children Bathing* appeared at the National Academy of Design was "G. M. Williamson," Shinn's "modest, elderly man."[30] George Millar Williamson (1849–1921) indeed resided in Brooklyn. The 1880 census lists him, his wife, and son all living with his mother and stepfather and four other family members, along with one live-in servant, on Madison Street,[31] in Brooklyn (this in spite of Williamson reportedly having built in 1874 a large Shingle-style house called "Heart's Desire" in an area of Sparkill, New York, called Grand View).[32] An extant letter from Sargent to "Mr. Williamson" could conceivably be a prelude to this commission:

> At just this time I am very irregular at my studio, and when the salon opens shall be still more so, and in case I don't find you in this afternoon when I intend going round to you, I shall have to beg you to make a rendezvous or else communicate by a note.[33]

Although undated and without return address, the note seems to be written to someone whom Sargent had not yet met and it is self-evidently from the years of Sargent's residence in Paris.

There are, however, difficulties reconciling Shinn's report with what little we know of Williamson. First, he was not "elderly" at this time, being only about thirty.[34] Second, the letter from Sargent to Williamson, if it dates from 1878, is evidently written before the Salon has opened, and so Williamson cannot yet have seen Sargent's *En Route pour la pêche* before seeking an appointment with the painter.[35] Nor can Williamson be aptly characterized as a naïve admirer and possessor of a single work.[36] Likewise Shinn's account of the commission of *Neapolitan Children Bathing* being the single factor that convinced Sargent of his vocation is demonstrably false; in addition to portrait commissions, he had already sold the small *Fishing for Oysters at Cancale* from the first Society of American Artists exhibition and knew so.[37]

The germ of Strahan's tale, however, merits consideration. First, what he writes of Sargent's peripatetic upbringing, his attention to music and literature, and his ability with languages rings true, and while this is not specific enough to signal privileged information, this was not yet widely known outside Sargent's circle. Moreover, while Williamson evidently had not seen paintings at the Salon before seeking out the painter, it is wholly conceivable that he had visited the Society of American Artists in New York earlier that spring, admired the smaller *Fishing for Oysters at Cancale*, and asked for a "smaller

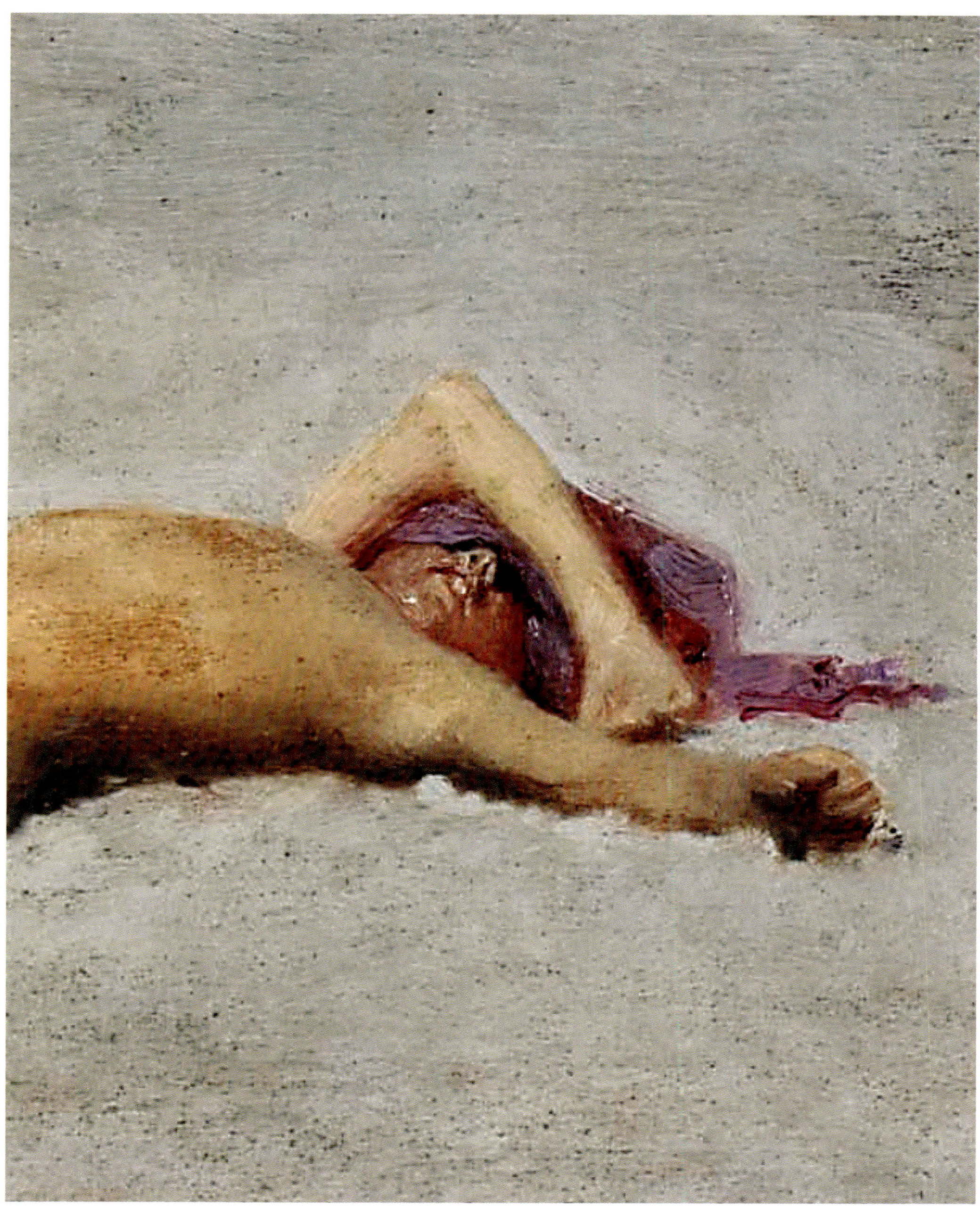

Fig. 169 Detail of fig. 172, *Boy on the Beach*, 1878. Collection of Isabel Fonseca, London. (Exhibition)

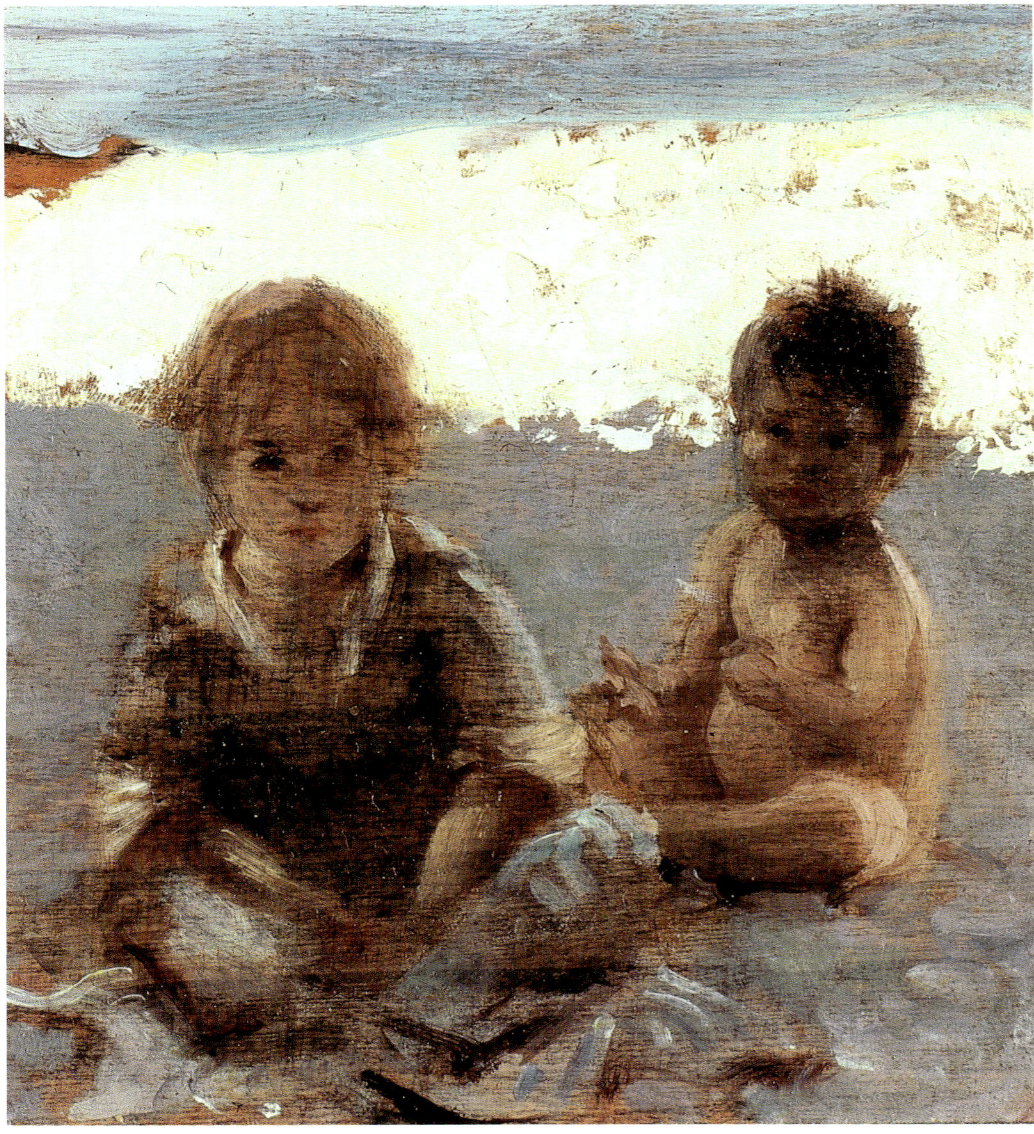

Fig. 170 Detail of fig. 166, *Beach at Capri*, 1878. Fine Arts Museums of San Francisco, Bequest of Frederick J. Hellman to the California Palace of the Legion of Honor, 1965.32. (Exhibition)

but similar" version of that much-lauded painting, which could prompt a work of the scale and general theme of *Neapolitan Children Bathing*. The distinction between the Society of American Artists or Salon versions of the same theme seems the type of detail that a journalist or friendly source could get wrong.[38] Further, some set of comparable circumstances—a commission direct to the painter on the basis of an exhibited work—is one of the only ways to explain how Sargent was able to leave Paris in late July; spend several months in Naples and Capri; go then to Nice to spend late October and November with his family; return to Paris only in December; paint this little picture and finish it sometime in early 1879; send it to the owner; submit it (with the owner's permission) to the National Academy;[39] and have it judged, passed, and on the wall in time for the 1 April opening. While Sargent was engaged in these activities, he was also at work on what he must have considered his principal tasks: the *Portrait de M. Carolus-Duran* (1879, Sterling and Francine Clark Art Institute) and *Dans les Oliviers à Capri* (1878, Private Collection) that were to be his Salon entries, and the ur-version of the latter (1878, Museum of Fine Arts, Boston), which he sent to New York for the Society of American Artists annual.[40]

So if there is truth to Shinn's construction of events, a third impetus for *Neapolitan Children Bathing* suggests itself. It is neither a delightful scene observed and spontaneously sketched by the painter, nor the studio confabulation using the fruits of a working holiday to produce a saleable painting. Rather, it evolves from a collector commissioning Sargent to make a picture "smaller but similar" to *Fishing for Oysters at Cancale*. To achieve it, Sargent followed the course he had set for his Cancale work: travel to an appropriate site, trial of various vistas, and then plein air figure studies. We know that he lodged, when he first arrived in Capri, in the Marina Grande rather than in the island's towns more distant from the sea.[41] Presumably he made his decision of what the seaside painting would consist, gathered his vocabulary of sketches, and then packed all these away to be further considered, assembled, and modified when he was back in his studio. For much of the rest of his stay on the island, he focused attention away from the water, on the olive groves and distinctive architecture of the place, emphasizing in particular Rosina Ferrara, the model who for Sargent (and many other artists) came to embody the spirit of the island.[42]

It is possible that this manner of working—methodically gathering materials for a campaign to be brought to fruition later, once back in Paris—is what prompted Sargent to make the otherwise anomalous *A Boat in the Waters off Capri* (fig. 173). One larger view of the Caprese waterfront on canvas with a light ground, comparable to what he anticipated for Williamson's commission and testifying to the improbable veracity of water shading from sapphire to emerald, juxtaposed with opalescent sand glinting like diamonds, would be useful as he worked in the gray light of a Parisian winter.

Nor is it certain that Sargent had the final composition of *Neapolitan Children Bathing* clearly in mind as he made his studies. In their thinness of application and complementary simplicity of background *Two Boys on a Beach, Naples* (see fig. 161) and *A Nude Boy on a Beach* (see fig. 162) bear a connection and clearly point to the direction he ultimately chose. The distinctive, more identifiably Caprese backgrounds of *Nude Boy on Sands* (see fig. 163), *Two Boys on a Beach with Boats* (see fig. 165), and *Beach at Capri* (see fig. 166) show options that could have led profitably in the direction of a dramatic work of light and shade, including a more recognizable view of the famous place. *Boy on the Beach* (see fig. 172), eyes covered and no hint of water, could have served in either, a link between the two options—as could *A Boat in the Waters off Capri* (see fig. 173). *Fishing Boats* (fig. 174), too, might

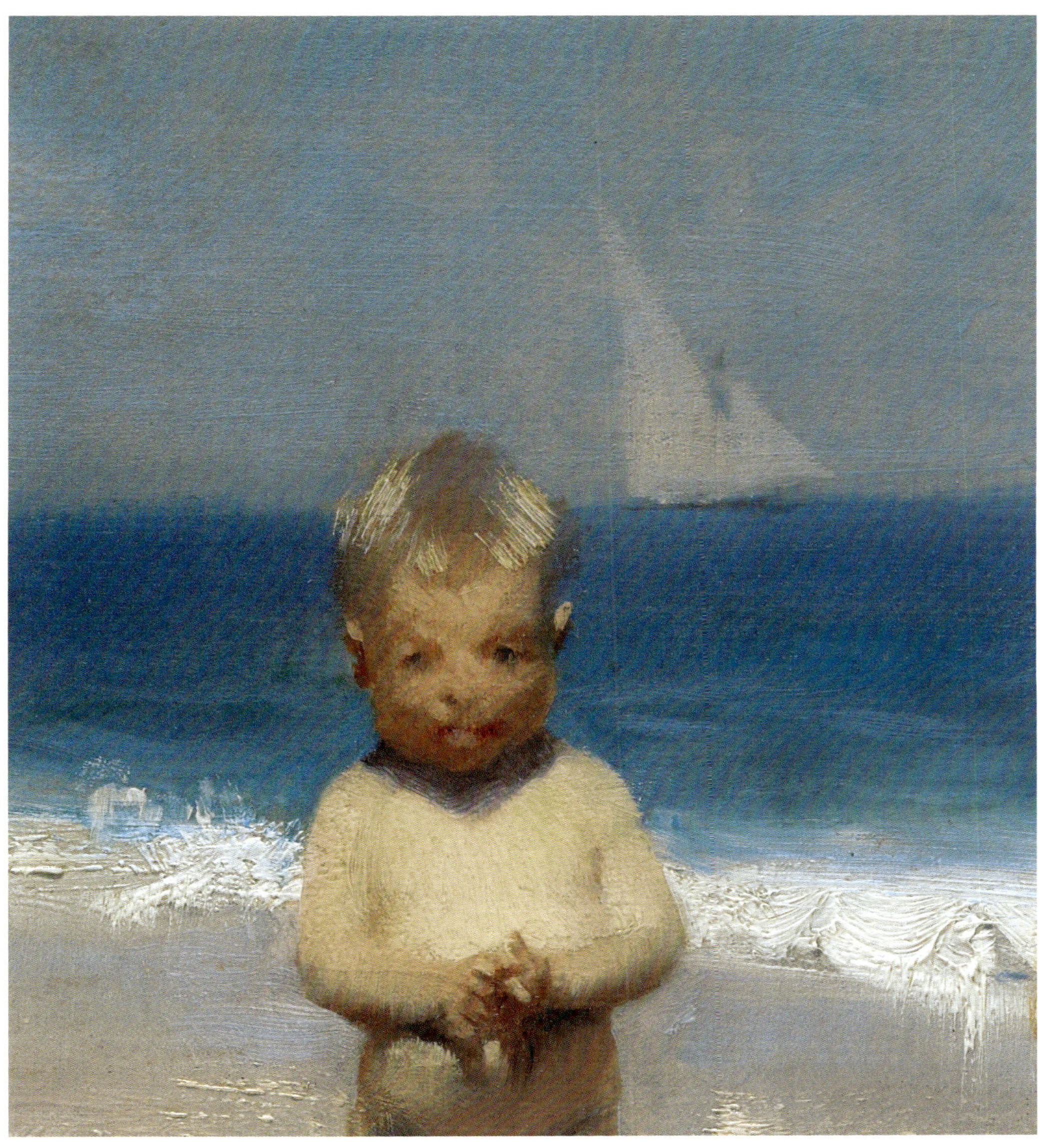

Fig. 171 Detail of fig. 160, *Neapolitan Children Bathing*, 1879. Sterling and Francine Clark Art Institute, Williamstown, Massachusetts, 1955.852. (Exhibition)

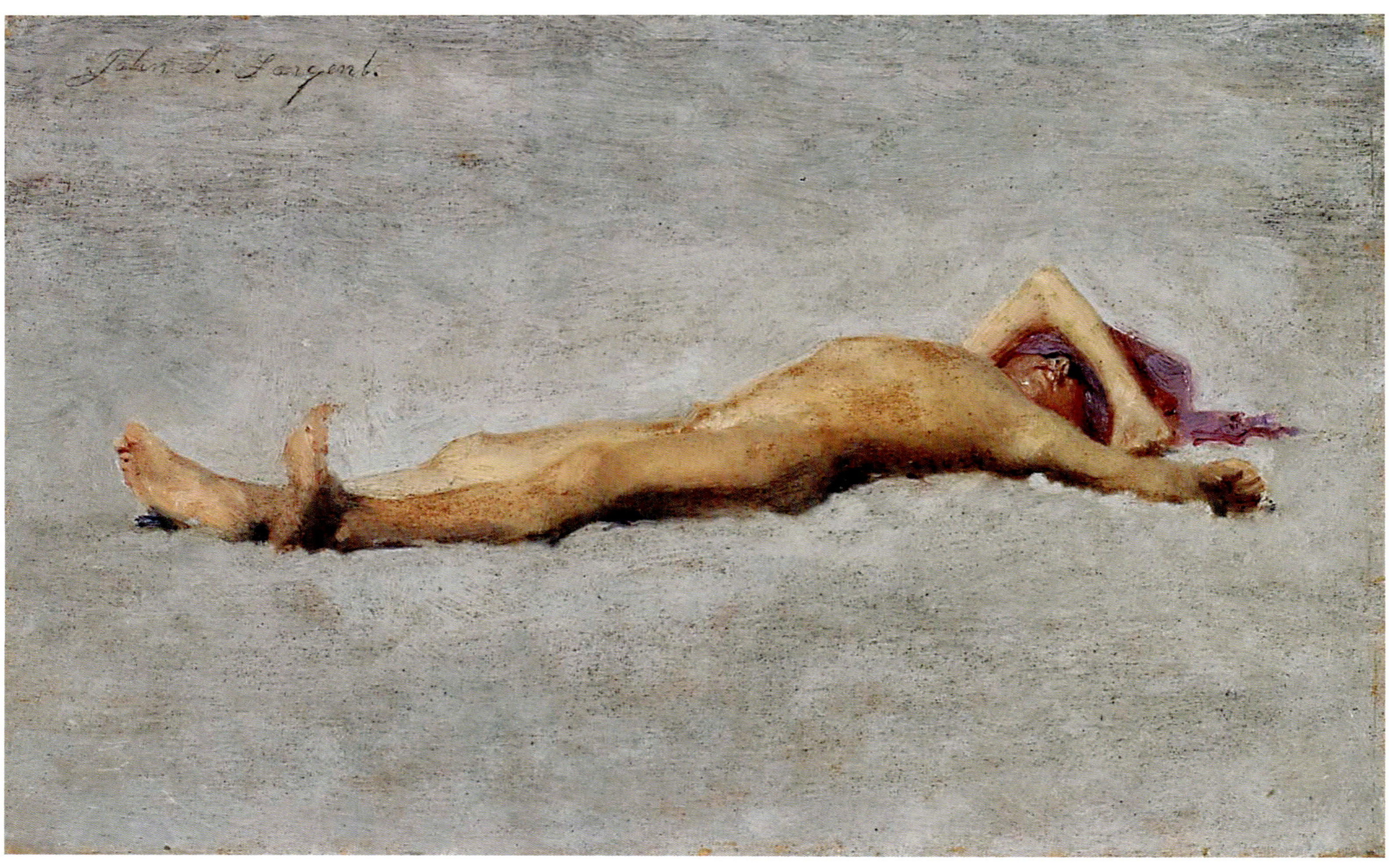

Fig. 172 *Boy on the Beach*, 1878. Oil on panel, 7½ × 11¾ in (19 × 29.8 cm). Inscribed, upper left: *John S. Sargent*. Collection of Isabel Fonseca, London. (Exhibition)

witness another variant that Sargent briefly considered and then abandoned (although he found twilight an apt time of day in which to set several of his architectural Capri scenes).

In this scenario *Neapolitan Children Bathing* reflects not so much Sargent's own fascination with the Caprese sea as Williamson's charge to create a work akin to the *Fishing for Oyster at Cancale*. The patron, rather than the artist, set the general template of sea and shore, while Sargent substituted a Mediterranean *dolce far niente* for the brisk communal commerce of the Breton seaside village. *Neapolitan Children Bathing* becomes, in this reading, not unlike the blond boy with the water wings, a child of the north temporarily set out in the hot Mediterranean light.

Sargent's decision to populate *Neapolitan Children Bathing* with little boys rather than a mixed group of women and children, as in the Breton paintings, may have been prompted by a comment from Williamson, the ready availability of models, the current fashion among academic artists,[43] or as a response to Sargent's own aesthetic (two boys figure prominently in the Cancale pictures). It might also, however, reflect Sargent's friendship, first in Paris and then perhaps in Naples, with a painter who specialized in painting the *scugnizzi* (street urchins) of the region, Antonio Mancini. Mancini later recounted that he had met Sargent (who would come to own several works by the Italian and, in later decades, serve as an intermediary for sales at an

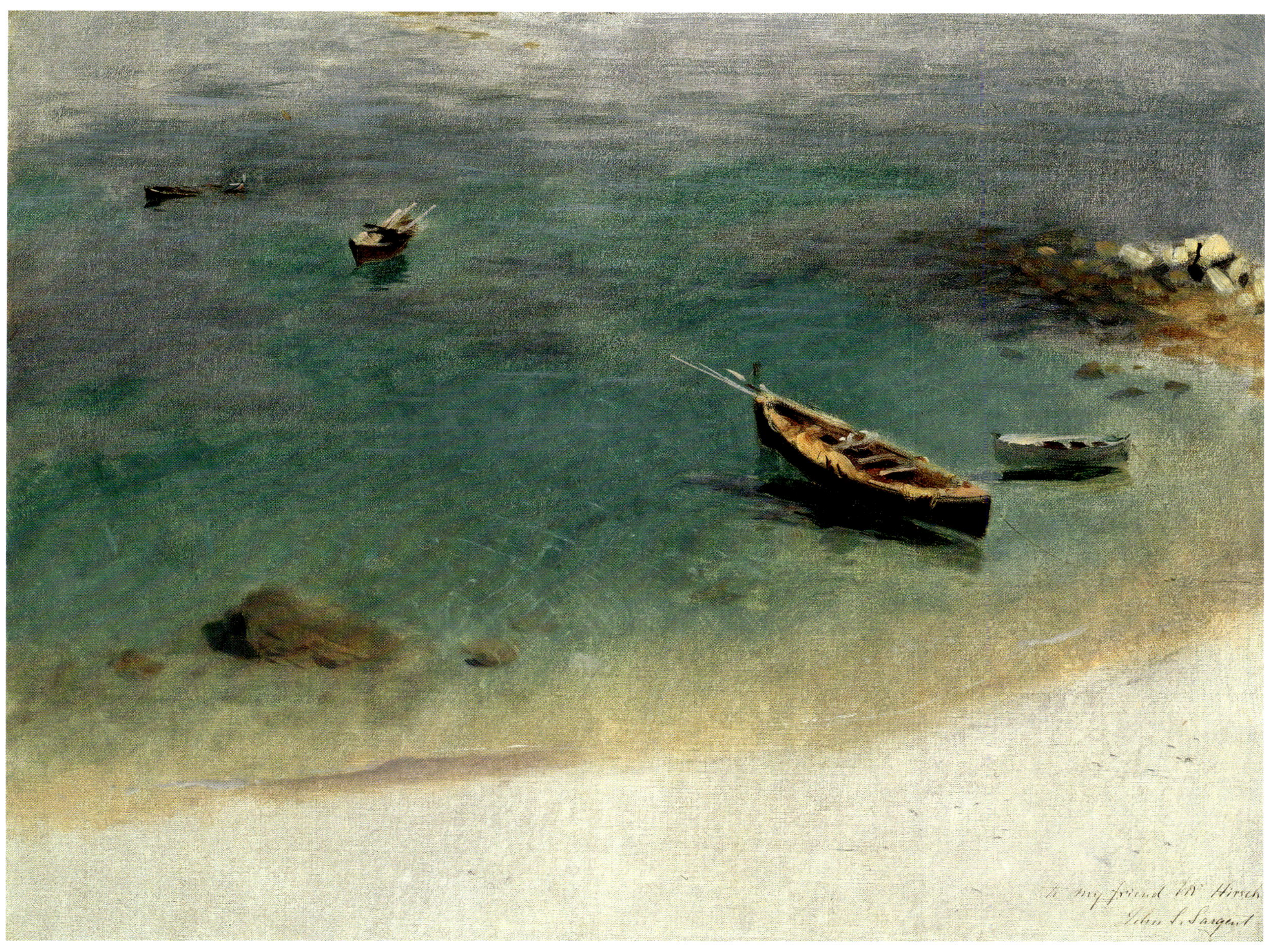

international level) during his stay in Paris from March 1877 to May 1878: "In Paris I knew everyone, Sargent and Paul Bourget brought me everywhere. I knew Boldini, De Nittis, Manet, Degas, and many others."[44] Sargent, in Naples for a week before leaving for Capri, could conceivably have found Mancini (himself just arrived in Italy from his stay in Paris) or, at the least, had him and his characteristic subjects in mind. Moreover, such a study as Mancini's *Children on a Sunny Beach* (fig. 175) seems akin to Sargent's Caprese panels in its bright color and bold facture.

Once it was in New York, both the subject and the handling of *Neapolitan Children Bathing* prompted writers to think of, if not Mancini, then of other contemporary Italian artists as they strove to write about the Sargent canvas. This was natural since the Hispano-Roman School, exemplified by the lamented Mariano Fortuny, was a powerful force in both the New York and the Parisian art worlds. The

Fig. 173 *A Boat in the Waters off Capri*, 1878. Oil on canvas, 18 × 23½ in (45.8 × 59.7 cm). Inscribed, lower right: *to my friend M. Hirsch/John S. Sargent.* Private Collection. (Exhibition)

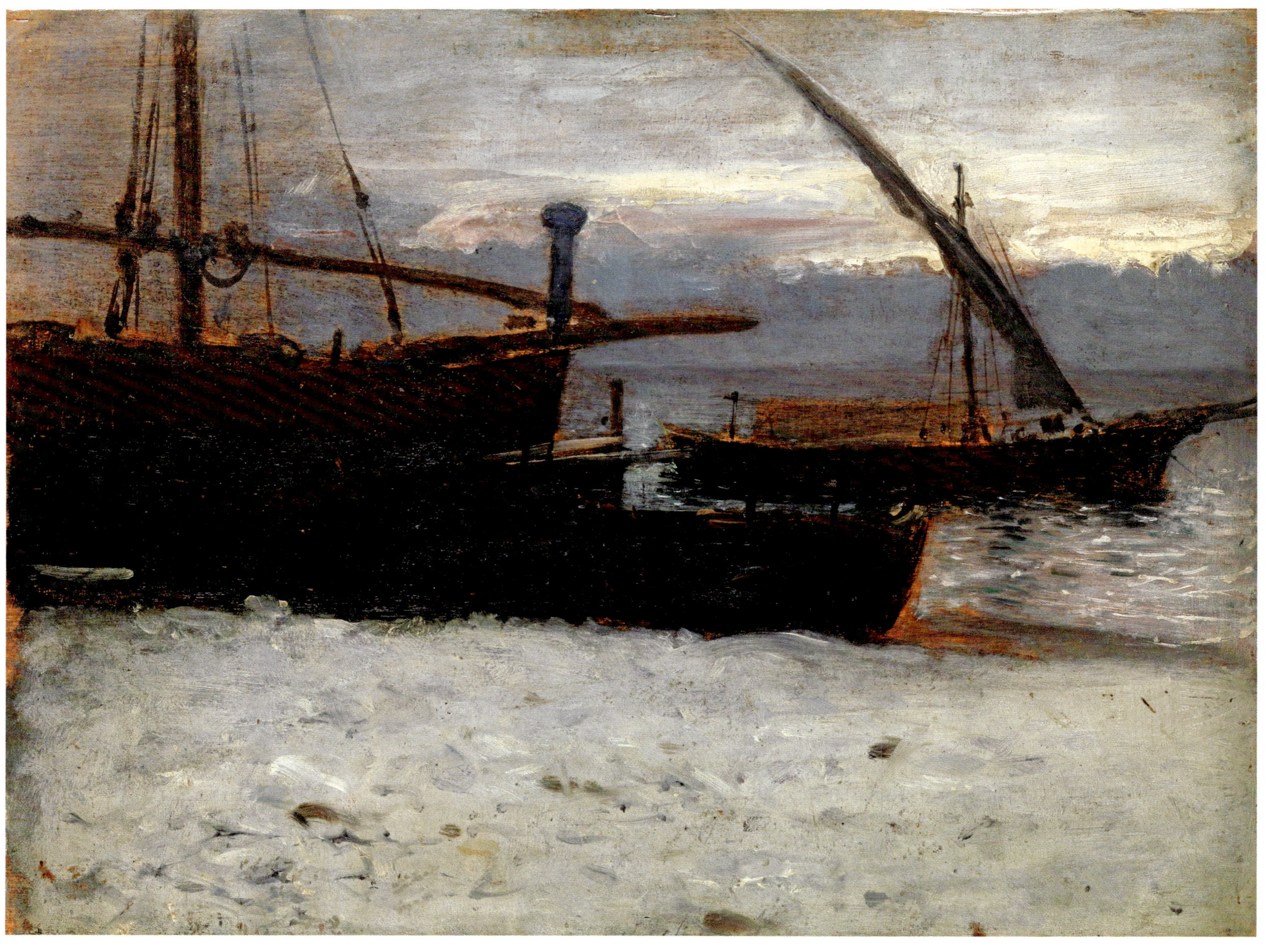

Fig. 174 *Fishing Boats*, 1878. Oil on panel, 10⅜ × 13⅞ in (26.4 × 35.2 cm). Private Collection. (Exhibition)

writer for the *Atlantic Monthly* surveyed New York's art scene in the winter of 1877–78 and found that throughout the commercial galleries "there are numerous examples of the Roman-Spanish school."[45] Shinn, surveying art treasures held throughout America, even concluded in 1879 that Fortuny "has afflicted his age with a whole school of parodists."[46] We know from his scrapbook that Sargent, too, if not a parodist, was an admirer, finding inspiration from the Spaniard.[47] Although Fortuny and his followers have been largely ignored in the history of nineteenth-century taste in the United States, their presence and influence in the years around 1880 was palpable.[48]

Among American responses to *Neapolitan Children Bathing*, references to Hispano-Roman work moved from the general to the pointedly specific. The critic for the *Art Journal* declared that Sargent's "most delightful little painting . . . is an imitation, or, perhaps we should say, an adaptation, from some of the Spanish-Roman work."[49] The writer for the *New York Daily Tribune*, praising the canvas for its truthfulness to Mediterranean light and color, felt prompted by the picture to generalize that the "whole school of Italian-Spanish artists, with their French and American imitators," were rightly seeking truths of natural observation rather than artistic convention. "To this school belongs Mr. Sargent, and he does not merely promise to be one of its most brilliant men, he already is such."[50] More concretely, the writer for the *Nation* made his case with testimony reportedly from the painter: "Mr. Sargent's 'Neapolitans' (431)—'too much like Michetti,' as he says himself—is a very lovely study."[51] The *Atlantic* critic made the connection to the same Italian and specified why:

> Before Sargent's . . . Neapolitan Children Bathing, Michetti's very singular Springtime and Love [fig. 176], at the Paris Exposition, cannot fail to be remembered. This is not at all so full of figures, and they are boys instead of girls, but the same bluish and violet shadows are scattered about among them, and it is the same vivid blue sea against which the rosy flesh tints are projected.[52]

Both Sargent's subject and handling harkened to the slightly older, then slightly more famous Michetti, known for "brilliant stuffs and dazzling flesh tints, conjoined to shadows of dark cobalt . . . delicious child faces caressed patiently by a cunning brush."[53]

On seeing *Neapolitan Children Bathing* at the National Academy of Design, numerous writers noted the "bluish and violet shadows" as particularly important in lending the picture its energy and outdoors feel. The New York *Daily Tribune* applauded "the daring of the blue shadows, no more audacious, though, than Nature herself, who, alike on northern snow and tropic sands, thus pays with *lapis lazuli* for the light she takes away"; the writer for the *Nation* judged "the effect of strong daylight with its blue shadows being quite deceptively dazzling . . . not a literal rendering of a natural effect, but . . . a highly poetical and inspiring one."[54] Sargent would employ this sensitivity to blue shadows throughout his career, making it a notable feature in nearly all his outdoor oils and watercolors.

The nakedness that Sargent chose to depict as a common state among southern Italy's children was also commented on by many others and reflects the expectation of the visitors to that place. In the last year of his life, living near Naples, Fortuny had

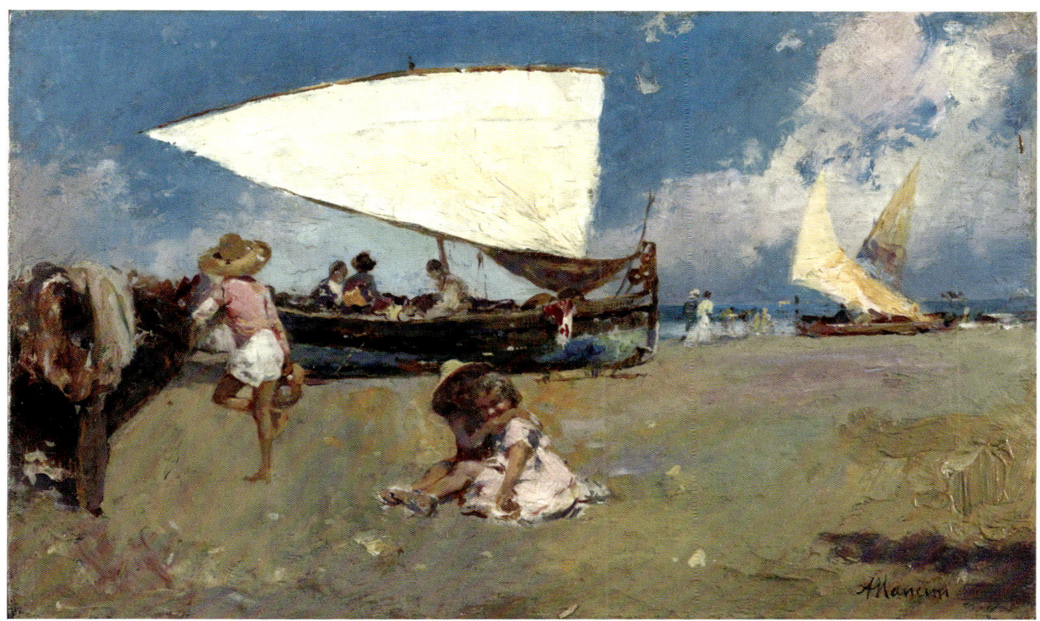

Fig. 175 Antonio Mancini, *Children on a Sunny Beach*, *c.* 1880. Oil on panel, 5¹⁵⁄₁₆ × 9½ in (15.1 × 24.1 cm). Philadelphia Museum of Art: Vance N. Jordan Collection, 2004-108-10.

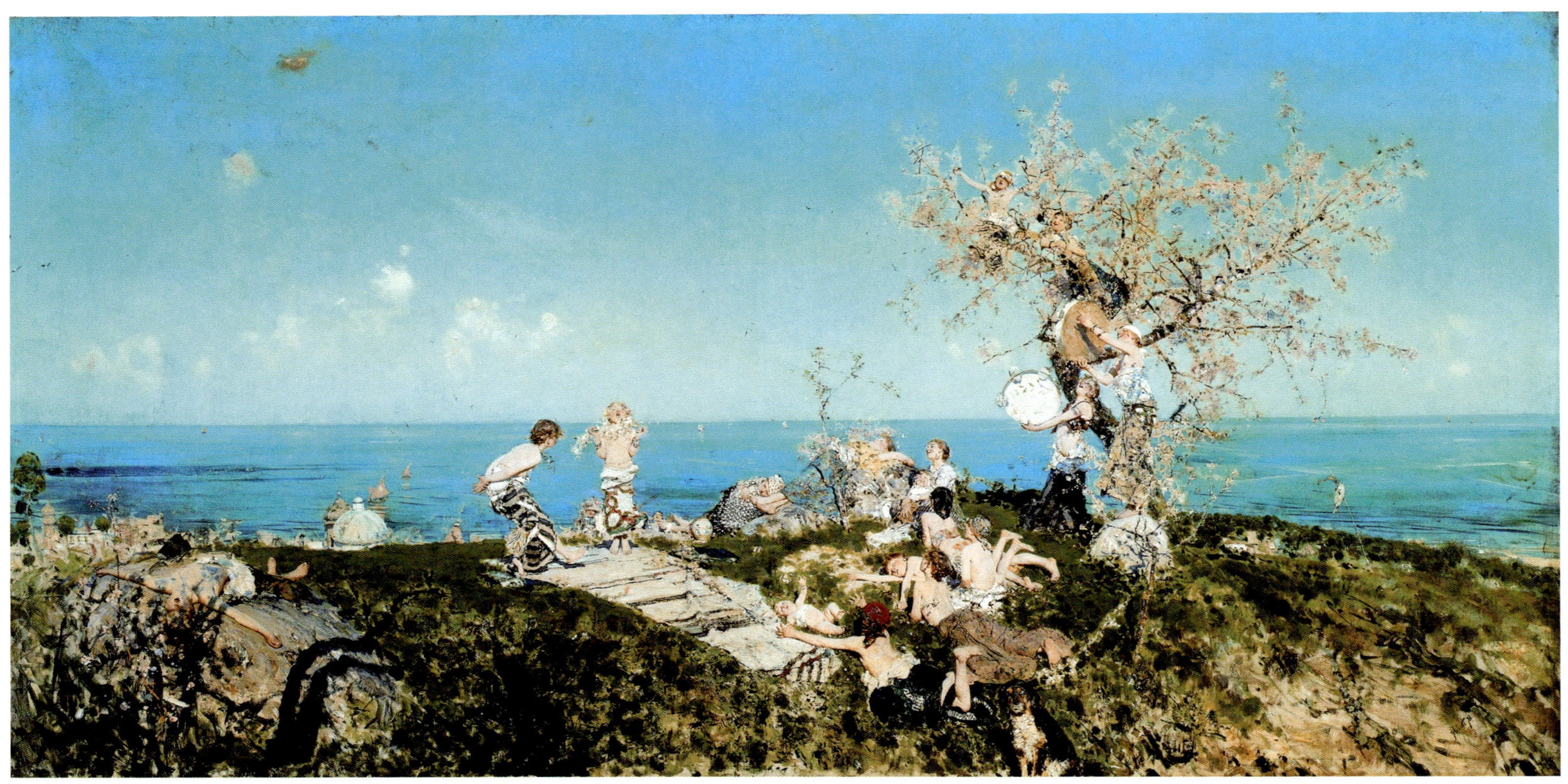

Fig. 176 Francesco Paolo Michetti, *Springtime and Love*, 1878. Oil on canvas, 37½ × 72¾ in (94.6 × 184.3 cm). The Art Institute of Chicago, A. A. Munger Collection, 1901.429.

painted a vivid sketch—*Nude on the Beach at Portici*—that resonates with Sargent's studies of a few years later (fig. 177).[55] Michetti, at work on the Adriatic at about the same time as Sargent was on Capri, made nude children scampering in the waves part of his larger scene of *La Pesca della Telline* (fig. 178), itself closely related to Sargent's Breton oyster-gathering views. At least one American painter, talking with Sargent and seeing his works, came to perceive the nude as a crucial element of Capri's allure. George de Forest Brush wrote to a colleague on 20 December 1878:

> I have just been in to see Sargent's work he has been all summer at Capri the sketches which he has brought back are splendid more than that, perfectly lovely . . . certainly he is a promising fellow. I fancy I shall go to Italy next year and spend the summer in Capri, the chances to paint from the nude are so fine . . .[56]

Even in prose, and limiting the search to Caprese references for a single year in one American periodical, there are multiple references to Capri's unclothed children: children "guiltless of garments playing in the water or sunning themselves at intervals on the long stretches of sand," and the "children are quite as much at home in the water as out of it. Half their life is spent in a condition of nudity" (January); "They . . . had exhausted their vocabulary of enthusiasm over the naked golden-brown children and warm-hued women . . . that flitted to and fro" (October).[57] Sargent, in a place where children cavorted naked on the shore, painted plein air studies that not only recorded what he saw around him but emulated in subject and bright Hispano-Roman manner the pictures that brought fame to his colleagues Fortuny, Michetti, and Mancini.

More than simply reflecting the sartorial nonchalance of boys on Neapolitan and

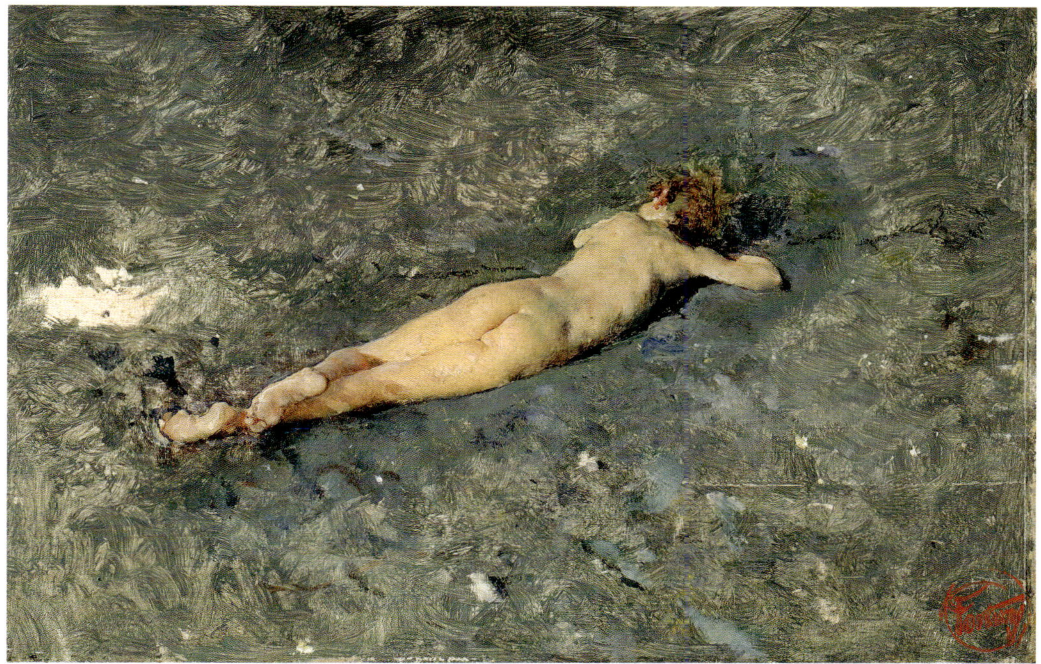

Fig. 177 Mariano Fortuny, *Nude on the Beach at Portici*, 1874. Oil on panel, 5¼ × 7½ in (13 × 19 cm). Museo Nacional del Prado, Madrid, Legacy of Ramón de Errazu, 1904, P02606.

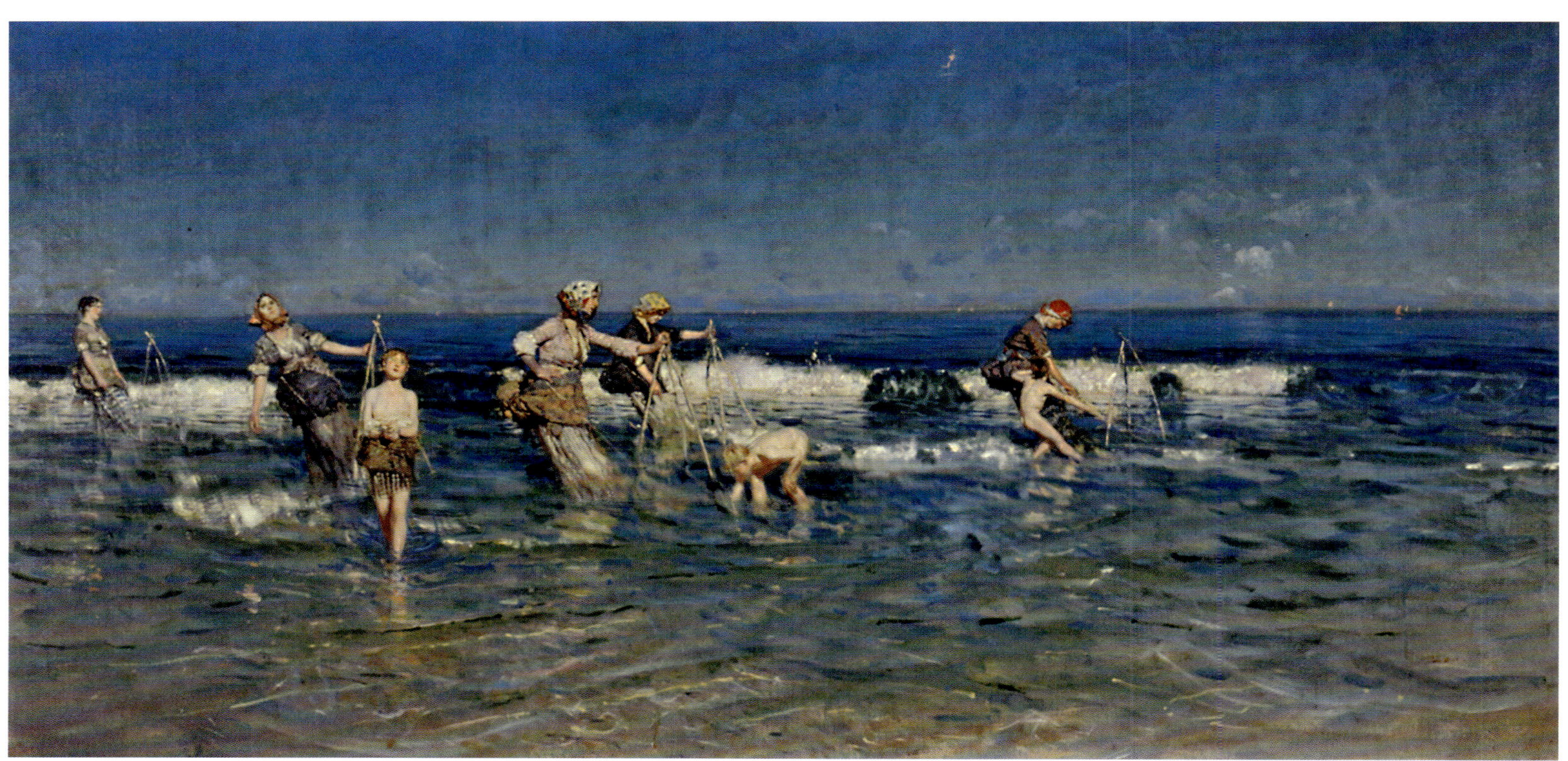

Fig. 178 Francesco Paolo Michetti, *La pesca della telline*, 1878. Oil on canvas, 28¾ × 59⅛ in (73 × 150 cm). Courtesy of the Embassy of the United States of America in Rome. Donated by Count Gaetano Marzotto in 1966.

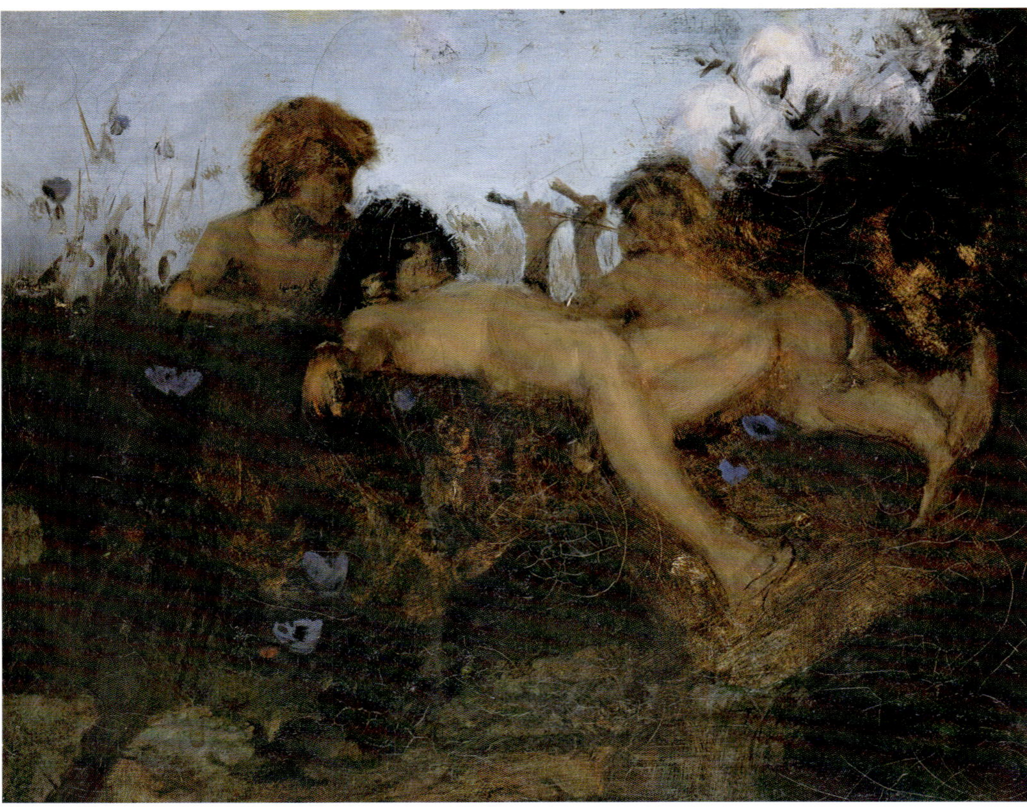

Fig. 179 *A Summer Idyll*, *c.* 1877. Oil on canvas, 16¼ × 28¼ in (41.3 × 71.7 cm). Inscribed, lower right: *To my friend Walton / John S. Sargent.* Brooklyn Museum, John B. Woodward Memorial Fund, 14.558.

Caprese beaches, or the predilections of either patron or artist, it seems possible that the young Sargent chose the naked children—with their direct links to putti and cherubs of previous centuries' art—as relatively neutral material to support stylistic exploration.[58] Indeed, if we turn to two of the most perplexing and idiosyncratic of his works from the late 1870s, *A Summer Idyll* (fig. 179) and *Nude Oriental Youth with Apple Blossom* (fig. 180), they, too, show undressed boys.[59] That they and the Capri pictures are—barring model studies obviously set in the studio—the only others of his works of the time to show naked children alerts us to a potential link between the particular subject and Sargent's experimentation with a variety of artistic voices. Prompted by this conjunction, we can begin to recognize that *Neapolitan Children Bathing*, too, in its overt homage to the Hispano-Roman school, is unlike almost all other Sargent paintings of the time. Only its truth effects and viewers' instincts to read it as a sketch or study have camouflaged its divergence of manner from the rest of Sargent's work.

We have looked at *Neapolitan Children Bathing* and posited four different catalysts that conceivably impelled Sargent to create it: a splendid sight; a pragmatic compositing of sketches from a working stay on Capri; a collector's specific request; a response to the stylistic preferences of one or more other artists. This is a cold and calculating approach to any work, especially one like *Neapolitan Children Bathing* wherein color combines with direction and weight of brushstroke to enrapture the eye and beguile the mind. To examine the surface of the painting is to wonder at Sargent's chromatic perceptions and at the deftness of his brush. To stand at a slight distance from it and imagine it as a scene beyond the frame is to be transported onto the warm beach, squatting or lying (because of the lowered point of view) beneath the hot sun and momentarily joining, without a care in the world, "the young boys who sprawl upon the sand, joyously and comically playing together."[60] Sargent's motivations in conceiving such a work elude explanation. Surely the site, the inspiration of the people that Sargent found there, his own working processes, outsiders' appreciation of his professional achievements, and the sense of himself within a cadre of ambitious contemporary painters—and much else—played a role in its creation. Looked at in sequence, however, these disparate bits of information and contradictory impulses that the picture necessarily calls to mind can perhaps begin to accommodate themselves within our sense of wonder at Sargent's achievement.

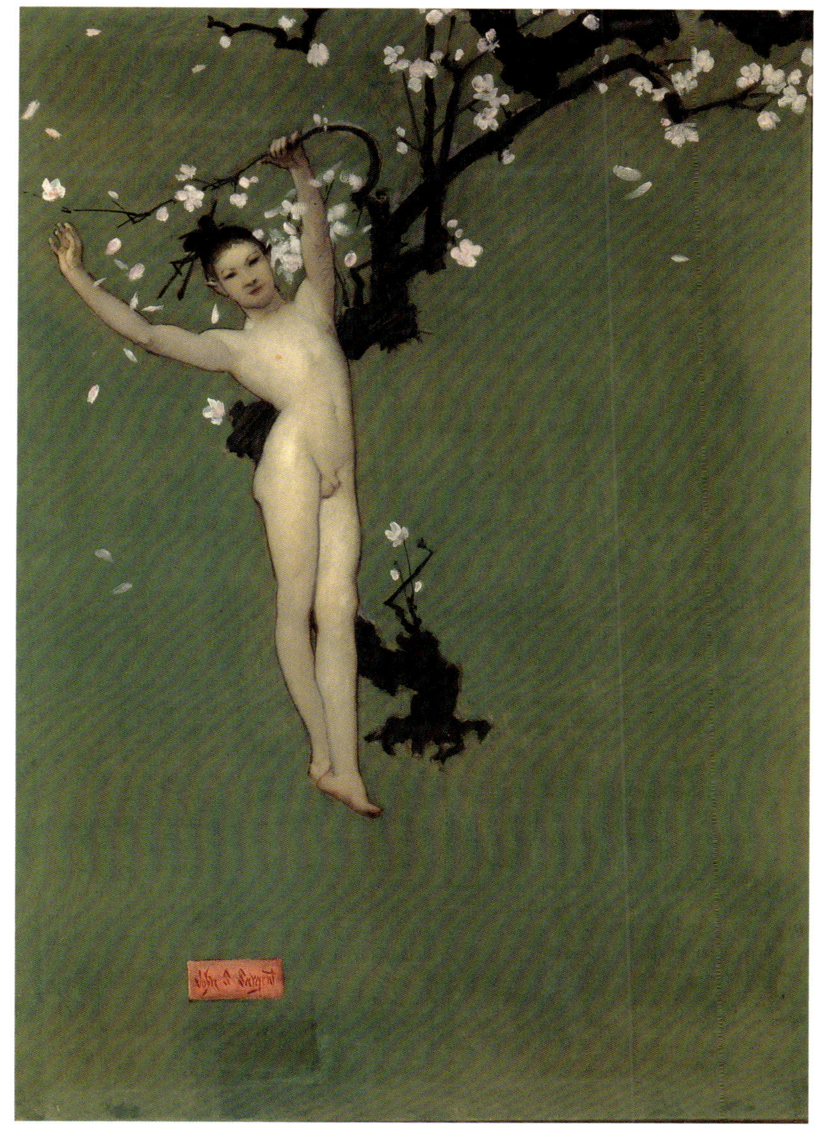

Fig. 180 *Nude Oriental Youth with Apple Blossom*, *c.* 1878–79. Oil on canvas, 35 ½ × 25 ½ in (90.3 × 64.8 cm). Inscribed within a block, lower left: *John S. Sargent*. The Western Reserve Historical Society, Cleveland, Ohio, 76.46.5.

Notes

Sargent and the Sea: Introduction
Richard Ormond

1 See Richard Ormond and Elaine Kilmurray, *John Singer Sargent: Figures and Landscapes, 1874–1882*, vol. 4 of *The Complete Paintings* (New Haven and London: Yale University Press, 2006), chapters IV and V.
2 Three other children died in childhood, Mary Newbold, Mary Winthrop (Minnie), and Fitzwilliam Winthrop.
3 See Sally M. Promey, *Painting Religion in Public: John Singer Sargent's 'Triumph of Religion' at the Boston Public Library* (Princeton: Princeton University Press, 1999), and Mary Crawford-Volk, "Sargent: Boston Public Library Murals," *Sargent/Sorolla* (Madrid: Fundación Colección Thyssen-Bornemisza, 2006), pp. 170–93.
4 See Carol Troyen, *Sargent's Murals in the Museum of Fine Arts, Boston* (Boston: Museum of Fine Arts, 1999).
5 For the genealogy of the Sargent family, see *Epes Sargent of Gloucester and his Descendants*, arranged by Emma Worcester Sargent (Boston: Houghton Mifflin Company, 1923).
6 Vernon Lee, "J.S.S.: In Memoriam," in Evan Charteris, *John Sargent* (London and New York: Charles Scribner's Sons, 1927), p. 240. In June 1864 the Confederate warship *CSS Alabama* sank the *USS Kearsage* off Cherbourg, an event commemorated in a famous painting by Edouard Manet (1864, Philadelphia Museum of Art).
7 Vernon Lee in Charteris, p. 240.
8 Sargent's letters to Gus Case are in a private collection, and those to Charles Deering in the Library of the Art Institute of Chicago.
9 Letter of 16 April 1865, quoted in Charteris, p. 6.
10 Letter of 18 May 1865, quoted in Charteris, p. 7.
11 Letter of 13 October 1865, quoted in Charteris, p. 9.
12 See the drawings in The Metropolitan Museum of Art, New York, catalogued by Stephanie L. Herdrich and H. Barbara Weinberg, *American Drawings and Watercolors in The Metropolitan Museum of Art: John Singer Sargent* (New York: The Metropolitan Museum of Art, 2000), nos. 9ee, 9ff, 9ll, 9oo, 9pp, 14, 16ll, 16mm, 17rr; and those in the Fogg Art Museum, Harvard University Art Museums, Cambridge, Massachusetts, 1937.7.1, f. 12; 1937.7.2, f. 19; 1937.7.6, f. 16; 1937.7.7, ff. 16v, 20; 1937.7.9, f. 10; 1937.7.12, ff. 2, 3, 22.
13 Vernon Lee in Charteris, pp. 239–240.
14 Charteris, p. 14. Silsbee was drawn by Sargent in a charcoal portrait of 1899 (Bodleian Library, Oxford).
15 Bemis papers, Massachusetts Historical Society, Boston.
16 The drawing is in the École Nationale Supérieure des Beaux-Arts, Paris (PC 8628), ill. Ormond and Kilmurray 2006, p. 32, fig. 12.
17 Quoted in Charteris, pp. 38–39.
18 See his letter of 21 August 1875, Bemis papers, Massachusetts Historical Society, Boston.
19 See Lloyd DeWitt, "Manet and the Dutch Marine Tradition," in *Manet and the Sea*, ed.

Juliet Bareau-Wilson and David Degener (Philadelphia: Philadelphia Museum of Art, 2004), pp. 1–14; and Frances Suzman Jowell, "Impressionism and the Golden Age of Dutch Art," *Inspiring Impressionism: The Impressionists and the Art of the Past*, ed. Ann Dumas (Denver: Denver Art Museum, 2008), pp. 79–109.

20 Letter from Thorne to Royal Cortissoz, 8 May 1930, Cortissoz papers, Beinecke Library, Yale University, New Haven, Connecticut, Box 1603A.

21 For the two paintings Sargent gave to Lemercier, see Ormond and Kilmurray 2006, nos. 665, 801.

22 Two versions of the subject are known, one in the Art Institute of Chicago, the other in the Museum of Fine Arts, Boston; see Ormond and Kilmurray 2006, nos. 723–24.

23 Chabrier owned Sargent's *Spanish Gypsy Dancer* (private collection); see the entry on that picture in Ormond and Kilmurray 2006, no. 768, for the story of their friendship.

24 Theodore Reff, *Notebooks of Edgar Degas* (Oxford: Oxford University Press, 1976), vol. 1, p. 133.

25 Sargent's drawing is in the Worcester Art Museum, Massachusetts. *L'Étoile* belongs to the Musée d'Orsay, Paris. In the 1881 exhibition, Degas showed one of the versions of *The Ballet from "Robert le Diable,"* and Sargent sent two Venetian studies. Marc Simpson discovered that Pierre Auguste Renoir had sent his large and important canvas, *Luncheon of the Boating Party* (Phillips Collection, Washington, D.C.) to the same exhibition, almost a year before showing it at the seventh Impressionist exhibition. See Marc Simpson, "The Earliest Public Exhibition of Renoir's 'Luncheon of the Boating Party'," *Burlington Magazine,* vol. 139, no. 1129, April 1997, pp. 261–62.

26 See Richard Ormond and Elaine Kilmurray, *John Singer Sargent: The Early Portraits*, vol. 1 of *The Complete Paintings* (New Haven and London: Yale University Press, 1998), nos. 21, 40, 56, and 114.

27 For contemporary reviews of the painting, see Ormond and Kilmurray 2006, no. 671.

28 For the three versions of *A Capriote*, see Ormond and Kilmurray 2006, nos. 702–704.

29 See Ormond and Kilmurray 2006, nos. 702–10.

Uncharted Waters
Erica E. Hirshler

1 Santayana's essay was published posthumously; see George Santayana, "The Philosophy of Travel," *The Virginia Quarterly Review* 40 (Winter 1964), pp. 8, 9.

2 Vernon Lee (Violet Paget) to her mother 16 June 1881, in *Vernon Lee's Letters*, ed. Irene Cooper Willis (London: Privately printed, 1937), p. 61; Henry James, "John S. Sargent," *Harper's New Monthly Magazine* 75 (October 1887), p. 683.

3 "Going Abroad," *Putnam's Magazine*, new series, 1 (May 1868), pp. 530–31.

4 Price Collier, *America and the Americans from a French Point of View* (New York: Charles Scribner's Sons, 1898), pp. 6–9. While Collier was an American writer, his critique and observations are in keeping with those recorded by French travelers to America; see Jacques Portes, *Fascination and Misgivings: The United States in French Opinion, 1870–1914*, trans. Elborg Foster (Cambridge: Cambridge University Press, 2000).

5 See for example Judy Bullington, "Henry Bacon's Imaging of Transatlantic Travel in the Gilded Age," in *Nineteenth-Century Studies* 14 (2000), pp. 63–91; and Mark Rennella and Whitney Walton, "Planned Serendipity: American Travelers and the Transatlantic Voyage in the Nineteenth and Twentieth Centuries," *Journal of Social History* 38 (Winter 2004), pp. 365–83.

6 Clarence Buel, "Log of an Ocean Studio," *Century Magazine* 27 (January 1884), p. 356.

7 Charles Dickens, *American Notes for General Circulation* (Boston: Ticknor and Fields, 1867), p. 15.

8 Henry Bacon, *A Parisian Year* (Boston: Roberts Brothers, 1882), pp. 201–07.

9 Richard Whiteing, "Henry Bacon," *The Art Amateur* 7 (November 1882), p. 116.

10 For the four paintings given to Bacon, see Richard Ormond and Elaine Kilmurray, *John Singer Sargent: Figures and Landscapes, 1874–1882*, vol. 4 of *The Complete Paintings* (New Haven and London: Yale University Press, 2006), nos. 663, 668, 669, and 681. Sargent's choice to give such informal sketches to Bacon seems somewhat unusual unless they commemorate a shared experience. The details of Bacon's 1876 trip from France to the United States are unknown. He did not travel with the Sargents on his return to Europe, for

Bacon is recorded as a passenger on the steamship *Ohio*, and he arrived at Paris in December 1876, much later than the Sargents. See Sara Caldwell Junkin, *The Europeanization of Henry Bacon (1839–1912), American Expatriate Painter* (PhD. diss., Boston University, 1986), pp. 162, 188.

11 James Carroll Beckwith Diary, 13 October 1876, as quoted in Pepi Marchetti Franchi, "Carroll Beckwith, Passionate Conservative of American Art," in *Intimate Revelations: The Art of Carroll Beckwith (1852–1917)* (New York: Berry-Hill Galleries, 2000), p. 15.

12 Another painting, *The Sailor's Procession*, remains unlocated. See Ormond and Kilmurray, 2006, pp. 81–83 and nos. 662–666.

13 Mark Twain, *The Innocents Abroad* (Hartford, Connecticut: American Publishing Company, 1869), p. 33; Charles Dickens, *American Notes*, p. 14.

14 The canvas is French, and there is a full-length study of a nude underneath the current composition, which reinforces the conclusion that *Atlantic Storm* was painted in Paris. See Ormond and Kilmurray, 2006, no. 662.

15 *Moonlight on Waves* could also be a sketch after a painting Sargent had admired. The sheet is inscribed with a pencil border, a device Sargent often used in his sketches after paintings (see for example his 1870s pencil sketches after Jean-François Millet's paintings; the drawings are in the collection of The Metropolitan Museum of Art).

16 Gustave Flaubert, *Dictionnaire des idées reçues*, quoted in John House, *Impressionists by the Sea* (London: Royal Academy of Arts, 2007), p. 15. See also Steven Z. Levine, "Seascapes of the Sublime: Vernet, Monet, and the Oceanic Feeling," *New Literary History* 16 (Winter 1985), pp. 377–400, and Nancy Locke, "Manet's Oceanic Feeling," *Nineteenth-Century Art Worldwide* 4 (Spring 2005), http://www.19thcartworldwide.org/spring_05/index.shtml.

17 There are a few other images of the mid-Atlantic; see for example Arthur Quartley's *Petrels Following in the Steamer's Wake*, which was painted on his own transatlantic voyage; it formed part of a decorative ensemble of works created over the course of the journey by eight artists (including Sargent's friend Beckwith) for the captain's cabin of the ship. See Buel, "Log of an Ocean Studio," pp. 356–71; Quartley's painting is reproduced on p. 370.

18 James Sprunt, *Derelicts* (Wilmington, North Carolina: Privately printed, 1920), pp. 3–4.

19 See the discussion in House, *Impressionists by the Sea*, pp. 26–27.

20 Jean Sutherland Boggs, "The Artist's Voyage to America, October 1872," in Gail Feigenbaum et al., *Degas and New Orleans* (New Orleans: New Orleans Museum of Art, 1999), pp. 177–85.

21 See Evan Charteris, *John Sargent* (London and New York: Charles Scribner's Sons, 1927), pp. 20–21. There is no other known documentation for a meeting between the two American painters at this time; other scholars date Sargent's first encounter with Whistler to the early 1880s in Venice.

22 Courbet to Whistler, 14 February 1877, Glasgow University Library, MS Whistler C/96 (BPII C/64), as quoted in Margaret Macdonald and Joy Newton, "Letters from the Whistler Collection: Correspondence with French Painters," *Gazette des Beaux-Arts* 108 (December 1986), p. 203.

23 Hamilton Minchon quoted in Ormond and Kilmurray, 2006, p. 55.

24 Claude Monet quoted in Charteris, *John Sargent*, p. 130.

25 James, "John S. Sargent," p. 684.

Sargent's Scrapbook of the 1870s
Stephanie L. Herdrich

1 The scrapbook (50.130.154) was donated to the Metropolitan by Sargent's sister, Mrs Francis (Violet) Ormond, in 1950. While other scrapbooks or albums were part of his estate, none of those surviving contain the variety of materials of the Metropolitan scrapbook. Only the Metropolitan book was definitively created by Sargent. For an inventory of the Fogg Art Museum's scrapbooks or albums, see Miriam Stewart and Kerry Schauber, "Catalogue of Sketchbooks and Albums by John Singer Sargent at the Fogg Art Museum," *Sargent at Harvard, Harvard University Art Museums Bulletin* 7 (Fall/Winter 1999–2000), pp. 16–38.

2 Sargent purchased (or received as a gift) the empty book some time after his arrival in Paris in spring 1874. With a few exceptions, most of the datable material included in the scrapbook seems to have been created or collected by Sargent

between 1874 and about 1880. The album bears a label on the inside back cover from a *Librairie – Papeterie* just blocks from the atelier of Carolus-Duran (81 Boulevard du Montparnasse) and the studio he would share with friend James Carroll Beckwith from the summer of the following year (73 Rue Notre Dame des Champs). The label reads: "Librairie – Papeterie / Maison Gosset / 152 Rue de Rennes / en face la Gare / Paris."

3 Sargent did include two sketches pertaining to his painting *The Rehearsal of the Pasdeloup Orchestra at the Cirque d'Hiver,* see note 10.

4 Fitzwilliam Sargent to Emily Haskell Sargent (Switzerland?), 21 September 1861, quoted in Stephanie L. Herdrich and H. Barbara Weinberg, *American Drawings and Watercolors in The Metropolitan Museum of Art: John Singer Sargent* (New York: The Metropolitan Museum of Art, 2000), p. 40.

5 The Metropolitan owns three sketchbooks from before 1874: Switzerland 1869 (50.130.147), Switzerland 1870 (50.130.148), and Splendid Mountain Watercolors, 1870 (50.130.146). The Fogg Art Museum has at least ten sketchbooks from before 1874. For an inventory and description, see Stewart and Schauber, "Catalogue of Sketchbooks and Albums by John Singer Sargent at the Fogg Art Museum," pp. 16–38.

6 The Museum of Fine Arts, Boston, also has a large collection of Sargent's works on paper but contains fewer of these pre-1874 works. A general synopsis of Sargent's thirty-eight sketchbooks in the Fogg Art Museum and the Metropolitan reveals that more survive from earlier in his career than later. In his early years, the sketchbooks seem to cover shorter time periods, and were often used for distinct periods of travel such as the Splendid Mountain Watercolors sketchbook (50.130.146), which records the young Sargent's travels through the Alps during the summer of 1870. Later in his life, the sketchbooks are more difficult to date.

7 For Sargent's drawings in the Metropolitan, see Herdrich and Weinberg, *American Drawings and Watercolors in The Metropolitan Museum of Art: John Singer Sargent*. For Sargent's drawings at Harvard, see http://www.artmuseums.harvard.edu/sargent.

8 Will H. Low, "The Primrose Way," typescript, "revised and edited from the original MS by Mary Fairchild Low, with the collaboration of Berthe Helene MacMonnies" (Albany, New York: Albany Institute of History and Art, 1935), p. 56.

9 See Richard Ormond and Elaine Kilmurray, *John Singer Sargent: Figures and Landscapes, 1874-1882*, vol. 4 of *The Complete Paintings* (New Haven and London: Yale University Press, 2006), pp. 31–34.

10 There are only two drawings that appear to be studies for a finished painting, *The Rehearsal of the Pasdeloup Orchestra at the Cirque d'Hiver* (1876, Museum of Fine Arts, Boston): *Compositional Study* (50.130.154c) and *Musicians* (50.130.154c2).

11 Fitzwilliam Sargent to George Bemis, Hotel Imbert, Beuzeval, Calvados, France, July 26 [1874], George Bemis Papers, Massachusetts Historical Society, Boston.

12 Fitzwilliam Sargent to George Bemis, St Énogat, August 21 [1875], George Bemis Papers, Massachusetts Historical Society, Boston. According to contemporary guidebooks, hourly ferry service covered the short distance between St Énogat and St Malo across the estuary of the River Rance as it meets the English Channel. John Murray, *A Handbook for Travellers in France*, 10th edn. (London: John Murray, 1867), p. 105.

13 The twelve sheets affixed in the Metropolitan scrapbook are *Schooner and Bark in Harbor* (50.130.154p); *Waves Breaking on Rocks* (50.130.154q); *Rocky Coast* (50.130.154r); *Coastal Scene* (50.130.154s); *Sailors in Rigging of Ship* (50.130.154u); *Two Sailors Furling Sail* (50.130.154v); *Two Small Boats Moored to Beach* (50.130.154hh); *Two Men and a Hayrack Drawn by a Horse* (50.130.154ii); *Two Men in Ship's Rigging, Two Scenes with Sailboats* (50.130.154jj); *La Pierre du Champ Dolent* (50.130.154kk); *Sailors and Reapers* (50.130.154mm verso); *Boy and Girl Seated by Tree* (50.130.154mm recto); and *Windmills and Reapers* (50.130.154oo). The drawing in the Corcoran is *Ramparts at St Malo - Yacht Race* (49.148c). See figs. 69–74, 76, 77, 80, 81, 83, and 87.

14 This drawing was removed from the scrapbook to reveal the image on the verso, *Sailors and Reapers*. Sargent mounted the drawing in the album to show *Boy and Girl Seated by Tree* (50.130.154mm recto).

15 I am grateful to Mary Margaret Chappell of Cancale for suggesting this location and

to Sarah Cash for sharing the information with me.

16 See Ormond and Kilmurray 2006, p. 96.

17 For example, *The Nurture of Bacchus,* after Nicolas Poussin (50.130.154f); *Noon,* after Jean-François Millet (50.130.154d); *Night,* after Michelangelo (50.130.154a).

18 H. Barbara Weinberg, "Sargent and Carolus-Duran," in Marc Simpson, *Uncanny Spectacle: The Public Career of the Young John Singer Sargent* (Williamstown, Massachusetts: Sterling and Francine Clark Art Institute, 1997), p. 27.

19 See Herdrich and Weinberg, nos. 50–52, 61, 125–34.

20 Elizabeth Anne McCauley, *Industrial Madness: Commercial Photography in Paris, 1848–1871* (New Haven, Connecticut: Yale University Press, 1994), p. 273.

21 John Singer Sargent to Ben del Castillo, Sorrento, 23 May 1869, quoted in Evan Charteris, *John Sargent* (London and New York: Charles Scribner's Sons, 1927), p. 12.

22 There are (at least) five albums from Sargent's estate. Three were given to the Fogg by Sargent's sisters in 1937. Two were given to the Metropolitan by Sargent's sister Violet Ormond in 1950. Of these five albums, only the one in question shows direct evidence of having been assembled in some part by Sargent himself.

23 John Singer Sargent to Violet Paget, Florence, April 23, 1870, Vernon Lee Collection, Colby College Special Collections, Waterville, Maine. Sargent would later add several of these photographs into the Metropolitan scrapbook. Photographs of Sicily are on pages 17–20 of the scrapbook.

24 Jessie E. Ringwalt, "Fun for the Fireside: A Help to Mothers," *Godey's Lady's Book and Magazine* (April 1880), p. 363.

25 John Singer Sargent to Violet Paget, Pontresina, Switzerland, August 12, 1873, Vernon Lee Collection, Colby College Special Collections, Waterville, Maine.

26 John Singer Sargent to Mrs Austin, Florence, March 22, 1874. Quoted in Charteris, *John Sargent,* p. 18.

27 For a biography of Laurent and a history of his studio, see *J. Laurent, un fotógrafo francés en la España del siglo XIX = un photographe français dans l'Espagne du XIXème siècle* (Madrid: Ministerio de Educación y Cultura de España, 1996), pp. 9-21.

28 In the Metropolitan's collection, Sargent's *Mystical Marriage of Saint Catherine* (50.130.143h) was copied or traced after a photograph of Tintoretto's painting in the Palazzo Ducale, Venice, by the photographer Carlo Naya. See Herdrich and Weinberg, no. 41.

29 In 1896, following du Maurier's death, Sargent selected some of the illustrator's drawings for Sargent's friend Charles Deering (Sargent to Deering, 18 November 1896, Library of the Art Institute of Chicago). I am grateful to Richard Ormond and to du Maurier scholar Leonée Ormond for this information.

30 The earliest and latest du Maurier *Punch* cartoons in the scrapbook appear to be: "Ratiocination" (19 April 1873), p. 160, and "A Chapter on Natural History" (1 February 1879), p. 42.

31 Henry James, "Du Maurier and London Society," *Century Illustrated Magazine* 26 (May 1883), p. 56.

32 James, "Du Maurier and London Society," p. 65.

33 Katherine Ott, Susan Tucker, and Patricia P. Buckler, "An Introduction to the History of Scrapbooks," *The Scrapbook in American Life* (Philadelphia, Pennsylvania: Temple University Press, 2006), p. 6.

34 "Editor's Study," *Harper's New Monthly Magazine* (September 1892), p. 639, quoted in Eleanor Gruber Garvey, "Scissorizing and Scrapbooks," in Lisa Gitelman and Geoffrey B. Pingree, eds., *New Media, 1740–1915* (Cambridge, Massachusetts: MIT Press, 2003), p. 211.

35 "Of Scrapbooks," *Harper's Bazaar* 12 (12 July 1879), p. 438.

36 Rev. A. Parke Burgess, "What to do with the Newspapers," *New York Evangelist* (2 December 1875), p. 1.

37 The reproduction is on page 60 verso of the scrapbook. For a discussion of contemporary reproductions of *Fumée d'ambre gris* see Ormond and Kilmurray 2006, no. 789.

Testing the Waters: Sargent and Cancale
Sarah Cash

1 Among the Sargent sources discussing the completed Cancale paintings are Trevor J. Fairbrother, *John Singer Sargent and America* (New York: Garland Publishing, 1986), pp. 28–35, and Carol Troyen, catalogue entry in

Elaine Kilmurray and Richard Ormond, eds., *John Singer Sargent* (Princeton, N.J.: Princeton University Press, 1998), pp. 62–66. The entire group of Cancale pictures and the relationships between them, as well as Sargent's 1877 trip to Brittany, were not discussed in depth until Richard Ormond's pioneering and comprehensive examination in Ormond and Elaine Kilmurray, *John Singer Sargent: Figures and Landscapes, 1874–1882*, vol. 4 of *The Complete Paintings* (New Haven and London: Yale University Press, 2006). See Ormond, "Cancale, 1877," pp. 83–86, and nos. 670–681.

2 On 21 June 1877 Sargent's father Dr Fitzwilliam Sargent wrote to George Bemis that John was about to leave for Brittany. George Bemis Papers, Massachusetts Historical Society, Boston, quoted in Ormond and Kilmurray 2006, p. 85.

3 Emily Sargent to Violet Paget, 5 June 1877, Vernon Lee Collection, Colby College Special Collections, Waterville, Maine, quoted in Ormond and Kilmurray 2006, p. 85.

4 Sargent and Lachaise were in Cancale until about 20 August, as Dr Sargent wrote in a letter of that date to his sister Anna Maria Sargent. Fitzwilliam Sargent Papers, Archives of American Art, Smithsonian Institution, quoted in Ormond and Kilmurray 2006, p. 85.

5 A boat trip to or near Cancale would not have been out of the question; in an August 1875 letter to George Bemis, Dr Sargent mentions occasional cruises to some of the islands (George Bemis Papers, Massachusetts Historical Society, Boston, quoted in Ormond and Kilmurray, 2006, p. 80); these may have included the smaller Îles Chausey and Les Minquiers in the Gulf of Saint-Malo, or the larger Channel Islands of Guernsey and Jersey. The magnificent Mont-Saint-Michel, which lies just east of Cancale, was then, as now, a major tourist attraction, and was designated a French historical monument only one year earlier. The Sargents also could have visited Cancale by land. The village lies 17 miles (28 kilometers) east of Saint-Énogat, 9 miles (15 kilometers) east of Saint-Malo and Saint-Servan, and 13 miles (22 kilometers) north of Dol, all towns that the Sargents visited that summer. See Herdrich essay, p. 62.

6 Fitzwilliam Sargent to Anna Maria Sargent, 20 August 1877; see n. 4.

7 Ormond and Kilmurray 2006, p. 83, discusses and reproduces works by the Feyen brothers, and on p. 85 suggests that Sargent may even have met one of them.

8 On average the Salons between 1874 and 1877 included about seventeen fishing scenes each, with twenty-one in 1874, eighteen in 1875, fourteen in 1876, and fourteen in 1877; still lifes featuring oysters were also popular, with six shown in the Salon of 1877.

9 The Bay, whose width spans over 13 miles from La Pointe du Grouin just north of Cancale across to Granville to the northeast, is equally broad, measuring from the Îles Chausey to the mouth of the Cousenon river, located at Mont-Saint-Michel.

10 See Joseph Pichot-Louvet, *The Oysters of Cancale* (Les Éditions du Phare for Musée de l'Huître et du Coquillage/Les Parcs Saint-Kerber, 1994); I am grateful to Pichot-Louvet's son, François-Joseph Pichot, of Les Parcs Saint-Kerber, for this booklet and for his kind introduction to Cancale, its topography, and its oystering history.

11 See "Cancale and its Fisheries," *The New York Times*, 20 August 1882, p. 3. The water's continual freshness is particularly conducive to the production of oysters, delivering constant nutrients to the bivalves as well as clean surfaces to which oysters can easily attach.

12 In 1868 an enormous staff of the French government's Ministry of Marine set out to enforce anew, in Cancale and elsewhere, longstanding regulations that forbade the sale of oysters for consumption from May through August. See Robert Neild, *The English, the French, and the Oyster* (London: Quiller Press, 1995), p. 92. These regulations date back to 1787, when the government imposed stiff restrictions on Cancale, including one prohibiting oyster fishing from 1 April to 15 October (Neild, pp. 77–82). I am grateful to John McCabe of Milton, Washington, who maintains the informative website www.oysters.us, for his extensive e-mail correspondence with me on the topic of oyster harvesting in Cancale and on the subject of Sargent's paintings (15–18 August 2008, Corcoran). It is not impossible, however, that there

were occasional infractions of these regulations.

13 I am grateful to Joseph Pichot-Louvet of Cancale, whose remarks were translated by Mary Margaret Chappell, also of Cancale, for this observation.

14 E-mail correspondence with John McCabe, see n. 12.

15 The title *Oyster Gatherers of Cancale* apparently was assigned to the painting after the artist's death, as its first known use was in the "Memorial Exhibition of the Works of the Late John Singer Sargent" held at the Museum of Fine Arts, Boston, from 3 November to 27 December 1925 (cat. no. 14). This title was changed to the present one in November 2008. The painting's nearly identical appearance to *Fishing for Oysters at Cancale* has led both paintings, incorrectly and often confusingly (see Ormond and Kilmurray 2006, p. 111), to be called *Oyster Gatherers of Cancale*.

16 Unlike the Feyen brothers, Sargent chose to include the distinctive topography and landmarks of Cancale, which would have been recognizable to at least some Parisian Salon-goers. As Ormond notes (Ormond and Kilmurray 2006, p. 84), tourists in Sargent's time, as now, enjoyed watching the activity on Cancale's oyster banks and were often outfitted with *sabots* (clogs) to protect their feet at low tide. Eugène Feyen documents this pastime (albeit involving shrimp-fishing and not oyster-gathering) in his *Parisiens à la pêche aux crevettes*, sold at Sotheby's, Olympia, 17 July 2002, lot 413.

17 See Mark Kurlansky, *The Big Oyster: History on the Half Shell* (New York: Random House, 2006), *passim*. Oysters had a similar popularity in other East Coast cities; like New York, Philadelphia (and possibly Newport) offered the popular "Canal Street plan," promising customers all the oysters they could eat for only 6 cents. See Kurlansky, pp. 158–59, and Joseph Dubow, "Consider the Oyster," *American Heritage Magazine* 31 (February/March 1980), AmericanHeritage.com.

18 Among such articles were William H. Rideing, "How New York is Fed," *Scribner's Monthly* 14 (October 1877), pp. 729–43, esp. p. 730; Albert Rhodes, "What Shall we Eat?," *The Galaxy* 22 (November 1876), pp. 665–74 and particularly p. 667 which remarks on the indelible impression the American passion for oysters made on the Prince of Wales when he visited the United States in 1860; "Something about Oysters," *Harper's Weekly* (September 16, 1882), p. 582; and especially James Richardson, "American Oyster Culture," *Scribner's Monthly* 15 (December 1877), pp. 225–39. Kurlansky, *The Big Oyster*, p. 214, observes that this period "was one of the few moments in culinary history when a single food, served in more or less the same preparations, was commonplace for all socio-economic levels."

19 "Something about Oysters," *Harper's Weekly*, p. 582.

20 See Kurlansky, *The Big Oyster*, *passim*, as well as pp. 57–171 for oyster cellars and pp. 172–97 for oyster markets and mania; and also Kurlansky, "City Lore: When the Oyster Was their World," *New York Times*, 24 June 2001, nytimes.com. For a thorough article on the oyster barges, see Michael J. Chiarappa, "New York City's Oyster Barges: Architecture's Threshold Role along the Urban Waterfront," *Buildings & Landscapes: Journal of the Vernacular Architecture Forum* 14 (2007), pp. 84–108.

21 See Marc Simpson, "Sargent and his Critics," in Marc Simpson, ed., *Uncanny Spectacle: The Public Career of the Young John Singer Sargent* (New Haven and London: Yale University Press for the Sterling and Francine Clark Art Institute, 1997), pp. 31–69.

22 There may have been other preparatory works that are no longer extant, or perhaps all the figures in the completed paintings were alterations from the known studies. It seems especially odd that there is no oil study for the red-haired woman in the Boston and Corcoran canvases. Although Ormond, in Ormond and Kilmurray 2006, p. 119, traces her to the Terra study showing a woman in a red kerchief (fig. 140), the present author believes this study more directly related to the figure third from left in the finished paintings; see this volume, pp. 100–101.

23 Fitzwilliam Sargent to Anna Maria Sargent, 20 August 1875, see n. 4.

24 Emily Sargent to Violet Paget, 29 July 1877, Vernon Lee Collection, Colby College Special Collections, Waterville, Maine, cited in Ormond and Kilmurray 2006, p. 85.

25 Ormond and Kilmurray 2006, p. 85.

26 Sargent's training at the École des Beaux-

Arts, and with Carolus-Duran and Léon Bonnat, prepared him well to make preparatory studies in pencil and oil; see Monique Nonne's entry on Sargent's portrait of Carolus-Duran in *Carolus-Duran 1837–1917* (Paris: Réunion des musées nationaux, 2003), p. 196. For Sargent's methods in creating *Neopolitan Children Bathing* (1878–79), see Marc Simpson's essay in this catalogue.

27 The woman's leaning, apparently weight-bearing pose, and the fact that she is seen from behind, also suggest her possible relationship to the figures in *Fisherwomen Returning*. In spite of its inscribed date of 1875, which may have been added later, this assured sketch surely dates to Sargent's 1877 summer in Cancale. Sargent was interested in the figure type as early as 1875, however, when he sketched a Niçoise peasant dressed similarly to the Cancale women and holding a basket (see Richard Ormond's essay, fig. 130).

28 I am grateful to Brittany native Arnaud Perreau, executive chef at Pesce Restaurant, Washington, D.C., for providing the term *marinière* and for his kindness in explaining the oyster-harvesting process.

29 This sketch, close in width to the four Terra sketches but 6 to 8 inches shorter, at some point may have been cut off at the bottom, but evidence of this was not discovered during the painting's recent conservation treatment. I am grateful to Harriet Irgang, Rustin Levenson Art Conservation Associates, for her input on this question.

30 The figure of the woman in the right middle ground of the Boston canvas, behind the little boy, may be based on some combination of the similarly clad woman in fig. 141 and that in fig. 143.

31 Ormond and Kilmurray, 2006, p. 112, states that the Boston version was most likely begun in Cancale. Both Fairbrother, *John Singer Sargent and America*, p. 32, and Troyen, catalogue essay in *John Singer Sargent*, p. 62, refer to the Boston canvas as a final study for the Corcoran work; Meg Robertson, in "John Singer Sargent: His Early Success in America, 1878–1879," *Archives of American Art Journal* 22 (1982), p. 22, discounts this idea, noting that it is a smaller version of the same scene and that, significantly, Sargent deemed it worthy of exhibition and sale.

32 In a letter to Helena de Kay Gilder of 12 October 1877, Saint-Gaudens reported having told a group of American artists in Paris of the SAA plans the prior Sunday, noting that he had secured their eager pledges to send works to the exhibition. Papers of Augustus Saint-Gaudens, Rauner Special Collections Library, Dartmouth College, Hanover, New Hampshire, reel 7, frames 653–55, courtesy of the Library of Congress, Washington, D.C.; cited in Jennifer A. Martin Bienenstock, *The Formation and Early Years of The Society of American Artists: 1877–1884* (City University of New York Ph.D. dissertation, 1983), pp. 34–35. As this letter states that the "following gentlemen have pledged themselves to send to the A.A.A. [SAA] . . . pictures . . ." but no list follows, the list referred to almost certainly is that written in Saint-Gaudens' script on three undated slips of paper in the same collection, reel 13, frame 41–43; Sargent's name is listed at the top of the sheet pictured in frame 41.

33 These are Ormond and Kilmurray 2006, nos. 702, 703, and 704.

34 The letter to Case (private collection) is cited in Ormond and Kilmurray 2006, p. 112, where Ormond also proposes the two paintings were "developed alongside each other." Much later in his life Sargent recalled executing both versions of his 1879 Luxembourg Gardens painting at the same time, calling them "the original sketch" and the "replica"; see Ormond and Kilmurray, 2006, p. 185. It seems most likely that at this early and ambitious point Sargent created two finished versions of the Cancale painting for purposes of promoting his career, reinforcing evidence so admirably set forth by Marc Simpson in *Uncanny Spectacle* (see n. 21). However, aesthetic and experimental reasons for this repetition (and others, see p. 108 and n. 42) should not be ruled out altogether. See Simon Kelly, *The Repeating Image: Multiples in French Painting from David to Matisse* (Baltimore: Walters Art Museum, 2007), p. 72, for a discussion of how Millet and Corot "navigated a course between aesthetic and market-driven motivations for repetition." See also Patricia Mainardi, "Copies, Variations, Replicas: Nineteenth-Century Studio Practice," *Visual Resources* 15 (1999), pp. 123–47.

35 In addition, in the Terra sketch corresponding to the woman at the far left of both the Corcoran and Boston paintings (fig. 133), the figure is nearly identical in contour to her counterparts in the completed canvases. In the Terra sketch of the figure third from left in the central group (fig. 140), the outlines of the figure correlate loosely to those of her counterpart in the Boston painting, but her head is at a different angle than the figure in the Corcoran's canvas.

36 Patricia Favero, Conservation Fellow at The Phillips Collection, performed an infrared reflectography examination of *En route pour la pêche* in February 2008. Museum of Fine Arts, Boston, Associate Conservator of Paintings Lydia Vagts has confirmed that *Fishing for Oysters at Cancale* does not exhibit graphite grid lines or underdrawing.

37 I am very grateful to Lydia Vagts and to Jean Woodward, Conservator of Paintings, Museum of Fine Arts, Boston, for sharing their Photoshop observations with me, and for their and Erica Hirshler's ideas about how Sargent may have executed the transfer. Vagts believes that Sargent may have used a magic lantern when making his murals for the Museum of Fine Arts, Boston, in the 1890s; since his collaborator on that project, the architect Thomas Fox, had one in his possession along with other Sargent materials (email to the author from Vagts, 30 September 2008). Devices such as the magic lantern were readily available by the mid-1870s in Paris, as were negatives for projection in them. See Mark Tucker and Nica Gutman, "Photographs and the Making of Paintings," p. 229 and notes 20–22, and W. Douglass Paschall, "The Camera Artist," p. 242 and notes 19–20, in Darrel Sewell, et al., *Thomas Eakins* (Philadelphia: Philadelphia Museum of Art, 2001). I am grateful to Paschall for further discussion on this point.

38 In an undated letter, Sargent wrote to Watts that she could order prints of the painting from Perichet (private collection, cited in Ormond and Kilmurray, *John Singer Sargent: The Early Portraits* [New Haven and London: Yale University Press, 1998], p. 42). According to Richard Ormond, the letter may date from as early as 1877 and, if so, at some point later may have been inadvertently inserted in its current envelope, postmarked 23 November 1881; it is unlikely that Sargent would have arranged for photography of the painting as late as four and a half years after it was completed and at that point notified Watts that she could order prints. August Perichet (life dates unknown) is listed as having his studio on rue de Notre-Dame-des-Champs beginning in the late 1870s in J.M. Voignier, *Répertoire des Photographes de France au Dix-Neuvième Siècle* (Chevilly-Larue, Le Pont de Pierre, 1993), p. 200. I am grateful to Malcolm Daniel, Curator in Charge, Department of Photographs, Metropolitan Museum of Art, and Amanda Maddox, Assistant Curator of Photography and Media Arts, Corcoran Gallery of Art, for the Perichet information.

39 The photographs are preserved in large registers, probably used by Braun, Clement & Cie. for publicity purposes, in the Centre Rhénan d'Archives et de Recherches Economiques (CERARE) in Mulhouse, France (emails from Graziella Claerr, Director, 6 January and 16 and 19 February 2009). *Fumée d'ambre gris* (1880, Sterling and Francine Clark Art Institute, Williamstown, Massachusetts) and several later paintings are listed in Braun's 1887, 1892, and 1896 catalogues. I am grateful to W. Douglass Paschall for suggesting Braun as a possible photographer of Sargent's work and to Maureen O'Brien, Curator of Painting and Sculpture, Museum of Art, Rhode Island School of Design, for leading me to Christian Kempf, independent scholar. Kempf directed me to CERARE and shared facsimiles of these Braun catalogues (email of 2 October 2008).

40 Also in this scrapbook, which entered the Metropolitan's collection in 1950 as part of the large Sargent gift from his sisters, are photographs of his 1879 portrait of his teacher Carolus-Duran and *Fumée d'ambre gris* (1880; both, Sterling and Francine Clark Art Institute, Williamstown, Massachusetts). I am grateful to Stephanie Herdrich for this information.

41 The letter is in a private collection.

42 See Ormond and Kilmurray 2006, nos. 702, 703, 704 (*A Capriote*); 705, 707 (*Capri Girl on a Rooftop*) (the third version, in a private collection, was discovered after the catalogue raisonne's publication); 721, 722 (*Luxembourg Gardens*); and 723, 724

(*Pasdeloup Orchestra*). Interestingly, it is only the Pasdeloup pair (besides the Cancale duo) whose dimensions differ significantly from each other.

43 "Fine Arts. The Lessons of a Late Exhibition," *Nation*, 11 April 1878, p. 251. The critics' preoccupation with the issue of finish (or lack thereof) manifests their readiness to embrace the tenets of the SAA, and perhaps even the organization's own marketing success.

44 "Fine Arts," *New York Herald*, 5 March 1878, p. 10. Even Sargent's father called the painting a sketch (after correcting himself from describing it as a picture); Fitzwilliam Sargent to Tom Sargent, 3 April 1878, Archives of American Art, Smithsonian Institution, roll D317, frames 553–554. Also during the SAA exhibition in 1878, Charles E. Dubois wrote to Julian Weir, alerting him to look out for ". . . a good sketch by Sargent . . . some Cancale women on the beach, very luminous." Weir Papers, Archives of American Art, cited in Fairbrother, *John Singer Sargent and America*, p. 34.

45 "Fine Arts," *New York Herald*, 10 March 1878, p. 8.

46 *Boston Daily Advertiser*, 12 March 1878, issue 61, col. D, "The Fine Arts." This review noted that "here, for the first time in New York, one may see pictures which were painted for the sake of painting them. Here, at last, says Mr. Clarence Cook, is Art for Art's sake!," and that most of the paintings are "studies or 'bits of realism'", but that "this studying, this preparation for work, cannot go on forever!"

47 C.C. [Clarence Cook], "American Artists. The Society's First Exhibition," *New York Daily Tribune*, 23 March 1878, p. 6. Cook, along with *New York Times* critic Charles de Kay, effectively served as a press agent for the SAA, writing articles to convince the public of its value while criticizing the traditional tendencies of the National Academy of Design. See Bienenstock, *The Formation and Early Years of The Society of American Artists: 1877–1884*, p. 36.

48 Edward Strahan (Earl Shinn), "The National Academy of Design," *Art Amateur*, June 1879, pp. 4–5.

49 "Fine Arts, The Society of American Artists, I," *New York Evening Mail*, 5 March 1878, p. 4.

50 This, perhaps, was not surprising for an exhibition that featured 2,330 works and for reviewers who were familiar from recent Salons with the subject of fish or oyster gatherers on the seashore. See Roger Ballu, "Le Salon de 1878: Deuxième et dernier article," *Gazette des Beaux-Arts*, July 1878, pp. 179 (illus.), 185.

51 It is unknown whether Sargent's 1877 portrait of his friend Fanny Watts, which is not inscribed to the sitter or her mother, was a commission.

52 In a letter to his brother Tom of 3 April 1878 Fitzwilliam Sargent noted that the painting "was very much thought of, apparently by two artists who drew lots as to who should purchase it for $200, the price [Sargent] had put upon it." Fitzwilliam Sargent Papers, Archives of American Art, Smithsonian Institution, Washington, D.C.

53 G.W. Sheldon, *American Painters* (New York: Cassell, Petter & Galpin, 1879), p. 72, quoted in Ormond and Kilmurray 2006, pp. 112–13.

54 Case participated in the Wilkes Expedition of 1837–42 that discovered Antarctica, as well as the Mexican War and the Civil War, and commanded several squadrons.

55 Apparently at first somewhat nervous that the admiral wanted to purchase the painting as a favor to a family friend, Sargent was reassured by Case's son Dan that his father "wanted it for its own sake." See letter from Sargent to Gus Case, 18 July 1878, private collection, quoted in Ormond and Kilmurray 2006, p. 111.

56 This work was formerly known as *Oyster Gatherers Returning*, and, prior to that, *Mussel Gatherers*, and gained its current title during the fall of 2008 based on the French laws against oyster-gathering during the summer months, noted elsewhere in this essay. See Ormond and Kilmurray 2006, no. 678, as well as Randall R. Griffey's insightful entry on the painting in Margaret C. Conrads, ed., *The Collections of The Nelson-Atkins Museum of Art: American Paintings to 1945* (Kansas City, Missouri: The Nelson-Atkins Museum of Art, 2007), vol. I, pp. 473–75.

57 This regulation was cited by Joseph Pichot-Louvet, Cancale, who said that the women would have been able to walk to Cancale from Le Porcon because the ocean bottom was sandy, not muddy as today. Email from Mary Margaret Chappell, Cancale, 6 October 2008.

58 I am grateful to Mary Margaret Chappell and to photographer Hervé Lambrecht, also of Cancale, for their assistance in identifying and photographing this site; they shared their findings with me in a series of emails from September through December 2008.

59 It is interesting to note that in the 1874 Salon (where François-Nicolas-Augustin Feyen-Perrin's *Retour de la Pêche* was shown, see p. 92 and fig. 126) the Belgian artist Félix Cogen (1838–1907) exhibited a pair of paintings entitled *Départ pour la pêche* and *Retour de la pêche*.

60 The boy may be naked because he is not finished. However, his appearance also relates this panel to that of *Two Nude Figures Standing on a Wharf* (see Ormond, fig. 35); the two pictures also appear to share short, light brushstrokes on patches of bare panel in the water and sky.

Bladders and Blue Shadows: "Neapolitan Children Bathing" Marc Simpson

1 The fullest account of Sargent's work and activities while in Naples and Capri, as well as the most extended consideration of the cultural context he found there, is Elaine Kilmurray, "Naples and Capri, 1878," in Richard Ormond and Elaine Kilmurray, *John Singer Sargent: Figures and Landscapes, 1874–1882: Complete Paintings* vol. 4 (New Haven and London: Yale University Press, 2006), pp. 136–79, 398–401. Seminar work undertaken by Gretchen Sinnett and Katie Steiner (M.A. 1996 and 2008, respectively) at the Williams College Graduate Program in the History of Art, focused on *Neapolitan Children Bathing*, has been of material aid in the writing of this essay.

2 Sargent refers to the USS *Vandalia*, which, because of its being the transport used by former President Ulysses S. Grant on his tour of the Mediterranean from December 1877 until March 1878, had been much in the news (http://www.history.navy.mil/photos/sh-usn/usnsh-v/vandla2.htm). That Sargent had been invited to dine suggests the social set in which he and his family moved.

3 Transcribed in Evan Charteris, *John Sargent* (New York: Charles Scribner's Sons, 1927), pp. 47–48. Sargent had planned the trip so as to spend time in Capri. He wrote on 18 July: "The man who in July is just going to start off for Naples ought not to say anything about heat. I am that man and in a week or two I expect to be [sweating?] at Capri. I want to spend a month or two there painting. After that I shall rejoin my people wherever they will be, and I hope that your father & mother will still be with them" (Sargent to Augustus Case; quoted in Ormond and Kilmurray 2006, p. 138). Sargent was probably urged to this goal by the recommendations of his friends and studio mates Auguste-Alexandre Hirsch, who had spent time in Capri in August 1877, and J. Carroll Beckwith, who was there in April 1878 (see Ormond and Kilmurray 2006, p. 138).

4 Ormond and Kilmurray 2006, nos. 692 through 720; elsewhere in the catalogue, however, the authors note that various oils and watercolors of indeterminate locale might be from his stay there.

5 This was Sargent's debut and, for a decade, only submission to the pre-eminent exhibition venue in the United States. Also during his lifetime the picture was shown at a charity fair in Brooklyn in 1883 and at the Pennsylvania Academy of the Fine Arts annual show in Philadelphia in 1902.

6 "Fine Arts. Fifty-fourth Annual Exhibition of the National Academy of Design – Second Notice," *New York Herald*, 31 March 1879, p. 5.

7 Ormond and Kilmurray 2006, pp. 150–51, 398; Margaret C. Conrads, *American Paintings and Sculpture at the Sterling and Francine Clark Art Institute* (New York: Hudson Hills Press, 1990), pp. 163–66.

8 This is smaller than many of the plein air and model studies that Sargent made to train his hand and eye. Indeed, the figure studies he had made for the *Fishing for Oysters at Cancale* (figs. 133, 137, 140, 141) were each roughly nineteen by eleven inches – considerably larger than the canvas of *Neapolitan Children Bathing*.

9 Emily, Sargent's elder sister, wrote of the Carolus-Duran portrait and Sargent's travel plans to Violet Paget (Vernon Lee) on 24 July 1878: ". . . he told John he would sit for his portrait, & John has begun it but expects to go to Capri in a few days, so will not be able to finish it now" (quoted in Richard Ormond, "John Singer Sargent and Vernon Lee," *Colby College Library*

Bulletin, series 9, no. 3 [September 1970], p. 162).

10 "The Academy Exhibition. A Creditable Display of the Work of American Artists," *Daily Graphic*, 29 March 1879, p. 207; "Fine Arts. Exhibition of the Academy of Design – II," *The Nation* (22 May 1879), p. 359; "The National Academy of Design. First Notice," *Art Amateur* 1, no. 1 (June 1879), p. 4. Others again called it "an out of door study" ("Fine Arts. Fifty-fourth Annual Exhibition of the National Academy of Design – Second Notice," *New York Herald*, 31 March 1879, p. 5) and complained "we could have wished to see a picture from the hand of John L. [*sic*] Sargent in addition to his superb little study" ("Fine Arts. Fifty-fourth Annual Exhibition of the National Academy of Design – The Reception and Private View – Third Notice of the Collection,"*New York Herald*, 1 April 1879, p. 6).

11 R.C., "Art in Philadelphia," *New York Tribune*, 19 January 1902. Richard Ormond, *John Singer Sargent: Paintings, Drawings, and Watercolors* (London: Phaidon, 1970), p. 22 (see also p. 235). A decade later, in 1980, it was called "one of several [charming little sketches] executed at this time," *John Singer Sargent: His Own Work*, exh. cat. (New York: Coe Kerr Gallery, 1980), cat. no. 4.

12 Ormond and Kilmurray 2006, p. 151.

13 "The Academy Exhibition," *New York Times*, 2 May 1879, p. 5.

14 "Sargent . . . thought that the artist ought to know nothing whatever about the nature of the object before him ('Ruskin, don't you know – rocks and clouds – silly old thing!'), but should concentrate all his powers on a representation of its appearance. The picture was to be a consistent vision, a reproduction of the area filled by the eye." Edmund Gosse, quoted in Charteris, *John Sargent*, pp. 77–78.

15 Emily Sargent to Violet Paget, 22 December 1878; Vernon Lee Collection, Colby College Special Collections, Waterville, Maine.

16 Conrads, *American Paintings and Sculpture*, p. 163; Ormond and Kilmurray 2006, p. 150. It would be like Sargent, in common with many artists, to leave a sketch or study unsigned. Throughout his life owners of canvases would ask him to sign and date such works that had come to them, and he did so with a certain cavalier attitude toward dates that has caused perplexity for chroniclers ever since. See, for example, Ormond and Kilmurray 2006, cat. nos. 628 and 644.

17 Both the Cancale pictures shown in 1878 are labeled "Paris," as is the Luxembourg Garden painting sold to John Sherwood in 1879; *Fumée d'ambre gris* (see Herdrich, fig. 12), shown in the Salon of 1880, is prominently inscribed "Tanger"; and the most detailed of the early Venetian genre scenes, *A Street in Venice* (c.1880–81, Sterling and Francine Clark Art Institute), proclaims itself as done in "Venise." In this latter, the inscription uses the French spelling of the city name, not the English version as recorded in Ormond and Kilmurray 2006 (nos. 670, 671, 721, 789, and 810). Of the three portraits he showed from 1877 to 1880, the only one with an outdoors setting – of Marie Pailleron – gives the locale as "Ronjoux" in the inscription (Richard Ormond and Elaine Kilmurray, *John Singer Sargent: The Early Portraits* [New Haven and London: Yale University Press, 1998], no. 25).

18 Ormond and Kilmurray 2006, nos. 702, 705, 707, and 719, along with 710 and 720. Of the six, all but the two replicas *Dans les oliviers à Capri*, one of which was the Salon painting of 1879, give a place name on their faces.

19 Eleven of the twenty-nine works that the authors of the catalogue raisonné assign to Sargent's stay on Capri are on such panels or boards (and another two are on what might be half panels).

20 It was documented as in the collection of the New York-based textile and art merchant Edward Runge by 1902. We do not know how Runge came to have the painting. Sargent did not inscribe it to him as he did the gifts to Edelfelt and Strettell, although it is signed – the only one of the six to be signed without an accompanying dedication. Runge's position in the New York art world, however, suggests that it was a private one-to-one transaction with an insider from the art world. Runge's obituary notes that for nearly thirty years he was one of the most discriminating connoisseur-collectors of Oriental rugs and porcelain in the city, working with the Morgan, Havemeyer, Altman, and other notable New York collections, as well as with the firms of Herter Brothers in 1885

and with Thomas B. Clarke from 1891 to 1911 ("Edward Runge Dead," *New York Times*, 21 November 1916, p. 11). The collection of seventy-six American pictures that he sold in 1902 included a number of small works of high quality by such fashionable painters as Robert Blum, Charles Curran, Joseph Decker, and Charles Ulrich, as well as pictures by Frederic Church, Winslow Homer, and George Inness. *Boy on the Beach*, then called *The Sun Bath*, was Runge's only work by Sargent (as reported in *American Art Annual*, 1903, pp. 21–23).

21 Ormond and Kilmurray 2006, p. 155.

22 "The Academy Exhibition," *Art Journal* 5 (1879), p. 159.

23 "The Academy Exhibition: Sales of Paintings, *New York Times*, 2 May 1879, p. 5; "Fine Arts. Fifty-fourth Annual Exhibition of the National Academy of Design – Second Notice," *New York Herald*, 31 March 1879, p. 5.

24 "The Two New York Exhibitions," *Atlantic Monthly* 43, no. 260 (June 1879), p. 781.

25 "Academy of Design. Fifty-fourth Annual Exhibition. Fourth Article," *New York Daily Tribune*, 26 April 1879, p. 5. This column mistakenly called the painting *Little Wanton Boys*.

26 "Academy of Design. Fifty-fourth Annual Exhibition. Fourth Article," *New York Daily Tribune*, 26 April 1879, p. 5. A note in the Clark's object file reports a visitor in 1986 who declared that at least some of the boys in the picture were from the Butler family, and that one of them, Harry Butler, was resident on Capri as late as 1965. Staff members then tried but were unable to pursue that line of investigation.

27 The exhibition in 1879 ran from 1 April to 31 May.

28 The incident is in Thomas Couture, *Méthode et entretiens d'atelier*, 2 vols., 2nd ed. (Paris: privately printed, 1868), vol. 1, pp. 112–27. Nicely, Shinn makes the millionaire an old man, which is not quite how Couture told the tale: "il paraissait avoir de vingt-huit à soixante ans" (118). It turns out, as well, that Couture's visitor is the son of the family in Rouen – a status parallel, we now know, to George Millar Williamson's own status in Brooklyn. Shinn, it seems to me, likely made the parallel transformation intentionally, allowing those in the know to recognize his bending of fact. Even for others, however, since the English version of Couture's text appeared in 1879 the reference had immediate relevance.

29 Edward Strahan (pseudonym of Earl Shinn), "The National Academy of Design: First Notice," *Art Amateur* 1, no. 1 (June 1879), pp. 4–5.

30 Maria Naylor, *National Academy of Design Exhibition Record, 1861–1900*, 2 vols. (New York: Kennedy Galleries, 1973), vol. 2, p. 822.

31 There was indeed no trolley on Madison Street. The *New York Times* in 1893 carried an article on the subject that described the formation of the Madison Street Property Owners' Protective Association to fight plans for a trolley thoroughfare on the street; the article described it as "now a most desirable place of residence, owing to the fact that business has made little encroachment upon it" ("Fighting a Trolley Road," *New York Times*, June 9, 1893, p. 8).

32 1880 United States Federal Census: Kings (Brooklyn), New York City-Greater, New York, roll T9_855; Barbara Dayer Gallati, *Great Expectations: John Singer Sargent Painting Children*, exh. cat. (Brooklyn Museum, 2004), p. 248.

33 Noted in Ormond and Kilmurray 2006, p. 151. The letter also includes the information that Sargent is having work done on the studio: "I am in tomorrow in the day-time though I don't expect to be much at my studio, as some workmen are just finishing some separations and the place is not in order." The fact that J. Carroll Beckwith, with whom Sargent had shared a studio at 73 rue Notre-Dame-des-Champs from August 1875, planned to return to the United States and did so in August 1878 (after spending the midsummer in Normandy), makes it plausible that Sargent would have workmen in, in the late spring 1878, to accommodate changes involved in transforming the space from a shared to a single-studio accommodation. Sargent did not stay there long, moving in spring 1880 to another studio at the same address, which he shared with Auguste Alexandre Hirsch. Indeed, the fact of there being no printed return address helps narrow the likely date of the letter, since Sargent had stationery with his address printed after his move to Boulevard Berthier in 1883. The

letter is now in the collection of the Huntington Library, Arts Collections, and Botanical Gardens, San Marino, HM 25218.

34 The 1870 census lists him as a "bank clerk"; that of 1880 as a "clerk in store." By the 1910 census, when he and his wife and sister are listed as residing in the village of Grand View on Hudson, in Orangetown in Rockland County, he has his "own income."

35 The Salon, in part perhaps due to the "Exposition universelle," opened late and ran longer than usual (25 May to 19 August 1878, as opposed to 1 May to 20 June 1877 and 12 May to 30 June 1879). From what Sargent writes, it seems likely that his note dates from the penultimate week of May 1878.

36 Over the decades Williamson assembled a notable collection of literary manuscripts and first editions, with particular emphasis on the works of Walt Whitman and Sargent's friend Robert Louis Stevenson. In 1888 Williamson sent a Christmas gift of $5.00 to Whitman, prompting the poet to wonder aloud, "How is it George M. Williamson is one of us? Has he come to the conviction by his own vision or has it been pumped into him?" Horace Traubel, *With Walt Whitman in Camden*, Saturday, December 22, 1888. Immediately before this Traubel wrote: "Williamson was always W.'s good friend in more ways than W. was aware of." (www.whitmanarchive.org/criticism/isciples/traubel/WWWiC/3/med.00003.52.html).

The Stevenson Collection was sold as a single owner sale in 1901, the Whitman Collection in 1903, and there was a general sale of the "extremely choice collection of first editions of English and American authors and association books formed by George M. Williamson of Grand-View-on-Hudson" in 1908. Moreover early on – by January 1883 – Williamson was recognized as an art collector of sufficient depth and quality to be a lender to a charity art fair held at the Brooklyn Academy of Music. He lent four works to the exhibition (22–27 January), which was a benefit for the Sheltering Arms Nursery: the Sargent painting; two paintings – *At the Spring* (date, location unknown) and *Tête à Tête in Cairo* (c.1880, location unknown) – by the fashionable and, with Sargent, arguably most promising of the young Americans in Paris, Frederick Arthur Bridgman; and an *Ideal Head* (date, location unknown) by the Frenchman Henri Gervex. These all represent advanced, fashionable taste (*A Boke of ye Arte Loane Fancie Bazaar, in ayde of ye Sheltering Arms Nurserie*, exh. cat. [Brooklyn: Academy of Music, 1883], cat. nos. 168–171). Later Williamson commissioned Sargent to paint his own portrait as well as, in 1900, that of his daughter Dorothy. All three Sargent paintings were in the Pennsylvania Academy of the Fine Arts annual exhibition of 1902. Williamson's portrait is currently untraced; that of Dorothy is in the Dallas Museum of Art. A letter from Williamson to Harrison Morris, the head of the Pennsylvania Academy of the Fine Arts, and dated 9 July 1902 (including the lines "How you must have enjoyed the trip. It was worth going for if only to have the pleasure of meeting J. S. Sargent"), indicates that the relationship of artist and patron was a pleasant one for the patron (Archives of American Art, Pennsylvania Academy of the Fine Arts Papers; I am grateful to Gretchen Sinnett for bringing this letter to my attention).

37 Sargent's father wrote of the sale in early April 1878 – nearly two months before the Salon opened and thus well before Williamson's purported visit. Fitzwilliam Sargent to his brother Tom, 3 April 1878; quoted in Ormond and Kilmurray 2006, p. 113.

38 The notion of an intermediary seems likely, and the most probable candidate for this is J. Carroll Beckwith, Sargent's Parisian studio-mate until 1878. He was a close friend of the artist and his 1878–79 diary includes a notation listing Williamson and giving his address as "6 Wall Street," perhaps a business address (Ormond and Kilmurray 2006, p. 151). Beckwith seems certainly to have served as the intermediary with the October 1879 purchase of Sargent's *In the Luxembourg Gardens* (1879, Philadelphia Museum of Art), which his uncle the art dealer John H. Sherwood acquired and held for just a few months before sending it to auction (see Ormond and Kilmurray 2006, p. 187).

39 I much appreciate Abigail Booth Gerdts's counsel in this matter, in which she concludes that any action on the part of Williamson to submit the work, without Sargent having taken the initiative, was

"Highly improbable" (letter to author, 30 August 2008).

40 The latter was done so as to be on the walls in New York by early March. Sargent doubtless felt pressure to be well represented in that show, since he had been elected one of the Parisian jurymen for the SAA in 1877.

41 Ormond and Kilmurray 2006, p. 139.

42 See Ormond and Kilmurray 2006, pp. 143–46.

43 "The slender figures of young boys may be noted as an especial preference for the moment," noted the writer for the *Atlantic Monthly*, considering particularly sculpture in the Paris "Exposition universelle" of 1878. "They are swimmers, fishers, – one in a straw hat with a brim, – Davids, Saint Johns" ("Pictures at the Exposition," *Atlantic Monthly* 42 [1878], p. 709).

44 Leandro Ozzolà, "Antonio Mancini," *Pegaso* 3 (June 1931); quoted and translated in Ulrich W. Hiesinger, *Antonio Mancini: Nineteenth-Century Master*, exh. cat. (Philadelphia Museum of Art, 2007), p. 35.

45 Raymond Westbrook, "Open Letters from New York," *Atlantic Monthly* 41, no. 243 (January 1878), pp. 96–97.

46 Edward Strahan (Earl Shinn), *Art Treasures of America*, 3 vols. (Philadelphia: George Barrie, 1879–1880), vol. 1, p. 36. Shinn's *Art Treasures of America*, which contains this lament, is a compendium of the greatest collections of paintings in the country; tellingly, it flows with the names of Boldini, Fortuny, de Madrazo, Michetti, de Nittis, Pasini, Rico, and Simonetti.

47 See Herdrich essay, p. 83, regarding the reproductions of two Fortuny watercolors Sargent included in his Metropolitan scrapbook: *Le Marchand de Tapis* (1870, Museu Montserrat, Barcelona, scrapbook p. 5 verso) and *Chef Kabyle dans la mosque de Tangier* (location unknown, scrapbook p. 53 verso).

48 As one telling example, Thomas Eakins expressed his admiration of Fortuny several times, both in memoranda to himself and in his interview of 1879 with William Brownell, saying "There are no lines in nature, as was found out long before Fortuny exhibited his detestation of them; there are only form and color." That Eakins cited Fortuny in this absolute sense, for an interview to be published in the popular periodical *Scribner's Monthly*, is testimony to the currency he thought Fortuny had in the eyes of the American public. For a full discussion of Eakins's views on Fortuny, see Kathleen A. Foster, *Thomas Eakins Rediscovered: Charles Bregler's Thomas Eakins Collection at the Pennsylvania Academy of the Fine Arts* (Philadelphia: Pennsylvania Academy of the Fine Arts, 1997), pp. 46, 72, 92–95.

Notable exceptions to the general ignoring of Fortuny's influence include Edward Sullivan, "Fortuny in America: His Collectors and Disciples," in *Fortuny 1838–1874*, exh. cat. (Barcelona: Centre Cultural de la Fundació Caixa de Pesions, 1989), pp. 101–17; and Carles González López, "Fortuny and the Phenomenon of 'Fortunyism' in Europe and America," and Mercè Doñate, "Fortuny in the Collections of the Nineteenth Century," in Mercè Doñate et al., *Fortuny*, exh. cat. (Barcelona: Museu Nacional d'Art de Catalunya, 2003), pp. 545–48 and 551–54 (English translations; originals pp. 387–95; 407–15). Fortuny attained particular fame after the estate sale of his studio in April 1875 at the Hôtel Drouot, which earned the newsworthy sum of over 600,000 francs. Doñate et al., *Fortuny*, p. 467.

49 "The Academy," *Art Journal* (New York) 5 (1879), p. 159.

50 "Academy of Design. Fifty-fourth Annual Exhibition. Fourth Article," *New York Daily Tribune*, 26 April 1879, p. 5. The critic for the *Times* approached the same observation from the other direction, praising *Neapolitan Children Bathing* as an "out-of-doors, sunshiny picture . . . It is very natural, home-like, and out-of-doorsy. In the next room," he continued, "two Italians strive for out-of-doors effects . . . but they do not express it half so well as the young Parisian" ("The Academy Exhibition. Sales of Paintings," *New York Times*, 27 May 1879, p. 5).

51 "Fine Arts. Exhibition of the Academy of Design. – II," *Nation* no. 725 (28 May 1879), p. 359. If indeed this is true, and the writer had a direct conversation with Sargent (or perhaps Beckwith) on this point, it would be interesting to know the means and in what context the subject arose. Although the article is unsigned, Edward Strahan (Earl Shinn), who wrote for the *Art Amateur* about the "elderly, modest man" who lent the painting to the

National Academy of Design exhibition in 1879, was also writing art criticism for the *Nation* during these years.

52 "The Two New York Exhibitions," *Atlantic Monthly* 43, no. 260 (June 1879), p. 781.

53 For near-contemporary considerations of Michetti, see Helen Zimmern, "Michetti," *The Art Journal* 39 (1887), pp. 16–19, 41–43.

54 "Academy of Design. Fifty-fourth Annual Exhibition. Fourth Article," *New York Daily Tribune*, 26 April 1879, p. 5; "Fine Arts. Exhibition of the Academy of Design. – II," *Nation* 28, no. 725 (22 May 1879), p. 359.

55 The painting, although only a sketch, was a highly valued one. At the studio sale in 1875, it sold for 6,900 francs, far more than other panels its size. Doñate et al., *Fortuny*, p. 318, cat. no. 120.

56 George de Forest Brush to Douglas Volk, 20 December 1878, Douglas Volk Papers, Archives of American Art, Smithsonian Institution, Washington, D.C. The letter is partially quoted in Nancy K. Anderson, *George de Forest Brush: The Indian Paintings* (Washington, D.C.: National Gallery of Art, in association with Lund Humphries, 2008), p. 191. Many thanks to Nancy K. Anderson, Curator of American and British Paintings, National Gallery of Art, Washington, for bringing this letter to the attention of Sarah Cash.

57 Dwight Benton, "The Artists' Island," *Lippincott's Magazine* 23 (January 1879), pp. 19, 25; Margaret Bertha Wright, "Rambles of Three: Summer Idyll," *Lippincott's Magazine* 24 (October 1879), p. 395.

58 In spite of all that naked flesh, the lack of apparent sexual energy in *Neapolitan Children Bathing* prompted the work to be exhibited at the Pennsylvania Academy of the Fine Arts in 1902 as *Innocence Abroad*, in smiling homage to Mark Twain's European travel account, published in 1869. And some critics then took the allusion further, writing of the painting as *Innocents Abroad* ("Studio Talk," *The Studio* [London] 26 [June 1902]: 52, 62).

59 Ormond and Kilmurray 2006, nos. 638 and 643. The authors call 638 "an isolated experiment" and cite Carolus-Duran and Böcklin as possible inspirations; they introduce 643 as "This odd picture," and, after noting its many Japanesque elements, observe, "One can only speculate on the reasons that led the artist to experiment with such an unusual subject."

60 "The Academy," *Art Journal* (New York) 5 (1879), p. 159.

Suggestions for Further Reading

NOTE TO THE READER

Additional sources appear in the notes to the essays in this catalogue. For a comprehensive Sargent bibliography, and the definitive catalogue of the artist's work addressed in the present volume, see Richard Ormond and Elaine Kilmurray, *John Singer Sargent: Complete Paintings Volume IV, Figures and Landscapes, 1874–1882* (New Haven and London: Yale University Press for The Paul Mellon Centre for Studies in British Art, 2006).

Adler, Kathleen, Erica E. Hirshler, H. Barbara Weinberg, with contributions from David Park Curry, Rodolphe Rapetti and Christopher Riopelle. *Americans in Paris 1860–1900*. London: National Gallery, 2006.

Adelson, Warren, Donna Seldin Janis, Elaine Kilmurray, Richard Ormond, and Elizabeth Oustinoff. *Sargent Abroad: Figures and Landscapes*. New York: Abbeville Press, 1997.

Alisio, Giancarlo, ed., *Capri nell'Ottocento: da meta dell'anima a mito turistico*. Naples: Electa Napoli, Edizioni La Conchiglia, 1994.

Bourguignon, Katherine M., ed., with essays by Nina Lübbren, Kathleen Pyne, and Margaret Werth. *Impressionist Giverny: A Colony of Artists, 1885–1915*. Giverny: Musée d'art Américain; Chicago: Terra Foundation for American Art; Distributed by the University of Chicago Press, 2007.

Fairbrother, Trevor. *John Singer Sargent and America*. New York, 1986.

Fink, Lois Marie. *American Art at the Nineteenth-Century Paris Salons*. Washington, D.C.: National Museum of American Art, Smithsonian Institution, and Cambridge: Cambridge University Press, 1990.

Gerdts, William H., with D. Scott Atkinson, Carole L. Shelby, and Jochen Wierich, *Lasting Impressions: American Painters in France 1865–1915*. Evanston, Illinois: Terra Foundation for the Arts for the Musée d'Art Américain, Giverny, 1992; also published as *Impressions de toujours: les peintres americains en France, 1865–1915*.

Herbert, Robert L. *Monet on the Normandy Coast: Tourism and Painting, 1867–1886*. New Haven and London: Yale University Press, 1994.

Herbert, Robert L. *Impressionism: Art, Leisure, and Parisian Society*, New Haven and London, Yale University Press, 1988.

Herdrich, Stephanie L., and H. Barbara Weinberg, with an essay by Marjorie Shelley. *American Drawings and Watercolors in The Metropolitan Museum of Art: John Singer Sargent*. New York: Metropolitan Museum of Art; Distributed by Yale University Press, 2000.

Hills, Patricia, with essays by Linda Ayres, Annette Blaugrund, Albert Boime, William H. Gerdts, Patricia Hills, Stanley Olson, and Gary

A. Reynolds. *John Singer Sargent*. New York: Whitney Museum of American Art in association with Harry N. Abrams, 1986.

House, John, with an essay by David Hopkin. *Impressionists by the Sea*. London: Royal Academy of Arts, 2007.

House, John, with contributions from Ann Dumas, Jane Mayo Roos, James F. McMillan. *Landscapes of France: Impressionism and its Rivals*. London: Hayward Gallery, 1995.

Kilmurray, Elaine, and Richard Ormond, with essays by Richard Ormond and Mary Crawford Volk, contributions by Erica Hirshler, Theodore E. Stebbins, Jr., and Carol Troyen. *Sargent*. London: Tate Gallery, 1998.

Olson, Roberta J. M. *Ottocento: Romaticism and Revolution in 19th-Century Italian Painting*. New York: American Federation of Arts, 1992.

Quick, Michael. *American Expatriate Painters of the Late Nineteenth Century*. Dayton, Ohio: Dayton Art Institute, 1976.

Sellin, David, and James K. Ballinger. *Americans in Brittany and Normandy*. Phoenix: Phoenix Art Museum, 1982.

Simpson, Marc, with contributions by Richard Ormond and H. Barbara Weinberg. *Uncanny Spectacle: The Public Career of the Young John Singer Sargent*. Williamstown, Massachusetts: Sterling and Francine Clark Art Institute, and New Haven: Yale University Press, 1997.

Stebbins, Theodore E., Jr., with essays by William H. Gerdts, Erica E. Hirshler, Fred S. Licht, and William L. Vance. *The Lure of Italy: American Artists and the Italian Experience 1760–1914*. Boston: Museum of Fine Arts, Boston, in association with Harry N. Abrams, 1992.

Stowe, William W. *Going Abroad: European Travel in Nineteenth-Century American Culture*. Princeton, N.J.: Princeton University Press, 1994.

Weinberg, H. Barbara. *The Lure of Paris: Nineteenth-Century American Painters and Their French Teachers*. New York: Abbeville Press, 1991.

Wilson-Bareau, Juliet, and David Degener, with contributions by Lloyd DeWitt and others. *Manet and the Sea*. Philadelphia: Philadelphia Museum of Art, 2003.

Index

NOTE
Page references in italics indicate illustrations. The abbreviation JSS refers to John Singer Sargent.

Photo Credits

Photography © The Art Institute of Chicago: 176

Provided courtesy HarpWeek, LLC: 47, 52, 131

Image Source, Toledo: 60

Photo: Imaging Department © President and Fellows of Harvard College: 75, 101, 142

Photograph by Robert Lorenzson: 29

Photo: Allan Macintyre © President and Fellows of Harvard College: 9, 134

Photograph by Joseph McDonald: 3, 145, 146

Image © The Metropolitan Museum of Art: 11, 16, 18, 20, 35, 39, 55, 64, 65, 66, 68, 70, 71, 72, 73, 74, 76, 77, 78, 79, 80, 81, 83, 84, 86, 87, 89, 90, 91, 92, 93, 94, 95, 96, 97, 102, 103, 104, 105, 106, 107, 108, 109, 110, 111, 112, 113, 114, 115, 116, 117, 118, 119, 120, 135, 138

Photograph by Jamison Miller: 150, 152

Photograph © 2009 Museum of Fine Arts, Boston: 23, 30, 48, 98, 99, 100, 122, 147, 155

© National Museums Liverpool: 46

Collection of The New-York Historical Society: 6, 7, 130 (neg. no. 74384)

Photo: D. Sole and Son: 25, 53

Photograph by Paolo Soriani—Fotografia e Comunicazione Visiva: 178

© Sterling and Francine Clark Art Institute, Williamstown, Massachusetts: 31, 159, 160, 164, 171

© Tate, London 2009: 22, 162

Courtesy Lydia Vagts, Associate Conservator of Paintings, Museum of Fine Arts, Boston: 148

© V&A Images / Victoria and Albert Museum, London: 61

Courtesy Yale University Library: 49